S0-BZB-175

IMAGINING THE EDGY CITY

IMAGINING THE EDGY CITY

Writing, Performing, and Building Johannesburg

Loren Kruger

Oxford University Press is a department of the University of Oxford.
It furthers the University's objective of excellence in research, scholarship,
and education by publishing worldwide.

Oxford New York
Auckland Cape Town Dar es Salaam Hong Kong Karachi
Kuala Lumpur Madrid Melbourne Mexico City Nairobi
New Delhi Shanghai Taipei Toronto

With offices in
Argentina Austria Brazil Chile Czech Republic France Greece
Guatemala Hungary Italy Japan Poland Portugal Singapore
South Korea Switzerland Thailand Turkey Ukraine Vietnam

Published in the United States of America by
Oxford University Press
198 Madison Avenue, New York, NY 10016

Cover: The City from the South, Johannesburg. Undated. Courtesy of David Goldblatt.

Library of Congress Cataloging-in-Publication Data
Kruger, Loren.
Imagining the edgy city : writing, performing, and building Johannesburg / Loren Kruger.
p. cm.
Includes bibliographical references and index.
ISBN 978–0–19–932190–2 (hardcover : alk. paper) — ISBN 978–0–19–932191–9 (updf)
1. Johannesburg (South Africa)—History—20th century. 2. Johannesburg (South Africa)—Intellectual life—20th century. 3. Art and society—South Africa—Johannesburg—History—20th century.
4. Motion pictures—Social aspects—South Africa Johannesburg—History—20th century.
5. Literature and society—South Africa—Johannesburg—History—20th century. 6. Theater and society—South Africa—Johannesburg—History—20th century. 7. Urbanization—South Africa—Johannesburg—History—20th century. I. Title.
DT2405.J6557K78 2013
968.22'105—dc23

2013003218

9780199321902

9 8 7 6 5 4 3 2 1

Printed in the United States of America on acid-free paper

Dedicated to the memory of Deborah Lee Kruger (1962–2013).

CONTENTS

Johannesburg Map from *Gold in Graphite: Jozi Sketchbook*. Graphite on paper copyright by Zafrica Cabral. Reprinted with permission.

PREFACE AND ACKNOWLEDGMENTS

I remember, as a very young child, sitting on the curb in front of the San Francisco—the apartment building where we lived until we moved to the suburbs—watching, fascinated, as motorized and pedestrian traffic went by, echoing between the multistory buildings. This scene of a child sitting unattended in front of a building on Clarendon Place, the busy thoroughfare that marks the edge between the dense district of Hillbrow and the spacious mansions of Parktown on the Witwatersrand ridge, may be a screen memory, or a mix of images and narrative absorbed from my parents or others in the neighborhood. Nevertheless, the picture of a white female child absorbed in the sights and sounds of city traffic, observed most likely by a black watchman, suggests both the attractions and the contradictions of the place, even if the shops, cafés, and nighttime entertainments—all of which made Hillbrow South Africa's most cosmopolitan district—would have been beyond the child's horizon. While the San Francisco, like many of its midrise midcentury peers, had no particularly distinguishing features, the Hillbrow skyline has in the decades since the 1960s been defined by two iconic structures. These are the Post Office Tower (1971), the tallest structure in Africa, known today as the Telkom Tower and as the signature emblem on the official Johannesburg website, and Ponte City (1975), a fifty-four-story cylindrical apartment tower built to attract white singles to the district, described by boosters—despite its decline toward the end of the last century and several aborted renovation attempts—as the icon of Johannesburg's past, present, and future (Bauer 2012). The rise, fall, and possible resurgence of Hillbrow is only one of several narratives pursued in this book, but it is an ideal example of the edgy city and its stories of boom and gloom, which have seized the attention of many generations and of people of diverse backgrounds from different parts of South Africa and the world beyond.

One of Johannesburg's most famous and most ambivalent chroniclers, the writer Alan Paton, had the narrator of his anti-urban novel *Cry, the Beloved*

Country (1948) acknowledge that, despite his aversion to it, all roads lead to Johannesburg. Taking its cue from this acknowledgment, *Imagining the Edgy City* argues that, contrary to some recent boosters who present their celebration of the "African world-class city" as a novel idea against an allegedly long tradition of fear and loathing, it is rather the vacillation between the heights of enthusiasm and the depths of condemnation that has characterized commentary on Johannesburg by natives and newcomers alike since the upstart city first emerged from the mining camp more than twelve decades ago. Nobody can say for sure which of several men called Johannes—Rissik, Joubert, or Paulus Johannes Kruger, last president of the South African Republic, all of whom had city streets named after them—made the strongest stamp on the mining camp or lent his name officially to the city. Perhaps for this reason, or perhaps because the city's ongoing attraction of transnational capital makes it expedient for politicians to leave its name alone, Johannesburg has not been the target of the kind of political animus directed toward other major cities named for icons of the old regime. The executive capital Pretoria, named unambiguously after the Voortrekker leader Andries Pretorius, has been absorbed—albeit with controversy—into the municipality of Tshwane, which is the Tswana name of the river that flows through the city and possibly also the name of a historic African clan leader. In contrast, the labels that people have given to Johannesburg—from the boosterish heights of *Egoli* (place of gold) or *Gam Saan* (gold mountain) to the lower depths of the old *duiwel's dorp* (devil's town) or the new *Johazardousburg*—reflect experience of or anticipation of the city's real and imagined dangers, as well as the desire lines that natives and newcomers alike have traced, pushed, and even forced along the city's edges and fissures or through even its most impenetrable barriers. The names in everyday use, however, tend to be affectionate abbreviations like "Jo'burg" or "Jozi," whose varied pronunciations, depending on the languages of the speaker, reflect the city's vernacular cosmopolitan character.

Johannesburg natives can find the key roads easily enough on the map from Zafrica Cabral's *Gold in Graphite: Jozi Sketchbook* (2010 see p. vi of this text), even without street labels to guide them, but readers unfamiliar with the city should note the directions here and throughout the rest of this book that point to streets and other edges between the district labels that Cabral provides. Roads play particularly important roles in both the early definition of the city and in its present dimensions, functioning, like Clarendon Place (visible on the map as a diagonal line just left of Hillbrow) as boundary markers; as thoroughfares through the city; as symbols of new political dispensations; as the names of short local streets (such as Miriam Makeba in the Newtown Cultural Precinct) that commemorate cultural icons; or as the names of longer highways (such as Joe Slovo Drive, running south between Hillbrow/Berea and Yeoville) that foreground more contested political leaders. In the current context, it is noteworthy that major thoroughfares running into the city from the affluent north still carry the names of neocolonial officials. Louis Botha Avenue, on the eastern side, retains the name of the Boer general who negotiated the Peace of Vereeniging at the end of the Anglo-Boer War in 1902 and the Union of South Africa in 1910. Running northeast from Clarendon Place, then above Yeoville past Slovo Drive and the Wilds, a rocky park of mixed indigenous flora (represented like other parkland on the map by a black shape, in this case on the far eastern end), it goes on to Orange Grove, Highlands North, the storied African settlement of Alexandra in the north off the map, and eventually to Pretoria. Its western counterpart, Jan Smuts Avenue, travels north from the University of the Witwatersrand in near-central Braamfontein (via Parktown West and Saxonwold and the dark patch that marks Herman Eckstein Park, better known as Zoo Lake, between them) toward the city's wealthiest districts well beyond the bounds of this map (Sandton and Bryanston), and still farther north as the William Nicol Highway. Jan Smuts, Botha's successor in the South African Party (now defunct), was an avowed internationalist but effectively authoritarian prime minister, who was present at the 1919 Versailles peace conference at the conclusion of World War I but went on to bomb the rebels of the Rand Revolt in 1922 and to endorse more vigorous segregation. Even as rumors spread in the early twenty-first century that the inner city's main east-west thoroughfare, Commissioner Street, the site of the city's first stock exchange (1887), and its regional extension the Main Reef Road (running just north of the apparently empty area of the old mining properties on the map), will shed its name and with it the legacy, shared with shorter streets like Nugget, Quartz, and Banket, of Johannesburg's gold mining history, most street names persist. Despite changes in the shapes of streets and even in entire districts, there remain enough intact points of reference to allow returning natives and other explorers to navigate the city and its extensions.

Although one writer cannot presume to cover every last corner of a conurbation that houses close to four million people, this book draws on material gathered over half a century, including formal and informal archives, published history and fiction, interviews and discussions with family and friends, film, television, visual art, performance, and the urban spatial and temporal practices, actual and invented, official, public or intensely personal, which have woven these elements together over the city's twelve decades and more. In addition to well-known cultural figures like Paton and Makeba, Nadine Gordimer, David Goldblatt, and William Kentridge, I give due attention to those who are less well known abroad, including Herman Charles Bosman, Achmat Dangor, Ahmed Essop, Mannie Feldman, Michael Hammon, Zubair Hassem, Stephen Hobbs, Herman Kallenbach, Kleinboer, Rex Martienssen, Maja Marx, Zola Maseko, Todd Matshikiza, Emily and Griffiths Motsieloa, Phaswane Mpe, Gabi Ngcobo, Sello Pesa, Bernard Sachs, Sipho Sepamla, Mary Sibande, Barney Simon, Lewis Sowden, Can Themba, Guy Tillim, Miriam Tlali, Ivan Vladislavić, and Marlene van Niekerk, among others. This is an eclectic list, and many a Johannesburger would likely want to supplement or contest it, but it suggests nevertheless the sheer variety of cultural production in the city over its short history. Mixing writers, theatre-makers, photographers, filmmakers, artists, architects, and entrepreneurs, this list of people who will reappear in the pages to come is intentionally promiscuous. I hope that my attention to the work of those who are less well known both in this book and in those that have preceded it, especially *The Drama of South Africa: Plays, Pageants and Publics since 1910* (1999), demonstrates to Johannesburgers, scholars, and general readers elsewhere the value of linking, juxtaposing, and occasionally even throwing together people, works, and traces from all over the map.

In addition to those whose contributions to *Imagining the Edgy City* will emerge in the subsequent chapters, I would like to acknowledge people who have shaped this work directly or indirectly. Growing up in a middle-class but not particularly intellectual environment, I was nonetheless exposed to shards of experience that provoked curiosity, even if the provocation registered only long after the event. If the image of the child on the curb came back into focus only when I worked one summer at the now-vanished Hillbrow branch of South Africa's dominant chain Exclusive Books on Pretoria Street, and visited a rare all-night eatery, the Fontana Bakery, across the road, others had more immediate impact. Marching with other students outside Wits University on the day after the Soweto uprising in June 1976 follows a by-now familiar script; the event brought the violent impunity of the state into closer quarters than most participants had experienced before and resonated for years thereafter. A family memory also carries with it something of a public charge: one of the rare exceptions to the white Jewish mourners at my grandmother's funeral a week or so after the Wits march in June 1976 was the Muslim owner of a clothing shop in Pageview, the near-inner-city district (separated from Auckland Park on the map by the Brixton Ridge) at the time recently declared "white," who was allowed to keep his shop open only by employing a white front. That white front was my grandfather, who had invited his colleague to carry my grandmother's coffin for part of the way to the gravesite in the West Park Cemetery (the large black shape on the map due north of Brixton); but what I remember from the event was the matter-of-fact, but evidently warm, interaction between the two of them. This small event, along with local projects in Johannesburg, from working with students at a Soweto primary school sponsored by my privileged high school on their annual "concert" or variety show, to, some years later, tutoring black high school students in mathematics, have stayed with me more than the perhaps more obvious student political activities on the other side of the country—working in the editorial collective of a routinely banned student paper, marching in opposition to the Cape Town iteration of the 1976 uprising or to government evictions of the organized informal settlement at Crossroads—in part because of the strands linking these moments to the spatial and temporal coordinates of Johannesburg's warped but tenacious urban fabric.

Turning to more formal acknowledgments: extended research trips in 1994 and 2007 were funded respectively by the US National Endowment for the Humanities and Wits University, and by the US Department of Education Fulbright-Hays Program. Shorter trips in 1996, 1998, 1999, 2002, 2005, and 2012 were supported in part by the American Society for Theatre Research, the Association for Theatre in Higher Education, and the University of Chicago. At Wits, several people offered help, insights, and suggestions on different occasions: Jillian Carman, Tim Couzens, Christo Doherty, Kelly Gillespie, Liz Gunner, Isabel Hofmeyr, Greg Homann, Peter Horn, Cynthia Kros, Hannah le Roux, Alan Mabin, Achille Mbembe, Lwazi Mjiyako, Sarah Nuttall, Gerrit Olivier, Bhekizizwe Peterson, Michael Titlestad, and Jill Waterman. Others in Johannesburg made important contributions: Pippa Stein, Barney Simon, Jo Ractliffe, Malcolm Purkey, Sonja Narunsky-Laden, Irene Menell, John Matshikiza, Minky Lidchi, Dorothea Kreutzfeldt, William Kentridge, Stephen Gray, Angus Gibson, Joseph Gaylard, Harriet Gavshon, Jane Doherty, and Achmat Dangor. Several former Johannesburg residents deserve thanks for reading, advice, or provocation: David Attwell, Neville Hoad, Ismael Mahomed, Jacqueline Maingard, Reingard Nethersole, Lewis Nkosi, and Ian Steadman. Beyond Johannesburg, several people in other places have read or edited parts of or the entirety of this project: Kim Solga, Tom Sellar, Willmar Sauter, Mark Sanders, Heike Roms, Leon de Kock, and Ian Baucom. Others were interlocutors at various events around the world: Christopher Balme, Catherine Cole, Vicki Cremona, Joachim Fiebach, Mark Fleishman,

Shannon Jackson, Simon Lewis, Gay Morris, Barbara Orel, Jennifer Robinson, and Benjamin Wihstutz. Others assisted me in Chicago: Catherine Sullivan, Agnes Lugo-Ortíz, David Graver, Theaster Gates, John Comaroff, Jean Comaroff, Dipesh Chakrabarty, Rose Bank, Ralph Austen, and the participants in my seminars on South African literature and visual culture.

The works cited at the end of this book compose a complete list of published sources available in print, on video, and online, as well as unpublished archival material, but I would like to draw the attention of readers and researchers to South African presses that have published local writing and images. Several presses that have since disappeared, such as Bateleur, AD Donker, Renoster, and Ravan Press (the last of which survived into the twenty-first century), pioneered local work, despite suffering from banning orders as well as other forms of harassment. Those that are currently active include art publishers Double Storey, Fourthwall, and David Krut; as well as publishers of prose, fictional or otherwise, such as David Philip, Kwela, Jacana, Jonathan Ball, STE, Umuzi, and Zebra Presses. University presses, especially Wits University Press and the University of KwaZulu-Natal Press, also deserve mention.

Portions of this research have appeared in earlier versions in the following publications:

South Atlantic Quarterly, Special Issue: Atlantic Genealogies 100: 1 (2001): 111–43; *Research in African Literatures* 37: 2 (2006): 141–63; *TDR–Journal of Performance Studies* 51: 3 (2007): 19–45; *Journal of Southern African Studies* 35 (2009): 237–52; *Contesting Performance: Emerging Sites of Research* (New York: Palgrave-Macmillan, 2009); *Critical Arts* 24: 1 (2010): 75–98; *The Drama of South Africa: Plays, Pageants, and Publics since 1910* (London: Routledge, 1999); and *Post-Imperial Brecht: Politics and Performance, East and South* (Cambridge: Cambridge University Press, 2004).

These earlier versions have since been revised, updated, and recontextualized in the present work.

Finally, I am grateful to the photographers and graphic artists whose work made a substantial contribution to the argument of this book. The images from the archives housed at Wits Historical Papers were assembled for me on different occasions by Carol Archibald, Gabriele Mohale, Michele Pickover, and Zofia Sulej. The photographs and captions of David Goldblatt, Jürgen Schadeberg, and Guy Tillim share intimate knowledge of Johannesburg buildings and people over most of the decades of this book. The location shot from Michael Hammon's film *Wheels and Deals* suggests the shadowy outlines of the city at its edgiest, and the documentation of public art work by Stephen Hobbs and Maja Marx illustrates a few examples of the many projects that have enhanced sites in the city, from Diepsloot to Soweto in the light of day. Zubair Hassem (a.k.a. Zafrica Cabral) provided the comparative sketch of high rises from Johannesburg's building boom and the map that will give readers signposts and other clues for navigating key sites and routes in the pages ahead.

ABBREVIATIONS, GLOSSARY, AND LINGUISTIC CONVENTIONS

Note: In keeping with sociolinguistic convention (see Mesthrie 2002), this book refers to other languages (e.g., Zulu) without importing prefixes (e.g., isiZulu) into English except when translating multilingual elements would be ambiguous without distinguishing between language (isiZulu) and people (amaZulu). The glossary includes South African words in several languages and English words that have historically taken on meanings peculiar to the South African context.

ACMS African Centre for Migration and Society, Wits University.

African Historically refers to speakers of Bantu languages; more recently claimed by South Africans of different ethnic backgrounds.

Afrikaans Native language of about 15 percent of South Africans and lingua franca for many more, derived historically from Dutch with lexical and other elements from Melayu, the lingua franca of slaves brought to the Cape Colony from the Dutch Indies, and indigenous Khoi languages (Roberge 2002).

Afrikaner (Afrik.) Historically the name claimed by white speakers of Dutch, and later of Afrikaans, to replace the derogatory *Boer*. Since the name means "African," Afrikaner ideology effectively deprived blacks of African identity.

AmaKwerekwere (Nguni: "those who speak funny"). Derogatory term used by black South Africans to denigrate black migrants as foreigners.

ANC African National Congress: active from 1912; exiled 1960–90; ruling since 1994.

Apartheid (Afrik., "apart-ness"). Official Afrikaner Nationalist government policy from 1948 to 1994. Distinguished from prior segregation by systematic deportation of black people from desirable land, racial classification of the entire population, and racial discrimination in education, housing, and public services of all kinds.

Banning orders Apartheid government directive confining a dissident individual to a single magisterial district or even to house arrest. Usually accompanied by restrictions on work, public appearances, writing or quotation by others, and sometimes also by the prohibition on talking with more than two people at the same time.

Bantu (Nguni: *abantu* = "people"). Historically, people speaking Bantu languages. Under apartheid, official government label for institutions controlling the lives of the black majority, e.g. Bantu Administration, and thus understood as abusive by the majority who used the prefix to register dissent; e.g., "Bantustans," which renamed the tribal polities that the government called "homelands."

BCM Black Consciousness Movement, most active in the 1970s and 1980s; is today supported by those who identify with Stephen Biko's legacy.

Beeld Afrikaans-language Johannesburg daily paper (1974–). Followed the government line in the apartheid era but its coverage of Johannesburg news and urban life was (and is) generally more substantial than other Afrikaans papers.

Bioscope Local, somewhat old-fashioned word for cinema or movie theatre.

Black Lowercase *black* usually refers to Africans. Capitalized, *Black* was the name claimed by BCM to represent all people demeaned by the official labels "non-white" or "non-European," including those South Africans labeled *Coloured* or *Indian*.

BMSC Bantu Men's Social Centre: club and performance venue (1924–60).

Boer (Afrik. "farmer"). Historically Dutch and later Afrikaans speakers; today often used in a derogatory way, as in "Kill the Boers."

BOSS Bureau of State Security (1965–76), known earlier as the Special Branch of the South African Police, and later (1976–90) as Internal Security Service.

Bushmen Contested term for South Africa's first peoples. The anthropologically sanctioned alternative, *San*, is also contested because it may have been coined by herder Khoikhoi to denigrate hunter-gatherers as tramps.

BW *Bantu World* (later *World*): Johannesburg newspaper targeting black readers.

CAD Central administration district. Neologism used here to mark the transformation of the conventional central business district (CBD) of Johannesburg into a center for government and corporate administration.

CJP Central Johannesburg Partnership: public/private initiative to generate inner-city development (1991–2003).

Clever (*Flaaitaal*: a man considered "too clever by half"); usually used by township toughs to put down Africans with intellectual aspirations.

Colour Bar The laws and practices reserving skilled work for whites. Promulgated already in the colonial period and solidified by apartheid laws governing "job reservation."

Coloured Lowercase still in use by people who identify themselves as neither black nor white. Under apartheid, Coloured (capitalized) was the official designation that conferred privileges denied to Africans, such as better education, housing and employment opportunities, and exemption from the requirement to carry passes. Not a synonym for US *colored*.

Concert Since the 1920s, a variety show including not only instrumental and choral music but also dramatic sketches and comic gags. Term still in use in black communities.

Coolie Derogatory term applied in the British colonial period to indentured Indians and by extension to Indians broadly. Resisted by entrepreneurs, especially Muslims, who sought, aided by Gandhi, to represent themselves as "Arabs" and thus as exempt from the Alien Act restricting "Asian" businesses and immigration.

COSATU Congress of South African Trade Unions (1985–); successor to the likewise anti-apartheid Federation of South African Trade Unions (FOSATU).

COSAW Congress of South African Writers (1980–).

CPSA Communist Party of South Africa (1919–50). After the CPSA was banned under the Suppression of Communism Act, the SACP reconvened in exile and returned to local politics in 1993.

Dam In Johannesburg, dams or lakes are usually reservoirs, as in Emmerentia and Moroka Dams and Bruma and Zoo Lakes.

DOCC Donaldson Orlando Community Centre, one of the very few art and performance venues in apartheid-era Soweto.

Egoli (Nguni: *eGoli*: "place of gold"). Popular vernacular name for Johannesburg.

ESCOM Electrical Supply Commission (parastatal company).

European Official designation in the nineteenth and twentieth centuries for whites, including those born in South Africa. Opposed to "non- Europeans" or "non-whites."

Flaaitaal (Eng: fly = "sly"; Afrik: *taal* = "language"; Stone 2002, 396). Street lingo used by urban black men, combining Afrikaans morphology with lexical elements from Bantu, English, and other sources. Although some speakers use the term *tsotsitaal*, most prefer *flaaitaal* or *iscamtho* (Makhudu 2002, 398).

Flatland Vernacular term for dense apartment districts in the Johannesburg inner city, which are hilly rather than flat.

FUBA Federated Union of Black Artists (1970s–).

Gauteng (Sotho/Tswana: "place of gold"). Historical counterpart to *eGoli*. Used today as the official name of the province of which Johannesburg is the capital.

Homelands Apartheid designation for Bantustans, nominally self-governing ethnically distinct states, but effectively rural slums housing mostly the elderly, women, and children whose male adult family members worked as migrants in the cities.

ISCOR Iron and Steel Corporation (parastatal company).

JAG Johannesburg Art Gallery; opened 1915.

JDA Johannesburg Development Agency (a city agency since 2002).

Jozi Popular nickname for Johannesburg used by speakers of all South African languages.

JSE Johannesburg Stock Exchange (founded 1887; moved to Sandton in 2000).

Kaffir This word derives from *kafir* (Arabic: "infidel"), which in its original meaning included all non-Muslims and therefore most whites, but it was used by white colonists to refer to blacks and remains a highly contested term to the present.

Kwaito Urban South African musical response in part to American house music; techno sound with some hip hop elements in Zulu, Sotho, or other vernaculars or sometimes in English; dates from the 1990s to the present.

Kwela-kwela Urban South African music of the 1950s associated with the penny whistle; featured in the films *The Magic Garden* and *Come Back Africa*.

Laager (Afrik: "fortified enclosure"). Historically, the circle of wagons fortified against hostile intruders on the trail. In the twentieth and twenty-first centuries applied metaphorically to the isolationist mentality of Afrikaner Nationalists.

Liberal Closer to the British than to the US meaning. South African liberals like Alan Paton described themselves as defenders of individual liberty and the rule of law. Leftists and African Nationalists tended, and still tend, to criticize liberals as capitalist, individualist, or elitist rather than broad-minded, socially inclusive, or progressive.

M&G *Mail and Guardian* Johannesburg weekly paper since 1994. Founded by journalists who published the anti-apartheid *Weekly Mail* after the *Rand Daily Mail* was banned in the 1980s.

Native Under British colonial (1806–1910) and Union (1910–48) governments, narrowly applied to institutions controlling the lives of blacks and thus to the people so controlled, e.g., Native Administration. This book attempts to restore the term to its broader application to those born in a particular location.

Nguni Bantu language group, including South Africa's most prevalent languages Zulu and Xhosa, and the less common Ndebele and Swati (Swazi to Zulu and English speakers). Xhosa is the earliest language to be written down; Zulu is a lingua franca for speakers of other Bantu languages such as Tsonga; Swati is the official language of Swaziland; and Ndebele resembles the Ndebele spoken in Zimbabwe (Herbert and Bailey 2002).

NP Afrikaner National Party, in power 1948–94. Dissolved by the end of the century.

PAC Pan-Africanist Congress: active 1950s; exiled 1960–90; splintered since 1994.

Pass Officially called a "reference book," the pass (Afrik. *dompas*: "stupid pass") was used to regulate the residence, movement, and employment of black South Africans (but not those designated Coloured or Indian).

Passage Interior hallway in a house or apartment, as well as a partially covered walkway linking apartments.

RAU	Randse Afrikaanse Universiteit; founded in 1975 as an Afrikaner university; now the integrated University of Johannesburg (UJ).
RDM	*Rand Daily Mail* (twentieth-century daily paper; banned in the 1980s).
Reef	Historically, the gold seam (now largely depleted) that ran parallel to and beyond the Witwatersrand; refers by extension to the settlements alongside the deposits, as in Main Reef Road or Main Reef Line.
RSA	Republic of South Africa (since 1961).
SAAR	South African Architectural Record.
SABC	South African Broadcasting Corporation.
SACC	South African Council of Churches; affiliated with the World Council of Churches and a conduit for overseas funding for anti-apartheid work.
SAIRR	South African Institute of Race Relations. Office in Braamfontein, near Wits.
SASM	South African Students Movement: organization of high school students active in Soweto in the Eastern Cape before and briefly after the Soweto uprising.
SASO	South African Students Organization: Black organization of university students formed when Stephen Biko and associates broke away from the white-run National Union of South African Students (NUSAS) in 1968.
Shebeen	In the apartheid era, when the government attempted to enforce a monopoly on liquor sales to blacks, the shebeen was an unlicensed township bar serving a range of drinks from traditional sorghum beer to cocktails made of dangerous solvents. In the post-apartheid era it applies more often to a licensed establishment trading on nostalgia for the old illicit gathering places.
Sotho(/Tswana)	Bantu language group comprising North Sotho, South Sotho, Pedi and Tswana.

SPRO-CAS Special Programs for Christian Action in Society; anti-apartheid NGO supported in part by the World Council of Churches, which provided funding for Black Community Programs and Ravan Press.

SSRC Soweto Students Representative Council.

Star *Johannesburg Star* (daily paper founded by the Chamber of Mines).

Suburb In South African as in British parlance, a subsection or district within a city, as opposed to the US designation of separate municipalities outside a major city.

Township Apartheid designation for a recognized peri-urban black residential area (e.g., Soweto). In the vernacular: "location" or *lok'shin*. Distinguished from informal settlements, although the latter often have settled cores and the former usually include shanty areas.

Tsonga Bantu language spoken in northeastern South Africa and in Mozambique. The language and its speakers are sometimes called *Shangaan*.

Tsotsi (*Flaaitaal*: "urban gangster" or "thug"); lingua franca: *tsotsitaal*: see *flaaitaal*.

UDF United Democratic Front (1983–93): Coalition of unions, civic organizations, anti-conscription activists, and other anti-apartheid groups.

Uitlander (Afrik. "foreigner"). Used by the Afrikaner leaders of the South African Republic to denigrate international migrants attracted by the Witwatersrand gold fields. Rendered moot when the British gained control of the territory in 1902 after the Anglo-Boer War.

UwB *Umteteli wa Bantu* (Nguni: "mouthpiece of the people"): Chamber of Mines–owned paper with a black readership (1930s and 1940s).

Venda Bantu language spoken in northern South Africa and southern Zimbabwe. Related to Shona, the most prevalent language in Zimbabwe.

Wits University of the Witwatersrand, founded 1922.

Witwatersrand (Afrik. "white watershed"). The ridge, or rather series of ridges, on which Johannesburg was built. Also, the divide between rivers that flow north and then east to the Indian Ocean, and those that flow south and then west to the Gariep (a.k.a. Orange) River and the Atlantic.

Zulu and Xhosa See *Nguni.*

IMAGINING THE EDGY CITY

INTRODUCTION: IMAGINING THE EDGY CITY

After apartheid, South Africa rejoined the world, and its cities invited celebration and criticism in a global context. Johannesburg has received special scrutiny as a city distinguished both by innovation and illegality, praised by its boosters in the mayor's office as a "world class African city" (Masondo 2007), and censured by its critics as a "city of extremes" (Murray 2011), or as one beset by intractable problems of unequal access and development (Beavon 2004). The epithet "world-class city" expresses the views of current boosters keen to compare post-apartheid Johannesburg to southern hemisphere cities with worldly aspirations, from São Paolo to Sydney, as well as to established global cities of the North, from London to Tokyo to Los Angeles. The turn to superlatives is not new, however. In keeping with Johannesburg's penchant for both reinvention and amnesia, recent comment tends to generalize from the post-apartheid "Afropolis" (Nuttall and Mbembe 2008), or reference a rather foreshortened view of the apartheid past without glancing much further back (Tomlinson et al. 2003; Bremner 2010). Focusing on the rapidly changing present and its relationship to the recent past may make sense for current stakeholders—policy-makers, planners, artists, and activists attempting to make the city more habitable—and to critics and citizens evaluating their efforts, but this tendency to highlight the now and compress the then repeats the gestures of amnesia and reinvention that have characterized boom and bust cycles in Johannesburg and its neighbors on the Witwatersrand (the white watershed) from the days of gold.[1]

As Johannesburg's history shows, the city provoked extreme responses from the very beginning, since the gold-mining camp became an official municipality in September 1886. Reflecting on developments around 1896, English observer William Butler displaced the already popular epithet "golden city" with the disparaging label: "Monte Carlo on top of Sodom and Gomorrah" (Butler 1911, 400).[2] William Plomer, who wrote the controversial novel *Turbott Wolfe* (1925) in his twenties and later libretti for Benjamin Britten, mixed aversion and admiration when he recalled the Johannesburg of his childhood as the "upstart city" (1984, 94). Similar mixed feelings laced the fortieth anniversary speech by the liberal Afrikaner J. H. Hofmeyr, who called Johannesburg "Peter Pan among cities" with the "rakishness and relentless energy" of youth (Hofmeyr 1986 [1926]). Even the outright boosterism of "Africa's Wonder City" (*Rand Daily Mail* [RDM] 1936e) on display at the Empire Exhibition in honor of Johannesburg's fiftieth anniversary jubilee was accompanied by stories of embezzled funds and other scandals. Achille Mbembe and Sarah Nuttall distinguish emphatically between their positive spin on the "*Afropolis*" (2008, 1) and an allegedly "long tradition of loathing" (2008, 33) but the archive compels us instead to balance the history of fear and loathing with an equally long tradition of bullish appraisals, and thus

1. The term "Witwatersrand" is often abbreviated as "Rand," which is also the name of South Africa's currency. Although the Afrikaans word is usually rendered in English as the "ridge of white waters," this poetic translation reflects typical Johannesburg boosterism rather than actual topography. While a few streams do originate in the fissures of the ridges that make up the watershed—such as the Braamfontein Spruit, which traverses locations as different as the central rail yard and the city's bird sanctuary and, joined by the slightly broader Jukskei River the dense settlements of the historic black township of Alexandra—the ridges are on the whole rather dry. The accurate translation of "white watershed" highlights the outcrops of light granite and the drainage divide between streams that flow north, eventually to the Limpopo River and the Indian Ocean and those that flow south, eventually to the Gariep (formerly known as the Orange) River and the Atlantic Ocean.

2. The phrase "Monte Carlo on top of Sodom and Gomorrah" has been credited to Butler's contemporary Winston Churchill, who visited South Africa during the Anglo-Boer War (1899–1902; see Ricci (1986, 16n3); Kruger (2001a, 223); Nuttall and Mbembe (2008, 33) but the comment appears nowhere in Churchill's voluminous writings. Butler's attribution to a well-known Cape politician hints at the most powerful Cape politician of the time, Cecil John Rhodes.

to recognize that the persistent mixture of aversion and admiration, rather than loathing, has been the dominant response to the upstart city. While the twenty-first-century Afropolis is arguably more African than the wonder city of 1936, and certainly more so than the apartheid city of 1956 or 1976, the terms of praise (energetic, rapidly changing, cosmopolitan) and those of blame (disorderly, violent, plagued by unwelcome migrants), often expressed in the same breath, have remained remarkably constant. The designation "Sodom and Gomorrah" may be out of date, but Butler's quip shows that the notion of dirty secrets beneath glittering surfaces is as old as the hills, or the Witwatersrand ridge.

Focusing on the *edgy city* rather than the old idea of depth and surfaces highlights the historical as well as present conditions of extreme contrasts in plain view (for those who choose to look), between the shopping mall and the shanty town, natives and foreigners, and between grandiose claims of cosmopolitan modernity reflected in glass-curtain skyscrapers and the intractable problems of inequality, scarcity, and xenophobia that lodge in their shadows. I introduced the epithet "edgy city" more than a decade ago in an essay on theatre and the city (2001a) to describe the pervasive nervousness expressed by blacks and whites in the face of crime and grime in the 1990s, before the post-apartheid city had begun to build institutions like the Inner City Office (1999–2001) and the Johannesburg Development Agency (JDA; since 2002), which would find "light" in "bleakness" (Morris 1999) and begin to "tame the disorderly city" (Murray 2008) so as to return urban spatial practices, especially in the central zones, to a state of productive play and innovative work that might earn the place the title "world city." Although my initial sense of edginess emerged from this particular period of uncertainty, I will show that the term delineates the literal as well as figurative shape of the city over the course of history.

Beyond the expression of subjective edginess, the term "edgy city" describes the objective layout of oddly shaped and unevenly developed districts, an urban form that has defined the city from the start. Johannesburg's growth and slump through cycles of speculation and retreat over unevenly joined parcels of real estate has always eluded the order of a rational street grid. This irrational order has in turn provoked calls for reform, argued eloquently in the fortieth anniversary year by British-born, Johannesburg-based architect and planner Stanley Furner in the *South African Architectural Record* (1926b). Even earlier, after victory in the Anglo-Boer War in 1902 secured British colonial control of Johannesburg until the Union of South Africa was established in 1910, the outlines of suburbs carved out of the veld but as yet unconnected to established districts or visible infrastructure demonstrate that speculation rather than orderly planning ruled the day (Beavon 2004, 65).[3] By 1939, undeveloped space in staked-out districts had been largely filled in, but the districts retained their uneven sizes and edges into the twenty-first century, and continue to retard the rational planning advocated by Furner and his colleagues nearly a century ago. Union (1910–60) and Republican (1960–90) governments implemented residential segregation and economic discrimination at the national and local levels, and thus sharpened the discontinuity of Johannesburg's urban form, but economic factors, over and above apartheid, shaped the city. Real estate speculation in boom periods such as the 1930s and the 1960s, and the exploitation of cheap labor, were the primary engines of capital flow and of suburban sprawl (Goga 2003; Beavon 2004, 197–235). Well before the end of the twentieth century, capital migration had hollowed out the historic central business district (CBD) in the inner city and created a de facto CBD in the office parks and simulated city squares of Sandton.

"Edgy city" also highlights the links between two apparently contrary tendencies in more recent times. On the one hand, there is the globalized phenomenon of the edge city, ex-urban developments of office parks and gated residential clusters whose sprawl even beyond established suburbs or exurbs like Schaumburg beyond Chicago (Garreau 1991), or Sandton beyond Johannesburg, enabled by car ownership, has accelerated the hollowing out of city centers from Los Angeles (Soja 1997) to São Paolo (Caldeira 2000, 2009) in addition to Johannesburg (Czeglédy 2003; Goga 2003; Beavon 2004; Bremner 2004). On the other, an informal but complex streetwise order has emerged in Johannesburg as in other cities with similarly sharp income disparities, within which internal as well as external migrants to the city create their own infrastructure (Simone 2004a), developing pedestrian matrices of "belonging and becoming" (Götz and Simone 2003) that push beyond the boundaries defined by residential gates and limited motorized access to (not so) freeways. Concerns about safety and security of property have shaped not only the fortress architecture in the historically wealthy northern suburbs (Czeglédy 2003, 32), but also the development of shopping malls and gated residential clusters in the former state-administered black townships, from

3. Local commentators use *suburb* in the British and South African sense of a subsection of a city, as opposed to the American application of the word to separate municipalities, perhaps better described as "exurbs," outside the city boundaries. Except when citing or paraphrasing another writer (here, Beavon), I will therefore use the planning term "district," so as to avoid confusion.

Soweto to other black districts between Johannesburg and contiguous municipalities, such as expanding Ekurhuleni on the East Rand (Boraine et al. 2006; Alexander 2010). The urban improvement projects sponsored by the JDA over the last decade have shaped urban space in different ways, from the quotidian—enhancing parks and government and community surveillance, and cultivating "desire lines," or informal pedestrian pathways (Shepherd and Murray 2007)—to the spectacular landmark institutions such as Constitution Hill. Nonetheless, overall planning has been hampered by organized resistance (such as the taxi companies' aggressive acts against Bus Rapid Transit structures and employees), as well as apparently disorganized but persistent practices of irregular and dangerous occupation of inner-city property as well as the illegal networks that enable this irregularity.

Experiencing Edges and Exceptions in the Ordinary World City

Although the edgy city invites the rhetoric of extremes, the normalization of edges marked by established district boundaries and the points of comparison with cities of the so-called global north like Los Angeles, characterized also by sprawl, limited access roads, and gated estates, suggest that Johannesburg's edginess is more ordinary than exceptional. As Jennifer Robinson argues in *Ordinary Cities between Modernity and Development* (2006, 93–115), it is metropolitan theory, particularly the theory of the elite global city of high finance and high culture, that constitutes the exception or the claims of exceptionalism, as against the actual mix of formal urban structures and informal networks that characterize the ordinary modernity of the world's cities.[4] While "global city" may have become "the aspiration for cities around the world" (Robinson 2006, 112), including sprawling mega-cities like Mexico City that even resident researchers call a "monstropolis" (García-Canclini 2009, 87), the "global city" label functions as a "regulatory fiction" (Robinson 2006, 113), rather than as a term that might take account of the range of transnational networks from below as well as above that shape cities in the world. *The Endless City*, the Urban Age project sponsored by the London School of

4. Saskia Sassen has extended her initially narrow group of global cities—principally the centers of high finance of New York, London, and Tokyo (see Sassen 1991)—to acknowledge the migrant workers on whose labor the high-tech transactions of transnational capital depend and to allow for the participation of a second tier of cities of the South in these global flows (Sassen 2000), but her model of urban form is still the classic one, in which the central core, high-status site of the concentration of economic, social, and cultural exchange dominates over marginalized peripheries.

Economics and the Deutsche Bank (Burdett and Sudjic 2007), does not cite Robinson but it recognizes Johannesburg's status as a world city by including it in the company of London, New York, and Berlin, and so confirms the contribution of Johannesburg, Shanghai, Mexico City, and other cities of the "global south" to the concept as well as the content of "world city" and of the ideas and practices of modernity from which the world city has emerged.

Recognizing that Johannesburg and other cities of the South are modern world cities entails more than belated inclusion in an exclusive club. Rather, this recognition challenges both the normativity and apparently normality of modernity as habitually defined by the North. As Robinson argues, modernity involves more than modernization. In addition to and sometimes in the absence of the concentration of capital and the development of productive capacity, modernity means the aspiration to and the "enchantment with novelty and innovation"; it also requires the acknowledgment that "novelty can be dangerous, disruptive" (2006, 7). As Max Weber reminds us, however, modernity may begin with enchantment, but modern agents must ultimately confront the "de-enchantment" (*Entzauberung*) of the world (Weber 1989, 13; 1992 [1921], 89)—in other words, the pressures of individuation and social disruption, as well as technological innovation, on urban dwellers in a world without gods or stable norms.[5] For Henri Lefebvre, whose formation combined sociology and phenomenology, this de-enchantment does not mean disenchantment, the usual translation of Weber's *Entzauberung*, but rather aspiration to its opposite, to the rights and freedoms that might lead to the good life. In his view, citizens claim their "right to the city" through active engagement that involves play and imagination as well as work (1968, 107; 1996, 147). Lefebvre's reflections inspired the serious play of the Situationists, who remapped and reimagined mid-twentieth-century Paris against the grain of capital. They could also be applied to the productive combinations of politics and performance in other upstart cities as apparently different as Chicago—from the anarchist uprisings under the Haymarket banner of the 1880s to the civil and uncivil activity of 2011, the year of the Occupy Movement and the 125th anniversary of the Haymarket confrontation between protestors and the police (Kruger 2012)—or Bogotá, whose mayor deployed mimes and other artists to begin the challenging task of rendering

5. *Entzauberung* is translated as "disenchantment" in *Science as Vocation* (1989) as in previous translations but, while the standard translation captures the disillusionment of a fall from grace or magic, it misses Weber's sense of the power of scientific thinking made possible by the critique of superstition, which is captured by "de-enchantment."

civil the uncivil urban practices of drivers and walkers alike (Sommer 2006). Following Lefebvre's contemporary, phenomenologist Maurice Merleau-Ponty, South African–born landscape architect and historian Jeremy Foster highlights the dialectic between human subjects and the lived environment they inhabit and, by calling this phenomenon *spac-ing* (2008, 82), highlights the spatial practices by human bodies and by the bodies of corporate making and remaking environments. While focusing mostly on terrains identified as the hinterland or the heart of the country, Foster's treatment of landscape, including the occasional urban site as well as the "socio-nature" of the cultivated park, as "an assemblage of material and cultural practices" (88), highlights the contribution not only of perception but also of imagination to the creation of lived environments and thus, in Lefebvre's terms, the real impact of "structures of enchantment [*structures d'enchantement*]" (Lefebvre 1968, 139; 1996, 173). More recently, South African literary critic Michael Titlestad has argued that literature of the city is "well placed to mediate between analytic maps and particular pathways of meaning" and thus between the "psycho-geographical understanding" of particular cities and the imagined narratives that rewrite these maps from new perspectives (Titlestad 2012: 679). These observations together highlight the dialectic between phenomenal understanding and structures of enchantment.

In the edgy city of Johannesburg, any claim of rights or even of new perspectives comes up against a history of refusal of such claims under the aegis of both official policy and customary behavior during segregation and apartheid, and against the hard facts of violent exclusion as well as habitual marginalization of unwanted others in the present, when more than 17 percent of the population has no visible income in the city that contributes 17 percent of the entire country's GDP (Burdett and Sudjic 2007, 198)—facts that suggest anything other than enchantment. This history of exclusion is not new. Strangers have haunted the imagination of Johannesburg's residents and rulers, whatever the names that they have been called, from the *Uitlanders* ("foreigners") that built the mining camps to the "citizens of Bantu homelands" whom the architects of apartheid wished to "endorse out" of the city (in the bureaucratic jargon of the day), to the *amaKwerekwere* ("those who speak funny") demonized by post-apartheid nativists. Their identities have never been fixed, however. The shifting boundary between kin and stranger, native and foreign, us and them, invites critical reflection on the aspirations toward civility and cosmopolitanism in the present-day city's aspirations to remedy a long history of exclusion while still policing economic and political borders.

Civil, Cosmopolitan, and Other Terms of Urban Hospitality

Upstart cities in the North as well as the South have challenged the norms of modernity and civility in the North by demonstrating the constitutive character of tensions between civil and uncivil modernity in urban life. This challenge is also a potential critique of the normative association of cosmopolitan agency with a global elite. The cluster of terms around edgy city, from innovation to illegality, urbanity to incivility, provides an idiom that is visual as well as verbal, cultural as well as political, playful as well as productive for representing hospitality as well as hostility. In Johannesburg, past and present, top-down attempts at creating formal order have had to contend with what Asef Bayat calls the "uncivil practices of little people" (1997, 53), but as AbdouMalique Simone's influential reflections on "belonging and becoming" (1998, 2004a, 2004b; Götz and Simone 2003) suggest, uncivil modern practices of migration from squatting to smuggling are still modern and, as a persistent response to unequal access to the goods of modernization, paradoxically civil in the sense that these and other informal transactions form part of city life and of inalienable city rights, despite the attempts of elites to alienate them. Language describing this uncivil modernity need not be xenophobic; it can accommodate cosmopolitan affiliations as they are expressed in exchange, whether economic, social, or imaginative. In thinking about cosmopolitan affiliations in process, I am drawing on Ulrich Beck and Natan Sznaider, who distinguish between the normative-philosophical concept of Enlightenment cosmopolitanism represented by the leisured and cultivated *Weltbürger* on the model of J. W. Goethe—citizen of the world who transcends national conflicts and ethnic differences—and what they call the "realistic cosmopolitanism" of transnational migrants, a cosmopolitan condition born of "unintended and unseen side-effects of actions which are not intended as cosmopolitan" (2006, 7). While I share Beck's and Sznaider's interest in a cosmopolitan condition whose subjects may or may not aspire to the leisure and the wealth of the *Weltbürger*, I disagree with their emphasis on unintended side effects, since this formulation eclipses the agency of those who have to negotiate the volatile persona of the stranger while seeking more amenable roles in new environments.

This tension between normative cosmopolitanism and realistic or "tactical" cosmopolitan agency has received much attention, as twenty-first-century Johannesburg grapples with migrants both internal and external (Landau and Haupt 2007; Hassim et al. 2008; Segatti and Landau 2011a; Segatti 2011; Landau 2012), but the colonization of whole neighborhoods by so-called foreigners that has provoked this recent attention is not a new phenomenon. In the 1880s and 1890s, South African Republic President Paul Kruger and his fellow Afrikaners refused citizenship to the *Uitlanders* (foreigners), whether they were the English-speaking mining elite or working-class migrants speaking German, Yiddish, Cantonese, or Gujarati, as well as different British dialects. *Uitlanders* outnumbered Afrikaners in the city by 1890, only four years after the discovery of gold; the grievances of mining magnates encouraged the so-called Jameson Raid, the attempted coup by Leander Starr Jameson and associates including Frank Rhodes, the brother of gold and diamond magnate Cecil Rhodes. The end of the Anglo-Boer War in 1902 brought newcomers to Johannesburg from across the world, to join those already there such as anti-imperial dissident Mohandas Gandhi, whose international stature grew in part as a result of his political and legal work in Johannesburg. The Rand Revolt, led by white miners against the Union government in 1922, included workers from the British Empire and beyond. By the time Johannesburg celebrated its fiftieth anniversary in 1936, the presence of foreigners, including black mine workers from South Africa's colonial neighbors such as British Basutoland or Portuguese East Africa, had become essential for supporting the capital investments that enabled the conspicuous symbols of cosmopolitan aspiration in modern architecture. Capital also enabled the import of high-profile culture brokers like Belgian director, writer, and Pageant Master André van Gyseghem, who brought European innovation in the 1930s and 1940s. Even under the parochial rule of Afrikaner Nationalism and apartheid (1948–90), when the country's isolation was reinforced by the anti-apartheid boycott of cultural and economic exchange, cosmopolitan links persisted. African Nationalists from the ANC (1950s) to the Black Consciousness Movement (from the 1970s on) drew inspiration from international trends derived from communism, socialism, and Gandhian civil disobedience in the earlier period, to American Black Power movements and postcolonial African state formation in the later. The attributes that Loren Landau and colleagues at the African Centre for Migration and Society (ACMS) find in current trends—in particular, the increase in mobility that has left inner-city districts mostly populated by African migrants, and which has created the phenomenon of improvised governance that Landau calls "hospitality without hosts" (Landau 2012)—represent the intensification of historical phenomena rather than the utterly new. Recalling these histories of cosmopolitan exchange, as well as of their xenophobic disavowal since the nineteenth century, counters the rather amnesiac language of exception and emergency with which both cosmopolitanism and xenophobia have been treated in the early twenty-first century.

By treating cosmopolitan as an attribute rather than a concept or an institution, I wish to show the improvised, performative quality of cosmopolitan agency, affiliation, or practices. By focusing on imaginative exchange, I mean to highlight not only performance in the narrower sense, but also the production of culturally and ultimately socially compelling narratives through fictions that capture the imagination of city dwellers at home and abroad. Imaginative representations in fiction, whether prose or film, as well as other verbal and visual arts, may give us an opportunity to test the subjunctive narratives of belonging, becoming, and encounters with strangers that have yet to secure a place in reality. This understanding of urban civility takes "cosmopolitan" in its broadest senses as the acceptance of multiple affiliations and the reimagining of citizenship and civility to draw strangers in to what I would call the *drama of hospitality*. This drama is not so much a fully formed work or script as a combination of affiliations and practices whose improvisation might enact new ways of interacting across multiple desire lines. The term "desire lines" joins the planner's understanding of "informal paths that pedestrians prefer to [. . .] using a sidewalk or other official route" (Shepherd and Murray 2007, 1) with the pedestrian's improvisation and the performers's imagining of new trajectories through the city. In Johannesburg, these practices have included collaborations across class, language, and national identities, among both artists and traders. Their actors include speakers of South African languages from Afrikaans, English, and Zulu to Tsonga and Portuguese. The latter two may be perceived as foreign (identified in this case with Mozambique, formerly Portuguese East Africa) but have been spoken in South Africa for generations. They have been joined since the end of apartheid by newcomers speaking languages from Amharic and Wolof to French and Mandarin. The languages in use at the present moment may therefore be different from those spoken at the turn of the last century, but the nativist perception of foreign invasion and the challenge of hospitality alike call for, at the very least, critical comparison of earlier and more recent decades.

What Time Is This Place? Excavating and Imagining the City Past, Present, and Yet to Come

The conflict over the production and experience of the modern city has in Johannesburg, like other edgy cities that grew quickly, fueled by speculation rather than planning, been repeatedly enacted in the creation and the contestation of the built environment. Innovation in the built environment, especially with the building boom in the 1930s, expressed in part the diversification of mining capital into real estate, but also the symbolic dimensions of these structures, whether expressed in imaginative acts or performance, imaginative writing, or visual representation. By performance I include embodied spatial practices that take in parades, marches, and inaugurations, but would also argue that the force of these practices draws not only on their social appearance but also on the sense of performance as the embodied practice of imagination, or what Raymond Williams called the subjunctive, perhaps utopian dimension of performance against the oppressive weight of actual or indicative reality (1981, 219). Performance deserves close attention not only from performance studies specialists, but also from all people interested in urban form and culture, because of the performative turn in urbanist writing as well as the embodied dimension of urban spatial practice. Urbanists since Lewis Mumford, who saw the city circa 1936 as "the scene of social drama" (1996 [1937], 185), routinely use the language of theatre, from tragedy to playfulness, but do not ground their metaphors in performance and its contexts. The persistence of performance in urbanist discourse highlights not only the contribution of embodied practices to the life and meaning of the city, but also the tension between order and disruption, between the modern civility of the urban planners and the uncivil modernity of the edgy city. Further, as Foster has more recently argued, the imagination of particular places in narrative fiction and visual depiction has shaped the ordinary perception of place in the world outside the fiction, so that the significance of the place becomes a synthesis of the terrain and of "subjective meanings" applied to it not only by "generations of authors" (2008, 88), but also by generations of readers, viewers, and others whose daily spatial practices produce the city they inhabit.

Even if the built environment is not alive in the ecological sense with which Richard Schechner begins *Environmental Theatre* (1994, x), the structures of the urban landscape not only bear traces of life as it was, but act as shaping environments of life as it is now and may yet become. As urbanist Kevin Lynch argues in *What Time Is This Place?* the historicist desire to "arrest the past" by "restoration" alone "cannot easily reconstruct the circumstance that created it" (1972, 32), nor allow that any such place may bear traces not only of different times but also of a series of imaginative acts that may have created, changed, or buried a succession of structures and environments. As Mike Pearson and Michael Shanks suggest, performative archeology includes not only the excavation of buried structures, but the reconstruction of performances that inhabited, shaped, and contested those structures (2001, 5) and, I would argue, those that imagine future alternatives. Johannesburg's Park Station, a central site (just east of Newtown on the map) marking historic times as well as a key place of urban arrival, invites this imaginative archeology. Heralding the gold-driven building boom of the 1930s, the building by Gerard Moerdijk and Gordon Leith, decorated with murals of flora, fauna, and white pioneer history (Foster 2008, plate 38), replaced the 1897 Victorian structure whose cast-iron skeleton still stands on concrete pilings on open land south of the train tracks and the Newtown Cultural Precinct (Cabral 2010, 4–5; 2011). The new structure celebrated "Johannesburg's economic importance" as well as "the romance of long-distance travel" (Foster 2008, 203, 204). It was also the threshold for the tens of thousands of black migrants who poured into the city from the 1930s, despite increasingly draconian Urban Areas Acts that tried to exclude them, and the site of wonder and disillusionment imagined in narratives as apparently different as Alan Paton's novel *Cry, the Beloved Country* (1948) and Lionel Rogosin's film *Come Back Africa* (1959). Even long after this Park Station building was replaced by the New Station Complex in 1965 (Chipkin 1993, 254), its ghost haunted Zola Maseko's 2002 film of Paton's 1960 story "A Drink in the Passage," represented in that film by the neoclassical City Hall on Market and Rissik Streets—in the center of the dense grid above the City Centre label on the map and also sketched in *Gold in Graphite: Jozi Sketchbook* (Cabral 2010, 10). Thus, the multiple times that swirl around the station and its surrogates enable the investigation of competing representations of a city notorious for obliterating its history.

The pertinence of Lynch's book-title-as-question, *What Time Is This Place?* can best be seen in those rare sites that have, against the odds, survived many decades of demolition that felled imposing structures such as the two successive Park Stations discussed above. The Drill Hall (located just south of Hillbrow on Cabral's map) has survived for more than a century and thus offers what is for Johannesburg a rare repository of the city's history. Indeed, Lindsay Bremner and Pep Subirós go so far as to claim that "the rise, fall and ultimate triumph of the Drill Hall narrates the history of the city" (2007, 58; photographs 59–61). Opened in 1904 to house the Rand Light Infantry and other British Imperial forces, whose troops assembled on the adjacent Union Grounds to quell rebellion by the recently defeated Boers, it functioned as barracks during World War I and World War II, a temporary factory manufacturing artificial limbs for veterans of World War I, the state's headquarters for counterinsurgency action against the white workers' uprising known as the Rand Revolt of 1922, and the initial site, in 1956, of the Treason Trials against members of the African National Congress (ANC) and their allies, until public demonstrations in Twist Street outside the hall prompted the government to move the trials to the executive capital (and Afrikaner stronghold) of Pretoria in 1957. While commemoration of the Treason Trials (whose capitalization highlights their official importance) and their defendants, including Nelson Mandela and associates, remains permanently in the exhibition space that has been the Drill Hall's most visible function since its renovation in 2004, in 2012 the building housed tenants who run the gamut from community services such as Johannesburg Child Welfare to the artists and researchers in the Keleketla Media Arts Project. The work undertaken by these organizations includes the negotiation of formal and informal rights for a variety of stakeholder claims to coveted spaces like the Union Grounds across the road, once a parade ground and now a hotly contested minibus taxi rank, and the investigation of informal occupation and employment in contiguous areas of concern such as the garment district to the east and Africa's densest square kilometer, Hillbrow to the immediate north.[6]

Other sites similarly combine visible and invisible traces. Newtown may be identified as the location of the internationally renowned Market Theatre in the former Fruit Market, but the district's other buildings, whether renovated, such as Turbine Hall, or new, such as the Brickfields mixed-income housing development, hark back to moments of uncivil modernity: to the explosion of dynamite that leveled not only the nearby brick warehouses but also a large part of the city in 1896, or to 1922, when the district was one of many sites of confrontation between police and strikers in the Rand Revolt, even though these traces are harder to see than the theatre or the renovation of the district as cultural precinct that began with Johannesburg's centenary in 1986 and has accelerated since 2000 (Gaule 2005). Still other sites represent, in imagined memory, city managements' penchant for neglect and demolition: across the road from the renovated City Hall (now the Gauteng Provincial Legislature) the Rissik Street Post Office (sketch: Cabral 2010, 9), which featured fleetingly in writer Herman Charles Bosman's account of political street processions in the 1930s (Bosman 1981) and was vacated in the 1990s but reappeared in various guises in film, for instance as a newsroom in the television series *Hard Copy* (Harber and Purkey 2002–5), only to fall between the cracks created by disputes between city and state agencies

6. For a summary history of the Drill Hall, see Ben-Zeev et al. (2006) and Chapters 2 and 5 of this book.

responsible for heritage. While Drill Hall, like the few traces of the 1936 Empire Exhibition still standing on what is now the west campus of Witwaersrand University (the apparently open space to the east of the Auckland Park sign on the map), invites the investigation of multiple times of particular places, a more recent development makes heritage a commodity. Main Street Life (2010), a multiuse site in the southeast inner city, in the optimistically named Maboneng (Place of Light) precinct (south of Doornfontein, west of Jeppestown, and to the near-northeast of the City Centre label on Cabral's map), which encompasses a cluster of galleries known as Arts on Main (2009), includes residential and retail spaces, an art cinema, and a hotel with rooms decorated with bric-a-brac representing each of the twelve decades of Johannesburg, from the 1890s to the 2000s. In combination with a website that features self-presentation and advertising by artists and entrepreneurs in residence, this site offers both the brazen commodification of heritage as kitsch and inadvertently ironic commentary on Johannesburg's habitual destruction and exploitation of same.

The promotion of Arts on Main and Main Street Life (two sites that disguise their actual entrances on Fox Street in order to claim the symbolic centrality of a Main Street address) also highlights Johannesburg's practice of urban simulation, or the simulation of urbanity as well as civic order in built environments that are often both more and less than they seem. From the Beaux Arts buildings whose structural material (steel and wrought iron) had to be imported from Britain, through local concrete replications of several iterations of Chicago style art moderne in the 1930s, high modernity in the line of Skidmore, Owings, and Merrill in the late 1960s, and postmodern Helmut Jahn in the 1980s, to the simulated Main Street in the privately owned and fully policed Melrose Arch in the 2000s (on the northern edge of the map but well within the limits of Johannesburg), built environments in Johannesburg often appear to simulate urbanity rather than to reinvent it. Nevertheless, these simulations have provoked controversies not only about the historically uneven deployment of resources, but also about the symbolic ownership of territory reflected in street names. While Main Street seems neutral, even bland, its use to simulate public thoroughfares that are neither public nor truly thoroughfares—streets named after people, particularly colonial and apartheid officials—provides easy symbols of transformation in the post-apartheid era, when substantial redistribution of resources has not been forthcoming. Although renaming a major thoroughfare through Afrikaans neighborhoods after the dissident Beyers Naudé to replace the apartheid-era prime minister D. F. Malan makes for persuasive politics, as does the renaming of smaller streets in the Newtown Cultural Precinct after key figures like Miriam Makeba or Henry Nxumalo and the dedication of the bus terminal square to Gandhi, threats to replace names that mark the city's gold mining history in a non-controversial manner, such as Commissioner Street, the longest east-west thoroughfare, and its extension in both directions as the Main Reef Road, which roughly follows the old gold seam of the Rand, would be a spendthrift as well as grandiose act of willful amnesia.

Although Johannesburg's cycles of demolition and renovation every generation may deter archeologists, performative or otherwise, recent work on particular sites of historical enactment as well as historical amnesia demonstrates its potential. As the above examples of the Drill Hall and the Market Theatre suggest, those rare structures that have survived the wrecking ball, and even those that linger only in memory, mark the *placing of time* as well as the complex interplay of documented or "declarative memory" and the "non-declarative" or "phenomenological" memory, as noted by Foster (2009, 209), of the corporeal experience of colliding times in the place occupied, visited, or imagined. Especially in the last two decades, theorists and practitioners of urban spatial practices in contemporary Johannesburg, including the imaginative practices of fiction alongside the practice of building and demolishing, have activated and analyzed productive networks bringing together play and work, management and imagination, planning and performance, belonging and becoming. The creativity and crime that defined the city in the uncertain years of the interregnum, which in terms of governance extended well after the historic national election of 1994 and the municipal elections in Johannesburg and other cities, inspired fiction writers (Hope, Vladislavić, Mpe, Beukes), theatre-makers (Purkey, Slabolepszy, Grootboom), filmmakers (Hammon, Tilley, Maseko, Matabane), the mutable collective creative teams producing television serials, and their critics to capture the edgy city (Kruger 2001a, 2004b, 2006, 2009a, 2009b, 2010a). In the new century, initiatives included the Joubert Park Project (JPP; Kurgan and Ractliffe 2005), which combined the work of artists, planners, and youth organizers in the inner city (2000–2009), and the contributions of international organizations, especially their collaboration in 2007 with Cascoland, a Dutch organization committed to facilitating social as well as artistic renovation out of the particular form and forces of specific sites with local cultural and social workers. The Cascoland project included practical work in projects like building new iron fencing that created both a secure perimeter and a series of incorporated work benches for entrepreneurs around their headquarters in the inner-city Drill Hall, as well as pedestrian direction and choreography outside and performance and skills training inside (De Bell and Schoenmakers 2008). JPP has since ceased operations, but another organization, which began with Stephen Hobbs and *Tour Guides of the Inner City* (2000), continues as the design company Trinity Session, which was officially incorporated in 2002 and is at the time of writing involved directly or indirectly in most work at the interface between art and planning in Johannesburg.

By encompassing the arts of writing and performing, and narrative fiction and film, and by attending to the evolution of these forms in the urban environment that has shaped them across the twentieth century and into the twenty-first, this book speaks to readers interested in art and architecture, history, literature, performance, and other media in Johannesburg and in other cities across the world. It offers analysis of the urban imagination and its social contexts of upheaval and transformation in Johannesburg, from the Empire Exhibition (1936) through the violent refashioning of the urban as well as the political geography, and resistance to it in the apartheid era (1948–90), to the innovation and turmoil of the early twenty-first century. Building in the city serves as a focal point because it brings together in concrete (and other materials) the physical and social transformation of the environment with the aesthetics of modernity, from the skyscraper to the cinema, and thus functions as an agent of urbanization as well as an actor on, rather than a mere backdrop for, fictional characters immersed or lost in the city. Analyzing cultural forms, high or low, mass or arcane, from literary fiction and theatre to street performance and television and their representation of the city in turn, requires the analysis of the roles played by particular buildings and other built elements in planned and unplanned districts and neighborhoods in these representations. As I suggest in "Filming the Edgy City" (2006), a particular edifice might begin by functioning conventionally as an index of modernity or decay (or both), but by the end of the film anticipate transformation, even against the odds. The Ponte City tower (1975) on the edge of Hillbrow above Doornfontein, for instance, provides the establishing shot for Zola Maseko's trenchant short film *The Foreigner* (1997), and documents both the imposing exterior and dilapidated interior of this apartment tower built for white yuppies but housing, in the 1990s when this film was made, predominantly Francophone African migrants. As the site for a dream-epiphany of the young boy befriended by the eponymous foreigner, the space transcends this documentary frame to evoke not only the past of a segregated and thus stunted modernity, but also a future of cosmopolitan exchange that might overcome pervasive xenophobia in the striving toward a pan-African modern city.

Returning to the term "edgy city" in the second decade of this century, after inventing it to capture the sense of the final decade of the last, I would argue that "edgy" registers not only nervousness, but also an awareness of unpredictable opportunities, and thus may sound a note of provisional optimism that we might capture the "elusive metropolis" (Nuttall and Mbembe 2008). In my view, Johannesburg's cultural forms are more *allusive* than elusive and tend to cite rather than merely mimic their sources in the manner implied by the "aesthetics of superfluity" (Mbembe 2008, 38–42). For instance, the exposition buildings of the 1936 Empire Exhibition called forth arguments against the import of "Chicago styles" (in particular those of the Century of Progress exposition, 1933–34), while Ponte City (1975), comprising shops and a health club as well as apartments in a cylindrical tower, paid homage to Bertrand Goldberg's Marina City (1964), twin sixty-story cylindrical apartment buildings in Chicago, but the Johannesburg projects also responded to the specific conditions of the highveld environment, specifically, bedrock, moderate climate, and sunshine (as against the clay, extreme temperatures, and intermittent grey skies of Chicago) and, in 2012, the newly renovated Ponte presented its revival from a nadir of illicit sex work, drug dealing, and asset stripping in typical Johannesburg boosterish language as a "fourth coming" (Bauer 2012). Further, the aesthetics and politics of this citational practice cannot be exclusively measured by internationally acclaimed artistic work (such as the Johannesburg images of William Kentridge) but ought also to engage with popular culture, in particular the avid local consumption of film and television serials that use variations on the Johannesburg skyline as their signature punctuation. Soap operas like the long-running *Generations* (1994–) also engage city history, even if their citation of the built environment is more cavalier than cerebral (and shorter-lived) series like the finance capital drama *The LAB* (2006–8; see Kruger 2010a). The mid-twentieth-century feature that gave its name, *Jim Comes to Joburg* (1949), to the defining genre of Johannesburg narrative film, recalls gangster icons like Humphrey Bogart as well as African American showmen like Cab Calloway. The "American" gangster in 1950s Johannesburg, however, whatever his allusion to Humphrey Bogart or to Richard Widmark, spoke Zulu, Sotho, or *tsotsitaal* (gangster lingo; a.k.a. *flaaitaal*) as well as English and listened to music that was, as composer and writer Todd Matshikiza pointed out in *Drum*, local as well as international in its modernity; his heirs in the twenty-first century still speak variations on *flaaitaal*, even if they listen to *kwaito* rather than jazz.

As the late writer and actor John Matshikiza (son of Todd) reminded his readers, Johannesburg does not just mimic movie images. Its own form—jagged edges, incomplete projects, sharp contrasts, as well as aspirations to greatness, nonetheless—resembles an "unfinished movie" (2008, 222) or, as Nestor Garciá-Canclini said of Mexico City, "a rough draft" (2009, 81). The city transforms the narrative structure and content that it appropriates from many sources and superimposes them on the built environment, literally as well as figuratively, to recreate its image and its inhabitants. Kentridge's short films, with their charcoal lines and visible erasures, animate images and figures from Johannesburg's early days to enact both the force and the evanescence of this superimposition. His protagonist Soho Eckstein recalls mining magnate Herman Eckstein in contrast with the rumpled figure of the artist disguised as Felix Teitelbaum, in landscapes marked by mine dumps and mining headgear, as well as native and imported flora, and penetrated by objects that morph from coffee-pot plungers to drills to shovels digging up corpses. Titles like *Johannesburg, 2nd Greatest City After Paris* allude to the Beaux Arts dreams of the first generation of builders, while *Woyzeck on the Highveld* deploys Büchner's pioneering proletarian tragedy, Kentridge's animations, and the poignant figures of Handspring Puppet Theatre to portray the plight of black migrants. Kentridge's ironic allusion to Paris may be tempered by the softened blur of hand-erased charcoal drawings, but the display of his work at Johannesburg sites that both inspired and reflect it—for instance at the now-shuttered Top Star Drive-In on top of an old mine dump as part of the *Tour Guides of the Inner City* in 2000—highlights the material ground of his figurative archeology. More recently, Mary Sibande's Sophie, a maid in royal blue Victorian costume, inhabited gallery exhibitions as a life-size figure based on the artist's performance of the character as homage, in *Hail to the Dead Queen*, to generations of black women in domestic service, and provoked ordinary pedestrians with nineteen images, multiple stories high, draped on inner-city buildings in July and August 2010. These images not only evoked the history of domestic work hidden behind suburban walls, but also exposed this work to the public eye, as the images amplified the symbiosis of art and labor in the built environment. In the shadows of these public images, domestic and other workers support the city's material and human infrastructures. The claims made on the city by these workers and the many migrants who yet aspire to work here may be less visible and more precarious, but theirs is a *sustained precarity*, a tenacious habitation real and imagined, which persists despite the odds against them.

Organization and Chapters

Working against the willful amnesia that has passed for memory in Johannesburg, this book excavates the history of the city and builds new links among recurring themes and forms in the literary, visual, and built representation of the urban imagination, in this city and in others with which it invites comparison. The projects sketched above and others discussed below remind us that, even in twelve decades, Johannesburg's answers to Lynch's question (*What time is this place?*) multiply across temporal and spatial coordinates, as they produce after-images and echoes from half-remembered periods and buried strata. The five chapters may thus be read in several ways. The most obvious would be in chronological order, following the signposts that lead from 1936, the year of the Empire Exhibition and of Johannesburg's first explicit claim for cosmopolitan modernity, prompted by half a century of growth, as well as its inevitably contradictory realization within the increasingly rigid racial segregation marked by the Slums Act of 1934 and the Representation of Natives Act (which effectively disenfranchised African voters) in 1936. While acknowledging key earlier dates such as 1896 (the year that began with the failed Jameson Raid and went on to the massive Brickfields explosion), 1910 (the Act of Union and the move from colonial to dominion status), 1922 (the Rand Revolt), and 1926 (the year of the city's proposed and abandoned Civic Survey), the book begins substantially with 1936 and continues thereafter with dates marking anniversaries at roughly twenty-year intervals. The year 1956 encompasses not only the Treason Trials, which began in Johannesburg's Drill Hall, but also the cultures of liberal dissent and radical resistance, expressed in fictional and film narrative, and the demise of both movements under the heel of an ever-more-powerful police state. More familiar to most readers, 1976 signifies a new generation of resistance, expressed above all in poetry and theatre, and 1996 examines representations of the anxiety and anticipation around the transition represented by the first post-apartheid city election of that year. For practical reasons, the final chapter breaks with this pattern of two-decade intervals, but 2012, as the centennial year of the ANC and of one of Johannesburg's most storied districts, Alexandra, offers a compelling alternative. While key events did not always happen on these dates, they are sufficiently auspicious to work as touchstones for events in their proximity. In addition to using Zafrica Cabral's map and comparative sketch of Johannesburg skyscrapers as points of reference throughout, each chapter also features photography or, in some cases, a particular photographer whose insights into the period in question illuminate the texts under discussion, as well as images of performance, art, and location shots.

Readers interested in forms and links other than linear progression might note that the first and last chapters focus on spatial practices, especially architecture and urban design or the gaps in design, mediated by imaginative representation, and thus deconstruct the ahistorical claims for the newness of the "world class African city" in the twenty-first century by juxtaposing it with its largely unacknowledged predecessor, "Africa's Wonder City" of the Johannesburg Jubilee in 1936. Building on this architectural base, Chapters 2 and 4 lay out the contribution to understanding and imagining the city from narratives in fiction and film, recounting the violent transformations and predictions of catastrophe circa 1956, with the imposition of the apartheid police state on the ruins of integration, or, in 1996, the emergence of post-anti-apartheid, if not yet fully post-apartheid, integrated institutions. This focus on narrative movement in space and time highlights the formal and historical entwinement of storytelling and migration in both periods of accelerated movement in which "all roads [and railroads] lead to Johannesburg" (Paton 1987 [1948], 52). In the center is the book's longest chapter, which takes as its point of departure 1976, the year when Soweto and the uprising erupted into the national consciousness, provoking radical rethinking of Johannesburg's limits and the rights to urban life. Focusing on the concentrated immediacy of theatre and of poetry, especially poetry in performance, while contrasting this immediate expression of powerful feeling with narrative recollections of the uprising and its aftermath, this chapter combines readings of texts and performances that capture the intensity of the moment with critical reflection on the legacy of a turning point that at that time "did not turn" (Kane-Berman 1978, 232) but that nevertheless eventually transformed the country. This critical reflection challenges the forgetfulness that leads even post-apartheid critics with access to recently uncensored archives to treat Soweto and the Soweto writers as phenomena without precedent or tradition. It also shows the cosmopolitan elements of the Johannesburg imagination even at the moment of South Africa's greatest international isolation, and thus the transnational dimension of the claim that "the Soweto uprising changed South Africa forever" (Orkin 1995, 72). As the following chapter summaries show, the theoretical armature of this book rests on the transnational legacy and interdisciplinary methods of comparative literature and comparative arts research to place the edgy city of Johannesburg in the multiple worlds of its imagination.

Chapter 1: 1936: Johannesburg Jubilee

This chapter examines competing claims to represent Johannesburg's modernity on the occasion of its fiftieth anniversary, the first occasion for claims of mature modernity without the apologias for urban adolescence that characterized earlier anniversaries as late as the fortieth. It includes not only the display of elite representation in the Empire Exhibition's "White City" and the transformation of the built environment in the city at large through localized versions of the international and art moderne styles of architecture, but also the attempts of urban blacks, or "New Africans," to assert their claims to the city from the formal Emancipation Centenary Celebrations of 1934 to acts of protest, on literary and legal stages, against a series of Urban Areas Acts that increasingly restricted their right to the city. The chapter also juxtaposes the debates about the Empire Exhibition and African modernity with the views of contemporary architects (Rex Martienssen, sole southern hemisphere associate of Le Corbusier's International Movement, and Hermann Kallenbach, friend of Gandhi and heir of German modernism) and their international mentors (Le Corbusier on the one hand, Peter Behrens and Walter Gropius on the other), as well as street demonstrations from the Rand Revolt in 1922 to Garment Worker Union parades into the 1930s, writer Herman Charles Bosman's reflections on "Johannesburg riots" in the 1940s, and the domestication of street revolt in *Red Rand*, the play by Lewis Sowden performed in the new theatre in the Johannesburg Public Library in 1937. The images for this chapter are drawn from the Empire Exhibition archive, but also illuminate the architectural and performance forms of the period.

Chapter 2: 1956: Genres of Johannesburg

Using as its point of departure the comment of the activist Anna Louw in Nadine Gordimer's novel *A World of Strangers* (1962) [1958], who lamented that Johannesburg had "no genre of its own," this chapter highlights responses in different narrative genres to a period marked both by regret for the passing of the "intercultural bohemia" that Lewis Nkosi found in the precariously integrated Sophiatown, dubbed the Chicago of South Africa, which was razed by apartheid's social engineering, and the mass resistance kindled by the resurgent ANC. While 1956 is officially remembered for the Treason Trials, in which the apartheid state attempted to indict more than a hundred political activists including Nelson Mandela, it also saw the celebration of Johannesburg's seventieth anniversary, which included a cantata for two hundred voices and seventy-piece orchestra by composer and *Drum* "Music for Moderns" columnist Todd Matshikiza. These exceptional events notwithstanding, the decade was marked at the beginning and end by longer-lasting transformations—not only the intensification of segregation and political repression but also, despite this state violence, the steady migration of blacks into Johannesburg and the vivid representation of this migration in photographic and cinematic images. From the powerful if sentimental social melodrama of *Cry, the Beloved Country* by the liberal Paton and its cinematic adaptation by socialist John Howard Lawson (1951), to *Jim Comes to Joburg* (1949), the film that gave its name to a genre that has persisted to the present, to the overtly political revision of the genre in *Come Back Africa* by way of the incendiary images of photojournalists like Bob Gosani and Jurgen Schadeberg, whose images are featured in this chapter, film and photography documented public politics and everyday life until the apartheid state clamped down on representation as well as activity in the 1960s.

Chapter 3: 1976: Soweto Erupts into Johannesburg

The year 1976 signifies above all the Soweto uprising, and thus retrospectively, the beginning of the end of apartheid, but it also marks the founding of the Market Theatre in Newtown, near the site of the Brickfields explosion of 1896, and the great number of political and cultural projects within universities and a host of nongovernmental organizations intended to reinvent an integrated city in the teeth of the apartheid state, ranging from champions of interracial collaboration such as the Christian Institute or the Wits History Workshop to avowed separatists like the Black Consciousness Movement, whose adherents nonetheless maintained ties to sympathetic whites. This chapter juxtaposes the horizontal vastness of Soweto's "matchbox" houses with the high-rise monuments of the apartheid building boom, including the Police HQ (and site of torture) at John Vorster Square, and the Carlton Centre, the tallest building in Africa and site of apartheid absurdity with its restaurant open to "international" blacks including Bantustan bureaucrats, but not to black township residents. These sites in turn provide coordinates for readings of poets and theatre practitioners inspired and also angered by Johannesburg and Soweto, and for the analysis of prose fiction by white authors (André Brink's *A Dry White Season* [1979], his sole novel published in Johannesburg) and black authors (the Soweto novels of Sipho Sepamla, including *A Ride on the Whirlwind* [1984b], and Miriam Tlali's *Amandla* [2005 (1980)]). It concludes with an examination of creative and critical writing that resonates with Njabulo Ndebele's call for a "rediscovery of the ordinary" against the "spectacular" tendencies of anti-apartheid protest writing in narratives of ordinary life, including writing about the inner city by Tlali and the Indian South African Ahmed Essop. The featured photographer in this chapter is David Goldblatt, whose documentation of Johannesburg dates from 1948 but whose pictures of Soweto and the inner city from the 1970s are particularly pertinent here.

Chapter 4: 1996: Edgy City

In 1996 the first free local elections (as against the national elections in 1994) took place and thus ushered in a delayed response to the problems that had troubled Johannesburg since the 1980s, from capital flight to unregulated in-migration, from the malign neglect of the built environment to the first attempts, on the part of the Inner City Office (1999–2001) as well as cultural and social groups, to make the city manageable and imaginable again. It thus represents less a fully achieved post-apartheid moment than a post-anti-apartheid interregnum, in which the clear lines of battle that characterized the anti-apartheid struggle had yet to be transformed into a convincing narrative of liberation. Most notable are cinematic and other visual treatments of the transition such as the films *Wheels and Deals* (Hammon 1991) and *Jump the Gun* (Blair 1996) and television series such as *The Line* (1994) and its contemporaries. Also key are prose texts, including exemplary fiction about the inner city not only in English, such as Phaswane Mpe's *Welcome to Our Hillbrow* (2001), but also in Afrikaans, such as the work of the writer known as Kleinboer, and of Marlene van Niekerk, whose *Triomf* (1994) was not only, since P. G. du Plessis's play *Siener in die Suburbs* (1974), the first Afrikaans text to tackle the lives and language of Johannesburg's white underclass, but also a taboo-breaking depiction of deeply buried stories of domestic and social pathology that have haunted urban Afrikaans history since the 1930s. Texts in English highlight narratives that blur the sharp boundaries between native and foreigner, whether explicitly as in the short but vivid film *The Foreigner* (1997), or in a more nuanced fashion in the fiction of Achmat Dangor and Phaswane Mpe. The chapter culminates with Ivan Vladislavić, whose minutely observed vignettes of Johannesburg in the apocalyptic 1990s appeared individually in that decade, but whose short story collection *Propaganda by Monuments* (1996) creates a language and a form in connected fragments for exploring the edgy city that comes to fruition in the notes from the 1990s and beyond assembled in the collection *Portrait with Keys* (2006). Photographs include Guy Tillim's photo-essay *Jo'burg* (2005).

Chapter 5: 2012: City in the World

The book concludes by reflecting on Johannesburg's aspirations to become an "African world-class city" from the perspective of 2012, the centenary of the ruling ANC and of the storied district of Alexandra, but without losing sight of the 1936 motto of "Africa's Wonder City." The post-apartheid present undoubtedly differs from the neocolonial moment, but they share optimistic projections of Johannesburg's cosmopolitan modernity, expressed in architectural landmarks and wider urban renewal, as well as ambivalent responses to extreme discrepancies between rich and poor. Focusing on the inner city, the chapter notes the self-representation of the post-apartheid government in Constitution Hill and in the permanent exhibition on the Treason Trial in the renovated Drill Hall, and goes on to examine more closely smaller but more penetrating explorations of urban spatial practices by artists, activists, and their interlocutors, from the Joubert Park Project (2000–2009), housed in Drill Hall, to Jay Pather's *CityScapes* (2003), dance sequences inspired by and performed at sites from the Carlton Centre to Sandton City, to *Hillbrow/Dakar/Hillbrow* by Trinity Session (2007). The last two events are particularly interesting for their engagement with migrants in the inner city and their attempt to employ as well as represent a drama of hospitality to reground cosmopolitan agency in the activity of the street, in concert with direct and indirect responses to migration from the analysis of the African Centre of Migration and Society and the city's Migrant Office (since 2007) to the interface between policy and "people as infrastructure" (Simone 2004a) in renovation projects in inner-city Hillbrow. These have included *Ekhaya* (At Home), which brings together tenant organizations, owners, and developers to renovate apartment buildings, to the joint efforts of artists, planners, and residents to reclaim city parks through the public acknowledgment of desire lines: artist Maya Marx's steps up the steep rise of Pullinger Kop (2008), for instance, not only memorialize the words of Mpe's *Welcome to Our Hillbrow* etched into the steps but also provide, albeit inadvertently, local students and their migrant kin with opportunities to practice English by reciting as they walk. This grounding of works of art in quotidian activity suggests the ongoing if unpredictable force of structures of enchantment by testing, as Lefebvre put it, "new models of appropriating space and time" (1968, 139; 1996, 173) and thus actualizing the imagined in real structures and practices.

Bringing together models, moments, sites, stories, and the networks, both real and imagined, that link them, this book does not pretend to unearth every item of significance in Johannesburg. Rather than attempting an exhaustive survey of the terrain, this book wagers that the juxtaposition of different genres, forms, and representations of urban spatial practices in this edgy, fragmented, but still distinctive city will provide affective and critical links among hitherto separate realms of experience and fields of study and shed new light on some of the city's darker corners. Retracing the edges between lived-in districts and their conjured others, as well as between and among the domains of urban history and design, and literary, filmic, and performance analysis will, I hope, illuminate not only zones of conflict but also the practices and people engaged creatively in reimagining Johannesburg. The edgy city has throughout its history balanced precariously between enchantment and disenchantment, aspiration to great heights and wonders and pedestrian navigation of the ground below, but a sustained precarity has testified, and continues to testify to the tenacity of those who persist in urban spatial practices from formal building to informal trade, from political parades to public art, to pedestrian negotiations as yet unnamed, and in temporal practices of narrative and storytelling in old and new media—in writing, performing, and building Johannesburg.

Although focused on a singular case, this exploration has not been bound by it. Johannesburg's ambivalent mixture of cosmopolitan and xenophobic elements, and transnational and intensely local moments and representations, invites comparison across regions and continents. Rather than simply replace the self-conscious adaptation of northern models from London, New York, or Chicago with a mandate to privilege south-south contacts, whether in the mock-belligerent manner of the Australian cartographer of the "corrective map of the world" who asserted "south is superior" more than thirty years ago (McArthur 1979, n.p.) or in the more recent provocation in Jean and John Comaroff's *Theory from the South* that "the global south is running ahead of the global north" (2012, 19). Looking beyond the confines of this particular project to other cities north and south that offer points of comparison, such as Berlin, Bogotá, Chicago, Dakar, Los Angeles, or São Paolo, I invite readers of this study of one city to take to heart Anthony King's remark that "all cities today are 'world cities'" (1990, 82), with the understanding that their citizens aspire in unequal but nonetheless significant measure to inhabit the world and to imagine and re-imagine that habitation as their right to the city.

1 1936: AFRICA'S WONDER CITY

In September 1936, the Empire Exhibition opened in the Witwatersrand Showgrounds in Milner Park between Empire Road and the University of the Witwatersrand (founded in 1922; hereafter: Wits). The first Empire Exhibition to take place outside Britain, the exhibition and performance events celebrated not only Johannesburg's fiftieth anniversary, but also the city's aspirations to modernity. Although modeled in part on the first British Empire Exhibition at Wembley in 1924 (Woodham 1989, 15) and on pageants and other commemorations of British civilization staged from Canada to Australia, the Johannesburg exhibit contested Wembley's emphasis on agricultural and raw materials by drawing on American models such as Chicago to highlight the industrial modernity of Africa's most rapidly developing city. Like Chicago—whose boosters invented the moniker "White City" for the Columbian Exposition of 1893 and fostered the creation of distinctively modern architectural forms, beginning with the steel-frame skyscraper in the 1880s and continuing with the white facades and futurist signage of the 1933 Century of Progress (Kruger 2007)—Johannesburg's turn toward modernism celebrated robust, brash, even uncivil innovation to create what Lewis Mumford called, with reference to Chicago, the drama of the "urban scene" (1996 [1937], 185). Johannesburg also resembled Chicago in that its aspirations to modern progress rested uneasily on the contradictions of racial segregation. On the one hand, the rising gold price enabled a building boom, the transformation of the skyline, and the employment of black as well as white workers in the renovation of the city. On the other hand, the implementation of the Urban Areas Acts (1923, 1930) and the Slums Act (1934) made it more difficult for Africans, dubbed "temporary sojourners," to find housing within city limits, even as they contributed in increasingly large numbers to building that city (Beavon 2004, 71–118). A tiny elite of educated Africans was exempt from the most draconian enforcement of the pass laws and thus able, within the shifting boundaries of segregationist custom, to participate in the city's cultural life by attending performances and exhibitions with white patrons, but 1936 ushered in greater restrictions to their rights in the city and the country as a whole with legislation like the Representation of Natives Act, which restricted African voting rights.

Although open only from September 1936 to January 1937, the Empire Exhibition reflected, in its built environment and in the formal and informal enactments in and around it, the contradictions of the surrounding conurbation, caught between modern aspirations to international trade and cosmopolitan culture, and neocolonial dependence on black labor and on British cultural prestige as well as industrial goods, which persisted well after South Africa became a dominion of the British Commonwealth in 1910. As a "miniature city" on display for "folk of all ages and divers races" (Crocker 1936, 45), as well as the inspiration for urban architecture in what architect and historian Clive Chipkin calls "Exhibition style" (1993, 110), the exhibition offered a touchstone for other, less visible expressions of modernity in forms ranging from street protest to theatrical performances to fictional and documentary writing. The building boom generated by a 50-percent increase in the gold price after South Africa decoupled its currency from the gold standard in 1933 (Beavon 2004, 93) transformed the central built environment from a hodgepodge of Victorian and Transvaal vernacular structures of the first generation, and a few later art deco and art moderne structures, to "the breeding ground of modernism in South Africa [. . .] a world city in the midst of a world depression" (Chipkin 1993, 89, 90). This boom depended on the labor of black construction workers and other workers who, over the decade, were compelled to abandon lively but overcrowded inner districts, like Doornfontein and Fordsburg, for the townships of Orlando, Pimville, and others whose rows of matchbox houses would form the nucleus of Soweto in the 1950s. Despite this reinforcement of segregation, however, city officials acknowledged the contribution of black workers to the Johannesburg Jubilee even if the national government disavowed it, and educated Africans shared a qualified enthusiasm for the city's steps toward modernity, expressed not only in participation at the Empire Exhibition, but also in the creation of new forms of cultural performance that drew on cosmopolitan trends as well as indigenous sources.

By cultural performance, I mean practices ranging from formal theatre events such as Eugene O'Neill's drama of alienated labor, *The Hairy Ape* (1922), performed first by the Johannesburg Repertory Theatre in 1932 and adapted to represent local urban Africans in 1936, through events like the *Pageant of South Africa* at the Empire Exhibition and the Emancipation Centenary Celebration two years earlier, to political demonstrations in the city streets. In order to set the scene for these events, we should briefly review the urban form, built and imagined, of Johannesburg at fifty. While some of the events discussed below appeared in previous publications (especially Kruger 1999, 2007), I return to them here in more detail as evidence for the long history of Johannesburg's aspirations to be Africa's wonder city.

Africa's Wonder City: Modernity, Imagination, and the Scenography of Progress

On the occasion of its fiftieth anniversary, celebrated on September 22, 1936, Johannesburg was dubbed "Africa's Wonder City," as the Jubilee supplement to the *Rand Daily Mail* (*RDM* 1936e) declared. For the city's boosters, the wonder consisted above all in the rapid transformation of the inner districts into a high-rise modern metropolis. Chipkin estimates that in January 1936, "more than two dozen large buildings in the city centre" were complete or nearing completion and "another two dozen" were about to begin construction (1993, 94). While he distinguishes between the minimalist modern movement spearheaded internationally by Le Corbusier and locally by Rex Martienssen, head of the Wits School of Architecture, and the art deco and other ornamental elements on the American skyscraper circa 1920, he notes their common and indisputably modern structure, centered on the reinforced steel frame or concrete core (90).[1] Like the steel frame that preceded it in the

1. Chipkin identifies New York as the source for art deco office and apartment buildings in Johannesburg. While the use of setbacks and towers to allow for greater height within existing regulations of bulk was indeed developed in New York, we should remember first that the Chicago School, represented by Sullivan and his predecessor, the engineer William Le Baron Jenney, pioneered the skyscraper, whose terra cotta cladding over steel, and art deco geometric floral ornament or more restrained art moderne rounded lines and edges hid its structural frame; and second, that debates about the architecture of the Empire Exhibition and the city of Johannesburg in the *South African Architectural Journal* and other periodicals in the 1930s attributed this architectural style to Chicago.

United States, the reinforced concrete core freed modern buildings in South Africa from the weight of load-bearing walls and enabled, as pioneer architect Louis Sullivan put it already in 1896, the tall office building to become a "a proud and soaring thing, rising in sheer exultation [. . .] from bottom to top [. . .] without a single dissenting line" (Sullivan 1988, 108). Notwithstanding rival definitions of modernism, diverse groups of city dwellers rallied to the idea of "Africa's wonder city" even if its realization in the era of segregation could be only partial and inevitably partisan.

The power of imagination as well as economics shaped the transformation of the cityscape. Skyscrapers in the central business district (CBD)—such as the Electric Supply Commission (ESCOM) House (21 floors; 1937; imploded 1983) and Anstey's Department Store (1937; still standing; sketch: Cabral 2010, 35)—and new apartment buildings near north-central Joubert Park expressed not only the prevailing taste for the "moderately modern" (Chipkin 1993, 140) building pioneered by the Chicago School, but also the aspirations of builders and inhabitants to cosmopolitan living, as exemplified by the urban apartment. Their architects included those whose formal modernism was matched by progressive politics as well as a contradictory association with the neocolonial state. Herman Kallenbach, for instance, had arrived in Johannesburg during the building boom of 1896, which followed the explosion of dynamite that destroyed 1,500 structures in so-called Coolie and Kaffir locations (Beavon 2004, 75), opening up space for the development of Newtown, and supported Mohandas Gandhi during the latter's ten years in the city (1903–13; Alfred 2003, 21–37). In the 1930s, he designed and built modern dwellings from the white-occupied center city apartments like Chatham Court to the black single-story housing of Orlando (van der Waal 1986, 171). A cluster of new cinemas by younger architects challenged the neoclassical and historicist taste of turn-of-the-century theatres, including those that were technically but not formally updated in the 1930s like His Majesty's (1939–41) (van der Waal 1986, 189–91). The most emphatically modern, with unadorned white facades and functional interiors, included the Plaza (1932–60), designed by Stanley Furner, a Kallenbach associate and author of the first defense of modern architecture in the *South African Architectural Record* (Furner 1925, 1926a), and the 20th Century (1939) by Douglas Cowin, who also designed many of the Empire Exhibition buildings. In keeping with Johannesburg architects' ambivalence toward the competing claims of American and British modernity, these cinemas offered a mainstream mix of Hollywood dramas and musicals leavened by more modest films from Britain, including occasional features filmed on South African locations like

Robert Stevenson's *King Solomon's Mines* (1937), which attempted to blend Rider Haggard's best-selling novel with Paul Robeson's voice and stature.

The creation of Africa's wonder city produced not only individually striking buildings, but the transformation of the disorderly legacy of the mining camp into an aspiring metropolis. A decade earlier, Furner had argued in a proposal for a Civic Survey that Johannesburg could realize its "great possibilities" only once it integrated traffic, building, and open space into a coherent whole (Furner 1926b, 31). The influx of capital from gold, once the country cut loose from the gold standard in 1933, made possible the renovation of a modern city center as well as the expulsion of the black working majority to the periphery, but it was in the twelve months leading up to the Empire Exhibition that this development accelerated. The *RDM* and the *Johannesburg Star*, which addressed English-speaking liberal readers (predominantly but not exclusively white), introduced the Exhibition by celebrating the transformation of the whole city. "A New Johannesburg in 50 Years" (*RDM* 1936a) asserted that £9 million was spent in those twelve months—as the city commemorated not only its fiftieth anniversary, but also the population milestone of half a million inhabitants. The "Romance of Johannesburg's Building Boom" (Hatfield 1936) and the *Star's* Jubilee supplement linked 1936 to earlier radical transformation, asserting that Johannesburg was "rebuilt from scratch" after the explosion of 1896 (*Johannesburg Star* 1936c, n.p.) and that slum clearance in 1904 transformed the crowded quarters of "Coolie Location" into Newtown for white workers. However, these publications omitted mention of social disturbances, from Afrikaner skirmishes against the British colonial government after the Anglo-Boer War ended in 1902, to the rising "for a white South Africa" against the introduction of cheaper black workers in the Rand Revolt of 1922, which was crushed by air attacks on strikers ordered by Prime Minister and would-be international statesman Jan Christiaan Smuts in 1922 (Krikler 2005).

The facts of segregation doubtless undercut the imagination of an integrated city, but this integration was not merely imaginary. Photographs of both city buildings and the exhibition structures showed blacks and whites working together on scaffolding high above the streets. The *Star* and *RDM* included tributes to black and white workers, suggesting that both had valid claims to modern agency. In *The Star* "the romance of Johannesburg's building boom" (Hatfield 1936) was illustrated by portraits of individualized black workers, and its Jubilee issue of September 22 included an article by the city's Native Affairs Department Head Geoffrey Ballenden thanking "the city's great army of native workers" (Ballenden 1936). The *RDM's* special edition for the exhibition praised "native industry" and "advancement" (*RDM* 1936c). The report on the "Three Mile Procession Celebrat[ing] Johannesburg's Jubilee" (*RDM* 1936d) tainted this praise with a typically patronizing view of "mine boys in their helmets" but nonetheless acknowledged their role in carrying a "bar of gold" to the pavilion exhibiting Johannesburg's dominant industry, the Chamber of Mines. The papers targeting literate Africans, *Bantu World* and *Umteteli wa Bantu* ("Mouthpiece of the People"), praised the "impressive record" of "Africans' Contribution to Development of the Witwatersrand" (*UwB* 1936, 5); the reporter for *Bantu World* paid particular attention to the "extraordinarily effective" appearance of mine workers in the procession, remarking "why the native's part . . . stirred the crowd is hard to say. Their presence and bearing seemed to say something which pleased everyone enormously" and linking this pleasure to the "remarkably good understanding" of the tightly packed but integrated crowd of "Europeans and Africans jammed together" (1936, 2). Allowing for some exaggeration on the part of an African journalist keen to promote African modernity, this account, along with the tributes to workers by white and black reporters, acknowledged urban Africans as modern agents and thus challenged the sharp difference between white and black, modern and traditional presumed by the Urban Areas Acts, the Representation of Natives Act, and other segregationist legislation.

Although the official Exhibition poster (fig. 1.1) depicted an evidently white and probably Afrikaner farmer gazing up at an exemplary skyscraper, the responses in the press suggest that this image captured the imagination of the city's "divers races." The accounts of the parades cited above also depicted, in the orderly coexistence of races and classes, a benign spectacle. This idealized portrait stood in sharp contrast to the strikes and other antagonistic gatherings of the time, from the segregationist Rand Revolt of 1922 to May Day demonstrations by precariously integrated unions like the Garment Workers in the late 1920s and early 1930s, to the clashes between fascists and anti-fascists that would mar South Africa's entry into World War II in support of Britain. Therefore, the spectacle of peaceful coexistence on the streets should be understood, like the events inside the exhibition, as a performance of the subjunctive hope for, rather than the full indicative realization of progress.

At the Milner Park showground itself, the Empire Exhibition strove to provide a "striking picture of the history, development and progress of the Union" (*South African Mining and Engineering Journal* 1935, n.p.), as well as of the place of South Africa in the British Empire. While certain elements—such as a

FIG. 1.1 Voortrekker and the City of Gold: J. P. Ullman's poster for the Johannesburg Empire Exhibition, 1936. Courtesy of Witwatersrand University Cullen Library: Historical Papers.

facsimile of a Cape Dutch house (now serving as the Wits Alumni House), as well as "native villages" including Bushmen, Southern Africa's original population, who preceded the migration of both Bantu and European populations—replicated the emphasis on colonial history established by the Colonial and Indian Exhibition in London in 1886 (the year of Johannesburg's founding), the organizers of the 1936 Exhibition commissioned buildings that announced Johannesburg's affinity with the international modern

FIG. 1.2 Art moderne columns line the Empire Exhibition entrance. *Empire Exhibition Souvenir Catalogue:* cover. Courtesy of Witwatersrand University Cullen Library: Historical Papers.

movement broadly conceived. Chipkin remembers art moderne style, with "large blank surfaces . . . modernistic horizontal and vertical" details (1993, 106) and futurist lettering that recalled the Chicago Century of Progress. The art moderne columns (fig. 1.2) lining the main entranceway and the Tower of Light—which still stands on Wits West Campus, unlike the office headquarters of its sponsor ESCOM, which was imploded in 1983—recalled similar structures at the Chicago fair, while others, like the unadorned building housing the Chamber of Mines display (fig. 1.3), eschewed ornament altogether to resemble something that might have been designed by Le Corbusier. Martienssen, editor of the *South African Architectural Record*, praised the winning exhibition designs by Douglas Cowin and Graeme Marwick for "originality and variety" as well as for representing the "younger members of the profession" (1935, 149). Even though some adjudicators, such as British exhibition

Fig. 1.3 Modernist mine dump housing Chamber of Mines Exhibition. Courtesy of Witwatersrand University Cullen Library: Historical Papers.

director B. M. Bellasis, complained that the "modernistic" designs were too reminiscent of Chicago and in his view "uncharacteristic of South Africa" (*African World* 1935b, n.p.), the city supported this venture in "gay modernism"; its official publication praised the winners also for their attention to local conditions, such as protection from the "harsh sun" offered by cantilevered canopies over the front entrance in a manner reminiscent of Mies van der Rohe's Barcelona Pavilion (1929; *Municipal Magazine* 1935, 1).[2]

2. Martienssen was the local representative of Le Corbusier's Congrès international de l'architecture moderne (International Congress for Modern Architecture, or CIAM). The winning designs earned Martienssen's praise for their allegiance to the unadorned style of the modern movement, rather than to the art moderne lines and curves that dominated the Century of Progress and appeared in the Empire Exhibition in several buildings of which only one remains: the Tower of Light. For artists' impressions of the winning entries see illustrations accompanying Martienssen's editorial (1935, 150–55). In keeping with his allegiance to Le Corbusier, Martienssen does not mention Mies van der Rohe or his more politically engaged contemporary Walter Gropius, but the article by Kurt Jonas, a German immigrant with more interest in the socially functional architecture practiced by Gropius, and to a certain extent, Mies (Jonas 1936), includes illustrations of Mies's Barcelona Pavilion.

Archaic Pageants and Modern Performances

If the exhibition buildings recalled the modern movement in Europe and the United States, the performances returned to the paradigms of British colonialism. Although directed by an avowed international modernist, the Belgian-born André van Gyseghem, whose influences included the avant-garde theatre of Vsevolod Meyerhold and other Soviet experiments (Kruger 1999, 221), the *Pageant of South Africa* owed its content (the colonial history of the Union) and its form (the parade of youth in historical costume—white men in dress coats or military uniform, white women in debutante ball gowns, and people of color in "traditional" garb, whether African or "Oriental") to the regional pageants that had emerged out of the Arts and Crafts movement and Masonic Lodge ceremonies in Edwardian Britain, and had flowered in South Africa with the Pageant of Union in 1910 (Merrington 1997).

Like the Pageant of Union, the Pageant of Southern Africa addressed the differences between Anglo and Afrikaner interpretations of history in order to reinforce their common roots in European civilization. The Pageant was performed only four times near the end of the Exhibition in December 1936, but its preparation and rehearsal commanded attention for over a year, from the initial plans in mid-1935 for an amphitheatre that would seat 12,000 people, through the selection of Van Gyseghem as a suitably bilingual Pageant Master (*RDM* 1935a), to the performance that coincided with the commemoration of Afrikaner victory over the Zulus on December 16. Indeed, the prestige associated with the Pageant and the Empire Exhibition is more palpable in the profiles of the young women applying for positions than in the commentary on the Pageant itself. The protestation in *Outspan*, the magazine organizing the selection of players, that "the Pageant is not merely a beauty competition" was belied by the portraits of would-be debutantes and the concession that good looks would play a role alongside "*some* elocutionary ability" (*Outspan* 1936; emphasis added). The Pageant Master Van Gyseghem was in turn feted as a metropolitan messenger bearing the latest fashions from Europe, rather than as a director whose theatrical style had more in common with the European and American avant-garde than with the drawing-room comedy that dominated the stage in London or Johannesburg, and who was also to become involved with African theatre groups such as the Bantu People's Theatre.[3]

3. Compare "Mr. van Gyseghem, Pageant Master" in the *Star* of March 5, 1936, with an article in the *Uganda Herald* (February 26, 1936), which discusses van Gyseghem's work in the Soviet Union and the United States (where he worked on the Living Newspapers, documentary plays about current social problems, produced by the Federal Theatre Project in the 1930s).

Like the 1910 pageant, the 1936 event comprised a series of scenes from South African colonial history culminating in the moment of Union. But, where the commemoration in 1910 relied on the opening of Parliament to depict South Africa's maturity, the 1936 pageant attempted to combine the triumphal dramaturgy of theatrical nationhood with the representation of the industrialization and modernization that had transformed South Africa since the Union. The latter aspiration was, however, at odds with the attempt to respect British, and especially Boer, myths of origin. The text was written by populist Afrikaans chronicler Gustav Preller, whose vivid accounts of the Voortrekkers in print and in film—*de Vootrekkers* (1916), scripted by him, was the first feature film in Dutch-Afrikaans—played a central role in the development of an Afrikaner Nationalist mythology.[4] The initial plan published in *Outspan* listed the episodes as follows:[5]

1. Zimbabwe the Magnificent
2. The Bushmen, at one time sole owners of the Continent
3. The Hottentots
4. The Beginning of History
5. The Landing of van Riebeeck [1652]
6. Simon van der Stel welcomes the Huguenots [1690]
7. The British occupy the Cape [1806]
8. The arrival of the British settlers in 1820
9. Chaka, King of the Zulus, presents the Charter of Natal to Lt. Farewell [1824]
10. Piet Uys and his party are presented with a bible by citizens of Grahamstown [1836]
11. Nagmaal [communion] after the Battle of Vegkop
12. Arrival of Louis Trichardt's trek party in Lourenço Marques
13. Vow taken to build a Church should the Boers be victorious over Dingaan [December 16, 1838]
14. Dingaan's Day: [Andries] Pretorius and Mpande [Dingaan's successor] on the Rock
15. Harry Smith's Solders and the Lady Kenneway Girls [1840s]
16. Discovery of Diamonds [1867]

---

4. "The Pageant," *Pretoria News,* May 8, 1936. Preller's work included *Piet Retief* (1906), an account of the Voortrekker encounter with the Zulu king Dingane, whose treatment of the Boer invaders as victims of Zulu aggression set the tone of later histories (see Hofmeyr 1988).

5. "Grand Pageant. Central Committee Decision," *East London Daily Dispatch,* July 10, 1936.

17. The Discovery of Gold on the Rand [1886]
18. Rhodes's indaba [conference] with Lobengula [king of the Matabele] [1889]
19. The Arrival of the first train in Bulawayo
20. Election of Paul Kruger . . . as President [of the South African Republic] in 1898
21. Final Tableau—Union—The National Convention Assembly in Cape Town. (*Outspan* 1936, n.p.)

These episodes reproduced a neocolonial view of South Africa, whose history supposedly began only with the arrival of Europeans. The original inhabitants appear either in prehistoric preludes or in capitulation to the imperial plan, as shown in Rhodes's indaba with Lobengula, which secured the best farming land for white settlers in the country that would become Rhodesia (and after 1980 Zimbabwe) or the scenes leading to the defeat of the Zulus at the Ncome (a.k.a. Blood) River. To emphasize this narrative of conquest, the pageant opened on December 16, 1936 (now known officially as the Day of Reconciliation).

New Africans, New Negroes, and Neocolonial Modernity in Johannesburg

While Afrikaner nationalists would go on to celebrate a nationwide centenary in 1938 at the Voortrekker monument foundation stone outside Pretoria commemorating their victory over the Zulus in 1838, Africans could draw only on modest resources to stage and stake their claims to modernity in the avowedly transnational city of Johannesburg. Even before the Empire Exhibition, "New Africans"—African writers and intellectuals in Johannesburg and other South African cities who were inspired by the "New Negroes" in 1920s Harlem, among them the writers and brothers Herbert and Rolfes Dhlomo and their cousin the composer Reuben Caluza—had commemorated another centenary with imperial consequence: the emancipation of slaves in British colonies in 1834.[6] African artists and intellectuals, American Board Missionaries, liberal whites, and a "New African" audience gathered at the Bantu Men's Social Centre (BMSC; 1924–60) at the southern industrial end of

6. On the aspirations of New Africans and their debt to the New Negro movement in the United States, see Couzens (1985). For the traces of this debt in New African performance, see Kruger (1999, 25–29).

Johannesburg's busiest commercial artery, Eloff Street, for National Thanksgiving. Speeches by American missionaries and leading Africans, such as R. V. Selope Thema (editor of *Bantu World*) and Dr. A. B. Xuma (later president of the ANC), preceded extracts from Handel's *Messiah,* Elgar's *Land of Hope and Glory*, hymns composed by Europeans, Africans, and Americans, including "Negro spirituals," and Abraham Lincoln's Gettysburg Address, delivered by African variety impresario and Trinity College (London) graduate Griffiths Motsieloa. It culminated in a "dramatic display," the subject of which was not, as might have been expected, the emancipation of slaves in British Africa or the West Indies, but rather the lives of slaves in the United States, who were freed only by the Thirteenth Amendment to the US Constitution in 1865, three decades after the emancipation of slaves in the British Empire.[7]

While its primary occasion was the commemoration of this emancipation, the celebration was also a reproach to the South African government for its disenfranchisement of Africans. The event responded not only to the then-current discrimination, but also to the racialist ideology of the first South African Parliament and its commemorative performance, the Pageant of Union in 1910. That pageant presented historical sketches on the European (Portuguese, Dutch, and British) "discovery" of the native inhabitants and the appropriation of their lands by treaty or conquest, epitomized, in the last episode of that pageant, by the meeting between Moshoeshoe and President Hoffmann of the Orange Free State in 1854, which allowed for Boer settlement of prime farming land. By ignoring the subsequent impact of the British annexation of Lesotho and that part of the Free State where diamonds were discovered in 1867, industrialization, and the forced proletarianization of African peasants to work in the mines, the pageant reenacted the familiar teleology of the Progress of Prosperity over "hordes of ignorance, cruelty, savagery, unbelief, war, pestilence, famine and their ilk" (Cape Town Pageant Committee 1910, 93), whereby Europe brought civilization to what Hegel notoriously called the "unhistorical, undeveloped Spirit of Africa" (1956 [1899], 99). The pageant acknowledged the historical role of some blacks, such as Moshoeshoe, but Africans were largely seen as timeless "natives" while Europeans and their surrogates in the new parliament were "historical heroes" (Cape Town Pageant Committee 1910, 95) flanked by "maidens in white" (94).

---

7. For the program, see the records of the South African Institute for Race Relations (hereafter: SAIRR), Witwatersrand University Cullen Library: Historical Papers Collection: AD843/B47.2.

The differences between these two events are noteworthy, but so are their points of contact. The modesty of the Emancipation Centenary Celebration exposed the relative powerlessness of even elite Africans, who were dependent on the Union government as well as liberal white patrons. At the same time, however, the participants in the Emancipation Celebration shared with those in the Union Pageant in 1910 and the South African Pageant in 1936 a belief in the universal value of European civilization, represented by the promise of enfranchisement and other liberal freedoms. Even those Africans who criticized the actual savagery of whites in Africa, and who therefore sought to "provincialize Europe" to a degree by relativizing its claim to the universal (Chakrabarty 1992, 20), used the language of the European enlightenment to defend the idea and practice of universal rights. The scripts of the Emancipation Centenary explicitly cast the participants as New Africans, as opposed to the so-called tribal Africans featured in the Union Pageant and the Savage South Africa show in London (1899–1900). By including Abraham Lincoln's text and African Nationalist songs, the program pointed beyond the nostalgia of the Union Pageant and toward a utopian democratic future for South Africa.

Although the Emancipation Centenary Celebrations focused on a representation of African modernity, the pathos of slave life in the manner of Harriet Beecher Stowe's *Uncle Tom's Cabin* (1852) complicates the heroic portrayal of black struggle offered by the ANC repertoire. Written by Zulu writer Rolfes Dhlomo and directed by his brother Herbert, a journalist, dramatist, and musician, the performance was called "The Life of the Lowly" in homage to the less-well-known subtitle of Stowe's best-selling novel. As reports in *Bantu World* and *Umteteli wa Bantu* suggest, "the suffering of the American Negroes on the slave market, in the cotton fields and at home, until the joyful news of the liberation" and the "feelings of joy and relief, which the right ending of the struggle for freedom had brought" highlighted the pathos of the slaves' misery and their gratitude for the act of emancipation (*BW* 1934; *UwB* 1934). This pathos was modified, however, by songs about the experience of urban workers, such as "Sixoshiwe" ([emsebenzini] "We are being fired [expelled from work"]) by Reuben Caluza, composer and collector of Zulu folksongs, and visiting fellow for a year at Columbia University in New York. While the full import of these songs might have been lost on the whites in the audience, it is likely that the Africans would have been familiar with these and other nationalist songs, such as "Silusapo" or "iLand Act" (the first ANC anthem, also by Caluza; Erlmann 1991, 119–47). Likewise, speeches such as the Gettysburg Address in the mouth of master elocutionist

Motsieloa resonated differently from the praise heaped on British "Emancipators" such as David Livingstone.

Politically charged as this event certainly was, it thus had no single political meaning. Tolerated by the state and applauded by white liberals, it was well received not only by the African elite at the BMSC, but by a more diverse audience in Eastern Native Township. The performance eludes the ideological dichotomy between white colonial hegemony and the oppressed black masses (or between high English culture and working-class practices), which some influential critics see in this period (see Kavanagh 1985; Coplan 2008). In this schema, members of the New African elite, the small class of clergymen, teachers, and other professionals, are distinguished by their attachment to European civilization and thus by their alienation from the masses of black people, whether or not this alienation is read as the result of their colonial assimilation and thus their distance from popular African culture. This retrospective judgment still haunts current debates, but it misses the fluidity of these class and ethnic affiliations and the unevenness of African identification with "European civilization" in the 1930s.

The uncertainties of New African life can be summed up by Shula Marks's phrase "ambiguities of dependence," which in her view was felt especially in the tension between the "mid-Victorian idea of progress" on the one hand and the "fact of subordination" on the other (Marks 1986, 54). The liberal ideals of the Enlightenment, particularly the concept of individual autonomy in the political and economic spheres, offered a compelling, if utopian, image and a weapon not only against segregationists but also against communism, which was feared by African conservatives as well as most Europeans. Selope Thema joined the American Board Mission in cautioning his readers to reject the unchristian tactics of the Bolsheviks and to "honor the great emancipators" such as Lincoln, whose example shows the way to "rescue [the world] from the thralldom of nationalist and racial passions" (Thema 1934b). Even Africans who expressed skepticism about European intentions to honor the promise of universal rights nonetheless used the language of the European enlightenment to make their case. For example, the editor of *Umteteli wa Bantu* wrote, "it is true that Natives can no longer be bought and sold . . . but they are still in bondage as a people and there is a determined stand by Europeans against the grant to them [*sic*] of that full liberty to which all men are entitled. . . . Natives are not slaves, but they are not freemen" (*UwB* 1933). In pointing to the entrenchment of racial discrimination despite formal freedoms, this editorial drew explicitly on the insights of W. E. B. Dubois, whose landmark work *The Souls of Black Folk* vividly described the oppression of

African Americans *after* emancipation (Dubois 1989 [1903], 28–29). In doing so, it not only challenged the authority of white segregationists but also criticized those Africans who, for various and not always consistent reasons, supported separate development as a form of African autonomy. The Emancipation Centenary Celebration was thus both more and less than a commemoration. It reminded its audience, white philanthropists as well as New Africans, of the lacunae in the narrative of liberation, while also speaking against attempts, on the part of some African leaders as well as the Union government, to restrict emancipation in the name of African autonomy.

The New African position in the 1930s was made even more precarious by African disagreements as well as white threats. The conservative wing of the ANC tended to see in the state's program of "separate development" an opportunity for what might be called *retraditionalization*.[8] Just as tradition has less to do with the "persistence of old forms, but more to do with the ways in which form and value are linked together" (Erlmann 1991, 10), retraditionalization implies not so much a return to premodern rural life as a reappropriation of clan custom as the means to achieving a tangible if limited autonomy in the present. In practice, it consolidated the power of the chiefs, which previously had been eroded by the mass migration of landless peasants to the cities.[9] This retraditionalist tendency collided with the convictions of New Africans, who held by and large to the belief that the benefits of modernity would ultimately outweigh the disruption of communal life. Selope Thema, for instance, defended African appropriation of the benefits of European civilization, such as literacy and individual rights, and, while acknowledging the value of precolonial communal organization, severely criticized tribal custom, especially ancestor worship, as the weight of the "dead . . . on the living" (1934a). Thema and his fellow New Africans shared with Frederick Douglass and other "defenders of the Negro race" in the United States a distaste for savage spectacles like "tribal dances," which in Douglass's view, "shamed" black people who considered themselves civilized (Douglass 1999 [1893], 9) and represented for Africans "uncivilized retrogression" rather than the progress, actual and desired, of the "enlightened Bantu" (Thema 1934a).

8. Mazrui and Tidy coined this term to describe a tactical appeal to tradition made by modern leaders (1984, 282).

9. While separate development appealed to chiefs keen to maintain their ebbing authority, there can be no doubt that the government's interest in segregation was firmly grounded in European interests, in the desire for a compliant labor reserve uncontaminated by the "usual antagonism of class war" (Dubow 1987).

Profoundly suspicious of European definitions of the authentically African promulgated by apologists for separate development along the "Native's own lines," New Africans such as Thema and the Dhlomo brothers did not, however, abandon traditions they saw as African. Rather, by participating in networks established by graduates of mission schools such as Lovedale (founded 1832), Adams (1855), and Marianhill (1884), as well as British-inflected cultural institutions such as the Gamma Sigma debating societies (1918), the BMSC (1924), or the Eisteddfodau (1931)—festivals of choral singing and dramatic monologues loosely based on Anglicized Welsh models—they hoped to enrich, elevate, and legitimate the African inheritance as well (Peterson 2000).

This negotiation of retraditionalization in the interests of African modernity came to the fore in contrasting African displays at the Empire Exhibition. While the exhibition featured displays of primitives—in particular, a village encampment of Bushmen hunter-gatherers, who were billed as "wonderful remnants of one of the oldest races in the world" (Gordon 1999, 267)—it also featured modern African performers. These included the avowedly modern musical variety concert group the Merry Blackbirds and the Darktown Strutters, whose name evoked New Negro Harlem and whose leader, Griffiths Motsieloa, had read the Gettysburg Address at the Emancipation Celebration. Less obviously but no less modern in their retraditionalizing intent were the "tribal sketches" of the mission-educated Mtetwa Lucky Stars. Founded in 1929 by Esau and Isaac Mthethwa, the Lucky Stars performed dances and sketches in reconstructed Zulu costume and in the Zulu language. The titles of such sketches as *Ukuqomisa* ("courting") and especially *Umthakathi* ("diviner, sorcerer") allude to the ambiguous legacy of the tribal sketch, which since the nineteenth century had included the "smelling out" of the diviner as an imposter impeding the civilizing mission (Caldecott 1853, 26). However, the several parts of this show—sketches, dancing, and choral singing of Zulu "folk" songs with a nationalist tinge, as well as quite varied places of performance—suggest a more complex mesh of occasion and meaning than either a reconstruction of precolonial practices or a replication of colonial prejudices. An account by a white observer of the Mthethwa brothers performing in Zululand is illuminating:

> This new departure among the black races is valuable in presenting to the public scenes of native domestic life with a realism which would be otherwise unobtainable. Such education of the white man is a necessary preliminary to his understanding of Bantu problems. . . . these

> plays are presented with a naivete which would be impossible for the white man to imitate. The style of acting is much more free than we have been accustomed to see on the more civilized stage. The producer is an educated Zulu [Isaac Mthethwa] but the players have only a rudimentary knowledge of reading and writing. Consequently, the parts are learned by word of mouth and no strict adherence to the original wording is insisted on. . . . This induces a freshness and vigor of presentation which is a welcome relief from the too conscious presentation of our own stage. (Lloyd 1935, 3)

This account replays familiar colonial themes in the opposition between jaded metropolitan culture, the "too conscious" artifice of the "civilized" actor, and the fresh naiveté of the "black races." At the same time, it concedes the artifice of this native naiveté, in the shape of Mthethwa's guiding hand, in the fact that the lines were learned, and in the possibility that the "education of the white man" might be the object and not merely the incidental result of this performance. The modern character of the show as a whole, over and above the content of the sketches, is confirmed by the "historical songs" that concluded the performance. Lloyd's description of the song—"they traced the record of the Zulu nation through their kings. They sang of those who had wielded supreme power, whether good or bad" (1935, 3)—suggests the historical consciousness of "Elamakosi" (Of the Kings), Caluza's song popular with Zulu audiences in the 1930s.

The Mthethwa brothers' performance in urban settings highlighted the modern character of the performance despite its ostensibly rural content. "Discovered" in Durban by Bertha Slosberg (Slosberg 1939, 194), a Jewish South African impresario and local talent scout for Stevenson's *King Solomon's Mines*, the Lucky Stars performed under her management at the BMSC in Johannesburg in May and at the Empire Exhibition in October 1936 (*BW* 1936a, 1936b). Their appearance before international visitors at the latter event also encouraged Slosberg to seek funding to take the show to London, but this project did not materialize. In keeping with modern practices of wage labor, Slosberg insisted that she paid the performers well and that she associated with them despite scandalized press responses (Slosberg 1939, 210–13), but her aspirations to honorary "Zuluness" have to be understood against the material advantages enjoyed by white South Africans. Isaac Mthethwa's acquiescence to this arrangement reflects above all the obstacles faced by Africans attempting to make a living as artists. Although producers such as Mthethwa and Motsieloa functioned as professionals, in the sense that they and their audiences took their performances seriously and they hoped to make a living from performing, they were unable to maintain full control over their work.

While the unnamed Venda iron workers on display for the exhibition in the Iron and Steel Corporation (ISCOR) building had even less control over their labor, their performance, like that of the Lucky Stars, complicates pat distinctions between modern and traditional. While scantily attired Africans elsewhere in the Exhibition—such as the Zulu dancers in *The Real Africa*, whose costumes were stripped of modern materials such as bright industrial cloth in the interests of "authenticity" (Kruger 1999, 42–43)—joined a long tradition of African "primitives" at modern fairs, which could be traced back to the Colonial and Indian Exposition in 1868 (see Corbey 1993; Erlmann 1999; Gordon 1999; Lindfors 1999), the iron smelters' functional industrial clothing (confirmed by a news photograph [*RDM* 1936b, 12]), no less than their smelting and smithing work, recalled a less familiar image of Africans as industrial workers, whose lineage included the "diamond Zulus" (in industrial drab despite the sparkling epithet) participating in diamond exhibits from the Chicago Exposition of 1893 (Kruger 2007). The iron smelters played a key role in what I would call an African modern series that opened with the "diamond Zulus," but their parts have been obscured by primitivist discourse that symbolically undresses them. As Jennifer Robinson argues, the Empire Exhibition made visible "the 'modern' . . . through its juxtaposition with 'tradition' " (2003, 770) but, despite the attempt to keep these poles "far apart" (770), the performance of African modernity brought them together. Robinson indicts the Afrikaans paper of record, *Die Burger*, and a report by writer Mimie E. Rothmann (known as M. E. R.), "By die Rykskou [At the Empire Exhibition]," but, while the exhibition of African iron smelters housed in the government's ISCOR might appear at first glance to confirm segregationist prejudice signaled by racist terms like "kaffir," closer examination suggests otherwise.[10] M. E. R's subtitle, "Bantu, Bushman and White Man," suggests a more ecumenical picture of South Africans than her casual use of "kaffir" implies (R[othmann] 1936, 14), and her account offers a more ambiguous juxtaposition, rather than a simple opposition between "the influence of science and its uses for humanity" and

10. Robinson sees *Die Burger* as an unambiguous representative of the "objectifying gaze and administrative dominance" of white supremacy (2003, 772) but, while this paper certainly supported Afrikaner advancement at the expense of Africans, its writers showed more awareness of the complexities of racial interaction than the rabidly nationalist papers *Die Vaderland* and *Die Transvaler*, which targeted so-called poor whites, unskilled and under-urbanized workers who were threatened by direct competition from blacks.

the "kaffirs . . . busy on one of the oldest industries in the history of man" (14).[11] Moreover, the location of the iron smelters in the art moderne ISCOR pavilion, rather than in a "native village," cements the historical connection between ancient iron smelting and modern steel manufacture.

The *Official Guide* and the official newspaper, the *Star-Mail News Bulletin*, rehearsed a familiar drama of "Africans awed by the white man's magic" (Empire Exhibition 1936b, 2) and thus ignored claims for African contributions to iron technology. In contrast, M. E. R cited historian G. M. Theal's praise for the "art of the iron-smelters" and argued, in noteworthy contrast to the patronizing remarks about "rude instruments" in the purportedly liberal *Star* (1936a, 12), that this technology, however "primitive," was also "effective [*doeltreffend*]" (R[othmann] 1936, 14). Contemporary archeological research by South Africa's preeminent paleontologist Raymond Dart and others (Dart 1931; van Warmelo and Lestrade 1932) confirmed that iron smelting was older than previously believed and that indigenous technology included the production of steel, but not as yet the tempering and quenching techniques required to maintain its strength and durability.[12] Instead of reasserting white supremacy, M. E. R. offers an acknowledgment of the universal import of the technology and a meditation on coexistence: "Standing next to the iron smelters one feels as though gazing on a path which will lead one to grasp the riddle of one's own existence" (R[othmann] 1936, 14). These comments on the part of an Afrikaans woman are not without condescension, but they nevertheless present a picture not of tribal primitives, but rather of people the newspapers called "urbanized natives" as no different from the men in trousers and shirts playing drafts in the photograph illustrating Ballenden's article on "The City's Army of Native Workers." While neither

11. M. E. R's relatively open-minded engagement with urban industry stands out also against the usual hostility to the city expressed by Afrikaans writers in this period such as Johan van Bruggen, whose *Ampie, die natuurkind* (1931; Ampie, the Child of Nature) set the standard of rural idyll against the evil city for the genre that became known as the *plaasroman*, or farm novel.

12. Dart, who advised the Empire Exhibition from his position as chair of Wits's paleontology program, argued that iron *smelting* (the extraction of iron ore through a high heat furnace dating to circa 1200 BC) and *smithing* (the production of implements in a forge) were not exclusively Venda; archeological remains indicated that these technologies had been practiced throughout Southern Africa for at least a millennium (Dart 1931, 392). More recent archeologists have investigated the perhaps unplanned production of steel (iron with a carbon content greater than 1 percent), which tended to be undermined by "less sophisticated" forging techniques, which did not as yet include tempering (reheating to lower temperatures) and quenching (rapid cooling with water so as to harden the steel), which would have maintained the high carbon content (Miller 2002, 1100–1101).

the Afrikaner M. E. R. nor the English-speaking Ballenden quite concur with the anonymous black reporter for the *Bantu World* who, as indicated above, found in the crowd observing the Johannesburg Jubilee parade "a remarkably good understanding" (1936d, 3), each affirms integrated urban modernity as a fact of life and thus complicates the standard narrative of the relentless march toward the rigid separation of apartheid. Although these instances of integration could not counter the increasingly draconian legislation restricting Africans in the city, they appear in retrospect as documents of the futility of segregation.

Performing Urbanity: City Drama on Street and Stage

While newspaper reports of the Jubilee parades made no direct comparisons between these displays of urban decorum and the strikes and other disturbances of civic order, the uncivil modernity of political demonstrations continued to define Johannesburg's upstart city. These demonstrations against the city elite, above all against the monopoly powers of mining capital, had diverse casts and purposes. The Garment Workers Union, for instance, combined young Afrikaner women with male tailors and workers of color, led by Jewish union secretary Emil Solomon "Solly" Sachs, father of later activist and constitutional court jurist Albie Sachs. Its public events, from strike processions to plays, combined the repertoire of international socialism with appeals to the anti-imperial struggles of the Afrikaner *volk* (Berger 1992, 95–101; Kruger 2004a, 226–31). The Rand Revolt of 1922, the most belligerent challenge to capital and the state, involved armed white miners among over twenty thousand strikers in battles with the police and the army as well as smaller skirmishes against unarmed blacks and other bystanders. The uprising led to the detention of thousands and the death of hundreds, mostly by state-sponsored counterattacks but, as historian Jeremy Krikler suggests, even an event of this scale invites comparison with drama and performance.[13] Krikler sees the event as a "tragedy," a conflict "heroic and cruel, ambiguous and doomed" (2005, 295) between white workers responding violently to perceived threats to their livelihood and the peremptory and far greater violence of the state. He describes particular elements such as demonstrations and funerals framed by "The Red Flag"—the international protest anthem as well as

13. Alfred (2003, 37–38) notes that a strike of black workers two years earlier had demonstrated the mass power of black labor, and thus intensified white workers' sense that they were under threat.

the cloth banner carried aloft—as performances that anticipated in their scale and fervor the anti-apartheid enactments of the 1980s, and notes the theatrical aspect of both the rebel and military staging areas at key landmarks on the Witwatersrand from the Brixton Ridge and the Fordsburg Market in the near west to Germiston in the east. The prospects afforded by the multiple ridges collectively known as the Witwatersrand encouraged spectators observing the rebels as well as the state's carnage (260ff.). In the city center, the Drill Hall served as a prison for captured strikers. After three months, the strike and the rebellion ended on March 18, 1922. Although March 18 also marks the start of the Paris Commune, the brief but famous revolutionary government of Paris in 1871, and the date was still commemorated by socialists in other parts of the world, no South African source makes this connection.

Nearly a century after the Rand Revolt, key staging areas are now formally dedicated to performance as well as to urban renewal—the Newtown Market has been the Market Theatre since 1976 and the Drill Hall has been a performance and exhibition space since 2004. However, the material record of workers who cited the *Communist Manifesto* and other expressions of international socialism while calling for a white South Africa has been eclipsed by the official history of the anti-apartheid struggle whose iconography dominates both spaces today. While the city of Johannesburg acknowledged the eightieth anniversary of the revolt in 2002, and plans were announced to clear the ground of a plant nursery in Braamfontein, which is also the site of unmarked graves which may contain the remains of strikers (Davie 2002), this site remains off the beaten track and the event has only been commemorated only once since, with an exhibition at the Workers Museum in Newtown honoring the event as a "Miners' Strike," in keeping with the labor history emphasis of that institution (Pabale 2011). Less centrally located memorials, such as the plaque commemorating the Irish dead in the revolt, which was erected on the ridge between the working-class district of Brixton and the affluent Auckland Park, have been forgotten, as have the dissenters from the white front, among them Bill Andrews, English-born head of the Communist Party of South Africa (CPSA), who had pushed for an integrated union based on class rather than racial alliances (Alfred 2003, 39; Krikler 2005, 112).

While rebellion on this scale would not recur until the emergency years of the 1980s, the Rand Revolt resonated in the more decorous 1930s in written, pictorial, and dramatic representations. Writer Bernard Sachs, brother of Garment Union secretary Solly Sachs, published essays in the *South African Jewish Times* and later the literary magazine *Trek*. "The 1922 Rand Revolt" and "The City Hall Steps" combine vividly dramatic recreation of dialogue and action drawn from Sachs's recollections as a teenager (he was sixteen in 1922) with retrospective reflection on the impact of these events.[14] Recalling the speakers and audience at the City Hall, a neoclassical building on Market (now Library) Square (Cabral 2010, 11), the second essay presents a cast of international activists, from Yiddish Bundists to English unionists like Andrews, to Oxford-educated South African historian Sydney Bunting, whose speeches on the steps were joined by the "volcanic surge" of the Rand Revolt's most fiery protagonist, Cornish miner Percy Fisher (Sachs 1959, 119). Sachs's longer essay on the revolt culminates with the key "battle of Fordsburg" but begins with a confrontation at the home of a miner who had broken with the strike and continues with a conversation mediated by an interpreter with black miners on the "strange behavior" of the whites (1959, 16), a depiction of strikers shooting at blacks leaving their compound, and a subsequent battle between strikers and police. A summary account follows of the government's bombardment of strikers holed up at the Fordsburg Market on March 14, 1922, the night Fisher died, and the trial of Fisher ally Samuel "Taffy" Long for allegedly killing a policeman.[15] Sachs returns to dialogue and dramatic action with the mass protest, in which English, Afrikaans, and Jewish marchers join Welsh miners in singing the Welsh anthem, "Land of My Fathers," and then the "Warszavianaka," which commemorates Polish resistance to the Russian Czars. Recreating Long's execution, Sachs uses the terms of theatre: the sketch "Each one in the drama had his part" has Long and his fellow prisoners each singing the "Red Flag" as he leaves his cell for the gallows (1959, 31). Krikler confirms that the anthem was sung at Long's funeral (2005, 284).

While the association with tragedy might be seen in retrospect to glorify the heroic agency of whites in revolt against blacks undercutting their wages, as well as white capitalists manipulating both parties, South African history is best served by acknowledging the "ambiguity at the centre" of this drama (Krikler 2005, x). Although Krikler and other historians make no mention of *Red Rand* (1937), by *RDM* journalist and Sachs contemporary Lewis Sowden, this play deserves attention for dramatizing the ambiguities of racial and class alliances and conflicts at the heart not only of the Rand Revolt, but

14. Johannesburg City Hall was erected after Union in 1910. Fronting rare inner-city green space, now known as Library Square in recognition of the Johannesburg Public Library (1935), the City Hall now houses the Gauteng Provincial Government and, like the Library building, underwent extensive renovation in the early twenty-first century.

15. Although Sachs misremembers the date of the final onslaught as March 8, the date Fisher made his will, his account of Fisher's last stand is corroborated by Krikler's analysis (2005, 180–91, 280–86). On Fisher, see also Alfred (2003, 32–44).

of the country as a whole.[16] Measured against early twentieth-century plays on Johannesburg themes—such as Stephen Black's *Helena's Hope Ltd.* (1984 [1910]), which satirizes capitalist real-estate speculators but tells a melodramatic (and predictably anti-Jewish) story of the dispossessed yet genteel Helena, who eventually outwits the villainous land-grabbers to reclaim her inheritance, or Bertha Goudvis's *Where the Money Goes* (1925), a tale of a woman's love for a gambler who embezzles money from the company where they both work, which was redeemed somewhat by its pioneering portrayal of Johannesburg working women—*Red Rand* is remarkable for its serious engagement with the social inequities of mining capitalism.[17] Yet its treatment of militant workers, their families, and their antagonists, while critical, remains within the bounds of "social concern" (the genteel Edwardian phrase applied to English playwright John Galsworthy), rather than revolution. Like Galsworthy's *Strife* (1910), which was hailed as a play of national importance at its premiere in London (Kruger 1992, 101–24), *Red Rand* portrays the militants as heroic but misguided manual laborers, whose grievances against capital—in this case, the Chamber of Mines—are justified, but whose armed resistance is shown to be the last resort of desperate men.

Red Rand also shares with *Strife* a predominantly private setting for the public drama that occurs largely off-stage. In both plays, the single public scene—a workers' meeting—reeks of barely suppressed violence. As Taylor, one of the instigators marked in *Red Rand*'s stage directions as a rabble-rouser and received as such by the anonymous reviewer (*Johannesburg Star* 1937), remarks in the manner that Sowden's colleague Sachs had attributed to the historical agitator Fisher: "I've got no time for moderate men. . . . Those who know history know that it is only by force that great reforms are effected" (Sowden 1937, I, 70). At the theatre in the new Johannesburg Public Library (opened 1935) in the former Market Square in the city center, Elsie Salomon directed this scene to intensify this threat of violence, deploying what the *Star* reviewer identified as "the new device of using the entire body of the hall" so that the "strike leaders harangued the audience and the strikers at the

16. *Red Rand* was the winning entry in an annual new play competition run by the Repertory Reading Group. It was performed at the new Library Theatre, December 2–3, 1937; Elsie Salomon also directed plays for the Bantu Dramatic Society. The manuscript is in the Wits Historical Papers collection (A406); page numbers begin anew for each of the three acts, which are identified by roman numerals, as in I: 3, for Act I, page 3.

17. In a plot similar to *Helena's Hope Ltd.*, Jan Grosskopf's *As die Tuig Skawe* (1926; When the Harness Chafes) offers an Afrikaans variation on the rural naif fleeced by cosmopolitan Jews.

back of the hall" until the strikers "rushed down the aisles to join their fellows" on stage (*Johannesburg Star* 1937, 26).[18] The violence of the Chamber of Mines and the military, on the other hand, remains off-stage, as shadowy but powerful forces whose machinations are impenetrable. This has the partial effect of generating sympathy for the underdog miners, but it also evades direct attribution of responsibility for the miners' grievances to the state or the Chamber.

Despite the ostensible focus on the labor struggle, the actual center of the play is not the labor leader, Will Mullins, but his educated brother, John, whose admonition to Will is echoed by the latter after John's death:

> That's the trouble with you strikers. You go about shouting and waving the Red Flag but you don't know the first thing about the force you set in motion. . . . You've got to know as much as the other side know before you can beat them. . . . And they've learnt a good deal from books. . . . Without geometry, you couldn't sink a shaft, without knowledge of history, you wouldn't know how to govern. You've got to learn and learn before you can have power. (Sowden 1937, II, 48)

The ending (John is shot by mine security goons while trying to retrieve his books, while Will reiterates his brother's plea for education rather than direct action) endorses an alliance between intellectual and manual labor, while saying little about the ongoing violence of the South African state and next to nothing about the fate of black workers caught between white state and white labor. The racist aspect of the strike, especially the miners' defense of the Colour Bar, is glossed over, as is the occasional reference to the deaths of black miners. The only black speaking part, Mrs. Mullins's house servant, Samuel, is portrayed as loyal but naive. He is willing to work for room and board (an ironic reflection of the miners' refusal to consider higher wages for their black coworkers) and is killed, not in heroic action but by a stray bomb, while watching the planes from the roof. Likewise, Zulu, spoken only by Samuel and Mrs. Mullins, features as a minor part of the domestic scene, rather than as one of the common languages of the mines. Thus, while this

---

18. Sowden's stage directions call for some actors playing strikers planted among the spectators, but his use of this "new device" may also reflect the influence of immigrants from the European avant-garde, such as Van Gyseghem or Kurt Baum, the latter formerly of Erwin Piscator's political theatre in Berlin and the founder of the leftist Johannesburg Art Theatre. Both were familiar with this and other staging devices common in experimental, socially engaged theatres in Europe and America since the 1920s; see Kruger (2004a).

play gives attention to conflicts among the workers and offers a relatively sympathetic portrayal of their grievances, racism remains its structuring absence. Africans were also excluded from the theatre event, since they were not admitted to the Library Theatre performance without special permit.

This dramatic silence on racism received a curious but telling endorsement in a contemporary article defending South African dramatists against criticism from abroad, in the person of an anonymous "Distinguished Visitor" looking for drama about the "particular problems of this country . . . between Boer and Briton, and between Black and White" (quoted in Celli 1937, 13). The author relies on the claim that "the reason our dramatists cannot write plays about either problem is the simple fact that . . . these plays would not be allowed to see the inside of a theatre." More telling, however, is her insistence that "the great South African play will need to deal with some aspect of the fundamental human being" rather than "national peculiarities." This appeal to the authority of universal art functions here, as Herbert Marcuse has argued, as a refuge from an unpalatable reality (1968 [1935], 118), as well as neocolonial resistance to the perceived inclination of distinguished visitors to reduce white South Africans along with blacks to raw material for the portrayal of particular problems.

In South Africa, as in Canada and Australia in this period, theatre art was defined by the metropolitan aspirations of a leisured class of tastemakers committed to the civilizing mission of the British Commonwealth.[19] To treat this class as a ruling class is misleading, however, since this ignores the gap between cultural and economic capital, the distance between metropolitan tastemakers and their followers at the periphery, and the ambiguous character of their relationship. Further, the greater *scale* of racial discrimination in South Africa may lead one to overlook the structural similarities among the Commonwealth dominions as well as the common aspects of neocolonial culture and its amateur practitioners. "Amateurs" should be understood in the full range of its meanings—as those who love theatre rather than those who sell it, associated informally with leisured patrons rather than the standardized production of a culture industry (Kruger 1992, 1–23)—but the amateur should also be distinguished from the unpaid African theatre-makers like Dhlomo, the Mthethwas, and Motsieloa, who did not enjoy the affluence

19. Like its South African counterpart, Australian theatre in the 1930s and 1940s was dominated by British tours under the practical monopoly of one company, in this case J. C. Williamson and Co; see Love (1984). In Canada, talk about a National Theatre began earlier but, as Alan Filewod writes of the "first self-declared National Theatre in 1915" (1990, 5), such talk emphasized the British aspirations of "English" Canadians.

of their white patrons. As Harley Granville Barker, chief sponsor of the English National Theatre, wrote: "Leisure is not so much an opportunity as a . . . quality of mind. . . . Although articulated in terms of a commitment to art as such, the theatrical activity of these leisured which art, with its sole concern for man's complete humanity, must make" (Barker 1922, 286–87). The case for art's complete humanity thus rests on the exclusion of the working majority, while offering the distant promise of inclusion.

Distant as it may have been, this promise of inclusion nonetheless moved New Africans to adopt theatre as an arena for staging social as well as artistic emancipation. Even before making informal contact with the white repertory companies, New Africans performed plays as an integral part of their mission-school education and received support from Commonwealth institutions such as the British Drama League to stage plays of contemporary as well as historical interest (Kruger 1999; Peterson 2000). While most productions of the Bantu Dramatic Society, led by writer Herbert Dhlomo and actor Dan Twala, followed British taste with plays like Oscar Wilde's *Lady Windermere's Fan* (1893), which was performed in 1932, its successor, the Bantu People's Theatre, strove, as its name suggested, to find plays more relevant to contemporary Africans. In this attempt, the Bantu People's Theatre (BPT) was supported by progressive visitors such as André van Gyseghem, who suggested American socially critical drama such as *The Hairy Ape* and *The Emperor Jones* (1920) by Eugene O'Neill and *Stevedore* (1934) by Paul Peters and George Sklar, and the English actress Sybil Thorndike, who used her tour to His Majesty's in 1935 to assert: "[i]n holding the black man back, we are holding back the best in ourselves. . . . We are not so clever that we cannot learn from him" (1935).[20]

While research on this period has highlighted the pioneering black playwright Herbert Dhlomo, especially his history plays on African kings (Couzens 1985; Kruger 1999; Peterson 2000), less attention has been paid to African adaptations of international drama on urban themes. The work of Eugene O'Neill found particular resonance. *The Hairy Ape*, which had its South African premiere performed by the Johannesburg Repertory at His Majesty's in 1932, may have been seen by Twala, who attended the company's dress rehearsals (Hoffman 1980, 39). Even though the representative of the

20. Thorndike and her husband, Lewis Casson, both veterans of the Old Vic Theatre, later the nucleus of the English National Theatre, were performing Shaw under the auspices of African Consolidated Theatres, a subsidiary of African Consolidated Mines, which owned His Majesty's in this period.

British Drama League thought the play "not sufficiently genteel" (Kelly 1938, 3), Twala approached van Gyseghem about *The Hairy Ape* in 1936. The play was performed under van Gyseghem's direction with Twala in the leading role of Yank at the BMSC in December and was revived at the Witwatersrand University Great Hall in June 1937.[21] Although set ostensibly in America, the play's dramatization of an absolute gulf between rich and poor, parasites and workers, clearly resonated in the context of racial and economic discrimination in Johannesburg and was praised for its "stark, symbolic treatment of the action" (Linscott 1937a, 15). This production signaled a departure from the practice of the genteel Bantu Dramatic Society at several points: its subject was the exploitation of urban workers, rather than the lives of precolonial tribes or English gentry; it used language more appropriate to this milieu, which a contemporary commentator heard as "American slang . . . translated into the Bantu idiom of English" (Kelly 1938, 3) and a more recent critic reads as Fanagalo, the pidgin spoken in the mines (Kavanagh 1985, 46); and it called for a performance style marked by staccato delivery and expressionist gesture quite different from the decorum of drawing-room comedy that provided the aspirational norm for the Bantu Dramatic Society performances of *Lady Windermere's Fan*.

This direction was certainly noteworthy, but it did not automatically put the Bantu People's Theatre in the vanguard of a new political movement. Twala reassured local white patrons that the company was "entirely dissociated from political movements and parties" (Twala 1937) and the company's constitution states its goal as the cultivation of art rather than politics:

(a) The Bantu Peoples Theatre stands for the cultivation of Bantu Art and Drama.
(b) It aims at improving the undiscovered talents of Bantu Art in Drama.
(c) It aims to be non-political. (Bantu People's Theatre 1936, 1–2)

The very terseness of the final sentence suggests an afterthought and a certain dissonance between the nationalist potential of the first two clauses and the disavowal at the end. In the political context of 1936, the draft constitution of the Bantu People's Theatre is likely to have been a defensive maneuver. The

21. The reason for the change in venue was a 1936 Johannesburg by-law that forbade African men from performing at venues at which white women were present, even if the venue—in this case, the BMSC—was supposedly run by and for Africans; see BMSC Annual Report 1937, SAIRR, AD843/B.73.1.

Representation of Natives Act of 1936 that stripped Africans of the franchise, the impotence of the All-African Convention (AAC) called at intervals since December 1935 in a vain attempt to halt this legislation, and the spectacle of European barbarity in Spain and Ethiopia combined to undermine the authority of "European civilization." As D. D. T. Jabavu, convenor of the AAC, had it:

> All Africans as well as other non-White races of the world have been staggered by the cynical rape of Italy of the last independent State belonging to indigenous Africans. After hearing a great deal for twenty years about the rights of small nations, self-determination, Christian ideals, the inviolability of treaties, . . . , the glory of European civilization, and so forth, the brief history of the last eight months [since the summoning of the Convention in December 1935] has scratched this European veneer and revealed the white savage hidden beneath. (Kabane 1936, 187)

What is striking about this speech is that, for all the fury of the attack on white savagery, the author sustains a certain faith in an ideal of civilization, which has been betrayed by some Europeans, in particular fascists in Italy and elsewhere, rather than by Europe as such. By stripping the "European veneer" from the faces of white savages, he can criticize the actual brutality of colonization while appropriating the values of modernity. The more conservative Selope Thema makes a related, though less corrosive, point when he writes "tribal life is not a peculiarity of the African race; it is a stage through which all the great nations of today have passed . . . we have a right to decide our own destiny and to make our distinctive contribution to the world's civilizations" (Thema 1936).

While these statements do not resolve the contradictory forces of neocolonial modernization, they do attempt to keep in view the idea of modernity as progress and enlightenment, even if European practice fell far short of the ideal. After the end of the decade and the outbreak of World War II, theatre provided more pointedly political groups with the raw material for critical adaptation to Johannesburg conditions and the aspirations of Africans. In their only drama festival, which took place in mid-1940, the Black Peoples Theatre performed two short plays by O'Neill—*The Dreamy Kid* (1918), set in "the Negro quarter of New York" and *Before Breakfast* (1916), set in "an American tenement house"—as well as two new plays by a veteran of the leftist Johannesburg Art Theatre, Guy Routh. *The Word and the Act* was set in "1937, at the height of the public controversy over the Native Bills," and dealt with the hypocrisy of the Representation of Natives Act, which in fact curtailed the right of African voters to elect their own representatives, and *Patriot's Pie* was set "in the early days of the Greater War 1939" (Bantu People's Theatre 1940, 3–4). It tackled the controversial subject of African conscription in World War II by dramatizing the plight of "a young African who attempted to fight for his King and Country" (Routh 1950, 21). Routh located both plays in the home of one *Sonke* [all of us] in order to emphasize the township context of urban African life; the domestic format was also intended to bring public political controversies closer to home. Despite the domestic setting, however, the black actors drew more on the presentational style of African variety "concerts" (still the local term), whose satiric and sentimental modes of direct audience address had been honed by experienced performers like Twala and Motsieloa, than on naturalist restraint, achieving, as Routh had it, "a more direct form of self-expression" (1950, 21).[22] Encouraged by modest success, the company changed its name to the African National Theatre (Routh 1950, 22). In this guise it encouraged the development of African plays on urban themes like *The Pass* (1943), a rare urban play by Dhlomo, about a journalist who spends a night in prison after the police pick him up for failing to carry a pass despite his exemption as a professional, which was unfortunately completed only after ANT folded. Even during its brief life, however, the African National Theatre offered a rigorously modern alternative to the genteel repertoire favored by the British Drama League in the 1930s, and it looked forward to the re-emergence of antiracist theatre in Johannesburg with Athol Fugard's debut play, *No-Good Friday,* produced with black collaborators in 1956.

Coda

After the war, street demonstrations, especially confrontations between hardline supporters of the Afrikaner Nationalist Party and the Communist Party and others on the left, erupted in the years leading up to the Nationalist political victory in 1948 and the subsequent abolition of the CPSA in 1950. The

---

22. African variety concerts drew on models from the Ziegfeld Follies to African American variety pioneers like Bert Williams and George Walker, but developed a distinctive combination of vaudeville gags, jazz, marabi music, nationalist hymns, and occasional social drama, such as *The 'Cruiter* by African American folklorist John Matheus, performed by Motsieloa's Pitch Black Follies in 1938; see Kruger (1999, 25–29, 44–47).

heroic portraits of cosmopolitan rebels captured by Bernard Sachs and others yielded to the more ironic treatment of political demonstrations by writers such as Herman Charles Bosman. Better known for his comic portraits of rural Afrikaners in the imaginary region of the Groot Marico, Bosman, who was a lifelong friend of Sachs since their time at Jeppe High School, began his career as an observer of Johannesburg, writing, for instance, about the annual Witwatersrand Show (later the site of the Empire Exhibition) in 1931 (Bosman 1986, 53–54). In the essay "Street Processions" (1947), he expresses a wry enthusiasm for political processions, dating from his early days in the "Young Communist League" (1981 2, 426), all the while avowing a "natural predilection for unpopular causes" (426), whether communist, fascist, or the "Peace Pledge Union" (427). In this promiscuous spirit, he follows a procession of striking miners down Commissioner Street, including an encounter with a man he calls "Grey-Moustache," a Crown Mines worker who professes to have been a member of the police force "shooting" miners in 1922 (428). Grey-Moustache may be a comic figure, but Bosman characterizes him as an untrustworthy actor in an ambiguous drama: "I couldn't help feeling that Grey-Moustache was still one of thems." "Thems" refers explicitly to the police corps of 1922, but Bosman's epithet also recalls South Africa's homegrown fascists of the 1930s, the Greyshirts, whose associates went on to form the anti-British sabotage organization *Ossewa Brandwag* (Ox-wagon Fireguard) during the war. More immediately, Bosman's report on "Johannesburg Riots" (also from 1947) applies the terms of dramatic conflict to his account of plebeian mayhem outside City Hall on the occasion of a speech by D. F. Malan, who would become the first Afrikaner Nationalist Prime Minister in 1948. Although this altercation reflected deep political and economic rifts, Bosman treats the occasion theatrically:

> A shower of bottles, half bricks, and pieces of masonry . . . thundered against the policemen's helmets. I breathed a sigh of relief. It was only the spirit of Johannesburg once more asserting itself. The undying spirit of the mining town, born of large freedoms and given to flamboyant forms of expression. (Bosman 1981, 2, 568)

Picking up the story inside City Hall, he places Malan in the unwelcome company of those trying to make Johannesburg respectable. He acknowledges that he did not actually hear Malan on this occasion but criticizes him nonetheless noting, "we who are of Johannesburg know this spirit [of large freedoms . . .] that is inside us and we resent the efforts which are being made to put a collar and tie on this city" (570). As historian Jonathan Hyslop suggests, this passage reasserts the "irrepressible" energy of the modern metropolis against the "anti-urban, anti-cosmopolitan Cyclops" in the shape of the Afrikaner Nationalist (Hylop 2008, 136) but, while he aptly alludes to James Joyce's lampoon of one-eyed nationalists in *Ulysses*, he misses the theatrical character of both Bosman's and Joyce's depictions of the conflict between nationalists and cosmopolitans, and thus the irony of the cosmopolitan Bosman playing the role of the plebeian accuser, indicting Malan's largely poor white audience of "trying to make snobs of us" (Bosman 1981, 2, 570).[23] In the decades to come, this irreverent play with the drama of politics would be eclipsed by the serious business of apartheid repression and anti-apartheid defiance but, as we shall see in the final chapter, the drama of a plebeian cosmopolitanism may yet provide a script for the edgy city.

---

23. The misquotation of Bosman's text by Hyslop (or his editor) undermines his otherwise useful reading; he adds "don't" to (inadvertently?) negate Bosman's emphatic declaration, "we resent the efforts," and turns Bosman's use of the standard phrase "collar and tie" into the unlikely phrase "collar and time" (Hyslop 2008, 136).

2 1956: GENRES OF JOHANNESBURG

While Johannesburg's Jubilee in 1936 heralded the Empire Exhibition and the celebration of Africa's wonder city by black as well as white denizens, the city's seventieth anniversary in 1956 took place in the shadow of government violence—in particular the elimination of "black spots," or remaining urban enclaves inhabited by black people, and thus the expulsion of those black residents from the city—amid increasing nationwide restrictions on political activity. In December 1956, 156 members of the African National Congress, the Congress of Democrats, the South African Indian Congress, and other anti-apartheid organizations were arrested by the apartheid police. Ninety-nine were charged with treason, but charges were dropped against all but thirty defendants, including members of the ANC such as Nelson Mandela and Walter Sisulu and of the former CPSA such as Ruth First and Joe Slovo; all were eventually acquitted in March 1961, at which time the government brought further charges and eventually sentenced Mandela and others to life in prison in 1964. The Treason Trial was the most visible clash in the struggle between the apartheid state and the anti-apartheid movement, and a turning point in the decade that had begun in 1950 with the four fundamental statutes of apartheid—the Group Areas Act, the Population Registration Act, the

Immorality Act, and the Suppression of Communism Act—which empowered the Afrikaner Nationalist government's program of racial segregation in private as well as public life while attempting to disable mass opposition. Despite the public protests (exemplified by the Defiance Campaign in 1952) and the ratification of the Freedom Charter by the Congress of the People gathered in Kliptown in 1955, the decade would end with the police killing unarmed protesters at Sharpeville on March 21, 1960 (now celebrated as Human Rights Day), the banning of the ANC and its rival, the Pan-African Congress (PAC), and the intensification of extrajudicial violence by the state (detention and torture) and by its opponents (acts of sabotage) in the decades to follow.

The court proceedings and the public demonstrations around the Treason Trial in the centrally located Drill Hall highlight the power of the built environment and spatial practices to make compelling drama as well as political acts, and to enable the image-repertoire of Johannesburg as modern city, epitomized by skyscrapers, trains, and crowded streets. However, the post-apartheid commemoration of the Treason Trial has all but eclipsed other mid-twentieth-century events that offered cultural, rather than strictly political, resistance to apartheid. The celebration of Johannesburg's seventieth anniversary in September 1956 with *Uxolo* (Peace), a cantata for two hundred voices and a seventy-piece orchestra in the City Hall, highlighted aspirations for integrated coexistence, represented by its black composer Todd Matshikiza and white arranger Gilbert Harris. Matshikiza combined the Western classical tradition, the diverse strands of African American music, and local jazz in his compositions for the bebop-inflected *Jazz Epistles*, and in commentary on "music for moderns" (the title of his column for *Drum*, by mid-decade the most popular English-language black-readership magazine on the African continent), and he directed the concert in formal tie and tails. Unlike his more aggressively anti-traditionalist *Drum* colleagues Can Themba and Lewis Nkosi, Matshikiza also deployed indigenous forms for modern purposes, as in the praise-song *uMakhalipile* (Xhosa: "undaunted one") in honor of Trevor Huddleston, anti-apartheid activist and Anglican pastor at the Church of Christ the King in Sophiatown.

Sophiatown, the lively and often lawless multiracial district, was planned for whites in the near west-north-west of Johannesburg (north-west of Brixton on Cabral's map) in 1896 but was leased to blacks because of its proximity to a water-treatment plant. By the 1950s it stood as the last enclave of African property ownership; it was home to people ranging from ANC leaders to the "American" gang. It was retrospectively dubbed an "exciting cultural

Bohemia" by Lewis Nkosi (1965, 24), writing later in exile, and has been celebrated since the 1980s republication of many previously banned authors as a meeting place of black political activists, bohemians of all colors, and organized and disorganized criminals (Stein and Jacobson 1986; Schadeberg 1987; Nicol 1991). In its overcrowded built environment (forty thousand people in a district built for a tenth of that number) and mix of respectable and shady characters, including the aspiring middle-class amid the working and non-working poor thrown together by segregation, Sophiatown resembled black American ghettoes during the same period such as Chicago's Black Belt—but in South African memory, it is the image of bohemia rather than ghetto that persists on stage and screen (Kruger 1999, 2006). Condemned as a "black spot" under the Group Areas Act and slated for demolition from 1955, it animated writing by William "Bloke" Modisane, Can Themba, and Nadine Gordimer, among others, and music by Matshikiza ranging from bebop to the musical *King Kong* (1959), whose performance in the Witwatersrand University (hereafter: Wits) Great Hall and later national and international venues would make some, like Miriam Makeba world famous, after Matshikiza himself had died in exile in Zambia in 1968.

Although the only record of *Uxolo* appears to be an unattributed picture and a brief comment by the German-born and formerly Johannesburg-based photographer Jürgen Schadeberg (1987, 52–54), this event and its composer deserve attention not only for blending European and African performance forms, but also for bringing together white and black audiences in the city center at a time when apartheid legislation confined similar events to Sophiatown or as yet non-segregated sites like Wits University. The cantata's seven parts paralleled Johannesburg's seven decades, from the discovery of gold to the era of apartheid, and ended, in Schadeberg's account, "with a prayer for peace" (1987, 54).[1] Unlike *Drum*'s more famous pictures by Schadeberg, Gosani, and others, of the dangerous but photogenic American gang in poses borrowed from Humphrey Bogart and Richard Widmark, or the jazzy nightlife in Sophiatown or on tour in city venues like *Shantytown in City Hall*, the image of Matshikiza in a tuxedo, framed by blurred images of black and white

1. Although Schadeberg notes that the cantata had seven parts, he attributes the commemoration to Johannesburg's eightieth birthday (1987, 52). The error, after a lapse of thirty years, is a measure of the obscurity into which this event had fallen. The photograph is not attributed to any particular photographer either in Schadeberg's photo-essay or in Nicol's subsequent book on *Drum* (1991). The event was advertised in the black newspaper *The World* as part of the Johannesburg Festival but received less press attention than the jazz concerts and ballroom dancing competitions that also took place on "non-European" nights in the same venue.

Fig. 2.1 Todd Matshikiza conducting *Uxolo* in Johannesburg City Hall, September 1956. Photographer unknown.

faces in the orchestra playing *Uxolo*, represented an integrated urban culture that would not be seen again until the end of apartheid (fig. 2.1).

Uxolo's blend of cultural forms, central urban place and occasion, and utopian message is exemplary because it conjures a bridge between the image of Africa's wonder city of the 1930s and the aspirations toward Africa's world-class city promoted in the twenty-first century, while tacitly acknowledging the political and economic realities that made utopian bridges impossible in the 1950s. The state's strict enforcement of segregation and the postwar economic expansion encouraged geographical as well as cultural separation.

Although the central business district (CBD) and adjacent districts saw new high-rise building in the International style, locally inflected by the legacy of Rex Martienssen and by the influence of Brazilian modernism (Chipkin 1993, 223–45), postwar Johannesburg and its peri-urban areas, like their counterparts in the United States, were characterized more by horizontal dispersal than vertical thrust. Increased prosperity and car ownership for whites in the 1950s enabled suburban decentralization that would accelerate in the 1960s and 1970s, when commerce and culture increasingly followed white affluence to the north, while the government's determination to remove Africans, Coloureds, and eventually Indians from inner-city districts led to the construction of standardized brick houses and administration buildings (but not commercial or cultural structures) in Dube, Meadowlands, and other townships southwest of Orlando, which would together become Soweto in 1964, and even further out over the next decade, Lenasia for Indian South Africans displaced from central districts Fordsburg and Fietas (the vernacular name used interchangeably for the districts officially labeled Pageview and Vrededorp).

However strong the impact of this decentralization on the political economy and social geography of Johannesburg, the representation of the city in politics as well as culture continued to draw on the idiom of urban modernity, including familiar inner-city structures and thoroughfares, as sites and backdrops for protests. The political campaigns of the anti-apartheid movement, while protesting the implementation of apartheid law across the country, concentrated their public displays of defiance on urban environments and amenities from train stations and bus lines to park benches and concert halls, and the mass demonstrations of protest that caught public attention were those that occupied, if only temporarily, the urban terrain around them. Widespread bus boycotts brought African commuters into public view, enacted through walking their right to the city, most spectacularly along major thoroughfares from far north Alexandra, whose commuters had staged bus boycotts at regular intervals since the 1940s.[2] The Drill Hall, which housed the Treason Trials until 1957 (when the proceedings were moved to the executive capital and Afrikaner stronghold Pretoria), drew thousands of observers from near and

2. While this was not the only route under boycott in 1956–57, Alexandra took on particular significance. Like Sophiatown, its inhabitants included a significant minority of African property owners and intellectuals who used the route into the city along the Pretoria Road and Louis Botha Avenue to turn the parade of walkers into a display of resistance. For the historical significance of Alexandra and the bus boycotts since the 1940s, see Bonner and Nieftagodien (2008, 59–124).

Fig. 2.2 "The Singing Box": Treason Trial prisoners on their way to Drill Hall, December 1956. Photograph copyright by Jürgen Schadeberg. Reprinted with permission.

far and front-page coverage from local newspapers. Prisoners brought to the site in police vans were said to have made each of their jails on wheels into a "singing box," so emphatic was their performance of protest songs (fig. 2.2). Street vendors hawked photographs that portrayed the defendants in cheerful defiance, with thumbs or fists in the air, and newspapers published pictures of ANC loyalists standing shoulder to shoulder in a phalanx of posters proclaiming "we stand by our leaders."[3] These demonstrations did not, however, prevent violence, as police began shooting in the air to disperse the crowds already on the second day and ceased only after protest by the mayor. The theatrical aspect of the proceedings was noted by international journalist James (now Jan) Morris, who compared the trial to a "long-running Broadway play"

3. For the phrase "singing box," see Archie Sibeko, Treason Trial defendant, quoted in *The Drill Hall* (Ben-Zeev and Gaylard 2006, 20). Newspaper coverage began in December with the announcement of "The Big Sweep: High Treason Suspects Crowded into the Old Fort" (*RDM* 1956a), but became more skeptical about "allegations" of treason and the ANC's aspirations to "set up a people's democracy" as the month progressed (*RDM* 1956c).

(Morris 1958, 28), but local writer and sometime playwright Lewis Sowden reminded readers of its potentially deadly outcome with the December 20 headline "At Start Songs; At End Drawn Guns" (Sowden 1956a, 1956b). The court's eventual dismissal of all charges brought in 1956 may have cast the prosecutors as (bad) theatre directors, but revised charges brought at the Rivonia Trial of 1964 led to life sentences for several ANC members, including Mandela.

Although these examples confirm the power of performance, social and political as well as theatrical, to contest the right to the city, the best-known medium for documenting this contest has been the photograph, especially pictures by photojournalists like Schadeberg and black colleagues like Bob Gosani working for *Drum*, as well as independent photographers such as David Goldblatt, who began documenting the city in the wake of the Nationalist victory of 1948. *Drum* was published by Jim Bailey, son of mining magnate Abe Bailey, and edited in its glory years between 1951 and 1960 by Anthony Sampson (1951–55), Sylvester Stein (1956–58), and Tom Hopkinson (1959–62), assisted by black journalists like Themba (1953–62; deputy editor first of *Drum* and later of the *Golden City Post*, under the same management) or Henry Nxumalo (a.k.a. Mr. Drum; from 1951 until his murder by tsotsis in 1955). Modeled in part on the (UK) *Picture Post* with racy stories and lavish photographs for consumers who were not fluent in English, the magazine managed to balance lucrative coverage, demanded by urban blacks, of city attractions like "jazz and film stars" (Sampson 1956, 20) with riskier exposés of prison conditions and coverage of the Defiance Campaign, the Treason Trial, and other political events, until censorship reduced it to inoffensiveness by 1960 (Chapman 1989, 185). In one exemplary report, which raised *Drum*'s circulation to seventy thousand in 1954 (Chapman 1989, 194), Nxumalo got himself arrested for violating the curfew banning Africans from the city at night (a common "crime" for urban Africans). He was confined in Number 4, the jail in the Old Fort that had housed political as well as common prisoners since the colonial era. While detained, he witnessed inhumane treatment, including humiliating searches in which naked men were forced to jump around an outdoor prison yard to show that they were not hiding contraband, known as doing the *tauza* dance (Themba 1985, 211–16; Nxumalo 1989b, 35–47). The famous photograph that Gosani was able to shoot from a nearby building and which has been reprinted in a book devoted to his pictures (Gosani 2005, 109–11) captured what Nkosi called the absurdly theatrical aspect of the regime (1965, 35), while the success of image and report showed the value of critical news to readers beyond the educated minority of the Sophiatown set.[4]

As direct documentation of abuse and resistance was always risky and became more difficult as the government piled up legislation to suppress critical speech and images, fiction and film, whose ostensible subjects were inoffensive enough to allow for critique in the margins, took on more significance. Even apparently frivolous films such as *Jim Comes to Joburg* (1949) and *The Magic Garden* (1951) were seen by black audiences to celebrate their lives in the city. Texts for print and stage also explored tensions between the dismal reality of apartheid and imagined stories and spatial practices that might conjure an integrated Johannesburg that, even if it appeared to have "no genre of its own," as a character in Nadine Gordimer's *World of Strangers* (1962 [1958]) had it, managed to celebrate the very practices that were anathema to apartheid ideologues. Theatrical collaborations between *Drum* writers and whites such as Athol Fugard working with Nkosi and others in *No-Good Friday* (1958) or Harold Bloom and Leon Gluckman with Matshikiza and others in *King Kong* (1959) offered a picture of migrants and natives in forms that drew on international as well as local sources. Completed the same year as *King Kong* but too overtly critical of the regime to be screened publicly in South Africa until the 1980s, *Come Back Africa* (1960) used the pretext of documenting the mines as a means to expose the exploitation of African migrants in Johannesburg, while also featuring African intellectual commentary on urban conditions.

"All Roads Lead to Johannesburg": Migration and Modernity in Alan Paton and Beyond

Before discussing these resolutely urban scenarios, however, we should look at a rather anti-urban, but nevertheless best-selling, text that provoked sharp criticism from black intellectuals, but also piqued Rogosin's interest

4. As Paul Gready notes, the editorial line at *Drum* was subject to several tensions. There was tension firstly between the publisher Bailey and the black journalists who felt that he exploited their talent with low pay. In addition, there were disagreements between the journalists and editors (at least the two more liberal ones, Sampson and Stein) on the one hand, who pushed for more critical exposés, and Bailey, who favored the kind of sensationalism that might compete with the non-political *Zonk*, and whose family connection to the Chamber of Mines was the most probable cause of *Drum*'s notable omission of any commentary on the mines, still South Africa's dominant industry in the 1950s (1990, 151).

in South Africa and prompted him to make *Come Back Africa*. Alan Paton's novel *Cry, the Beloved Country* (1987 [1948]) was published initially in the United States, where it has since achieved a kind of "hyper-canonical" status, as Rita Barnard suggests (2004, 87), featured in both middle-school curricula and Oprah Winfrey's Book Club. At the time of publication, it addressed in the first instance white liberals concerned about their own moral probity as well as the plight of black people. The novel's sharp contrast between Johannesburg, depicted as a place where people are lost and destroyed, and rural Ndotsheni, figured, despite its abject poverty, as a place of moral renewal, would seem to offer an unlikely source for the celebration of urban modernity. Nonetheless, even this avowedly anti-urban narrative included, in bus boycott organizer Dabula, at least one character committed to shaping the city and its people in terms other than Christian forbearance. Although the film version, scripted by the American leftist John Howard Lawson alongside Paton, omits Dabula, it amplifies the role of the urban priest Msimang and thus a key voice, embodied by Sidney Poitier, expressing outrage against injustice. Even as the apartheid state accelerated the destruction of urban integration, and even in a novel accused of complicity with the ideology of the "rural native" (Nkosi 1965, 4–7), the city proved irresistible.

Even though it condemns the city, *Cry, the Beloved Country* acknowledges that "all roads lead to Johannesburg" (1987, 52). The novel's long-suffering protagonist, Reverend Stephen Kumalo, seemed to angry young men like Nkosi an absurdly humble Uncle Tom, whose retreat from the vortex that turned his son Absalom into an accidental killer and his sister Gertrude into a prostitute back to impoverished Ndotsheni and dependence on white benevolence expressed a "distorted, sentimental, if ameliorative vision" (1965, 5). Nkosi recognized in Paton's account of his actual work with black youth at Diepkloof Reformatory (through which the fictional Absalom passes in the novel) an "unsentimentalised encounter with the dark and iron reality of the urban African" (6), but he argued that the novel's reconciliation based on charity exposed the "Christian liberal's dilemma: how to persuade an unwilling people to change for the good without revolution" (5). Zoltan Korda's film (1951), which was screened in South Africa in segregated venues, follows Paton's script in that it begins and ends in Ndotsheni and focuses on the changing relationship between Kumalo and James Jarvis, wealthy farmer, Kumalo's landlord, and the father of Arthur Jarvis, the liberal philanthropist killed by Absalom; it also depicts Johannesburg mostly through the eyes of a bewildered Kumalo as a turbulent hell, in contrast to the closing pastoral images of Ndotsheni nourished by the rain and Jarvis's promise to build a new church for "his" Africans.

Nonetheless, Korda and his American collaborators, including Lawson as unacknowledged (blacklisted) scriptwriter, the likewise leftist Canada Lee in the role of Kumalo, and Poitier as his angry colleague Msimang, as well as black South Africans like Lionel Ngakane as Absalom, changed the narrative sequence and the tone of urban scenes and characters to allow for a more critical treatment of the story.[5] The novel begins with Kumalo's journey to Johannesburg in search of Absalom and turns to Jarvis only in the second half of the book, once Absalom has confessed to killing Arthur in a botched burglary of the latter's Johannesburg home. In contrast, the film juxtaposes the lives of both fathers, establishing at the outset a sharp distinction between the conditions that shape these men, highlighting Kumalo's poverty as well as his humility, and Jarvis's wealth as well as his high-handed dismissal of his son's attempt to improve the lives of urban blacks through better housing. As Mark Beittel notes, the film adds dialogue that has the elder Jarvis (Charles Carson) express his initial disapproval of his son's activity by focusing not so much on the ends—"I understand the housing"—but rather on the image of a handshake, in a photograph illustrating a Johannesburg newspaper article, in which Arthur is shown shaking hands with black associates (Beittel 2003, 74–75). The narrative goes on to measure Jarvis's transformation by his new willingness to shake the hands of black well-wishers at Arthur's funeral, even if he fails, in the climactic encounter with Kumalo—who struggles to speak the words "my son killed your son"—to close the distance between them. Handshakes also function as a means of differentiating black characters. After the trial in which Absalom has been sentenced to death and his companions acquitted, including Matthew Kumalo, the son of Stephen's ambitious brother John (Trinidad-born English actor Edric Connor), John is shown playing the politician as he shakes the hands of men around him

5. Citation of the dialogue is from my transcription. Regarding the political background of the filmmakers: Zoltan Korda was more liberal than Alexander, his more imperial-minded brother and partner, and had a long-standing interest in South Africa (Beittel 2003, 73). Lawson had written leftist plays and scripts since working for the US Federal Theatre Project in the 1930s. He was blacklisted after he and the other so-called Hollywood Ten refused to answer incriminating questions posed by the House Un-American Activities Committee in 1951, and thereafter was denied credit for his contribution to this and other films. Although credited, Lee had suffered under suspicion of communist leanings (he had played Bigger Thomas in the stage adaptation of *Native Son* by Richard Wright, a former communist) and died relatively young in 1952. For more on this film and the Hollywood blacklist, see Viennalle (2000, 118).

and pronounces the verdict "justice." Msimang confronts him with the words, "keep your words in your mouth and when you open it again at your great meetings [. . .] spare us your talk of truth and justice," and, after inadvertently touching him, turns away exclaiming, "where can I wash my hand?" Whether or not Poitier's performance amounts to the "moving miracle of indignation" that James Baldwin praised in a film that he otherwise found "less than overwhelming" (1968, 52), it gives us a portrayal of righteous anger that exceeds the bounds of Christian forbearance to demand accountability from black as well as white would-be leaders in the wider world.

Although Beittel faults the film for eliminating bus boycott organizer Dabula, thus leaving John as the sole model of secular urban African leadership as against Msimang as the conscientious priest (2003, 76), he overemphasizes the role of John as a communist even while acknowledging that John is never identified as such. In the wake of the Suppression of Communism Act (1950), it would have been easy enough to demonize John as a communist in the film, but the fact that the script and Connor's portrayal present him rather as a manipulator of ideology for his own gain, and that the film elsewhere offers moments of muted but noteworthy analysis of class discrimination, suggests that Lawson's leftist views prevailed despite his invisibility and that Paton's genuinely liberal concern for free speech, reflected in his opposition to the Act (Beittel 2003, 77), remained relevant. Although Dabula is gone, the bus boycott and other economic questions still appear in the dialogue, beginning with comments made on the train to Johannesburg, where one passenger uses a phrase that echoes the stories of contemporary activist and writer Modikwe Dikobe, "they want six-pence for bus fare *and so the people walk*" (emphasis added), and another compares wages between factory and mine in a more pointed class analysis than John's later bluster.[6] The boycott also figures in the image-track, albeit by omission; we see black people on the train from rural KwaZulu to Johannesburg and later the suburban train on the horizon, as well as bicycles in the foreground, but there are no buses. Further, while the scenes shot in Sophiatown and, even more so, in the illegal but tenacious shanty settlement near Orlando, show Africans in wretched

6. Dikobe's story "We Shall Walk" is a lightly fictionalized account of the 1946 boycott, which was in progress when Paton was writing the novel, and features the leadership of Gaur Radebe, a former communist but by this time more closely associated with the nationalist youth wing of the ANC, led by Anton Lembede and Nelson Mandela. See Dikobe (1979, 104–8); for comment on Radebe's politics, see Mandela (1995, 71–74).

conditions, the shots in the city center show people of all races, implicitly contradicting the enactment of apartheid policy. This also suggests the limits of liberal good works by reminding the viewer of the unbridgeable gap between the shantytown and Arthur's compact but affluent house in suburban "Parkside" (most likely the near northwest suburb of Parkview). While the overarching story of *Cry, the Beloved Country* hews too closely to the sentimental pastoralism of the original novel to acknowledge the claims of secular Africans to urban modernity, even South African critics who dismissed the novel, such as Es'kia Mphahlele, writing about "encounters between Africans and African-Americans," admired the performance of black South Africans in smaller roles, such as Ngakane as Absalom (Mphahlele 2002, 162). More than the overt narrative, however, the film's location shots of the bustling city center suggest, despite the combined pressure of apartheid planning and sentimental pastoralism pushing Africans out of the city, black response to the film at venues like the Harlem Cinema (locally, bioscope) in Sophiatown (fig. 2.3), and their claim to the city depicted in it, that all roads and trains still led to Johannesburg.

While the film of *Cry, the Beloved Country*, like the novel, appealed mostly to white liberals, other films from the period deserve mention for

FIG. 2.3 Harlem Cinema in Sophiatown showing *Cry, the Beloved Country*, Johannesburg 1951. Photograph copyright by Jürgen Schadeberg. Reprinted with permission.

portraying urbanizing blacks, even if they have been dismissed by critics as patronizing African performers and audiences and therefore for being merely "superficially black" (Masilela 2003, 26). Although lacking a world-renowned literary source and favoring broad comedy rather than moral gravity, Donald Swanson's films *Jim Comes to Joburg* (1949) and *The Magic Garden* (1951) highlight the appeal of urban culture and mobility. Like other black-cast films of the period, such as *Zonk* (1950) and *Song of Africa* (1951), Swanson's films showcased black musical talent; however, unlike these films, which essentially reproduced the live musical revues on which they were based, *Jim Comes to Joburg* and *The Magic Garden* inserted demonstrations of urban African talent into narratives depicting encounters between not quite urbanized protagonists and the ways and wiles of the city. Despite an opening voice-over that introduces "natives" as newcomers to Johannesburg, and the slight narrative line that follows newcomer Jim as he is taken in by tricksters or seduced by showbiz glitz, *Jim* appealed to urban blacks with images that normalized as well as documented migration while celebrating the performance of urban savoir faire.

Although *Magic Garden* depicts a comedy of errors unleashed when money stolen from a church in Alexandra is apparently discovered in a vegetable garden, the comedy is affectionate rather than condescending, as indicated by the overtly ironic voice-over that introduces the setting as a "simple African village" known to the whites as Johannesburg and the "dark-skinned races as Egoli, city of gold." As Jacqueline Maingard shows, these films addressed an already well-formed community of black filmgoers (2007, 75–89) who saw the appearance of Africans on film, regardless of the flimsy narrative, as a vindication of black agency. Dolly Rathebe, who first appeared as an entertainer who charms the eponymous newcomer in *Jim* and later the main love interest in *Magic Garden*, was photographed numerous times for *Drum* and starred as a singer in musical revues (*Jazz on Wheels*, 1955; *Shantytown in City Hall*, 1956), returning late in life to film and television in, for instance, *The Line* (1994) and *Waiting for Valdez* (2002). While Rathebe's star power may not have been adequate recompense for the overall lack of freedom suffered by all blacks, her appearance on stage and screen and at related public events, and thus her and her colleagues' contribution to black urban life, provided audiences with models of modern agency, suggested by *Drum*'s caption description of her role in *Magic Garden* as a "location go-getter" (quoted in Maingard 2007, 87) and confirmed by the crowds who greeted her at the Durban premiere with the ANC motto *Mayibuye iAfrika!* (*Come Back Africa*; Coplan 2008, 166). As Jacqueline Stewart has written of African

American reinterpretations of stereotypes in early American film, "Black film images should be read as polyphonic, speaking of and speaking to constructions of Blackness" (2005, 31) produced by whites and blacks. If even crude blackface stereotypes might draw in black American filmgoers, then it is not surprising that the aspiring urban characters performed by Rathebe (Dolly) and her colleagues made a significant contribution to the development of a "black national film culture" in South Africa (Maingard 2007, 89). The appeal of these performances as well as the image repertoire of Johannesburg's modernity—from the train pulling into Park Station to the high rises and the street bustle in the city center, to the tenacious attachment of black arrivals to urban life, even when their share amounted only to crowded quarters in the dilapidated buildings of Sophiatown or the planned sterility of the townships—gave even the slight narrative of *Jim Comes to Joburg* the status of the genre exemplar that would be the reference point for future narratives, cinematic and otherwise, over several decades well into the post-apartheid era.

"House of Truth" and Irony: *Drum*, Sophiatown, and the Renaissance That Might Have Been[7]

Sophiatown in 1955, the year its demolition began, might seem—with its dilapidated, overcrowded, and thus hardly private housing and its precarious public spaces, from the Church of Christ the King to the Odin and Harlem cinemas to the dance halls infiltrated by rival gangs—a poor cousin to the urban modernity that white South Africans found in the affluence of the northern suburbs or in the renovation of high-rise Hillbrow in the image of Brazil. And yet, as suggested by Chipkin's provocative comparison between Martienssen, mentor to architects in the affluent white city, and Themba, mentor to writers in Sophiatown and beyond, both men gathered around them people who shared their attachment to the modern city, even if the privileged architects ensconced on the ridge at Wits had "little awareness of Sophiatown . . . virtually around the corner" (1993, 209). Despite the racial discrimination that restricted African cultural as well as political agency and led to the exile and early deaths of many, often accelerated by alcohol, Themba provided, as deputy editor of *Drum* and as host of the "House of Truth," an

7. My subtitle alludes to Nick Visser's groundbreaking essay (1976), which, despite its critical title "The Renaissance That Failed," renewed serious interest in the legacy of Sophiatown after nearly twenty years of neglect.

FIG. 2.4 Can Themba, Johannesburg, 1955. Photograph copyright by Jürgen Schadeberg. Reprinted with permission.

intellectual salon (which was also his bedsit), which acted as the very incarnation of the edgy city. Schadeberg's portrait highlights both Themba's modernity in clothing and intellectual pursuits and the gap between his modern aspirations and the twilight he inhabited, lit only fitfully by a kerosene lamp, rather than the electric light that whites could take for granted (fig. 2.4). Themba's retrospective comments on the "best of times and the worst of times" (1972, 5) do more than merely quote Dickens's *Tale of Two Cities*; the corollary, "we had everything before us, we had nothing before us," critiques the residual optimism of Nkosi's "bohemia" by reflecting ironically on the very real destruction of the structures that housed this bohemia while insisting stubbornly on the truth of imagined alternatives. When tsotsis mocked township intellectuals by calling them "clevers" (implying too clever by half) or "situations" (as in white-collar workers applying for advertised "situations vacant" rather than the menial jobs handled outside the pass office in south-central Albert Street), Themba and his associates responded by ironically embracing these labels that marked their in-between condition between white and black society. Comparing the precarious urbanity of Themba's generation to the "modernity of underdevelopment" that Marshall Berman associates with Fyodor Dostoevsky's generation in St. Petersburg (Berman 1982, 174), Paul Gready calls this milieu the "unreal reality" of Sophiatown (1990, 139);

its persistence as a point of reference for South African urbanity long after its disappearance testifies to the power of the imagination to shape perception of reality, and thus future action in the district that is now once again known as Sophiatown, as well as in urban spaces beyond its boundaries.

Themba is not the best-known intellectual to emerge from the *Drum* circle but his life and performance as host of the "House of Truth" and of the much-reproduced shebeen scene in *Come Back Africa* exemplify the hazards as well as the high points of the Sophiatown era. Like Ezekiel (later Es'kia) Mphahlele, Themba earned a BA with distinction and taught high school English until the Bantu Education Act (1953) reduced African education to training for menial labor—but there the affinities end. Mphahlele, a member of the ANC, led a sober, disciplined life, writing his MA thesis even while working for *Drum*; he later produced several books including memoirs, autobiographical fiction, and academic studies, and returned from exile with a US doctorate to take up a professorship in 1974, enjoying, despite the repression after the Soweto uprising of 1976, a long career at Wits well into the post-apartheid era (see Mphahlele 2002). In contrast, Themba shared with other *Drum* colleagues a satiric rather than politically committed perspective on the contradictions of urban black life under apartheid. Like Matshikiza, who preceded him at *Drum*, and Modisane and Casey Motsisi whom he mentored (the latter had been his high school student), he wrote in a style that Mphahlele, writing retrospectively of "landmarks of literary history in South Africa" described as "racy, agitated, impressionistic," quivering with "nervous energy and caustic wit" (2002, 309). While Matshikiza and Modisane are remembered for their collaborations on collective projects in music (Matshikiza), film (Modisane), or theatre (both), and for memoirs published in their lifetimes, Themba's writing resurfaced in South Africa only in the 1980s, well after his death in Swaziland in 1968, when apartheid censorship relaxed sufficiently to lift the ban on Sophiatown writers.[8] Before the publication of *The World of Can Themba* (1985), he was known in South Africa only by the few who had access to *Drum* and then chiefly by his journalism. Highlights include reports on "terror in the trains" (1985, 111–115) or the bus boycott as the "world's longest walk to work" (127–32), or essays on a recurring topic

8. See, in particular, Matshikiza's *Chocolates for My Wife* (1982 [1961]) and Modisane's *Blame Me on History* (1986 [1963]). Themba's work, along with that of his exiled contemporaries Matshikiza, Modisane, Mphahlele, and Nkosi, was banned in 1966 and remained unavailable in South Africa until the late 1980s. The anthology published by the African Writers Series in London (Themba 1972) was banned.

of personal as well as political interest, "Let the people drink" (158–65), which criticized the government's insistence that Africans drink only "traditional" beer bought from government-run beer halls, which excluded African women from the truly traditional practice of brewing beer and entrepreneurs of all races from selling liquor to black customers.

Themba's assessment of his own place in the *Drum* line-up, written in an obituary for his young colleague Nat Nakasa, who committed suicide in New York in exile in 1966, offers a useful starting point. In contrast to the voice of "protest and resistance" that he identifies with PAC leader Robert Sobukwe, Themba highlights Motsisi's "derisive laughter," Modisane's "implacable hatred," and Mphahlele's "intellectual contempt" and his own "self-corrosive cynicism" (1985 [1955], 219).[9] While "self-corrosive" applies more directly to Themba's autobiographical sketches like "The Bottom of the Bottle" (1985 [1955], 227–36) or autobiographically inflected fiction like "The Will to Die" (47–52) about a drunken former teacher, "corrosive cynicism" permeates his debut story, "Mob Passion," which won the *Drum* short story prize in 1953. Colored by overheated adjectives that suggest a penny-dreadful romance, allusions to Shakespeare's *Romeo and Juliet*, and the "racy, agitated, impressionistic" depiction of blood-letting, the story reads at first glance like a tabloid melodrama: young lovers are torn asunder when the Xhosa Linga is beaten to death by the relatives of his Sotho sweetheart Mapula, led by her uncle Alpheus for no excuse other than Linga's ethnic difference, provoking Mapula to kill her uncle with an ax before collapsing over Linga's corpse. On closer reading, however, the story reveals Themba's keen eye for the absurd but pressing facts of African life, as well as his canny deployment of colliding registers and dialects of English. The story begins with the key image of African urbanity, the journey by train, but to dispel any romance that might linger from cheerful instances like *Jim Comes to Joburg*, Themba sketches the real dangers that beset passengers on this ordinary journey, as the narrative includes the pickpockets, the *staffriders* (freeloaders hanging from the sides of the train), and the casual talk of yet another murder. This realistic note persists as he punctuates melodramatic lines about "ill-starred love" (Themba 1985, 11) and Linga's rant about black on black violence, "they butcher each other and they seem to like it" (12) with Mapula's pragmatic

9. Themba's judgment of his colleagues may be exaggerated: Mphahlele's criticism is sharp but usually moderate (Mphahlele 2002), and Modisane's "hatred" of racists was part of a contradictory mix of attachment and repulsion to white society (for definitive analysis, see Sanders 1994). Nonetheless his self-assessment rings true.

reminder: "Let us think about ways to handle my father" (13). It also comes to the fore in the spare narrative and dialogue that introduces Thabo as the messenger and Alpheus as the ringleader looking for an excuse to attack the "Letebele" (Sesotho for *umNdebele,* a speaker of *isiNdebele,* the Nguni language similar to *isiXhosa*).[10]

The equivocal power of language complicates this melodramatic schema in unexpected ways. As Alpheus plans his mischief, Themba highlights the contrast between the ringleader's theatrical manipulation of his audience—"Alpheus's voice went down softer and heavier, touching strings of pathos, rousing tragic emotions" (15)—to produce an "automatic movement in the crowd" toward "frenzy and fury" (16)—and Linga's attempts to defuse the tension by speaking to the crowd of attackers in fluent but plain Sotho, asking for directions. Although they initially take him for a "child of at home" (the English mimics South Bantu idiom), it is the return to melodrama, this time from Mapula, who screams Linga's name (whose meanings run from the neutral "try" through the ambiguous "test or tempt" to the outright devious "trick by magic") and thus reveals his Xhosa origin, that dooms the lovers, as Alpheus leads the attack against Linga for lying "so sleekly" (17). The story ends on a note that matches the writer's corrosively cynical signature; Mapula's weeping (her name means "rain") may touch every "breast" with a "sense of something wrong" but the speed with which, "their bravado gone," the members of the mob become "quiet and sulky" before also "crying piteously" (20) suggests contagious rather than cathartic emotion that might just as easily flare up into anger again. This cynical ending overlays a less obvious ironic counterpoint, however; Themba's play with Linga's name and talent for disguise, exemplified in Linga's initially pitch-perfect Sotho, and his attribution of Mapula's inadvertent but deadly betrayal to the strident mode of melodramatic revelation, undercuts the sentimental formula, even while delivering a "racy" story. This irony has satiric implications to the extent that the thoroughly urban Themba blames violence on blind tribal loyalties, but it is the corrosive undertone of irony playing on the unreliability of language, an irony that refuses to draw a political lesson from this problem of translation.

More than the *Drum* stories—which, whatever their undertones, fit the "racy" house style—Themba's later story "The Suit" is uncompromisingly corrosive. The story was written in exile and published in the first issue of *The*

10. I depart here from the standard sociolinguistic convention of avoiding imported Nguni and other prefixes into English in order to highlight Themba's multilingual irony playing off ethnic identity against language.

Classic, the independent magazine founded by Nakasa in 1963 and edited after Nakasa's suicide by Barney Simon, later founder of the Market Theatre. It exemplifies the corrosively ironic treatment of melodrama that made Themba both Sophiatown wit and Johannesburg's answer to Dostoevsky. Thanks to Nakasa's efforts, "The Suit" was reprinted abroad in several languages but, despite Nakasa's encouragement, Themba went on to submit only rough and unpublishable work, doubtless due to the alcohol addiction that would kill him in 1968.[11] The story has become better known through its stage adaptation (by Simon and Mothobi Mutloatse) for the Market Theatre (1993) and production by international maestro Peter Brook (2000), but the original story is simpler, starker—and more peculiar. Philemon discovers his wife, Matilda, in bed with another man who escapes, leaving behind his suit. To punish her, Philemon insists that she treat the suit as an honored guest. Despite her compliance, his demands become more extreme. At a party which Matilda hopes will mark the end of her torment, Philemon demands that she wait on the suit in front of their guests and then storms out for a night on the town. He returns to find her dead. From this synopsis a reader might immediately glean the story's debt to melodrama, but not necessarily the complex of allusions that bring together the penny-dreadful and the profound torment of Dostoyevsky's "Gentle One" with naturalistic depiction of daily trials for aspiring urban Africans. The opening pages lay out these contrasting elements. The first sentence and a half—"Five-thirty in the morning, and the candlewick bedspread frowned as the man under it stirred. He did not like to wake his wife lying at his side" (Themba 1985, 83)—give us Philemon's performance of a model modern husband of the sort featured not in the *Drum* stories of domestic mayhem but in the advertising, especially on the women's pages, whose images of proper urban domesticity encouraged middle-class aspirations, and contrast this aspirational image with the squalid reality of Sophiatown. Maintaining a middle-class appearance, with clean jacket and tie befitting a white lawyer's black messenger, requires Philemon to fetch coal and water from the muddy yard shared by "twenty . . . thirty other people" (84) so as to heat water to wash himself and to prepare an unlikely but romantic "warm breakfast" for "his wife, cuddled in bed" (85). Themba also uses the vignette to contrast his protagonist with "one of those who believed in

11. As the correspondence between Nakasa and Themba makes clear (Nakasa 1963–64, n.p), Nakasa's attempts to get Themba to revise two manuscripts, "The Genuine Article" and "The Refugees," received a truculent response, as Themba demanded that the stories either be published without "changing so much as a comma" or be summarily rejected.

putting your wife in her place, even if she was a good wife" (85) and thus to set everyday township brutality against his subtly cruel scenario of punishment.

Once Philemon finds Matilda and her unnamed lover *in flagrante*, the narrative stretches the tension between high melodrama and sharp irony. When Matilda ducks in anticipation of a blow, her husband, who has just threatened to kill her if anything happens to their "visitor," makes a crueler threat: "There is to be no violence in this house if you and I can help it. Just look after that suit" (89). Themba portrays Philemon's cruelty as the dark side of his model modernity: instead of bringing his wife breakfast in bed as he did before, he now reads books on "Abnormal Psychology" (92) to refine his torture technique. Matilda's attempt to "find absolution in some club doing good" (93) is likewise couched in modern psychological terms as a "whole new venture into humancraft" (94). Appearing to grant her a reprieve for a party in honor of her fellow club members, he turns the screws by demanding once again that she serve the suit alongside her guests, then leaves for a drinking spree with a friend. In the final paragraphs, in which Philemon returns to discover Matilda's dead body, Themba entwines melodrama, irony, and the realities of Sophiatown, moving from the spectacle of the drunken husband as he "crashed through the kitchen door" to sudden sobriety ("Then he saw her. [. . .] whatever whiffs of alcohol still wafted through his head were instantaneously evaporated and the man stood sober before stark reality") to a sentimental ending ("There she lay, as if just before she died she begged for a little love [. . .] just this once . . . just this once more") and finally: "In intense anguish, Philemon cried 'Tilly!'" (96). This conclusion may well invite a sentimental reading, and Sello Maake kaNcube, in the act of giving Stella Khumalo one last embrace in the 1993 stage adaptation, appeared indeed to redeem his character.[12] Nonetheless, Themba's final lines carry more than a

12. The Market Theatre's treatment used third-person narration juxtaposed with vivid enactment by actors to highlight competing points of view on the action—not only the conflict between husband and wife, but also the interventions of friends and passersby. This does not merely bring out the conflicts inherent in the plot; it also sharpens the irony of the retrospective view of present-day audiences. The melodramatic color of the aggrieved and later grieving husband, painted with relish by Themba, is in the performance complicated by the tone of Khumalo's and Maake kaNcube's exchanges: angry, ironic, and pathetic by turns. The narrative connecting moments of dramatic conflict also highlights the unglamorous social, economic, and racial discrimination that was the precondition for this story. Brook's production, by contrast, indulged in the nostalgia that had by 2000 become the standard treatment of Sophiatown. Played by the African American singer Princess Erika, Matilda gave a rendering of two songs, which, despite the false etymology linking one of the songs "Ntyilo, Ntyili" to Tilly, had nothing to do with the plot and seemed to be designed to wrap this actress in the garb of Miriam Makeba, who had made these songs famous in the 1950s.

whiff of his characteristically cynical view of sudden sobriety as more likely a step on the road to sodden defeat (as in "The Will to Die"). From the perspective of exile, the lines offer an ironic perspective on the protagonist's—and author's—quixotic attempt to escape the Sophiatown stereotype. This self-corrosive irony undoes catharsis; its vertiginous effect on the reader anticipates the kind of post-apartheid, even postmodern refusal of perspective, political or otherwise, which critics now associate with the late novels *Underground People* (2002) and *Mandela's Ego* (2006) of Nkosi, until his death in 2010 the longest-lived Sophiatown survivor and irredeemable cosmopolitan), but here depicts the contradictory aspirations that animated and finally destroyed both Themba and his subjects—lively, self-aware, and sometimes self-destructive denizens of the ghetto.

Alienation and Collaboration: *A World of Strangers, King Kong,* and *Come Back Africa*

While Themba's inside view of Sophiatown may today invite comparisons between his "House of Truth" and the more formally designed structures and visions of the more privileged Martienssen, the observations of outsiders dominated the contemporary field. Sympathizers in Britain and the United States were primed by Paton to be moved by the memoirs of liberal expatriates such as Sampson or Huddleston, or later, by Fugard's international breakthrough play, *The Blood Knot* (premiered in London in 1964) but Fugard's earlier collaborations with Sophiatown intellectuals in *No-Good Friday* (1958) and *Nongogo* (1959) became well known only after his breakthrough led to publication in the 1960s.[13] In contrast, *A World of Strangers*, Nadine Gordimer's second novel, reached overseas readers promptly when published in London in 1958. Despite its author's awareness of the ambivalent responses of her fellow liberals to their contradictory position between white power and black aspirations in South Africa, the narrative offers an outside view. The narrator Toby Hood is a male expatriate traveling to South Africa to represent his family's publishing house; his story begins on the ship "anchored at Mombasa" (1962, 7) on the way down the Indian Ocean coast to Durban and ends as Toby says goodbye to his friend Sam Mofokenzazi before boarding the train

13. I have discussed Fugard at length elsewhere; readers interested in the place of Sophiatown in Fugard's work may consult my *Drama of South Africa* (1999, 88–90, 156–63) and *Postimperial Brecht* (2004a, 215–53) and the work of Fugard scholars Dennis Walder and Albert Wertheim cited there.

out of Johannesburg, denying Sam's suspicion that something will prevent his return (266). Toby's story of their friendship, which he defines as eating and sleeping at Sam's house, nonetheless maintains a certain distance, as he acknowledges that he would "always be a stranger" there (162).[14]

Although it is undoubtedly fiction, the narrative draws its male characters from Johannesburg's history. Toby's profession and his initial pose of apolitical insouciance suggest in part the biography of Jim Bailey, who like his fictional counterpart went to Oxford and later represented his family firm in publishing, and in part the persona that British-born *Drum* editor Sampson created for himself. Toby's black associates Sam (writer, composer, and family man) and Steven Sithole (former writer, cynical drinker, and caustic observer of the Sophiatown scene) bear significant resemblance to Matshikiza in the case of the former, and Themba in the case of the latter. Steven, in particular, who dubs his Sophiatown bedsit the "House of Fame" and who guides Toby through the shebeens, recalls Themba in his "House of Truth." Most female characters tend to follow the satirical sketches of Gordimer's short stories: bright and brittle white women at home on the manicured lawns of Johannesburg's northern suburbs, for whom Sophiatown seems more remote than London. One of these women, the beautiful divorcee Cecil, becomes Toby's lover, but his affection and his curious sense that Cecil shares with Steven the "strange freedom of the loose end" (168) do not blind him to the fact that if he told Cecil that his "closest friends were black men," he "would lose her" (163–64). The notable exception to this stereotype is Anna Louw, an Afrikaans dissident whose comments on her legal work for blacks, her "steady" voice (79), and "sober" response to others' inebriation (91) reveal midcentury Johannesburg as a city whose fragmentation into a "world of strangers" makes it seem to have, as Anna puts it, "no *genre* of its own" (80).

Although Toby moves between the worlds of white ease and black deprivation that otherwise meet only intermittently in Johannesburg, he makes no attempt to bridge the gap between them. Anna, whose legal work brings these worlds together and demonstrates her rare ability to inhabit the frontier "between white and black" (175), offers a realistic assessment of the different kinds of alienation affecting the haves trapped in "the loneliness of a powerful minority" (80) as against the have-nots, or rather those one could call the "would like to haves," educated blacks like Steven or Sam aspiring to

14. "Sithole" is a common name, but "Mofokenzazi" splices together Sotho and Nguni fragments with too many consonants and is therefore rather implausible.

intellectual life. While recognizing the constraints under which these men must live, Anna criticizes them for what she sees as a "romantic" attitude to their misdemeanors, in their attempts to treat default on hire-purchase loans, for instance, as an expression of "Robin Hood" rebellion, "robbing the rich to give to the poor" (122), in contrast to organized political resistance. Yet this critical note seems oddly absent from the narrative when Toby romanticizes the poverty of Sophiatown as "more real" than the suburbs (158), and the dancing of its inhabitants as an expression of "joy" rather than "escape" (128). Here the character projects his enthusiasm on to the place for "having made me more myself" (163) in a manner common to a long line of white primitivists the world over, while the author, elsewhere so sharply critical of white liberals eager to "identify themselves with Africans" (169), seems to indulge him here. When Steven dies in a car crash while fleeing a police raid on a club run by his Indian South African gangster friend Lucky Chaputra, Toby finds himself struggling, as he drives through Sophiatown, to deal with Steven's death: "I had to keep drumming it into myself, *he* is not there, *he* is not there. He was made up of all this. If it existed, how could he not?" (251). Despite Toby's preoccupation with his own reactions—"I had to keep explaining death to myself" (251)—this fusion of character and milieu, whether Steven and his township, or Cecil and fellow northern suburbs women and theirs, and Gordimer's vivid depiction of these urban and anti-urban environments and the social lives they contain, creates a persuasive picture of Johannesburg, this "world of strangers" as *one world* whose denizens, however estranged from one another, cannot forever deny that they collectively inhabit.

Although Gordimer takes pains in her novel to satirize the collaboration between Sam and a white liberal she calls Brunner, the "African opera" that "had as much Africa in it as [gypsy operetta] Ruritania ever resembled any Balkan country" (1962, 211–12), the historical target of this satire, the "jazz opera" *King Kong* (1959), based on the life of the "Non-European" boxing champion Ezekiel Dhlamini, deserves more serious attention. Although I have discussed *King Kong* before (see Kruger 1999 and, for pictures, Schadeberg 1987), its collaborative mode of production, urban location, and syncretic form bear review, both as part of the life and work of the exemplary New African Todd Matshikiza, and as a point of comparison with the production relationships of *Come Back Africa*, which included local whites as well as the outsider Rogosin. It can certainly be said that the pressure of the "white hand" in the words of Job Radebe, boxing promoter, and one of the African advisors for *Drum* (quoted in Sampson 1983, 21) was a combination of handshake and manipulation, well-meaning liberalism and the search for profit, and also that venues for black/white collaborations such as the Bantu Men's Social Club, where Radebe served as secretary, were, as Gordimer's narrator suggests, "dreary" (1962, 211).

Nonetheless, the BMSC had provided a rare venue for black social and cultural gatherings for thirty years by this period, and Union Artists, the organization that supported the *King Kong* collaboration, managed, despite class and race contradictions, to support black artists and, in Nkosi's view, to fuse "African native talent and European discipline and technique" (1965, 19) at a moment when participants of both groups by and large acquiesced to this division of labor.[15] White associates, such as chairman Ian Bernhardt and producer Alfred Herbert, exaggerated when they claimed that they had discovered African talent, and their influence and capital led at least one critic to argue that the spectacle of multiracial harmony reflected the interests of the Union's most powerful sponsor, the Anglo-American Corporation, whose director, Harry Oppenheimer, had argued that the "disintegration of traditional African society" was a necessary step in the development of a "modern state and society built on European foundations" (quoted in Kavanagh 1985, 89). It is true that Anglo-Americans sponsored African entertainment but not the African franchise. But it is also true that Union Artists managers were able to marshal the capital to secure royalties and sponsor shows and that the white—predominantly Jewish—philanthropists, and amateur and professional artists who collaborated on *King Kong* did so with the encouragement of black colleagues. Despite the disdain expressed by Gordimer, herself Jewish, Lewis Nkosi read the participation of producer Leon Gluckman, musical director Stanley Glasser, writer Harold Bloom, and facilitators Clive and Irene Menell, as commitment to the "tenuous liberalism and humane values" that "tempered the harsh social order of apartheid" (Nkosi 1965, 19).[16] While we cannot deny the differences in wealth and privilege that separated Jewish and other white patrons, liberal or socialist, from Africans like Matshikiza or Nkosi, we ought to note that this alliance stemmed from a shared affinity for

15. The chair of Union Artists was advertising executive Ian Bernhardt; its members included Solomon Linda, who wrote the hit song *Mbube*, later rearranged by the Weavers (Coplan 2008, 172). Although both Coplan 2008 and Kavanagh (1985, 47) claim that trade unionist Guy Routh initially held the chair, Routh left for London in 1950, after the Suppression of Communism Act.

16. Art director Arthur Goldreich was more radical than liberal; he was an associate of Mandela who was arrested with his comrades in Rivonia but managed to escape prison into exile.

the cosmopolitan potential that made "Johannesburg alive and absorbent in a way no other city in the Republic was" (19).[17]

If Jewish South Africans were the catalyst that brought about "the fusion of Africa and Europe" (Nkosi 1965, 19), America was the base. On the one hand, the Manhattan Brothers followed local variety groups in borrowing from African American ensembles like the Inkspots. On the other, the producers of *King Kong* drew on the American musical. *West Side Story* (music: Leonard Bernstein; book: Stephen Sondheim, 1957) and *Threepenny Opera* (music: Kurt Weill; adaptation of Brecht's text by Mark Blitzstein, 1956) featured in discussion as well as in the musical idiom of *King Kong*.[18] The most telling exemplar was *Porgy and Bess* (1935); this "jazz opera" by George Gershwin and white Southerners Dorothy and Du Bose Heyward was reviewed in *Drum*—at the time of its world tour (1950–53)—as "the Negro show sweep[ing] the world."[19] *Porgy and Bess*'s influence can not only be seen in the subtitle, but heard in the overall orchestration as well as the echoes of Gershwin's "Summertime" in the overture. *King Kong* was not a simple imitation, however. Its musical numbers—and the Nguni lyrics—were written by Matshikiza; the English lyrics (by journalist Pat Williams) and the book (by Bloom, based on a synopsis by Williams and Clive and Irene Menell, with input from Matshikiza) drew on the distinctive English of *Drum* and especially the composer's own brand, Matshikeze.[20] Although Bloom, a theatre

17. Affluence was still a new phenomenon for most Jews in the 1950s. Eastern European Jewish immigrants had been subject to the same restrictions as Indians and other Asians under the British Colonial Aliens Act (1902), until pressure from the Anglicized minority led to the "white" classification of "Eastern" Jews as well; see Krut (1984). On Gordimer's disavowal of her Jewish background, see Leveson (1996, 172–94).

18. Schadeberg (1987, 177) mentions *West Side Story*, as does Irene Menell (1994). Bloom notes that *King Kong* was proposed partly because Union Artists was unable to secure the rights for *The Threepenny Opera*; see program for *King Kong* (February 1959) in the Johannesburg Public Library (Strange Theatre Collection).

19. See *Drum* (1953). For Langston Hughes, however, *Porgy and Bess* was "not a Negro opera but Gershwin's idea of what a Negro opera should look like" (Hughes 1976 [1966], 699). Even if it became the "biggest breadbasket for blacks in the history of the American theatre," "whites got the caviar and blacks only the porgies" (698). Hughes's poetry and essays were available in the BMSC library from the 1930s and he visited South Africa to work on the compendium *An African Treasury* (1960).

20. Despite Bloom's claim to sole authorship, Schadeberg (1987, 177) suggests a collaborative writing process. Menell's outline of the plot and lyrics and her recollection in interview (1994) went further. She noted that, after Bloom and Matshikiza sketched out a series of numbers based on the boxer's life, Bloom moved to Cape Town, leaving the rest of the team to produce a plot, which he fleshed out on a subsequent visit to Johannesburg. Menell also suggested that the *flaaitaal* in the play should be attributed to Matshikiza, flavored by his own version, Matshikese.

novice, and his associate Mona Glasser, *King Kong* "chronicler," described Matshikiza as an "unknown musician," the latter was not only an accomplished pianist who worked with several bands from the Harlem Swingsters to the Jazz Dazzlers, but was also *Drum*'s music editor, writing jazz reviews, social commentary, "How Musicians Die" (1953), and an informal history of African jazz, "Jazz Comes to Jo'burg" (1957).

Therefore, it is not surprising that black and white participants had different views of the storyline and the relative weight of text and performance. Nat Nakasa's account of Dhlamini's life in *Drum* follows the trajectory from mission school and petty crime to his triumph as a champion but undisciplined boxer, and on to his murder conviction and subsequent suicide by drowning while working in a prison labor camp. It also includes his secret humiliation by the white champion and the violence of the police, so as to highlight the contradictions in his social situation as well as his character (Nakasa 1989 [1959], 27). Bloom suggests that Dhlamini was a "symbol of the wasted powers of the African people" (1961, 17) and has King Kong's manager, Jack, comment bitterly on the discrimination against African champions (77), but his script focused on the decline from the winner (31) to "a man [with] writing on him—bad, rubbish, gangster" (78). The performance of Nathan Mdledle, lead singer for the Manhattan Brothers, complicates this melodramatic image of a muscle-man gone bad. A "tall rangy man with expressive hands" (Glasser 1960, 21), an image borne out by photographs, Mdledle's deft movement and supple baritone granted the character more subtlety than his "Marvellous Muscles" lyrics implied. Played by Moloi, the character of Jack acquired a reflective quality at odds with the swagger of the stereotypical boxing manager and at a certain remove from the other singing parts, particularly the outlaw glamour of the gangster Lucky (Manhattan Brother, Joseph Mogotsi) and his (briefly, King Kong's) shebeen queen Joyce (Miriam Makeba), backed by their signature tune, "Back of the Moon" (named after an actual Sophiatown shebeen).

These modifications by the performers reflect their understanding of the social context and the resources of dramatic and musical representation provided by the township musical, however allegedly inferior to the jazz opera. Most overt in Jack's bitter comment and in the intermittent chorus of washerwomen, whose remarks point to the discrepancy between King Kong's legend and the shabby reality of township life, social criticism also surfaces in the ironic use of musical themes and stage vignettes; thus, during King Kong's prison term, Joyce throws a party to a flashier version of "Back of the Moon," while Jack trains a substitute for King Kong to a "ragged version" of

"Marvellous Muscles" (Bloom 1961, 56–58). While this use of comic gesture and musical phrasing apparently reflected the difficulty some actors had with English (Glasser 1960, 17), it also drew on similar techniques used by African variety groups, with which the Manhattan Brothers and other older members of the cast would have been familiar, especially the Pitch Black Follies, the premier African variety group whose principal, Emily Motsieloa, was honored in *Drum* after the death of her husband and group leader Griffiths Motsieloa. The influence of the variety format, rather than "straight" drama, suggests that the stylistic and thematic references—from the American musical and European drama to African variety (itself a syncretic product of African American vintage)—available to cast and production team may have been heterogeneous but were nonetheless too intertwined to be reduced to simple oppositions between white and black.

If *King Kong* keeps the conventions of the American musical in contact with African variety, it also reveals the syncretic character of the forms that Bloom marks as traditional. The two songs with Nguni (Xhosa/Zulu) lyrics, written by Matshikiza, are important not simply because the text speaks to the African audience largely indifferent to "talky" theatre (Kavanagh 1985, 109), but because the music and lyrics in combination evoke a multilayered tradition of *Africanizing* performance that has historically absorbed outside conventions without being overwhelmed by them. The overture is identified in the program by the English title "Sad Times, Bad Times" but consists of a Xhosa saying in proverbial form, sung to *amakwaya* (jubilee choir) melody underlaid with the swing beat, as the gangsters cross the stage and disrupt the early morning routine:

Ityala lalamadoda	It is the fault of these men
nguAndazi noAsindim'..	It's "I don't know" and "it's not me" . . . .
Alaziwa-mntu	Nobody knows

(Bloom 1961, 27)[21]

While the lyrics allude to township passivity in the face of gangsterism in the present, the music resembles less the kwela-inflected jazz of King Kong's signature than the national laments written a generation earlier by composers

21. Bloom glosses the text as "The fault of these men/Lies in their ignorance"; Kavanagh corrects the Xhosa orthography and translates the named figures but not the key topic sentence (1985, 111). John Matshikiza, son of Todd, later claimed that Mandela read the line as a covert expression of support for ANC members on trial in 1959; see Matshikiza (1999).

like Reuben Caluza (trained at Columbia University) to music that combines church choir with ragtime. The Zulu song, "Hambani Madoda," which speaks to the trials of urban Africans plagued by tsotsis and impossible work conditions, likewise echoes these earlier songs:

Hambani madoda	Keep moving, men
Siy' emsebenzini	We are going to work
Sizani bafazi	Stand with us, women
Siyahlupheka	We are suffering
Amakhaza nemvula	cold and rain
Ibhas' igcwele	the bus is packed
Sihlutshwa ngotsotsi	we are preyed on by tsotsis
Basikhuthuza	they rob us of what we have
Siyaphela yindhlala	we are half-dead with hunger
Nemali ayikho	there is no money
Hambani madoda	keep moving, men
Isikhathi asikho	time is short
Hambani madoda	keep moving, men
Isikhathi asikho	time is short

(Bloom 1961, 82–83; Kavanagh 1985, 111)

Although it opens with the staccato rhythms and masculine bass of the migrant work song, this is not the choir of "a thousand [male] voices" that Kavanagh associates with mass struggle. Sung as a restrained lament, this song has more in common with the *isicathamiya* of Solomon Linda's Evening Birds (and, more recently, Ladysmith Black Mambazo) than the mass rallies of the Defiance Campaign. Combined with the women sopranos in the ensemble, an addition unthinkable in *isicathamiya*, the song acquires an intimate quality reminiscent of Caluza's Double Quartet, recorded in the 1940s.[22] Even though the song itself is not repeated, the note that is struck by this lament returns in the reaction to his death in an image that sings of both mourning and celebration.

Matshikiza's appropriation of the choir music of the New African elite does not mean that these songs have nothing to do with protest. On the contrary, they mine a long tradition of singing protest against the grain of the

22. For the history of modern African music and the career of Reuben Caluza, see Erlmann (1991).

apparently genteel choir melody, but they suggest tenacious survival rather than heroic defiance. It is also significant that the locus for this survival is not, in the first instance, the modern political organization, but the music and the subdued subversion associated with migrants, or to a certain degree with women. By including these songs in a musical environment that is otherwise thoroughly modern, Matshikiza is not retreating into a neo-traditional refuge of the kind promoted by Bantu Education, but rather extending the boundaries of the modern to include forms marked as traditional, just as he had filled the "traditional" form of the praise-song with modern content in *uMakhalipile*, celebrating Huddleston as the "undaunted one," or fused African and European forms in *Uxolo's* commemoration of the city of Johannesburg. Although this representation of urban complexity has been largely eclipsed by sentimental treatments of Sophiatown's gangster glamour on stage and screen, Matshikiza's experiments in collaborative creation with *King Kong* deserve attention alongside its better-known contemporary, *Come Back Africa*.

Directed by the American socialist Lionel Rogosin from a script developed with Modisane and Nkosi and with the further collaboration of Themba and other habitués of the House of Truth, *Come Back Africa* was conceived as early as 1957 but released in New York only in 1960. It was banned in South Africa shortly after its release, coincidentally on March 21, 1960, the day of the Sharpeville Massacre. In recent years, it has received due credit as a key South African film as well as a major contribution to the neo-realist docudrama that was Rogosin's signature genre (Davis 1996, 2004; Balseiro 2003; Maingard 2007). Gaining access to locations under a series of cover stories, claiming variously to be making a travelogue, a music film, or a documentary of the gold mines, Rogosin was able to film in the streets as well as on mine property, while also meeting dissidents, from progressive whites to black intellectuals, who could help him explore the city. Despite using the ANC's slogan "Come Back Africa!" as its title, the film allows its political impact to emerge less in the emphatic manner that would define anti-apartheid film in the 1970s Soweto era than in its depiction of what Peter Davis calls the "mundane torment of seeking work in a system of exploitation" and thus the "violence to human dignity" more than the occasional if brutal acts of physical violence (2004, 10).[23] As in his first film,

23. This citation is from Davis's introduction to his edition of comments by Rogosin and others in *Come Back Africa* (2004). Since Davis knew Rogosin for two decades and was charged by Rogosin's son Michael with editing and updating Rogosin's notes included here, citations refer to the volume as Davis (2004), with further attribution as needed.

On the Bowery (1957), Rogosin set up a loose fictional frame to create a persuasive if not strictly documentary narrative around actual inhabitants of Johannesburg and its environs. Zachariah Mgedi, who portrayed the migrant Zachariah, was himself a worker, picked by Rogosin and local production manager Morris Hugh out of a bus queue (Davis 2004, 56–58). Vinah Bendile, who played his wife, also in her own name, was a domestic worker, likewise without acting experience (54).[24] At all stages of Zachariah's story, the narrative shows the conditions that enable this "mundane torment." Viewers see the dangerous work on the mines and the confinement of the mine-worker compounds, the house work where Zachariah clashes with petulant white employers, and his own confined domestic space in Sophiatown, where Vinah comes to join him but where they must battle not only with the "system of exploitation" but also with the routine violence of the ghetto streets, where bullies both threaten and influence their son, and which throw up the adult bully, tsotsi Marumu, who provokes Zachariah and later kills Vinah.

Although this narrative draws on the *Drum* melodrama familiar to scriptwriters Modisane and Nkosi, the story as embodied by non-professional but evidently gifted actors allowed Rogosin to show and his target audience of conscientious viewers to "see the individual on the screen against the background of his real environment," as his notes on neorealism suggest (in Davis 2004, 58–60). The film's representation of the city goes beyond merely background or the protagonist's point of view, however, to show the complexity of this environment: from the opening sequence of high-rise structures, to the sequences in Sophiatown which show people in rural as well as urban dress at work as well as engaged in a mix of activities from playing music and drinking to doing the laundry. Sophiatown is shown as both a lived-in district and an area under demolition; a political poster ("Hands off Western Areas!") acknowledges the political struggle but leaves it at the margins of this story, as it would remain for people like Zachariah, who were more concerned about

24. Despite consulting Rogosin's notes, later published in Davis (2004, 48–120), Balseiro speculates that Bendile had acting experience on the grounds that her "smart European dress and fluent English render her characterization of a rural woman . . . hardly believable" (2003, 109). Although neither Rogosin nor his posthumous editor Davis provide an explanation, a woman of Bendile's generation could have acquired English skills and Western dress at one of the few (church-run) schools for girls and still not found anything other than domestic work.

survival than long-term political goals.[25] While African writers and photographers had documented this reality, *Come Back Africa* remains, as Davis claims, the "only record *on film* from that time not only of what the African reality looked like, but what Africans felt about it" (2004, 10; emphasis added), and, more importantly, how their analysis of the situation has set the standard.

The stature of the film is indisputable, as demonstrated by its ongoing influence on representations of the period. In museums, such as Museum Afrika near the Market Theatre, clips from the film form part of exhibitions on Johannesburg history, including clips from the mining scenes presented *as if* they were documentary. In the post-apartheid search for historical models for an integrated urbanity, films like *Sophiatown* (2004), by French filmmaker Pascale Lamche, rely on these clips, especially the famous shebeen scene which shows Miriam Makeba singing from the Manhattan Brothers repertoire. *Come Back Africa* contains more explicitly anti-apartheid scenarios than any other film of its time and place, beginning early on with Zachariah's discussions (in Zulu) of work conditions with his fellow mine workers, continuing with scenes of his humiliation by capricious employees that made one reviewer "feel ashamed to be white" (Davis 2004, 12), and culminating in the shebeen scene in which black intellectuals discuss tsotsis like Murumu and other anti-social agents, and South African politics generally, considered by Rogosin and many since to be the "climax of the film" (in Davis 2004, 84). Presided over by Can Themba, the scene recalls the "House of Truth," even if it could not have been filmed there. As host, Themba expected visitors to speak candidly about their experiences in Johannesburg. In the film, Themba moderates an argument between Modisane and Nkosi, who sharply criticize *Cry, the Beloved Country*, and Hugh, who defends the liberal point of view embodied by Paton (Rogosin 2010, ch. 10).[26] The critics win the argument, backed by Modisane's imitation of the abject Reverent Kumalo in a manner that exaggerates Lee's performance of the role, and by Nkosi's rejoinder to

25. As Gready notes (1990, 158), the ANC overestimated the power of political activists to mobilize tenants against the removals because they disregarded the fact that many paying high rents for small rooms, often to landlords of color in Sophiatown, welcomed the opportunity to rent single-family houses in Meadowlands, even if those houses and the township as a whole had minimal amenities.

26. All speakers appear as themselves in this scene. Citations of dialogue are from the 2010 DVD edition, which includes *An American in Sophiatown* (2007), a documentary with commentary from Rogosin, Nkosi, and other participants. Rogosin notes that Morris was "remarkably capable" as production manager but also behaved oddly, often "provok[ing] people to attack him" (in Davis 2004, 96).

Hugh "the liberal just doesn't want a grown-up African" (2010, ch. 10). As indicated by Modisane and Nkosi's later publications, and by key work by their associates, such as Henry Nxumalo's *Drum* article "Birth of a Tsotsi" (1989a), this critique reflected the actual views of these participants and evidently influenced the political tenor of the rest of the film, which was shot after this scene.

Keen to reinforce the authority of *Come Back Africa* as an "intensely political film" (Davis 2004, 12) on the one hand, and swayed by Modisane's and Nkosi's emphatic critique of Paton on the other, commentators from Rogosin to the present have overemphasized *Come Back Africa*'s break with *Cry, the Beloved Country* (Balseiro 2003, 94–100; Rogosin in Davis 2004, 58; Maingard 2007, 115–16). While the abject Kumalo certainly invites Nkosi's scornful response, "he never grew up," the film version managed to push the story beyond the "distorted, sentimental, if ameliorative vision" of the novel (Nkosi 1965, 5). Poitier's portrayal of the Reverend Msimang's righteous anger is the most obvious critical point, but there are more subtle points of comparison. Despite his rural naivete, Kumalo's conversation on the Johannesburg train elicits comments about the bus boycott and about urban African wages in the mines and elsewhere, which anticipate the comments Zachariah receives from his roommates in the compound, although the latter are more plausibly rendered in Zulu. Further, the sequences in African districts from Sophiatown to the shanty towns near Meadowlands depict not only the wretched accommodation, but also the attempts of its inhabitants to get by.

The impact of *Cry, the Beloved Country* on black spectators was more nuanced than the Sophiatown intellectuals allowed. When he auditioned for the role in *Come Back Africa*, Zachariah Mgedi described *Cry, the Beloved Country* as a "good film" (quoted by Rogosin in Davis 2004, 58). Although no doubt less sophisticated than Nkosi, Mgedi's opinion discomforted Rogosin, who had not seen the film but found the novel "maudlin and patronizing" (58). While Rogosin rightly anticipated that Mgedi would perform very well as Zachariah, his assessment of the actor as "someone in transition, who still retained some innocence and yet had enough experience to grasp the complexities of urban life" (56) seems rather patronizing coming from someone otherwise "astounded by Zachariah's ability to identify with" (59) and to *perform* his role. Further, while Rogosin's negative view of the novel was shared by some "African and American Negro intellectuals" (58), others, such as Mphahlele and Baldwin, came later to acknowledge the realism of elements in the film, and even Nkosi modulated his condemnation of the novel with a more nuanced view of Paton's "unsentimentalised encounter" (1965, 6) with urban Africans in his reformatory work and in later fiction. Lastly, while Rogosin expressed concern for Mgedi's ongoing problems with his employer, his own abrupt departure for New York after the shooting was over left Mgedi and others to fend for themselves. In contrast, Korda's stronger ties with film institutions enabled at least one South African actor, Lionel Ngakane, to go from writing for *Drum* to acting for Korda in *Cry*, to acting and directing in Britain (making, for instance, *Jemima and Johnny* in 1967) and participating in the founding of FEPACI (Pan-African Federation of Film Makers) in the same year (Ngakane 1997).

Epilogue: 1960/2002

Nkosi's more positive assessment of Paton's later work, in particular, "A Drink in the Passage," a story set in 1960 at the end of the decade that cemented apartheid law and disorder, provides an appropriate bookend to this chapter. Even though the narrator is a white observer, Nkosi praised the story as "recognizably modelled upon our [black urban] lives" (7), and despite its fictional characters, "a report of what actually happened in real life to one of us" (1965, 7). The story is notable not only for its reflection on this significant historical moment, but because of its post-apartheid resonance, expressed in the film treatment in 2002 by Zola Maseko, a young filmmaker who had previously attracted attention for documenting the repatriation of the remains of Sara Baartman from Paris, where she had been displayed and later dissected as the "Hottentot Venus" at the Musée de l'Homme after her death in 1815.[27] The adaptation of Paton's story is more modest; it deals with a fictional black sculptor, Edward Simelane, at a moment in the mid-twentieth century when actual black artists, such as Caspar Darare and David Koloane, had at best intermittent access to institutions like art schools or galleries. In the published story, the unnamed, presumably white narrator begins in a manner notably more ironic than *Cry, the Beloved Country*:

> In the year 1960 the Union of South Africa celebrated its Golden Jubilee and there was a nation-wide sensation when the one-thousand-pound

27. After *The Life and Times of Sara Baartman* (1998), Maseko went on to contribute to the Sophiatown nostalgia boom that *Drink in the Passage* avoids. His later film *Drum* (2005), a biopic about Henry Nxumalo, stars American actors in key roles, including Taye Diggs as Nxumalo (a.k.a. Mr. Drum) and Gabriel Mann as Schadeberg, and plays up the "racy, agitated, impressionistic" quality of Sophiatown personas that feed the nostalgia mill.

> prize for the finest piece of sculpture was won by a black man, Edward Simelane. His work, "African Mother and Child" not only excited the admiration but touched the conscience or the heart or whatever it is of white South Africa. . . . (Paton 1961, 87)

The narrator goes on to say that the committee received a "reprimand" for failing to add the words "for whites only" to the competition notice but decided after all to award Simelane the prize at the public ceremony marking the occasion. Nonetheless, the narrator notes ironically, Simelane "said mischievously to me" that his family decided that he wasn't "up to it" and so he decided not to go. Despite pressure from friends to take a public stand, he demurred: "Boys, I'm a sculptor not a demonstrator" (88). At this point the narrative frame of the story widens to the scene of the conversation between Simelane and narrator, allowing Simelane to shift from this overtly political debate to express appreciation for his host's largesse: "This cognac is wonderful [. . .] It is also the first time that I've drunk a brandy so slowly. In Orlando, you develop a throat of iron and you put back your head and just pour it down in case the police should arrive" (88). Despite his deflection of politics, the artist comes back to the political constraints on his aesthetic and epicurean life, as he invites his interlocutor to hear the story of the only other cognac he has had occasion to drink.

This invitation not only sets up Simelane's account of the "drink in the passage" (partially enclosed hallway that links the flats in most South African apartment buildings). It also provided the inspiration for Maseko's film and the occasion for reevaluating the legacy of a writer many have criticized for sentimentality in the twenty-first century, at a time when it is the Sophiatown legacy, including Rogosin's unsentimental film, that has been enshrouded in nostalgia. Introduced in the credits as "Alan Paton's *A Drink in the Passage*," this fifty-minute film adds a post-apartheid outer-narrative, which casts a critical light not only on the 1960 story but also on the post-apartheid moment; otherwise it follows the story quite closely. The film begins with a present-day celebration in the Johannesburg Art Gallery, in which the aging artist (played by anti-apartheid veteran actor David Phetoe) is feted by the gallery spokeswoman, the Minister of Arts and Culture, and other well-dressed notables in the stark-white addition (Meyer and Pienaar 1986) to the original building. Maseko does not show the exterior, but his image addresses those Johannesburg viewers who know that the building, designed by British imperial architect Edward Lutyens in 1910 in celebration of the Union of South Africa's creation that year, has always been unsettled on its site, turning its back on inner-city Joubert Park to face the gap that should have been a park over the railway line, and that it currently has a precarious relationship with the inner city around it.[28]

Just as the younger artist resisted his friends' injunction to "demonstrate," the older Simelane deflects the drama of oppression and liberation implied by the gallery spokeswoman's account of "art [that] can transcend race, color, religion even persecution." As played by Phetoe, his costume—black shirt with Madiba print (after shirts with jazzy rather than traditionalist prints popularized by Mandela) and Beatnik beret—signals his cosmopolitan affiliations. Retiring to a bench where he sits enjoying a goblet of cognac, he is approached by a young black journalist whose braids and formal suit speak to conventional globalized fashion, even as she asks him to reiterate the national narrative of triumph over racist discrimination: "Coming from a life of such oppression, where did you get your inspiration?" In response, the artist smiles skeptically and says instead, "this cognac is wonderful" (Paton 1961, 88), with which statement the film returns to Paton's story.[29] Even though the journalist looks barely interested in events that Simelane places "before [her] time," he tells the story not of struggle against oppression but of the personal encounter that led to his first ever cognac, the "drink in the passage."

The flashback that follows recalls in color the streetscape and fashion of Johannesburg circa 1960, which was captured in black and white in *Come Back Africa*. The recollection begins in a sentimental mode, as the younger Simelane (David Mohloki in a photojournalist's jacket but with the same artist's beret) makes his way to his government-issued township house in Orlando and informs his wife (Motshobi Tyelele) that he has decided to enter the Golden Jubilee competition.[30] This domestic sequence from the story

---

28. As art historian Jillian Carman points out (2003, 231), despite urban legend to the contrary, the gallery was *designed* to face away from Joubert Park toward what was to have been an extension of the park across an underground railway. But, because the railway remains exposed to this day, the building was left on the edge. The modern extension facing the park was added on the occasion of Johannesburg's centenary in 1986; for further comment on the district see Chapters 4 and 5.

29. Quotations with page numbers cite film dialogue taken directly from Paton's story; unattributed quotations cite dialogue added to the film adaptation, written as well as directed by Maseko (2002).

30. The music (piano composed by Witus du Toit) that accompanies the segue from recollection to flashback is not merely incidental. In echoing John Barry's theme for *Born Free*, James Hills's 1966 popular film about a wounded lioness nursed back to freedom, it highlights the gap in the present-day scene between Simelane's generation and the current generation that South Africans call the "born frees," too young to remember and often to care about the legacy of apartheid.

continues with another added by Maseko: father and son (played by real-life sculptor Darare's grandson, Zane) work together by candlelight chiseling the stone, which has not yet "spoken" to the artist but which will eventually become the work—*African Mother and Child*—that wins the competition. Nonetheless, the narrative establishes at the outset an ironic counterpoint to this sentimental note; the flashback begins with a voice-over reiteration by Simelane of the opening words of Paton's story, including the Golden Jubilee and the art competition. The sequence leaves out for the moment the "nation-wide sensation" (87) that introduced the story, possibly to create suspense but also to prepare a visual analog for the competition advertisement and, later, the newspaper announcement of the prize. Simelane's face is reflected in the frame of the competition poster as it is placed in the window of the "Alabaster Bookshop" (88) by a white shop clerk who tries to shoo him away. After the competition, Simelane returns at night to look at the winning sculpture on display in the window framed, as in Paton's story, by a newspaper headline "Black man conquers white world!" (88), but this time the sculpture occupies the central spot where before the artist's reflection had appeared. It is on this occasion that he meets a white man who arrives as Simelane is seen looking at the sculpture: a shy, self-educated Afrikaner, van Rensburg (Witus du Toit, who also composed the score). Mohloki and du Toit look in on the sculptured head of the woman looking back at her child. Capturing both men in the same shot taken from inside the shop, the camera shows their uneasy but compelling encounter as van Rensburg praises the piece for showing the mother as "someone guarding. She knows it won't be an easy life" (89). When van Rensburg offers his interlocutor (who does not admit that he is the artist) a conversation over a drink at his apartment, Simelane is skeptical but accompanies him nonetheless. Perhaps because his host anticipates an ambivalent welcome from his relatives, he and Simelane drink wine "in the passage" exposed to "impersonal doors" that might open to hostile residents "at any moment" (91). Despite the later appearance of van Rensburg's apologetic aunt carrying snacks and cognac, the artist feels compelled to down the drink quickly in anticipation of a hasty exit. He accepts an offer of a ride to the station but reflects in the voice-over that he was unable to explain to his acquaintance that as a "non-white" he would not be allowed to use the front entrance—possibly, he reflects, because he has already disappointed his interlocutor: "black men don't touch white men any more, or only by accident" (94–95).

While the story ends with Simelane's wife weeping in response to her husband's account, the film returns to the scene in the gallery. Even before the closing scene, however, the post-apartheid elements filter through the flashback at a number of points and so remind viewers of the links between past and present. One reminder is pointed, even heavy-handed: after Simelane recounts winning the prize, he reappears as his old self in the gallery to speak an abbreviated version of the lines that, in Paton's story, close the very first paragraph and thus set the ironic tone at the outset: "my work [as against Paton's 'his work'] not only excited the imagination, but touched the conscience . . . or whatever it is of white South Africa" (87). Others are more fleeting: despite the costumes and parked cars indexing 1960, several anachronistic elements stand out even in the city night. The present-day Out of Print Bookshop in the bohemian suburb of Melville (thanked in the credits) stands in for the "Alabaster Bookshop in Von Brandis Street" in the 1960 CBD, and the old City Hall (now Gauteng Provincial building) fronts for the long-since-demolished station building from 1930. These anachronisms may be inadvertent, but the appearance of the name of the actual bookshop and its neighbor Melville Meats unmasked in the frame when Simelane approaches to look at his sculpture in the window suggests otherwise; even if they do not follow the director's intentions, these elements invite the viewer to ponder the differences in the built environment and the racial and class geography of Johannesburg between the era of high apartheid and the current moment.[31]

These moments appear all the more significant in the bright light of the closing sequence. As Simelane's voice-over conveys the phrase "touch [. . .] only by accident" cited above, the scene changes from 1960, figured in a sepia long shot of Simelane overshadowed by the station, to a close-up of his older self in the blue-white light of the gallery. The next shot, which follows Simelane's gaze away from the young journalist at his side, frames an encounter between the sculpture surrounded by empty glasses from the now-concluded reception and the well-worn hand of the elderly cleaning woman pausing in her task to caress the sculpture's head. The journalist drops out of the picture as this close-up is succeeded by another showing Simelane's hand clasping the cleaning woman's as his off-screen voice greets her respectfully in

31. This Alabaster Bookshop is fictional but, while its name may add to the ironic tone of Paton's story, its display of the sculpture and the notice celebrating an integrated South African achievement recalls the Vanguard Bookshop, which had operated on the corner of Von Brandis and Jeppe Streets in the 1930s and 1940s but, by 1960, had moved around the corner into Joubert Street. This bookshop, which survived into the 1970s, was a haven for the free exchange of ideas in an increasingly closed apartheid city; for more on the shop and its Trotskyist owner Fanny Klenerman, see Klenerman's papers (1916–83).

Zulu. This focus on the handshake may seem overwrought, but, as a cinematic adaptor of Paton's fiction, Maseko may well be quoting the noted handshakes in *Cry, the Beloved Country*. In his 2002 film, the casual greetings between black and white notables at the gallery reception contrast poignantly with van Rensburg's apparent inability to shake Simelane's hand; he behaves, as the narrator has it in the story (and Simelane says in the film), "like a man trying to run a race in iron shoes" (Paton 1961, 95). In this film, the final handshake between the now-famous artist and the unnamed cleaner suggests both an intimacy between two people of an age to have suffered apartheid and a widening gap between their generation and the "born frees" who appear to take their success for granted. The rising generation may be immune to sentimentality in the edgy city as well as the gallery on the edge, but the final image suggests that brushing off sentimentality may entail the loss also of fellow feeling and collective responsibility for public space beyond designated precincts, without which public life in the city becomes all the poorer. We shall return to these questions around politics and fellow-feeling in the following chapters on the apartheid city and its demise.

3 1976: SOWETO ERUPTS INTO JOHANNESBURG

The year 1956 closed with the Treason Trials, and the next decade saw the apartheid regime's crackdown on legitimate mass opposition, life sentences imposed on Mandela and other ANC members at the Rivonia Trial of 1964, and the promulgation of laws that allowed for practically unlimited police powers of surveillance, detention, and torture. Against this historical backdrop, 1976 heralded the uprising not only of a new generation of political activists but also of cultural institutions that would play an important role in resistance to apartheid.[1] Even if it did not immediately

1. The Criminal Law Amendment Act of 1965 permitted detention without trial for 180 days (up from the 90 days permitted in 1963). The Suppression of Terrorism Act (1967) and the Internal Security Act (1976) broadened the terms of conspiracy and "racial hostility" further and allowed police in the special Bureau of State Security (BOSS) to detain suspects indefinitely (Kane-Berman 1978, 39) without charge or notification. This period was also marked by the forced relocation of blacks, Coloureds, and Asian South Africans from urban areas or farmland decreed "white." According to the sharply titled study *The Surplus People*, three and a half million people were "removed" under the Group Areas Act from 1960 to 1985; Africans forcibly identified with tribal ancestry were dumped with little hope of employment in Bantustans such as Transkei and BophuthaTswana (Platzky and Walker 1985, 10).

topple the apartheid regime, the student revolt against the imposition of Afrikaans as a medium of instruction erupted in Soweto in June 1976 with enough force to define a generation of black activists, as well as the culture of protest expressed in poetry, theatre, and retrospectively in prose. The revolt also transformed the views of the minority of whites who were active in anti-apartheid organizations in Johannesburg, Cape Town, Durban, and elsewhere. As Martin Orkin wrote in his introduction to the critical history of plays created after the uprising by Junction Avenue Theatre Company, "the 1976 Uprising changed South Africa forever" (1995, 72). Michael Chapman goes further in his introduction to *Soweto Poetry*, suggesting that "Soweto" has "metaphysical" as well as "social" meaning (2007, 11); it is not only the place (the consolidated Southwestern Townships, so named in 1964), but also the idea that shaped national and international understanding of South Africa under apartheid. The exact meaning of this idea remains in dispute, but even John Kane-Berman, who argued at the time that it represented "a turning point where South Africa did not turn" (1978, 232), acknowledged that the students, in combination with resurgent unions, recently released political prisoners, and many others who were no longer willing to submit to discrimination and state violence demonstrated that resisting apartheid was possible, even if a "long and taxing war of attrition" would be needed to overcome it (Karis and Gerhart 1997, 184).

These comments emphasize the contemporary impact and the ongoing resonance of Soweto while also acknowledging that the impact was propelled by pressures that had been building up before the uprising. Well before 1976, the social engineering of apartheid had already stretched the urban fabric to anti-urban limits. Already in the 1960s, the government moved to convert the last remaining mixed central neighborhoods like near-west Fietas (the vernacular name used variously for the districts of Pageview and Vrededorp ["peaceful village"]) into white suburbs like Triomf ("Triumph," which had been erected in 1960 on the ruins of Sophiatown farther west). By the early 1970s, the government was pushing the regimentation of Soweto, already fenced and subject to surveillance, even further by requiring residents to live in tribal groups that conformed with apartheid ideology but not actual township diversity. In addition, while the state and private corporations exploited the expanding population during the postwar boom that lasted until the world-wide oil crisis of 1973, the economic contraction after the global oil crisis prompted government to rediscover the ideology of separate development. Taking control of Soweto from liberal Johannesburg, which had subsidized its infrastructure (Kane-Berman 1978, 69), and handing it instead to the

West Rand Administration Board (WRAB), one of several boards countrywide dominated by bureaucrats loyal to Afrikaner Nationalism, gave the state full control over the taxes of more than a million Soweto residents. Under WRAB, much of the revenue from these taxes and the sale of government- monopoly beer was absorbed by the bureaucrats' salaries or diverted to the Bantustans such as Transkei. Dismissed as a sham by the rest of the world, Transkei "independence" in October 1976 deprived those identified by the government as Xhosa of their South African citizenship and rights of residence.[2] Nonetheless the "self-governing" Bantustan was promoted directly or indirectly as a sign of stability after the uprising. This was the message of the pro-government papers, including the *Johannesburg Beeld*, as indicated in the billboard featuring Transkei premier Kaizer Matanzima and Bantustan leaders-in-waiting Mangosotho Buthelezi (KwaZulu) and Lucas Mangope (Bophutatswana) appearing below the head of Henry Kissinger, ally of South African premier B. J. Vorster, on David Goldblatt's photograph (fig. 3.1). These policies deepened the chronic neglect of infrastructure, housing, and schools, and taxed schools still further by reviving an unworkable plan to require black teachers, most of whom were not Afrikaans-speaking, to teach math and social science in Afrikaans rather than in the more practical English.[3]

This anti-urban regime in the townships had its counterpart in the city, in the fortress architecture of the "great apartheid building boom" (Chipkin 1998, 248–67). This boom was anticipated in 1962 by the Herzog Tower (after Minister of Communications Albert Herzog), which was located on the Brixton Ridge, site of the Rand Revolt, and used by the reliably pro-government South African Broadcasting Corporation (SABC). However,

---

2. The "homeland" policy planned to make all Africans citizens of entities identified with their alleged tribal origins, even if they were born in urban centers of mixed parentage, and thus to treat them henceforth as foreign migrant workers in South Africa. For a summary of this policy and its consequences for urban blacks, see Karis and Gerhart (1997, 221–37).

3. According to the South African Institute of Race Relations, the so-called 50/50 rule requiring urban township schools to teach key subjects through the medium of Afrikaans had been part of the Bantu Education Act of 1953 but had been dropped for lack of teachers with adequate Afrikaans. It was revived in 1974 to appease hardline Afrikaners, despite expert linguistic opinion that mother tongue primary education (in Zulu, Xhosa, etc.) should be followed by middle and high school education in a single language, and evident preference for English among urban teachers, parents, and students. Despite the prominent role of high school students in the uprising, they were not directly affected by the rule; the government left high schools alone while trying to force the rule on middle schools, whose students began to protest months before the June uprising. See SAIRR (1977, 50–77) and the revisionist account by Sifiso Ndlovu, formerly at Pheleni Junior Secondary School (Ndlovu 1998). The Afrikaans requirement was dropped when schools reopened after the winter break in July 1976.

Fig. 3.1 This is our new world. Read the morning paper for the new generation—Beeld. Braamfontein, October 1976. Photograph copyright by David Goldblatt. Reprinted with permission.

the boom dates more precisely, in Chipkin's view, from 1966, when Minister of Police Balthazar Johannes "John" Vorster became prime minister, to 1976, when the uprising hastened the trend toward recession. The boom had its most concentrated expression in new apartment blocks in Hillbrow, where names like Highpoint or Highrise emphatically expressed their developers' aspirations, but it also included concrete representations of state power. Key structures included the deceptively transparent high-rise police headquarters at John Vorster Square near the western edge of the inner city; the Post Office (now Telkom) tower in Hillbrow erected in 1971 in advance of the launch of television in 1976; Ponte City, the tallest apartment building; and the Carlton Centre, the tallest building overall in Africa (fig. 3.2). Beyond the city center, the new SABC building and the Randse Afrikaanse Universiteit were the most notable among monumental Afrikaner Nationalist intrusions into the old Anglophile district of Auckland Park (est. 1896), just north of the Brixton Ridge. Although these institutions attempted to deflect the force of the uprising with instruments ranging from propaganda to brute force, and succeeded in postponing the moment of reckoning until the late 1980s, they

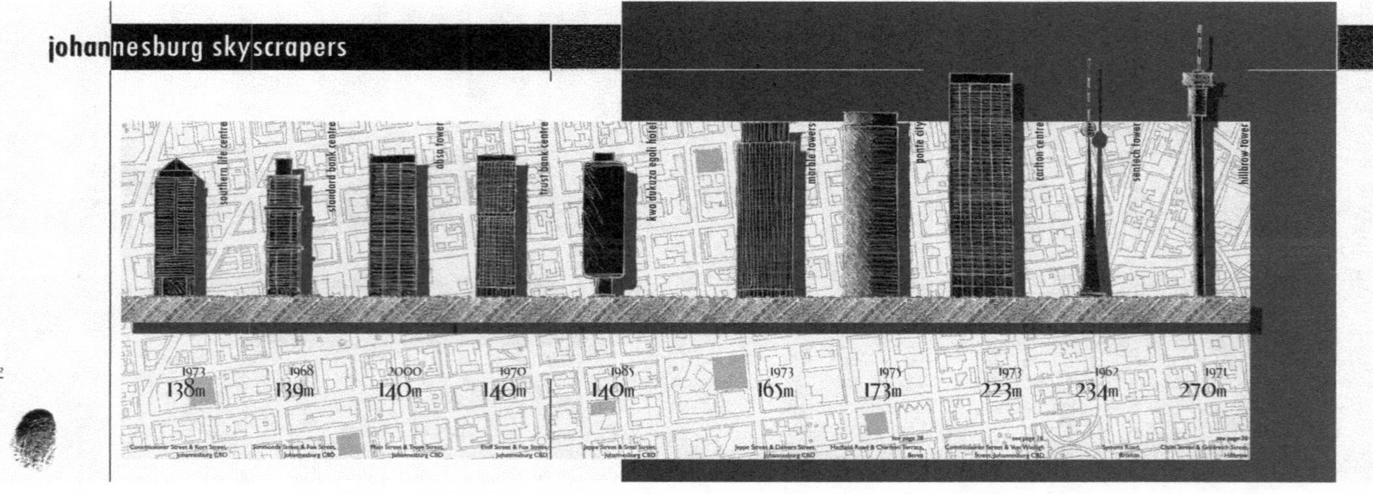

FIG. 3.2 Johannesburg Skyscrapers. *Jozi Sketchbook*, 2010. Graphite on paper by Zafrica Cabral. Reprinted with permission.

could not ultimately overcome the unsustainable expense of separate education, housing, and government administration, nor deal with the social and human costs of suppressing burgeoning resistance.

Although the uprising surprised the ANC in exile and the Bureau of State Security (BOSS) at home, students in Soweto and elsewhere did not create a movement from nothing. Soweto provides a reference point for a movement that emerged already in the late 1960s and dissented from the nonracial legacy of the ANC to focus on Black consciousness and Black empowerment. The impact of these ideas is a matter that has since been subject to debate between those who grant the Black Consciousness Movement (BCM) primary credit for the uprising and those who dismiss the BCM as an elite grouping whose ultimate impact did not match that of the unions that were reemerging in the 1970s.[4] Despite retrospective skepticism, however, many students and community members drew inspiration from the BCM and associated movements like Black Theology (Karis and Gerhart 1997, 89–188). The South African Students Organization (SASO) was founded by Stephen Bantu Biko, then a medical student at the University of Natal-Black section and joined by students from the University of the Western Cape (officially designated Coloured) and the University of Durban Westville (designated Indian); it broke with the white-run National Union of South African Students (NUSAS) in 1968. SASO engaged not only in student activism but in organizations like Black Community Programs (1971–77), which were dedicated to economic skills training, and community organizing in townships and rural areas, with the support of the South African Council of Churches (SACC), and the Christian Institute, a local organization run by the Afrikaans pastor Beyers Naudé. SASO's sources of inspiration for their program of Black self-reliance also included Black Power advocates in the United States from Malcolm X to Stokely Carmichael (Kwame Ture), as well as spokesmen for African independence from Ghana in 1957 to Mozambique in 1974; Biko, however, argued that being Black was "not a matter of pigmentation" but of "mental attitude" (1978, 48). His call to build Black institutions and thus Black "self-respect" (72) addressed not only Africans but also others demeaned by the apartheid label "non-white" (49). Even if only a minority of Coloureds and Indians joined the BCM, they made a considerable impact on Black cultural

4. David Lewis's contribution to Karis and Gerhart's study explicitly critiques Baruch Hirson's claim (1979) for a workers' vanguard, arguing that the student uprising had "a far more powerful impact on the working class and its unions than did the latter on the uprising" (Lewis 1997, 209).

institutions and their influence on their respective communities led eventually to widespread boycotts of segregated Coloured and Indian elections in the 1980s.[5]

SASO's vocal support for FRELIMO (Front for the Liberation of Mozambique) and other African independence movements provoked state harassment, beginning with the banning of key SASO and BCM officers in 1973 and culminating in trials for treason in 1975 (Karis and Gerhart 1997, 140–48)—the most spectacular of which charged activists such as Saths Cooper and Pandelani Nefolovhodwe with treason for performing political theatre. This trial in turn inspired the courtroom scenes in *Cry Freedom*, Richard Attenborough's fictionalized film about Biko and his supporter, Donald Woods, editor of the anti-apartheid Eastern Cape paper, *The Daily Dispatch,* which Cooper and Nefolovhodwe praise in their essay.[6] Despite this state harassment, SASO affiliates on segregated campuses such as the University of Natal-Black section, and the University of the North at Turfloop, had a durable impact on anti-apartheid activism in Soweto. Turfloop in particular included many students from Soweto and professors like Es'kia Mphahlele (who returned from US exile in 1974) who taught African and African American literature. Student Representative Council president Abraham Onkgopotse Tiro, SRC president Aubrey Mokoena, and Cyril Ramaphosa went from Turfloop to teach in Soweto schools, where they encouraged the development of the South African Students Movement.[7] While many students went into exile

5. On the influence of Durban students like Srini and Sam Moodly, Saths and Vrini Cooper, and others on the South African Black Theatre Union and anti-apartheid politics of the 1970s, see Kruger (1999, 129–47); for the contribution of Black writers like Achmat Dangor and Chris van Wyk, see van Wyk (1988) and Ngwenya (2012).

6. In a tribute to Biko, Cooper and Nefolovhodwe refer to not only political theatre but also to Richard Attenborough's film *Cry Freedom* (1987), in which Denzel Washington played the role of Biko (2007, 112–13).

7. The circulation of Black liberation texts—by figures including Kwame Nkrumah, Jonah Nyerere, Frantz Fanon, Malcolm X, and Carmichael—is evident in the writings of Stephen Biko (1978), in the SASO journal *Black Review*, and in the poetry and drama performed by Black consciousness groups in the 1970s. Mphahlele taught at Turfloop until 1978, when he became the first professor of African literature at Wits University. Although Tiro, Ramaphosa, and Mokoena were expelled from Turfloop without receiving their graduate degrees, government mandated self-management of Soweto schools still in place in 1972 (until 1975) allowed principals to hire them. See Karis and Gerhart (1997, 122–28, 156–67) and Mokoena's interview with Gerhart (Mokoena 1991). Tiro was killed in exile by a parcel bomb. Biko died in detention due to police torture. Ramaphosa became secretary general of the National Union of Mineworkers and later of COSATU. In the post-apartheid era, he moved into pension funds and other investments, including a sizable share of the Marikana platinum mine where police shot wild cat strikers in mid-2012, but returned to politics at the ANC convention in December 2012, where he was elected deputy president of the party.

in 1976 and some returned only in the 1990s, activists like Ramaphosa and Mokoena continued anti-apartheid work in South Africa, even though their allegiances diverged in the 1980s, as Ramaphosa and others moved away from Black Consciousness to integrated union work and the United Democratic Front (UDF; active 1983–93).

Cultural activists affiliated with the BCM were primarily interested in creating black-run institutions; their cultural expression favored more emphatic political content than previous generations, characterized by "stark English idiom" and "naked" unadorned forms (Chapman 2007, 11), especially in poetry and theatre. The sharp questions and ironic answer in "In Defence of Poetry" by Mafika Gwala exemplified this protest through poetry: "Tell me/ What's poetic/ about shooting defenceless kids/ in a Soweto street? [. . .] Tell me brother,/ What's poetic/ about defending herrenvolkish rights?/ As long as/ this land, my country/ is unpoetic in its doings/ it'll be poetic to disagree" (Gwala 1982, 10). As Chapman notes (2007, 13) and Thengani Ngwenya more recently confirms (2012, 500–501), these emphatic forms of expression were in part the product of apartheid policies. Unlike the Sophiatown intellectuals, whose access to liberal education and international literature encouraged fluency in English and brought forth writing characterized as much by irony as political critique, the Soweto generation had to contend not only with the Bantu Education curriculum—which was designed to limit them to vocational training—but also the effects of censorship. The Publication and Entertainment Control Board (1963–93) banned the circulation of Sophiatown literature in 1966 (restored in part in 1986) and liberation writing from Africa and the African diaspora in the Americas in 1974, after the work of Frantz Fanon and others had surfaced in black-activist speeches (Karis and Gerhart 1997, 108).[8] Nonetheless, the gap between Sophiatown and Soweto was narrower than these critics assume. Despite the assertion by editor Robert Royston that younger black writers had "no tradition to continue," (1973, 7), the poems in his own anthology, *To Whom It May Concern*, demonstrated that, to the contrary, poets like Gwala and contemporaries Oswald Mtshali, Mongane Serote, and Sipho Sepamla found inspiration in local and international sources, from Xhosa and Zulu praise poetry to Sophiatown writers like Can Themba, to African American music and writing.

8. In "Ideas under Arrest" (1981), exiled professor Daniel Kunene itemizes the laws that limited not only the publication of fiction and nonfiction deemed a threat to the state, but also those inhibiting gatherings and those that confined individuals to a given magisterial district or even to a single home, forbidding them to write or speak publicly or even to meet with more than two people at any one time (Kunene 1981).

Although the government's enforced separation between black and white residential areas and cultural institutions provoked arguments for Black self-reliance and resistance not only to state repression but also to white liberal interference, interracial collaboration persisted for pragmatic reasons including access to money and venues. While censorship and other kinds of state harassment also affected white-run institutions, from bookstores to campus associations, institutions with liberal capital backing such as Johannesburg's Market Theatre had more room to maneuver. Its predecessor, the Space in Cape Town (1972–81), the first integrated theatre to emerge at the height of Separate Amenities Act prohibitions against mixed assembly, presented provocative work like Athol Fugard, John Kani, and Winston Ntshona's play *The Island*, whose implicit setting in Robben Island Prison exposed it to censorship, but Fugard and his associates did not have to confront the persecution inflicted on militant groups such as Theatre Council of Natal (1969–73) and Peoples Educational Theatre (1970–73), whose members suffered detention, death, or exile.[9] The Market Theatre, established in June 1976 in the old Fruit Market in near-west Newtown, has been the most durable of these institutions, but its success as an anti-apartheid venue depended not only on white capital but also on the creative labor of pioneers and contemporary collaborators, both black and white. Opening a few days before Soweto erupted, the Market drew on the contributions of Sophiatown-era writers and performers, and younger people from groups like Workshop '71, MDALI (Music Drama, Literature Institute, whose acronym *umDali* means "creator"), and the Federated Union of Black Artists (FUBA). Market founding director Barney Simon, who had previously run the experimental but whites-only Arena Stage in central-east Doornfontein (one of Johannesburg's oldest districts, established in 1887) also worked with literary magazines like *Purple Renoster* (Purple Rhino, 1956–72), its short-lived spin-off Renoster Press, both edited by Lionel Abrahams, Simon's long-standing friend, and *The Classic* (1963–71), edited initially by *Drum* writer Nat Nakasa and after his exile in 1964 by Simon and others.

While these magazines had mostly whites at the helm, their successors had Black editors. *New Classic* (1975–78) and *The Classic* (revived in a new series; 1980–82) were edited by Sipho Sepamla, who began his editorial career with *S'ketsh* (1972–75), which he dubbed "South Africa's popular theatre and entertainment magazine." In contrast to these short-lived ventures, *Staffrider*

9. For the history of these theatres and the political affiliations of their members see Kruger (1999, 129–66).

lasted nearly two decades (1978–94). Launched in the wake of Soweto by Ravan Press and affiliated in the 1980s and 1990s with the Congress of South African Writers (COSAW), it was helmed initially by Mike Kirkwood, and later by Black writers Chris van Wyk and Andries Olifant. Although some organizations, such as MDALI, found accommodation in rare Soweto venues like the Donaldson Orlando Cultural Centre (DOCC), most tended to use private urban venues that did not require prior censorship of scripts. SPRO-CAS (Special Programs for Christian Action in Society), which funded the Black Community Programs and Ravan Press, had access to overseas funds through the World Council of Churches.[10] Even unaffiliated local whites had more capital than blacks and, while not immune, were less likely to suffer police harassment. Simon and Abrahams lived and worked in the near-east district of Kensington (established in 1897 around the rocky outcrop due north of Troyeville on Cabral's map), where Renoster Press resided until it was absorbed by AD Donker in the northern suburb of Craighall (established in 1902, but settled mostly after World War II). Sepamla edited *S'ketsh* out of a home office in Dube, Soweto, and the new series of *The Classic* from eastern satellite town Benoni, before moving to FUBA, which he directed in the 1980s out of a building directly opposite the Market Theatre.

This centralization of anti-apartheid cultural activity in Johannesburg was in large part due to the political economy under apartheid. Despite curfew laws that required blacks to vacate the city after dark and despite BOSS surveillance of dissidents across the city, the inner city offered a meeting point between the white suburbs and black townships. Further, the speculative expansion of office construction in complexes and malls in the northern suburbs of Johannesburg and in the northern satellite of Sandton (established in 1966) left cheaper spaces for rent in inner districts. Although the economic downturn after the uprising exacerbated capital flight to the northern suburbs, and thus the evacuation of office and residential space in the CBD and contiguous districts like Hillbrow and Berea, research by economically inclined historians has shown that the movement of capital began already in the 1960s, with speculative investment in real estate as well as a response to (white) consumer desire for leisure and shopping opportunities in the

10. Ravan Press was initially established by Special Projects for Christian Action in Society (SPRO-CAS) in 1973 and was directed by Peter Randall. By *Staffrider*'s first issue (1978), Randall had been banned from public life but Ravan continued to put out prose, poetry, and drama by new writers. The press also printed publications by other new presses, such as AD Donker's anthology of Black poetry *To Whom It May Concern* (Royston 1973), which was the first of its kind to be published in South Africa.

suburbs (Goga 2003; Beavon 2004). As inner-city vacancies were increasing in the 1970s, however, the government was focused on forcing out the last non-white (Coloured, Indian, Muslim, Hindu, and Christian) inhabitants of historically mixed inner districts, including Doornfontein and Bertrams in the near-east and Fordsburg and Fietas in the near-west, without providing adequate housing in overburdened segregated townships like Eldorado Park (Coloured), southeast of Soweto or Lenasia (Indian) southwest, both beyond the boundaries of Cabral's map.

This patent contradiction between the apartheid-era obsession with pushing people of color out of the inner city and the economic reality of owners of vacant properties needing tenants would by the end of the 1980s bring down the Group Areas Act and other laws enforcing segregation, but the edifice of apartheid began to crack already in the 1970s, undermining attempts to keep Johannesburg white. Some Coloureds and Indians who had lived in inner districts for generations and who did not have to carry the passbooks required for Africans resisted removal (the last Indian inhabitants of Fietas were evicted only in the 1980s), but others looked elsewhere in the city for housing. As early as 1971, even as developers were building more high-rises, including the massive Highrise on the rocky outcrop of Pullinger Kop off Nugget Street (fig. 3.3), some displaced people began surreptitiously to rent vacant apartments in Hillbrow and Berea (whether in their own names or behind a white front). This phenomenon came to be recognized in the 1980s as the "greying of Johannesburg" (Pickard-Cambridge 1989), but as Goldblatt's photographs attest, some Indians living in the inner city were willing to be photographed—hidden by newspapers—by 1978 (2010, 209) and to make their names and faces public by 1981 (236). In time, even Ponte City (architect: Mannie Feldman with Rodney Grosskopf and Manfred Hermer, also architect for the Johannesburg Civic Theatre), the fifty-four-story cylindrical apartment tower completed in 1975, was transformed. Like its evident (but not acknowledged) model—Bertrand Goldberg's sixty-story Marina City in Chicago (1966)—Ponte was built to attract affluent white singles or young couples (perhaps like those in the Highrise wedding party in fig. 3.3) to urban life; its dominant position on the edge of the ridge above the slope into Troyeville made it an icon of the urban glamour.[11] By the 1990s, however, Ponte would house not only South Africans of color but also migrants

11. To complement the schematic comparative sketch reproduced here, readers might consult Cabral's more topographically detailed map and sketch (2010, 38–39), which show Ponte's cylindrical shape and distinctive position in the city.

FIG. 3.3 A wedding on Pullinger Kop, with Highrise under construction, Hillbrow. February 1971. Photograph copyright by David Goldblatt. Reprinted with permission.

from Congo, Senegal, and elsewhere. The transformation of this iconic building and its more modest neighbors, which represented modernist styles from 1930s art deco to 1950s "Little Brazil" in Hillbrow (Chipkin 1993, 235–40), would generate more fictional representations in the edgy city of the 1990s, but already in the 1970s, writers from radically different parts of the Johannesburg conurbation—from the horizontal vastness of Soweto's standardized houses to the vertical density of Hillbrow's flatland—probed the fault lines that exposed the futility of segregation.[12]

In the high apartheid era of the 1970s, shaped by political repression and censorship on the one hand, and activism that encouraged avowedly committed writing on the other, the genres that came to the fore were those that favored direct expression rather than indirection, emphasis rather than subtlety, and short rather than long forms: in sum, poetry and performance rather than narrative prose. Nonetheless, novels depicting the uprising and

12. Since at least one researcher has assumed that "flatland" means level ground (Murray 2011, 66), readers should note that the term refers to the dense environment of high-rise buildings on the brow or the slope of the hill, whether apartments or flats or, in the post-apartheid period, former office buildings repurposed by squatters.

its aftermath began to appear at the end of the decade. These novels deserve attention not only because their fictions revise contemporary and present-day recollections of the uprising and its context, but also because they embed these events in detailed depictions of built and lived environments and communities in Johannesburg and Soweto. André Brink's *Dry White Season* was published at home in Afrikaans and abroad in English in 1979; Miriam Tlali's *Amandla* (Power, 2005 [1980]) and Mbulelo Mzamane's *Children of Soweto* (1982) were published by Ravan, and Sepamla's *Ride on the Whirlwind* (1984a) by AD Donker. Sepamala's novel and *To Every Birth Its Blood* (1981) by Mongane Serote, who was already in exile, were later published in England. All of these authors were censored (Brink only briefly) in South Africa because of their explicit representation of police brutality. While these fictional treatments of the uprising grabbed critics' attention at the time, quieter, more intimate stories about daily life under apartheid, whether in Soweto or in the contested districts of Fietas and Fordsburg, especially the work of Ahmed Essop, have more recently received notice. Before exploring the fictional representation of the urban environment, however, we should begin with testimonial writing for print or performance. Although this testimonial work expressed attitudes, emotions, and exhortations that could have emerged anywhere in the country, several texts of prose and poetry for performance speak of Johannesburg and are therefore the focus of the next section.

"Jo'burg, Sis!" Loathing and Living in "City Johannesburg" in the Age of Apartheid

This subtitle juxtaposes two Johannesburg writers: Barney Simon, whose *Jo'burg, Sis!* (1974), comprising stories and monologues, was published before he became better known as director of the Market and co-creator of the theatre's distinctive testimonial workshop form; and Mongane Serote, whose poem "City Johannesburg" appeared in his debut collection *Yakhal'inkomo* ("So Cries the Ox"; 1972) and was reprinted in the influential anthologies of black poetry *To Whom It May Concern* (Royston 1973), *The Return of the Amasi Bird* (Couzens and Patel 1982), and *Voices from Within* (Chapman and Dangor 1982).[13] Juxtaposing these two authors, whose lives intersected

13. Serote returned to poetry after devoting the 1980s to cultural work for the ANC in exile; his most recent poetry collection appeared in 2010. My discussion of Simon here focuses primarily on his own texts. For Simon's contribution to the collective workshop method of testimonial theatre, see Kruger (1999, 154–84) and the interviews and commentary by Simon's collaborators compiled by Stephanou and Henriques (2005).

but whose experiences were sharply divided by apartheid, may illuminate the spatial politics and the aesthetic modes shaping Johannesburg in the years leading to the crisis of 1976. Simon was born in 1936 and raised in Kensington by working-class Jewish parents; he had the freedom to finish school and to find theatre and related work in England in the 1950s and the United States in the 1960s before returning permanently to South Africa in the 1970s. His first published story, "The Birds," which appeared in the second issue of *The Classic* (1963), is a portrait of a pigeon breeder in what appears to be a London suburb.

Serote was born in Sophiatown in 1944 but was forced to move to Alexandra with his family when Sophiatown was demolished; he was later educated in British colonial Basutoland (now Lesotho) and in Soweto, although without completing high school (Serote 2007, 114). Nonetheless, he too published in *The Classic,* beginning with "Cat and Bird" in 1969, in a special poetry issue compiled by Nadine Gordimer and Audrey Cobden when Simon was general editor; he also contributed to the last issue (1971) with the poem "Alexandra." Both writers depict the nervous alienation of new arrivals to the city and both choose forms—Simon's proto-theatrical monologue and Serote's harsh, anti-lyrical apostrophe—that capture the unforgiving urban environment as well as their protagonists' uneasy response to it.

Despite this connection, the gulf between these two lives exemplifies both the impact of apartheid and the struggle to represent it critically. Simon's monologues feature female as well as male speakers on edge in the inner city, especially in Hillbrow, whose reputation as a cosmopolitan haven from the political and sexual restraints of Calvinism overshadowed its more diverse actual population, which included more working-class people than swinging singles, despite the nightlife glamour captured by photojournalists (Clay and Griffiths 1982). Although the press had registered the presence of Coloured and Indian pioneers and the government's attempts to evict them already in 1971 (Morris 1971–93), Simon's characters, like those in other stories of Hillbrow, such as those by Sheila Roberts in *Outside Life's Feast* (1975), are white but marginalized in other ways. The title monologue of *Jo'burg, Sis!* (1974, 129–36) portrays a middle-aged man who uses the expression "*Sis!*" ("yuck"), which is commonly used by children. Created by Afrikaans actor Marius Weyers at the Arena and reprised later at the Market, Bobby Ferreira was slighter and more vulnerable than Weyers's better-known role from the 1970s, the macho biker Jakes in P. G. du Plessis's drama about poor whites, *Siener [Seer] in die Suburbs* (1971), but Ferreira's allusion to his family environment in suburban Kempton Park (near the Johannesburg airport) might have struck audiences as similar to the blue-collar near-south setting for Du Plessis's play, whose population included settlers from Portugal via Mozambique, to which Ferreira may belong. Dressed in a "brightly checked sports jacket and a cravat," and surrounded by the furnishings of a small Hillbrow flat, including armchairs and a "Formica coffee table" (Simon 1986, 110), Weyers played Ferreira as a nervy queer talking to a younger man whom he had picked up in a pub.[14] The monologue begins with peevish remarks about strangers: "Jo'burg, sis! Honestly you know, you can't walk down the street without someone biting you" (111), whether "kaffir beggars" or "bladdy policemen" (113). He worries about burglars stealing his "tailor-made" suit (115) but, despite stating his desire to leave, plans to renovate his flat with white walls and "modern" curtains (111). The piece ends with Ferreira failing to persuade his companion to stay the night, in between comments about his itchy balls and big double bed: "But look, hey, why don't you try to come back? Just knock three times so I'll know it's you" (116). The audience is left with the sense that this character, while he evidently finds Hillbrow alienating, could not stomach living anywhere else. Although his sexual orientation is unmentionable in a regime that criminalized homosexual conduct (Gevisser 1995), Bobby Ferreira inhabited one of the few places where men might lead half-visible gay lives in the 1970s, two decades before members of Gays and Lesbians of the Witwatersrand (GLOW) could assemble the first LGBTQ rights parade in South Africa on these streets.

Although the other two monologues performed under the title "Hey Listen" are not set in specific locations, *Jo'burg, Sis!* includes two as-yet-unstaged pieces written for actors in Simon's company, "Monologue for Vanessa [Cooke]" and "Monologue for Danny [Keogh]," both of which are set in Hillbrow. The role created for Keogh, scripted as a pothead from Cape Town who turns to heroin in Hillbrow, resembles the panhandler character that Ferreira recalls accosting him with the demand: "Ag please my china, *gooi my* [throw me] five cents" (Simon 1974, 129). It might also echo an even unkinder portrait by Serote, whose poem "Hippy or Happy" (1972) portrays a hippy who may be a "piece of art walking around" but whose "arms are guns" (Serote 1982, 21), suggesting that, in this era of apartheid violence,

14. The performance text published in *Market Plays* (1986) includes a description of the actors and stage directions, which were not in *Jo'burg, Sis!* because the latter was published before Simon assembled his company.

all whites, even flower children, are dangerous to blacks.[15] The monologue for Cooke, who collaborated with Simon until his death in 1995 and continues today to work at the Market Theatre Laboratory, would have offered the petite, versatile actress a matter-of-fact city worker as a foil to the ditzy Miss South Africa has-been she played in the "Hey Listen" series. This monologue is striking not only because it is the only one in the series to mention a named black character, but also because its speaker's language is plain and its delivery apparently neutral, whether she is talking about her office job as "alright" (1974, 141), or pondering the plight of black miners shot by police during an underground dispute: "I read that they were angry because they did not get raises when other men did" (140). While this expression of liberal sympathy may not be unusual in this period, its juxtaposition with more intimate observations about the janitor working in the speaker's low-rent Hillbrow building is more disturbing. While she acknowledges that the janitor Phineas "earns a very small salary" (140), which might explain his habit of selling the building's coal "so that there is often not enough for the boiler" (139), she describes a man whose behavior flouts community as well as apartheid norms: "He rules the building" (139). He not only steals and resells tenants' clothes and liquor, including the speaker's gin, but also uses her flat for trysts: "Once I came home early and met him leaving the flat with a woman" (141). Unlike characters in the Market's later and more emphatically anti-apartheid testimonial plays, like *Born in the RSA* (1985; see Simon et al. 1997), this man is not a hero or a victim of the struggle against apartheid. Nor can he be seen as an avatar of a post-racial community. While the band of bohemians in the Market's whimsical *Cincinatti* (1977) maintained a multicultural face (despite misspelling the American city in its aspiration to American cool) and later found its way into a textbook (Simon et al. 1984), Phineas's behavior and the sinister impression he makes on the speaker—"I am grateful that he does not choose to take too much" (Simon 1974, 141)—may have strayed too far from anti-apartheid moral outrage to allow staging in the 1970s. His amorality rather anticipates the outlaw entrepreneurs trolling Hillbrow in the lawless 1990s.

While Simon was at home in Johannesburg even if his characters appear uneasy, apartheid law made Serote into a foreigner in his native city. His

15. Simon's "monologue for Danny" appeared for the first time in *Jo'burg, Sis!* (1974) after Serote's poem, which was published in his *Yakhal'inkomo* in 1972. Even if this is not a direct response, Simon would have been familiar with *Yakhal'inkomo,* since the volume was published by his friend Lionel Abrahams.

poem, "City Johannesburg," begins by starkly addressing this fact, as it opens with a "salute" to the city and a reflex action that suggests an automatic response to apartheid power born of fear and lots of practice: "This way I salute you/ My hand pulses to my back trousers pocket/ Or into my inner jacket pocket/ For my pass" (1982, 22). The personification of the city as femme fatale may not be new, but Serote makes it speak to the peculiar conditions of apartheid, enjoining his reader not only to see a city whose "neon flowers flaunt their way through the falling darkness" but to realize that this beguiling twilight is the hour of the law, when all blacks must leave Johannesburg and return to the townships. The unnamed township here is homely but also fatal, "my love/ My dongas [potholes], my dust, my people, my death," whose danger is stressed by the next line: "Where death lurks in the dark like a blade in the flesh." Despite apartheid attempts to cordon off township violence, the city is just as lethal, as the poem concludes—"Jo'burg City, you are dry like death" (23). Signs of nature are instruments as deadly as the arms borne by the aforementioned hippy, whose portrait precedes "City Johannesburg" in *Yakhal'inkomo* and in Serote's *Selected Poems*.

The poem that follows "City Johannesburg" in the *Selected Poems* is "Alexandra," which apostrophizes the poet's childhood home, the last freehold district for black homeowners in the Johannesburg area after the destruction of Sophiatown. In keeping with an old-fashioned homage to childhood or perhaps with a new appeal to pan-African images, the poem appears first to soften the brutality of black urban life with an opening portrait of Alexandra as a "most loving mother" (1982, 24). However, the poet's Alexandra is not a nurturing Mama Africa: "You frighten me, Mama/ When I lie on your breast to rest, something tells me/ You are bloody cruel" (24). South African readers may see in this image of a mother whose "breasts ooze the dirty water of your dongas" not only an indictment of the apartheid order that made Alexandra a slum, but also a riposte to white expatriate poet Roy Campbell whose "Zulu Girl" paints a picture of a black mother as a part of the rural landscape, nourishing her baby like a "broad river" (2002 [1930], 83).[16] Even when Serote does

16. Campbell's poem, which was standard fare in South African schools, both black and white, suggests that the boy imbibes a history lesson along with mother's milk: "The curbed ferocity of beaten tribes/ The sullen dignity of their defeat" (2002 [1930], 83). Nonetheless, the poet's reduction of the unnamed "girl" to a timeless feature of the landscape like a "hill" looming above the child diminishes the woman's agency, while his sentimental treatment of rural life betrays an ideological bent that hardened with his support for the Franco regime of Spain, where he chose to settle.

not directly address the city, as in "For Don M—Banned" (1973), dedicated to writer Don Mattera at the time under house arrest, his representation of the bleak and volatile historical moment takes its cue from Johannesburg: "the trees [. . .]/dry as steel" recall city skyscrapers, and the "dry white season" (1982, 52) alludes to the typical highveld winter, where frost bleaches grass white and electrical storms set it on fire.

Like Serote, Sipho Sepamla was born early enough—in Krugersdorp, on the West Rand beyond Florida on Cabral's map—to remember a childhood before the violent uprooting of black urban communities and to have gained access to Sophiatown culture. Sepamla first made this contact through theatre work with Union Artists, who had produced *King Kong* in 1959, but later turned his attention to writers, in particular to Can Themba (Sepamla et al. 1988, 303). Unlike Serote, whose poems forge sharp images from anger against apartheid, Sepamla's admiration for Themba comes through in his penchant for irony, sometimes in the service of satire but sometimes ambiguous, as in his poetic homage "Come Duze Baby" (1972). This poem borrows the *flaaitaal* and basic scenario (wannabe township "clever" or wise guy tries to pick up streetwise girl) from Themba's "Baby, Come Duze [near]," which appeared in *Drum* in 1955.[17] The homage is clear but the differences mark the distance between Sophiatown and Soweto: Themba's playlet was accompanied by photos by Gopal Narasamy; text and pictures reflected the racy dialogue and gangster glamour that delighted *Drum* readers, but gently mocked the tsotsi stereotype by having Ellen, the "baby" in question, initially reject Prettyboy's advances (Themba 1989 [1955], 110). Sepamla's poem has only a masculine voice and one that threatens his would-be date with violence: "Hela Sisi!/ Look sharp/ Otherwise [. . .]/ Jy val soos 'n sak kool [you'll fall like a sack of cabbage]" (1984a, 39), or attempts to blackmail her with rumors of a white lover "Hulle vang jou/ Sluit jou toe/ For Immorality [They'll catch you/ Lock you up/ For Immorality]," even as he tries to seduce her with sweet words "Jy's my number one" (40). Like Themba, Sepamla is undoubtedly playing with a

17. Mzamane claims that "Come Duze Baby" is the "first symptom of a new and vibrant South African English" (1984, 11); Ngwenya echoes this claim when he cites this poem as evidence that "Sepamla stands out in his experimentation with English" without mentioning Themba (Ngwenya 2012, 518). Only Vernon February, who was in exile, notes Sepamla's general debt to Themba (February 2007 [1982], 83), but does not mention this particular connection. While Mzamane's omission can be blamed on the fact that Themba's work was still banned in 1984, Ngwenya's cannot, since the ban was lifted soon afterwards and Michael Chapman's edition of *The Drum Decade* (1989) in which Themba's playlet was reprinted is still a widely used textbook. Ngwenya's oversight is thus testimony to the persistently uneven condition of literary transmission in South Africa.

persona rather than expressing himself directly, but the harsher swagger reflects the greater violence in private as well as public life that emerged with the hardening of apartheid. Unlike Themba, who died in exile, and Serote, who spent the apartheid years working for the ANC abroad, Sepamla endured the "dry white season" at home by turning to satire. The poem that gives the anthology *To Whom It May Concern* (Royston 1973) its title uses the brutally impassive language of apartheid bureaucracy, stripping its subject, an unnamed "Bantu," of everything but his ID number. While the man represented by ID no. 417181 may wish to settle in a particular place, "[h]e lives/ Subject to the provisions/ Of the Urban Areas Act of 1925/ Amended often" and may therefore only "acquire a niche in the said area/ As a temporary sojourner" (Sepamla 1984a, 19). Despite the official reduction of his persona to a number that would identify "remains" that might be granted a "plot/ Set aside for Methodist Xhosas," and the poem's allusion to the government's plan to turn South Africans of Xhosa extraction into citizens of "homelands" Transkei or Ciskei regardless of their place of birth, the poet managed to spend the decade and beyond living and working in Soweto and Johannesburg.

Sepamla's poems also mine African American poetry and song alongside local song forms to capture urban time and space in Johannesburg. "Work Song," which appeared first in his *The Blues Is You in Me* (1976) and then in his *Selected Poems*, combines complaint and protest:

> In Commissioner Street
> On the Main Reef Road
> In Prince's Avenue
> Down there where people are
> I've heard the anguish of a chant
> Heard rising in the air
> Like orchestrated screams of a big band
> The harmony of the labourer's voice
> Singing:
> abelungu [whites] goddamn
> abelungu goddamn
> basibiza bojim [they call us all Jim]
> basibiza bojim. [. . .]
>
> (Sepamla 1984a, 62)

The chant *basibiza bojim* is at once a plausible complaint that might be uttered by a work crew exasperated with white disrespect, and a riposte to all those

"Jim comes to Joburg" stories that paint blacks as naive newcomers to the city. Although Sepamla does not cite Todd Matshikiza's work song "Hambani Madoda" (see Chapter 2), his avowed familiarity with *King Kong* (Sepamla et al. 1988, 303) suggests that this song is present even as his poem repudiates lament in favor of defiance. This defiance in turn quotes the civil rights protest song "Mississippi Goddamn" by the African-American singer-songwriter Nina Simone, even as it locates the singers on Johannesburg streets. Despite the brief allusion to "anguish" to the traditional lament (*isikhalo*), invoked for instance in Serote's title *Yakhal'inkomo*, the rhythm and language of the work song suggest an incipient rising of an "army of tattered arms" (Sepamla 1984a, 62) "stirred into consciousness" (63) by the lazy insults of white bosses. Even if the workers do not make an outright threat, their song demands the right to their own names, just as the poet lays claim to Commissioner Street, the inner city's longest thoroughfare, and its suburban extension, the Main Reef Road, which links Krugersdorp in the west, the poet's birthplace, with Benoni, the East Rand town where he edited the revived *Classic*.

Although focused on Soweto, Sepamla's collection, *The Soweto I Love* (1977), includes a poem about Johannesburg that targets whites more directly than does "abelungu goddam." "All That Gold" indicts the "rush for gold" for which "so much blood has spilled" (1977, 28) but focuses the poet's ire on the Carlton Centre (in the block bound by Commissioner, Von Wielligh, Main, and Kruis Streets), a landmark of the apartheid building boom and the product of an international architectural team including Chicago's Skidmore, Owings and Merrill and locals Rhodes and Harrison (see fig. 3.2). Although there is no mention in the poem, the controversy around the Carlton Hotel restaurant—which admitted so-called international Africans, including officials from Transkei, but denied entry to local blacks—may have provoked the response, whose intensity exceeds any obvious prompt: "no wonder I hate the Carlton Centre/ with its winding stairs dipping into a pit/ a dome peeping stealthily into the sky" (28). This image not only captures the building's height as the tallest office building in Africa but also hints at its affinity, in bands of concrete alternating with windows, with the citadel of "peeping," the police headquarters building several blocks to the west, where Commissioner meets the M1. The pit at the bottom and the dome at the top of the Carlton may remind local readers of the site of an ice rink that was not only a novelty in 1975 Johannesburg, but also the stage for apartheid absurdity. Before the rink was moved to the top floor from its initial location in the shopping concourse, blacks who could work but were not allowed to play in the building habitually crowded the rails surrounding the rink to watch "European" South

Africans mostly failing to skate. Yet where a Sophiatown writer like Lewis Nkosi, who called apartheid "a daily exercise in the absurd" (1965, 35), might have played up the ridiculous element in this scene, the Soweto poet responds with "hate" (Sepamla 1977, 28), or at least with disdain.

In contrast to the detailed locations and concrete images of the city poems, the title poem in *The Soweto I Love* remains abstract, perhaps because the death of hundreds, mostly children, at the hands of the police defied image-making.[18] Drawing on the mode of Xhosa praise songs (*iibongo*), Sepamla salutes Soweto's sons "whose strength of character/ has been a source of pride" (1977, 22) and whose struggle to "shake off the restraints" of the "yoke of laws" produced a "great roar went up abroad" (23); however, the contrast between muscular sons and mothers "made widows" (22) uses patriarchal symbolism that seem recycled from SASM pamphlets rather than forged anew. The second poem in *The Soweto I Love*, "The Child Dies," is much more powerful. It distills the violence of the times with concentrated force—so concentrated, apparently, that it was deemed too strong to be reprinted in Sepamla's *Selected Poems*. While it may echo Ingrid Jonker's "The Child (Who Was Shot Dead by Soldiers in Nyanga)" (Jonker 2002 [1965], 167–68), made famous by Mandela's citation at his inauguration in 1994, Sepamla's poem paints a complex picture of the aftermath, when students and others set fire to government buildings but armed police initiated and perpetuated the violence:

> He was a mere kid
> consumed by curiosity
> [. . .]
> the fire raged before his eyes
> it was angry
> [. . .]
> then came an alarm
> because a monster was known to stalk the streets
> unthinking
> the child fled
> he just ran and ran

18. According to investigative journalist John Kane-Berman, police, hospital, and court records indicated that close to 50 percent of the dead on record were seventeen to twenty-three years old, while over 40 percent of the remainder were thirteen to sixteen years of age (1978, 7).

away from the fire
but his mind was engrossed by the fascination
his eyes fixed on the burning scene
unthinking
the child ran and ran
until he fell smack
into the hands of a towering giant
[...]
he was hurled to the ground
like grain
he was pounded and pounded
with a gun-butt

we buried the mess
another day

may his soul rest in peace (Sepamla 1977, 2)

Although Sepamla does not identify the arsonists, who could be students targeting beer halls or tsotsis looting stores, the child's view underscores the fascination of fire common to children everywhere, until the child, the poem, and the reader run "smack" into the unnamed but recognizable "monster," the armed policeman. Most of the more than three hundred who died in Soweto in June alone were shot by police (SAIRR 1977, 85; Kane-Berman 1978, 26–36)—most famously, thirteen-year-old Hector Peterson, who was accompanying his older sister Antoinette in Moele Street as the June 16 march went its way to Orlando High School when he was killed (and memorialized by photographer Sam Nzima)—but eyewitnesses also corroborated reports of deaths by beating (Kane-Berman 1978, 31).[19] By ending with the beating, the poem's conclusion captures the violent excess of the police response to the uprising in general, as well as to particular encounters with evident innocents as well as avowed militants. This "manifest display of violence and brutality" certainly exemplifies what Sepamla's contemporary Njabulo Ndebele would later call the "spectacular" character of anti-apartheid writing

19. Although Peterson was initially identified as such (Kane-Berman 1978, 1), the first student to be shot dead was Hastings Ndlovu (Cabral and Somayya A.E. 2010, 104). Antoinette (now Sibanda) is on the board for the Hector Peterson Museum (2002). The third person in Nzima's photograph, eighteen-year-old Mbuyisa Makhubo, who was carrying Hector's body, apparently disappeared in exile. For a photograph of the memorial in Maseko Street, Orlando West, see Bremner and Subirós (2007, 80–83).

(1991, 37–57), but, as Ndebele himself acknowledges, in the context of his appeal for a "rediscovery of the ordinary" (37), an image like this one of the dead and dehumanized child would be a fitting response to the "mindbogglingly spectacular"—even "exhibitionist"—excess of state violence (38). The poem registers the exhaustion as well as the grief of those left to bury "the mess/ another day" (Sepamla 1977, 2). The concluding lines, moving from the gruesome image to the burial and the prayer, evoke both the terrible reality of routinized violence and the extraordinary resilience of its survivors.

Acts Recollected in Anger, Analyzed in Sorrow: Re-membering Soweto

Immediate responses to the Soweto uprising balance, like Sepamla's dead child, on the razor edge between spectacle and testimony; those that remain compelling today achieve an even more difficult equipoise between anger and analysis. The poems thus far certainly depart from the Romantic axiom of emotion recollected in tranquility; their anger is directly expressed on the page without any apparent mediation. The poetry of the student generation, however, took cues from public performance, in part from militant theatre and in part from the hymns and praises accompanying funerals, including political funerals. The "theatre of determination" lauded by *Black Review* editor Benny Khoapa (1972, 201) favored plays that eschewed dramatic suspense in favor of declared defiance, whether calling for armed revolt, as in *Shanti* (1973) by SASO leader Mthuli ka Shezi, or, as in *Give Us This Day* (1975) by Mzwandile Maqina, a militant tribute to Abraham Onkgopotse Tiro, the former SRC president of the University of the North killed by a parcel bomb in exile. Even when banned after very short runs in university or township venues, these pieces received vocal support from audiences, whose enthusiasm provoked the security police to cite *Shanti* and other plays in their indictments of the players for terrorism (see Kruger 1999, 144–47).

Nonetheless, the most durable of these plays not only expressed defiance, but also differentiated and thus provided more dramatic testimony in several voices. *Survival*, by Workshop '71 members Fana Kekana, Selaelo Dan Maredi, Themba Ntinga, and Seth Sibanda, with leftist director and Wits academic Robert McLaren (a.k.a Robert Mshengu Kavanagh), opened at the Space in May 1976 and played at Wits and in Soweto before and briefly after the uprising in June. It was received by audiences and the police as part of the uprising, with the latter claiming that the play had the power to incite revolt.[20] But unlike *Shanti*, which projected the players' desire for armed revolt but not much of their actual experience, *Survival* was created in workshops out of the life narratives of black male workers and drew its method in part from the famous testimonial theatre pieces *Sizwe Bansi Is Dead* (1972) and *The Island* (1973), both by John Kani, Winston Ntshona, and Athol Fugard. But where *Sizwe Bansi* favored conversation leavened with comedy, *Survival* used terse dialogue to provide a functional frame for narratives delivered directly to the audience; where *The Island* focused on two individuals rather than the group of prisoners envisaged in the first draft of the play, *Survival* used four actors to represent both individual lives and the broader conditions of apartheid, the effects of which on the lives of black people could be fully understood only on a larger social scale. However brief its run before it was shut down and its performers dispersed into exile, the performance of this play participated in a "revolutionary situation" partly by opening the eyes and ears of white spectators, but also by assembling township audiences as participants in defiance of the laws against "riotous assembly" and "seditious speech" (Kavanagh 1981, 127).

Rather than a single plotline, *Survival* is structured around a place—prison—which is also an occasion for four prisoners to reenact their politicization in response to everyday life under apartheid. Although the prison could not be named, several references, including to *Drum* (Workshop '71 1981, 135) and "deep Soweto" (149), place the action in the Johannesburg area and thus suggest either the Old Fort in the city or Diepkloof Prison in Soweto. Each actor delivered a report in his own name, in which he reenacted, with other actors playing roles from family members to court interpreters, the events that led to the arrest of his character. This matter-of-fact presentation, coupled with fluid movement from one role to another, highlighted the collective impact of the action. Themba Ntinga, who played Leroi Williams, introduced a character who chooses an American name to reflect his interest in pan-African liberation; he alternates with other characters, allowing the actors to draw from the individual stories the shared analysis of oppression and resistance. As Williams comments, "Suddenly, at obstinate moments,

20. *Survival* is the most powerful piece of testimonial theatre from the period immediately before and after the uprising, but it is not the only one. For context, see Orkin (1991). My discussion here summarizes more detailed discussion of this play and comparable work in *Post-Imperial Brecht* (2004a), but the play's pioneering transformation of the testimonial form into a cultural weapon that remains theatrically vivid merits inclusion here.

these circumstances come together and trap a human being so tightly that for one moment the parts become a whole" (160). Drawing on particular circumstances—Edward Nkosi kills one of his mother's clients in a revolt against the conditions that pushed her into prostitution; Vusi Mabandla kills a black policeman trying to prevent him from driving his father to the hospital without a license; Slaksa Mphahlele is jailed for striking and Williams for political agitation—the plot gains analytic clarity as well as militant power in generalization. As the prisoners go on hunger strike, they shout:

> Phela, phela, phela [a]malanga
> Azophela, azophela [a]malanga
> [Enough, enough, enough of these days
> There will be an end to these days]
>
> (Workshop '71 1981, 167)

Despite the (mimed) beating of the prisoners that follows, the actors survive to "go forward" (168).

The action may have seemed "strong and ugly" to some white reviewers, but the final note of anticipation of liberation struck home with whites (including this writer) as well as blacks in the audience at the Nunnery, a former convert turned theatre near Wits University.[21] At township venues like the Dube YMCA, the players faced police in the audience but incorporated them into the show by opening with a comic impersonation of a policeman looking for "agitators" and by encouraging audience participation, especially in the finale, "We go forward." Rather than displaying politics merely as a theme, the players thus turned police threats into politically enabling performance—at least until the state shut them down. However brief its run, *Survival* participated in the enactment of an alternative public sphere generated not only by the student rebellion, but also by church organizations and industrial unions. The mode of performance pioneered by *Survival*, the anti-apartheid testimonial play, presented narratives of mostly black and male individuals urgently and directly to the audience, in English, punctuated by song, usually in the vernacular. This would be the definitive format after the uprising and in the shadow of the "emergency" in the 1980s for plays by black men like *Egoli* by Matsemela Manaka (YMCA Soweto 1978; Space and Market 1979) and *The*

---

21. Kavanagh (1981, 126). Roy Christie's positive comment on the "note of anticipation," in the *Johannesburg Star* (August 12, 1976) contradicts Kavanagh's generalization about a uniformly hostile white response.

Hungry Earth by Maishe Maponya (DOCC Soweto; Market 1979), as well as those done by men and women at the Market from *Cincinatti* (1977) to *Born at the RSA* (1985), and in Junction Avenue Theatre Company's plays from *The Fantastical History of a Useless Man* (1976), written and performed by white leftist students and graduates from Wits, to their collaborations on Johannesburg history, especially *Randlords and Rotgut* (1978) and *Sophiatown* (1986), with the Wits History Workshop and with black performers like Ramolao Makhene, who came to JATC when Workshop '71 disbanded.[22]

Although less immediately subject to surveillance than theatre, poetry after Soweto—especially but not only by black students and former students—was increasingly performed in public, from writing groups to larger audiences, such as those at funerals. This public delivery favored the terse expression of urgency as in the poetry published in *Staffrider*, which supplemented the work of seasoned poets with new writers from workshops at cultural organizations like MDALI in Orlando and the Creative Youth Association (CYA) in Diepkloof, where poets were encouraged to test their work on one other before submission (Van Wyk 1989: 165). In the first issue of March 1978, two poems by Oupa Thando Mtimkulu, who was detained as a student from 1976 to 1977, combine testimony with critique. "Baragwanath Hospital" addresses Soweto's hospital, the biggest in sub-Saharan Africa, asking "How many souls did you swallow/ Who were intentionally killed/ Who genuinely and sincerely died/ How many arrived satisfactorily dead/ Come Bara [. . .]/ . . . what do you have to say?" (Mtimkulu 1978, 21). Even though the poem has only one voice, the series of questions echoes unresolved debates about those who died in 1976, while recalling, in the personification of the hospital, Serote's portrait of Alexandra as fatal mother. In the second and final stanza the poet deploys police jargon to highlight the routinization of injustice suffered by the dead and the living: "Did they all have inquests/ Did they all claim indemnities?" This line shifts ambiguously from victims requiring inquests to perpetrators claiming indemnity. Meanwhile, the conclusion broadens the indictment: "Are you hospitable to testify to us all?"

22. We shall return to JATC at the end of this chapter. Those who regret the absence of the musical *Sarafina* in this discussion should note that despite its appearance on Broadway in 1986 and the film version starring African American Whoopi Goldberg as a teacher at Morris Isaacson High School, the play by Mbongeni Ngema does not engage seriously with the legacy of Soweto, but rather serves chiefly as a platform for dancing legs. In 1996 Ngema produced *Sarafina II*, which was supposed to educate audiences about AIDS but was instead a misogynist melodrama that misled audiences about sexually transmitted disease and cost too much to tour, thus wasting government money at the height of the AIDS crisis.

which suggests that all South Africans must confront the uprising and its consequences. The companion poem, "Nineteen Seventy-Six," has been anthologized twice, unlike "Baragwanath" (in Chapman and Dangor 1982, 176 and in Olifant and Vladislavić 1988, 173). It combines lament not only with indictment but also with retrospective critique: "Go nineteen-seventy-six/ We need you no more/ [. . .]/ Good friends we have/ Lost/ Nineteen-seventy-six/ You stand accused/ Of deaths/ Imprisonments/ Exiles/ And detentions./ [. . .]/ You were not revolutionary/ Enough/ We do not boast about you/ Year of fire, year of ash" (1978, 21). Inspiring the title and the thesis of Baruch Hirson's study of the "Soweto revolt" (Hirson 1979, 2), this poem puts the uprising in historical perspective while looking forward to a year yet to come that would be revolutionary enough to topple apartheid. This aspiration is restrained by reality: the year of fire inspired action but left ash in its wake. Although they make no reference to *Survival*, both poems recall the envisaged end to struggle while reminding audiences of the long road ahead.[23]

While Mtimkulu shows that even a short poem can offer political analysis as well as recollection of emotion, it was writers of prose fiction that took on the task of depicting the uprising's impact on the urban fabric of Johannesburg-Soweto, creating narratives that might enable local readers to re-member fractured experiences of the period and outsiders to comprehend the complexity of the story and of the struggle yet to come. André Brink's *'n Droë Wit Seisoen* (*A Dry White Season*) appeared in 1979, followed by novels by black writers. Miriam Tlali's *Amandla* (1980) and Sipho Sepamla's *A Ride on the Whirlwind* (1981) stand out because they portray conflicts among several characters, rather than depicting events from the perspective of a central character or a single political line. In this respect, they differ from the dominant mode of anti-apartheid fiction: the autobiographically inflected political *Bildungsroman,* exemplified by novels like Es'kia Mphahlele's *The Wanderers* (1971) as well as Serote's *To Every Birth Its Blood* (1981). The latter tracks Alexandra musician Tsi Molope as he moves from wayward rebelliousness

---

23. The analytic economy of "Nineteen-Seventy-Six" resembles Brecht's critique in his *Buckow Elegies* of the still-born revolution in East Germany and shares with a poem like Brecht's "Changing the Wheel" an analytic clarity that contrasts with the emphatic but incoherent declamations on "blackness" in some post-Soweto poetry, such as Gwala's "What is Black?/ [. . .]/ Black is point of TO BE OR NOT TO BE for blacks" (quoted in Watson 1990 [1986], 85–86), which Stephen Watson rightly lambasts for "intellectual poverty" (86). Mtimkulu's output was more modest than Brecht's, but the comparison highlights the potential of poetry as argument; the energy of Mtimkulu's poems, like Brecht's, emerges in the quest to forge language with which to examine the incomplete legacy of 1976, rather than the "formal" or "linguistic" originality that Watson's more belletristic taste demands (85).

to the disciplined focus of the revolutionary operative with a briskness that serves the telos of politicization rather than the motivation of character or the complexities of social conflict.[24] This singular telos leaves the few characters directly associated with the uprising, such as the student activist Oupa, undeveloped—or dead—and thus misses an opportunity to represent the historical role of students from Alexandra in Soweto politics, many of whom commuted to Soweto schools because there were not enough schools in Alexandra (Bonner and Nieftagodien 2008, 201–28). Despite this foreshortened narrative and scant attention to the uprising, Serote's novel received highest praise in Kelwyn Sole's article on the Soweto novels. In contrast, Sole calls Sepamla's *Whirlwind* a "conventional adventure novel" (1988, 66) that "downplays historical and sociological concerns" (67), while praising Tlali's *Amandla* for "plac[ing] historical events and [. . .] debates in Soweto" within a "web of familial experiences" (67). Above all, he favors Serote's *Birth* for moving beyond the "anomie and defeat of Tsi's monologues" (68) to his political baptism in the "sea" of the "Movement" (Serote 1981, 200). Writing in the era of the UDF alliance with socialists at home and the ANC abroad in the 1980s, Sole was undoubtedly keen to endorse Serote's vision of the "birth of a new post-revolutionary South Africa" (Sole 1988, 68). Nonetheless, his solidarity leads him to overlook on the one hand the narrative gaps in Serote's novel that leave Tsi's conversion unpersuasive, and on the other Sepamla's courageous if perhaps disconcerting depiction of the messy lives and mixed motivations of activists, stooges, and Sowetans of all ages caught up in the uprising.

Both Sepamla and Tlali deserve more attention but, before comparing their depictions of Soweto through the eyes of different characters, and their ability to shape the data of Soweto into a "narrative line" that takes the "reader's involvement beyond the act of recognition" as Ndebele wrote in the first serious critique of these novels (1991, 24), we should look at Brink's *A Dry White Season*. This novel is noteworthy not only because it was the

---

24. This conversion formula, which mandated the transformation of an immature rebel into a fighting force or good party man, dates from the First Soviet Congress of Writers in 1935, which set the tenets of socialist realism or, as Maxim Gorky called it, revolutionary romanticism, but continued to shape the literature of Soviet-sponsored liberation movements half a century later. The best examples such as Mikhail Sholokhov's *Virgin Soil Upturned* (Soviet Union, 1934), Ernst Neutsch's *Trace of Stones* (East Germany, 1964) or Pepetela's *Mayombe* (Angola, 1984) transcend the formula while reaffirming the ideals of socialist solidarity. For the ANC's ties to the Soviet Union and its allies, see Ellis and Sechaba (1992), and for the cultural dimensions of this solidarity, see Kruger (2004a, 8–12).

only Afrikaans novel on the subject (and Brink's only novel published in Johannesburg), but also because its compelling deployment of the political *Bildungsroman* (novel of personal growth and formation) provides a useful point of comparison with Sepamla's and Tlali's later attempts to transform the genre by broadening their scope from a singular hero to distinct members of the community.[25] As Brink acknowledges, *A Dry White Season* borrows its title from Serote's poem. The novel depicts not only the bleakness of the season, but also the story of one man's refusal to see injustice merely as a passing winter, and his decision to act against both culpable individuals and the state they represent. Using the device of the manuscript confided by the hero to an unworthy scribe, Brink has his narrator describe himself at the start as an "old hack" incapable of learning "new tricks" (Brink 1984a, 9), while his subject, Ben du Toit—husband, father, and teacher at a segregated Afrikaans school—is described as, in the original, a "doodgewone, onskadelike, onmerkwaardige mens" (1979, 1) and in the author's English, as "an ordinary, *good-natured*, harmless, unremarkable man" (1984a, 7; my emphasis to highlight the additional word in the English text).[26] But by the end, the narrator has been shaken out of his complacency by this ordinary man moved by extreme conditions to extraordinary commitment. Ben's attempts to clarify two deaths in police custody—first of Jonathan Ngubeni, a Soweto student detained after the uprising, and next of the boy's father Gordon, whom Ben knew as an upstanding former janitor at his school and whom he offered to help—lead to his estrangement from his wife and daughters, one of whom becomes a police informant, and to a friendship with Soweto "clever" and putative undercover activist Stanley Makhaya, a love affair with investigative journalist Melanie Bruwer, and ultimately to his own death, apparently by a hit and run motorist, after BOSS threats fail to deter his efforts on behalf of

25. Brink's previous novel, *Rumours of Rain* (1978), is set partly in Johannesburg and includes a trip to Soweto but, in keeping with his protagonist's dismissal of political commitment, Brink reduces the uprising to a very brief radio report near the end of the novel.

26. Since Brink wrote both English and Afrikaans versions of *A Dry White Season*, I will cite the English alone where possible but will return to the Afrikaans when the difference between them merits closer attention. When both versions are cited in the text, Afrikaans page numbers precede the English separated by a slash. As Brink himself notes in "English and the Afrikaans Writer" (1976), his English "must bear the weight" of his Afrikaans (1983, 115); but there are places, such as this first sentence, where his English flattens key notes in the Afrikaans. The latter does not include an equivalent of "good natured," the only cheerful attribute, and without it, paints a greyer portrait of Ben as an "*utterly* ordinary *person*" who is not only harmless but apparently "*unworthy of note*," all the more to highlight in retrospect the remarkable last year in the life of this ordinary man.

Gordon's widow Emily to "clean" her husband's name (1984a, 173). In the process, Ben comes to understand not only the impunity of the apartheid state, but also his complicity as an Afrikaner among Afrikaners, whose silence has allowed state operatives to continue killing people in the name of protecting the *volk* from communism and other alleged threats. The narrator in turn comes to see himself as a witness whose testimony challenges those who retrospectively try to justify inaction by ignorance: "Perhaps all one can really hope for, all I am entitled to is no more than this: to write it down. To report what I know. So that it will not be possible for any man ever to say again: *I knew nothing about it*" (1984a, 316).

Where the English edition closes on that final italicized "it," the last words in the Afrikaans edition leave the object of knowledge open: "Ek het nie geweet nie [I did not know]" (1979, 261). The novel thus ends with the unbounded imperative to know and to act, an emphasis Brink clearly prefers, quoting it in a lecture on the "intellectual and his world" (Brink 1983, 201). This existentialist strain is deliberate: Ben resembles Sisyphus (in *The Myth of Sisyphus* [1942] by Albert Camus) in that he chooses to act against hostile police and their professional allies (doctors and lawyers who perjure themselves in defense of the state) despite the obstacles in his way. Brink also invokes "man in revolt" (*homme révolté*) from Camus as an inspiration for writing against the silence imposed by the "state of siege" in the 1970s (Brink 1983, 5). Critics such as Richard Peck and Isidore Diala have identified existentialist traits in Brink's characters. However, they focus on other novels, like the earlier *Rumours of Rain* (1978), where the nouveau-riche protagonist Martin Mynhardt acts out a textbook case of bad faith when he exploits and betrays intimates including his activist friend Bernard Franken (modeled on the Afrikaner lawyer, communist, and martyr Bram Fischer) for his own gain (Diala 2006, 96–100), or the later *Wall of the Plague* (1984), in which Mandla (whose name means strength or power) exemplifies the *homme révolté* by insisting, against the passivity of white liberals, that everyone in South Africa can choose to act or not (Peck 1992, 73–82). While portraying a character committed to an authentic fight for justice, Brink grounds this imperative in the peculiar South African version of the police state, which not only allowed officials to get away with murder but also twisted the law to treat critics as outlaws unworthy of a fair hearing. Commenting briefly on *A Dry White Season*, Peck reads Ben's transformation "from lack of involvement to whole-hearted commitment" as an embrace of a "more authentic life" (1992, 74) but his analysis, limited by evident ignorance of Afrikaans, does not distinguish fully among different Afrikaner responses to apartheid, preferring to generalize "the powerful and uniform societal pressures of Afrikanerdom" (69). In between the poles of avowed support for the regime on the one hand and radical revolt by rare individuals like Fischer or Naudé, who were prepared to endure prison or worse for breaking ranks with the *volk,* on the other, Brink earned the title of dissident Afrikaner when his first emphatically anti-apartheid novel *Kennis van die Aand* (1973; translated and published as *Looking on Darkness* in 1974) became the first Afrikaans book to be banned.[27] His example and that of other dissident writers suggests that social pressures on Afrikaners were not uniform: they differed by gender, allowing men more freedom than women (as the suicide of Brink's contemporary Ingrid Jonker suggests); by class, in that well-educated Afrikaners were better able, if not always willing, to loosen the ties of family and *volk*; and by region, in that Cape Afrikaners (especially those with access to parallel-medium English/Afrikaans schools, which were a feature of the Cape Province until abolished in the 1970s in favor of Afrikaans-only schools) tended to be more enlightened (*verlig*) than the narrow-minded (*verkramp*) poor white, petit bourgeois, and nouveau riche in the interior (see O'Meara 1996, 135–67).

A just reading of *A Dry White Season* therefore requires attention not only to Brink's international inspirations, but also to the realism of a narrative that tracks the particular pressures on Afrikaners and others in Johannesburg during and after the Soweto uprising. Realist representation in this context involves not only exposing the government's lies, but also showing how responses to the "state of siege" emerge out of the daily lives of ordinary people. There are moments when the narrative deploys the jargon of state evidence given by police or police doctors exonerating torture as necessary interrogation techniques, or uses the language of anti-apartheid documents, such as the report on Gordon Ngubeni's torture and death, which borrows directly from actual reports on torture and even attributes the fictional report to the SAIRR (Brink 1984a, 104).

At other moments, the narrative gives concrete form to state power, as in this view of John Vorster Square: "At the wrong [*verkeerde*] end of Commissioner Street [. . .] where the city grows [. . .] down at heel with barely legible ads for Tiger Balm and Chinese preparations, [. . .] the building appears oddly out of place [*skoon ontuis*], tall and severely rectilinear, concrete

27. While the ban on *Looking on Darkness* was lifted only in 1982, nine years after publication, *A Dry White Season* was suppressed for only a few months (Brink 1983, 241). The censorship was undercut by circulation to Taurus subscribers, whose initial contributions had launched this small and short-lived Johannesburg press when *Darkness* was banned in 1974 (Brink 1983, 254).

and glass, blue, massive, yet hollow and transparent enough to offer an unreal view of the cars traveling on the high fly-over of the M1" (Brink 1979, 42; 1984a, 57; emphasis added; the freeway line runs north-south just east of Fordsburg on Cabral's map). This oddly transparent police bastion, whose design (by commercial firm Harris, Fels, Jankers and Nussbaum) drew from office rather than prison models, is more uncanny (like *unheimlich*, usually translated as uncanny, *ontuis* carries the sense of alienation from the homely and the familiar) than the more obvious police-thriller touches like the elevators "without buttons or controls [that] shoot upward to a predetermined floor the moment you enter" (1984a, 57). The building's unreal transparency reflects Ben's optimistic belief in plain dealing, which prompts his first visit to the security police and his expectation that he can talk to them man to man to explain their error in detaining the upstanding Gordon. This encounter is also the point of departure for Ben's gradual loss of footing in a world in which he can be persecuted by his fellow Afrikaners; his disorientation begins in this scene with his "neck itching" as the sinister Captain Stolz plays with an orange behind his back (60), and grows apace as BOSS agents search his house, tap his phone, take intimate photographs of him with Melanie, and block her re-entry into the country.

Although these thriller elements may create suspense (especially for those readers who might find BOSS methods incredible), the novel is most compelling when it slows down to track the steps by which the "minor ripples of Ben's preoccupation with Gordon" (63) begin to affect members of his family and other associates. In a context in which the state can make communication between blacks and whites nearly impossible, Ben's political transformation is measured by his efforts to bridge the gulf that separates him from the black people he comes to know—efforts that pull him away from the family home (whose location remains notably secret even though its bourgeois interior is meticulously described) to the dwellings whose character and inhabitants shape his political formation. These include the house Melanie shares with her dissident professor father in Westdene, then a blue-collar white district located northwest of Auckland Park between two monuments to Afrikaner power: Triomf and the SABC, the workplace of Ben's actress wife Susan. The story also takes Ben to very different spaces in Soweto, in particular Emily's house and Stanley's haunts. The views of Soweto that Ben sees from Stanley's car seem initially colored by the fear that characterizes his polar opposite, the rich, venal, and hypocritical Martin Mynhardt in *Rumours of Rain*, after the latter has been subjected to a tour through Soweto shebeens by the only black professional in his employ, Charlie Mofokeng (Brink 1984b, 342–45), and stamped by Ben's own reiteration of the common white perception of Soweto as "countless rows of low, squat houses" (1984a, 167) almost invisible in the dark, since 80 percent of Soweto homes had no electricity until the 1980s. This view notes the shanty areas that Stanley calls *Sofasonke* ("we shall all die") *City* (79) after James "Sofasonke" Mpanza, who appropriated government property to rent to fellow blacks desperate for housing in the 1940s, but misses completely the enclaves of limited home ownership in districts like Dube, Jabavu, or Moroka in central Soweto.[28] As Goldblatt's 1972 photograph of a wedding photo opportunity in Jabavu suggests (fig. 3.4),

FIG. 3.4 Wedding photography at the Oppenheimer Memorial, Jabavu, Soweto. September 1972. Photograph copyright by David Goldblatt. Reprinted with permission.

28. Mpanza emerged in the 1940s when the postwar economic boom drew tens of thousands to Soweto but before national or local government began to address the housing backlog with developments like Meadowlands in the 1950s (Kane-Berman 1978, 57–59). In the 1970s, the overwhelming majority of Soweto residents paid rent to the WRAB, but a few had bought their houses in the government's short-lived plan to use limited property rights (ownership of houses but not of land, which remained government property) to develop an African elite with a stake in the status quo. The plan was scotched when hardliners pushed the government to favor the Bantustans rather than "temporary sojourners" in the townships (61), and then reinstated when the government tried to placate blacks after the uprising (191–97).

along with numerous pictures in Soweto homes, and as Jacob Dlamini's autobiographical essay *Native Nostalgia* (2009) confirms, those few Soweto families with professional qualifications and some disposable income used whatever means available to distinguish themselves from the generally drab environment of the township.

Despite his ignorance of these distinctions, Ben's humanity, his genuine concern for Emily, and his deepening if uneasy friendship with Stanley, who mockingly calls him "lanie" ("rich whitey") but sticks with his quest, are measured by his personal pledge to Emily in her Soweto home, his awkward attempt to welcome Stanley to his home (despite his family's racial panic), and his desire to share in Stanley's prophecy, however ironically expressed after Robert's murder and Emily's death from grief leave little room for hope, that "Daardie dag sal kom [that day will come], sure's tomorrow [. . .] ons sal nog saam uitloop [we will walk out together] in broad daylight, man" (240/288). Stanley's characteristically multilingual speech marks him as a township "clever," fluent in *flaaitaal* and English as well as Afrikaans and Xhosa, but it also suggests his willingness, in contrast to younger angrier blacks like Emily's son Robert, who will not speak Afrikaans on principle (and who, like his brother, is killed by anonymous apartheid forces), to find humanity in the language of the oppressor. However unlikely, this encounter of apparently incompatible languages and people in the apartheid city conjures an oasis, the waters of which might one day quench the inferno of the dry white season.

Miriam Tlali's *Amandla* (*Power,* 1980) is in many ways the opposite of *A Dry White Season.* Her novel portrays only black Sowetans, and, while she includes avowedly politicized male characters, from students to elders, whose actions and arguments express the militancy implied by the title, she grants more narrative space to women than do most male writers: the old matriarch Gramsy Moeng; her difficult daughter Seapei, who will do anything to get back a handsome policeman who has abandoned her for another woman; her married nieces, Nana, an upstanding community leader married to a teacher, and Agnes, who struggles with a drunken husband; as well as a few female students. In addition to this focus on women, *Amandla* is distinguished by its evocation of the particularities of place; the Moeng clan and associates live in Soweto's Moroka district, also known as Rockville, where a reservoir and a white-owned shopping mall (which took blacks' money but admitted only white and Indian traders) broke the monotony of the rows of houses. They speak both English and Sotho, which suggests ties with kin similar to Tlali's own across South Africa and independent Lesotho, without however diminishing the family's attachment to Soweto. Gramsy's struggle with high blood pressure, stroke, and other stress-related health problems, and with the bureaucratic and financial hurdles that delay her quest to erect a tombstone on her late husband's grave in inner-city Braamfontein Cemetery, draw into the immediate Soweto plot the long history of black migration into, and removal from, central Johannesburg. It also provides a counterpoint to her grandson Pholoso's odyssey through Soweto, from his traumatic witnessing of the death of his friend Dumisani by police bullet on June 16, to brief trysts with his girlfriend Felleng, to his detention in prison. Pholoso, also known as Moses, is a charismatic leader from Sekano Ntoane High School and thus possibly modeled on the actual leader from that school, Dan Montsitsi, who was detained in 1977, but Tlali emphasizes Pholoso as a hero by giving him a "dramatic escape" (Tlali 2005 [1980], 240) from a police vehicle carrying him and others on a mission to collect evidence.[29] In the end, Pholoso goes into exile after a sentimental farewell with Felleng, but the parts of the novel that are compelling today are those focused on Gramsy and her female relatives.

Pholoso's dramatic escape, in combination with authorial explanations of past and present politics, reflects Tlali's stated goal to "deliberately" create a literary platform for the expression of opposition to apartheid (Tlali 1998, 144), and corresponds also to the promotion of the 2005 reprint of *Amandla* in a textbook series on "Creative History."[30] Despite the pedagogic value, especially for twenty-first-century students, of summary comments on various

---

29. Dan Montsitsi of Sekano Ntoane High School became president of the Soweto Student Representative Council in January 1977 after the first SSRC president, Tsietsi Mashinini of Morris Isaacson High School, where the June march was hatched, and his successor Khotso Seathlolo of Naledi High School fled the country (Karis and Gerhart 1997, 175–84). Montsitsi was detained in April 1977 after a successful boycott against rent increases, and held without charge until after the second Soweto anniversary in June 1978. Aubrey Mokadi's claim, in *Narrative as Creative History*, the only book-length study of the Soweto novels, that Pholoso in *Amandla* as well as Oupa in Serote's novel and Mandla in Sepamla's are "fictional counterparts" of Mashinini (2003, 31) slights the authors' distinctive treatments of the story. Mashinini's interview in New York (Mashinini 1977), noted retrospectively by then-SSRC Treasurer Murphy Morobe (Morobe 1991), reveals a person more self-aggrandizing than charismatic. By contrast, Tlali's character Pholoso ranges from impetuous to disciplined but is rarely if ever boastful, while Mandla evolves from naive attachment to his exile mentor Mzi toward more nuanced loyalty to his fellow students.

30. The Creative History series includes the four Soweto novels and Mokadi's study; its central claim that these novels "creatively record history through fiction" (2003, 17) prompted the press at the Vaal Triangle Technikon where he is rector to reprint the novels, which had been out of circulation.

aspects of apartheid from the Group Areas Act to workplace discrimination to the daily indignities of pass inspections, and the interest for older South Africans of the argument, over two chapters framed by the tombstone unveiling, between two men debating the merits of Black Consciousness versus the workerist line of the Unity Movement (a rival of the then more Soviet-affiliated ANC in exile), these didactic sections do not exactly "place historical events and [...] debates in Soweto at that time" within a "web of familial experience" as Sole claims (1988, 67). Rather, they interrupt the story, so that the events of the uprising and their consequences do not so much emerge from "the experiences and conversations" of the characters (66) as they stretch the narrative web to insert commentary that the author deems important.

Tlali was not bound to write an integrated narrative that might have met "so-called aesthetic standards" (Tlali 1998, 144) that she found inhibiting. Nonetheless, the unevenly integrated argument, in combination with the odd fit between moving exchanges among kin and melodramatic treatment of romantic moments—as in this description of the student lovers Pholoso and Felleng: "They kissed passionately. The moment they had longed for had ultimately arrived and all their cares, unease and heartache of the past weeks seemed to vanish" (Tlali 2005 [1980], 67)—create unintended dissonance that distracts, rather than either absorbing or instructing, the reader in the ways of the world inhabited by the Moengs.[31] Criticizing Tlali for disavowing the effects of novels on the "emotions of the reader" in the name of showing matters "just as they are," Ndebele suggests that *Amandla* is most effective when it puts its trust in narrative (1991, 30). The lovers' final parting is more affecting for being more restrained than the earlier encounter: "Pholoso stepped back. For the first time the lonely girl felt the freezing air about her. . . . She watched Pholoso as he turned and walked away, waving his woolen cap. . . . She looked at the receding figure until it was a mere dot against the horizon where the dawn of a new day was becoming visible and she too finally turned to go back home" (Tlali 2005 [1980], 256). The novel ends here with both a sense of loss and

31. While Mokadi attempts to ground the didactic elements of modern fiction in "traditional storytelling" and its emphasis on "moral lessons" (2003, 28–29), he acknowledges that the novels have different form and function than "oral tales" (24). One should note further that Tlali herself does not reach for tradition, but rather justifies her didactic form as a means to a thoroughly modern end: to make readers "conscious of the system" of apartheid (1998, 144). This emphasis on raising consciousness reflects Tlali's commitment to the Black Consciousness Movement but, like other intellectuals in that movement, she uses the international language of political debate and militant struggle rather than the informal storytelling language of "the people" (Lockett 1989, 277).

of ongoing life and struggle, and thus makes a more compelling claim on the political solidarity and the emotional empathy of the reader.[32]

In contrast to the dissonance between story and pedagogy that mars the political effectiveness as well as narrative power of Serote's and Tlali's representations of struggle, Sepamla's theatrical sense for vivid dialogue and the dramatization of group rivalries as well as individual streams of consciousness create a more compelling story and a more illuminating treatment of the political tensions that marked the student revolt. While Sepamla's novel shares with *A Dry White Season* the titular evocation of a violent natural phenomenon standing in for political turmoil, and with *To Every Birth Its Blood* a portrait of a black exile, *A Ride on the Whirlwind* differs from these novels' focus on the political education of a central figure. While it shares with *Amandla* a focus on the political experiences of apparently non-political women, it paints a more vivid picture of both the individual complexity and social exemplarity of its characters. To be sure, Sepamla begins his story with a singular male figure, Mzi, a guerrilla arriving in Soweto from training in exile to carry out a mission, and ends with his hasty departure after the operations expose several student activists to police scrutiny and detention, but Sepamla treats operation and operative with skepticism, contrasting Mzi's bold plans to "change the world" (1984b, 29) with his ignorance of Soweto, not least the location of his target, Jabavu Police Station (28). Far from being a "conventional adventure novel" (Sole 1988, 66), *A Ride on the Whirlwind* draws on Sepamla's experiences with theatre to create a narrative that uses dramatic conflict between characters to depict not only commitment, but also disorientation among the students, as they struggle to maintain momentum and to focus the energy generated by the uprising into effective action against apartheid.

Despite the epigraph (from Sepamla's own *The Soweto I Love*) that "salutes" the "young heroes" whose "bravery [. . .]/ Stormed the June winter" (Sepamla 1984b, 5), the novel illuminates the fears and missteps as well as the genuine courage of old and young alike, women as well as men, behind the images of "circumcised" [i.e., male] youth with "clenched fists" (5). It also mediates the militant slogans of struggle evoked by the poem through the more ambiguous

32. While Tlali may not know György Lukács's defense in "Narrate or Describe" (Lukács 1955 [1936]; 1971) of the greater realism of narration over description or didacticism, or even his surrogates that shaped ANC cultural policy in exile, Ndebele's call for writers to use the "subjective capacity" of characters to ground their sense of commitment in "knowledge of themselves" as well as the "objective situation" (Ndebele 1991, 57, 56) echoes Lukács's praise for writers who depict characters' inner motivation in narration, rather than merely describing that motivation from the outside. Even without direct citation, Ndebele is a professor of literature and therefore more likely to have read Lukács.

language of older characters as well as the discourse of the press—in particular in the sensational newspaper headlines that punctuate the narrative in a manner reminiscent of Richard Wright's *Native Son* (1940). The opening pages employ the pattern of the political thriller, in that they quickly sketch Mzi's arrival in Park Station, his memories of training in Dar es Salaam, East Berlin, and Moscow, and his focus on the assigned mission: "to eliminate Warrant Office Andries Batata," a black operative in the "Special Branch" (8). At the same time, Sepamla separates the Soweto activists from the "Movement" in exile:

> the children's revolution gripped the imagination of many people. [. . .] The office in Dar acted on the spur of the moment to dispatch someone like Mzi to take advantage of the situation. It did not much matter to the Dar office that the children were concerned with a complaint about the use of Afrikaans in their classrooms. This was read to mean a complaint against the whole fabric of the ruling forces. [. . .] What more fertile soil was needed for the accentuation of a situation always at boiling point? (Sepamla 1984b, 8)

The dissident note emerges clearly even though this reflection on the "mission" appears to be focalized through Mzi. Having demonstrated his skill in bending bureaucratic language to satirical ends in poems like "To Whom It May Concern," Sepamla here confounds readers who expect a heroic narrative by openly broaching the touchy topic of the ANC's initial surprise at the Soweto students' action, and its subsequent attempt to "insert itself into student decision-making networks" (Karis and Gerhart 1997, 280) and to deploy "young, politically immature guerrillas" to attack police stations and similar targets (284). The passive voice and the mixed metaphors lumbering from the "complaint against the whole fabric of the ruling forces" to the "accentuation of a situation at boiling point" aptly express Mzi's characteristic arrogance but also seem, in the present-day context of an ANC government calling for the "deployment of cadres" in private as well as public sectors, to offer a foretaste of post-apartheid bureaucratic jargon. The jargon here, focalized through the mind of a would-be hero, troubles the picture of unadulterated militancy that might be implied by the cover photograph (by Peter Magubane) of a man with his fist aloft.[33]

---

33. The novel was initially published by AD Donker in Johannesburg, but after being banned in South Africa, it was reprinted in London in 1984 in Heinemann's African Writers series with the photograph by Magubane in four iterations arranged in a square on the cover. The man in the photograph—whose jacket, tie, and glasses suggest a teacher—was not identified, but readers may see it as a portrait of Mzi's older ally in the Movement, Uncle Ribs.

Although the narrative begins with Mzi, it moves quickly to other characters, including the older activist Uncle "Ribs" Mbambo, and especially Sis' Ida Diradikayi, who does not claim to be an activist but who nonetheless harbors several students while earning a living selling cosmetics, and whose point of view over the course of the story provides perspective on the action. The students range from those close to Mzi, especially Mandla, to militants who are suspicious of him, such as Roy and Bongi (one of the few women involved), to Keke, who feels excluded from the inner circle. While all are fictional as the author's disclaimer insists, their conversation includes a reference to Hector Peterson (Sepamla 1984b, 60), the emblematic victim of the uprising, and their group includes one Dan Montsho (42), whose name resembles that of SSRC leader Dan Montsitsi, although this fictional Dan escapes detention. The plan to blow up the police station is consistent with documented activity in Soweto, and Mandla's impetuous support of Mzi's ideas makes him seem initially like the hot-headed first president of the SSRC, Tsietsi Mashinini. The confused arguments that Sepamla dramatizes in the meeting that follows their first attempt—in which their homemade bomb misses their target, killing an ordinary policeman rather than the security operative Batata—highlight rifts among the students. Mandla supports the operation initially, but he is challenged by Roy and Bongi, who worry that they are being used (60) and that Mzi might be "part of the system" (85). Mzi's recklessness leads Mandla to suspect that he is taking unnecessary risks at the expense of "a whole house of friends [now] in detention" (173). These arguments suggest multiple fractures in the group and provide a candid portrayal of the students' passion and courage as well as their naiveté and lack of political experience, which explode literally in their faces: Keke gets badly burnt in a kitchen experiment with bomb ingredients when he tries "to achieve something for himself" (107), but manages only to put the others in danger. Shortly before Mzi takes Dan to Botswana, the latter confesses to Dr. Kenotsi, who has tended to Keke's burns in secret, that "the show is no longer ours. [. . .] We shook the system by bringing classes to a halt [. . .] but now we are drifting" (164); he has no answer to the doctor's concern that Dan's departure will leave the weakened Keke a vulnerable target of the police.

This candid depiction of ambiguous behavior does not diminish the novel's commitment to representing the seriousness of the uprising or the fearlessness of students such as Bongi, who suffers sexual assault in detention (157), or Roy, described by BOSS operatives as "Mandla's no. 2" (212), who withstands torture from an infamous interrogator known only as *Praatnou* (Now Talk!), but who is killed in a staged altercation so that police can use his battered body as a warning to others (236). Nonetheless, Sepamla's critical departure from a model of epic heroism allows him to lay out a complex social matrix within which to dramatize the struggles of a range of characters whose involvement emerges more slowly. In particular, Dr. Kenotsi may be modeled on Dr. Nthata Motlana, chair of the Soweto Committee of Ten, which forcefully replaced the apartheid puppet Soweto Urban Council and established an independent township governance model that would later spread beyond Soweto to other townships countrywide (Karis and Gerhart 1997, 236–37). And Sis Ida, who bears no resemblance to any famous figure, follows a critical evolution to political consciousness without abandoning her core belief in Christian charity. While acknowledging the students' limits, Sepamla links their enterprise to the long-term struggle not only by having Ribs compare the plan to bomb the police station with his ANC sabotage activities in the early 1960s (1984b, 27), but by highlighting historical mass resistance like the miners' strike of 1947, as recalled by a sympathizer, the coal merchant Pop Duze (196). In drawing key characters from the ranks of the black professional and entrepreneurial class, especially residents of Dube, Sepamla not only taps his own knowledge of this district (southwest of Orlando on the main Soweto rail line) but also reminds readers, whether township activists or their white allies, that members of this precarious elite were not automatically the sell-outs that some militants claimed. Sepamla's interest in depicting the complexities of commitment is reflected in some outright surprising characters such as Sergeant Ndlovu, who works at John Vorster Square but attempts to deflect BOSS attention from Sis Ida, as well as Ida herself. The narrative uses her experience as a touchstone, returning repeatedly to her situation at home and in detention at key points, but integrates that experience into the social matrix around her, in which her motherly concern for students and even for younger policemen, as well as her experience in detention, highlight multiple strands of interaction as well as the evolution of engagement more substantial than Mzi's.

Although dismissed by Mzi, who is "sneering" when he presumes that she will "crack under pressure" (165), Sis Ida shows remarkable endurance under torture. Her staying power is contrasted both with those students who crack such as Boysie, whose lack of experience makes him more vulnerable to police manipulation, and those who do not, such as Roy, who is killed by police. She stands out because of her attempts to respond civilly to her interrogators and by her ability to draw on her Christian faith as a source of strength, even on those occasions when she falls for interrogators' tricks and reveals information that she thinks they already know. Having established her as a vividly drawn character in this drama, Sepamla is better able to make Sis Ida perform the role Tlali wants to give to Gramsy, that of witness to apartheid's destruction of black urban life. When Ida tells police she was born in "Fi[e] tas" (169), and even when they demand that she use the Afrikaans name Vrededorp, she persists in using vernacular names. Her reference to her schooling in Sophiatown has an unexpected if passing effect on the otherwise canny Colonel Kleinwater ("little water"; by implication, "small piss"): "he repeated the word [Sophiatown] as if he wanted to clutch at it at the very moment when it was receding from his grasp" (169), before he goes on to pry information out of her about student access to forged passports (171). This exchange illuminates the dynamics of the "good cop/bad cop" interrogation used by BOSS, while also absorbing the reader into the story as experienced by an inadvertent but courageous actor in the struggle. Sepamla's skill in encouraging the reader to identify with Ida makes even implausible events emotionally compelling; in her last encounter with Praatnou, after one more demand that she reveal Mandla's hiding place to which she responds as before that she does not know and "resigns herself to death," the narrator tells us: "Praatnou snapped" (225). As her tormentor collapses with his head in his hands, Ida feels "sorry for the cop" even if she is too exhausted to remember being led away (225). While this extraordinary moment may not answer to Ndebele's call for a "rediscovery of the ordinary," it is nonetheless grounded in a compelling portrayal of an ordinary woman under extreme duress. Sepamla remains true to realism by leaving Ida in detention to confront the less violent but still "unpredictable" Kleinwater (240), who threatens her with indefinite detention if she does not give him information (241), and by ending the novel with Mzi's cynical escape, facilitated by his naive white liberal sponsor Ann (244). Like Pholosa's "dramatic" escape in *Amandla*, Praatnou's collapse in front of Ida may be implausible but, unlike Tlali's attempt at epic heroic portrayal rather than, as she claimed later, telling things "just as they are" (Tlali 1998, 306), Sepamla turns what could have been merely melodramatic into a magic realist conclusion that testifies to the extraordinary power of this character and of actual if anonymous people, especially women, who survived similar ordeals in the 1970s and 1980s.

The Relevance of Relevance: Envisaging Ordinary Life in the Era of Extremes

If writing in the wake of Soweto usually exemplified what Ndebele saw as the "spectacular" and even "exhibitionist" character of anti-apartheid writing in response to the "mind-boggling" brutality of the apartheid state

(1991, 38)—exhibitionism Louise Bethlehem would later censure not only in novelists but also in critics in thrall to "the rhetoric of urgency" (2004, 95–116)—there were some exceptions, especially in short stories, including those of Ndebele himself in *Fools and Other Stories* (1983) and others whose work appeared in *Staffrider* and other venues. The first issue of *Staffrider*, in addition to introducing poets such as Mtimkulu, featured an interview with Miriam Tlali about her first novel, *Miriam at Metropolitan* (1979), and about an oral history project she initiated called "Soweto Speaks," which the editor (probably Mike Kirkwood) compares with *Working*, the oral history compiled by the American writer Studs Terkel (Tlali et al. 1978, 2). Although published in 1975 before the uprising and the state's spectacularly violent response, *Muriel at Metropolitan* paved the way for the return to everyday life in Johannesburg in short fiction of the 1980s. The novel brings together blacks and whites working at the fictional Metropolitan Radio shop in downtown Johannesburg, as well as customers, especially blacks but also poorer whites, buying radios and furniture on hire purchase. *Muriel* is at its best when the author allows the doings of her central character to illuminate the struggles of ordinary people exploited by salesmen pitching unaffordable goods as well as employers who pay legally but unfairly low wages. Since economic exploitation has outlived both apartheid discrimination and post-apartheid promises of "black economic empowerment," and since this ongoing relevance complements its creation of vivid characters and scenes in a realistically drawn Johannesburg workplace, *Muriel* better fits its author's claim to tell things "just as they are" than does her later novel *Amandla*.

Muriel's detailed attention to the impact of the laws on labor and leisure in Johannesburg set this novel apart from most emphatic critiques of apartheid. Despite anachronisms such as inconsistent references to pounds (the old British currency) and to rands (the South African currency since 1965), and despite didactic interruptions in which the author summarizes the broad scope of South African race relations, *Muriel* provides an absorbing depiction of daily business in a central Johannesburg store.[34] Although Tlali prefers the title *Between Two Worlds* (1998, 143), the title of the edition published in 1995 and reprinted in 2004, *Muriel at Metropolitan* (Ravan Press's choice) highlights multiple points of conflict and the location of the action, rather

34. The narrator attributes this confusion to the canny but disorganized boss, Mr. Bloch, who she claims "had never overcome the habit of dealing in sterling rather than in rands" (1987, 20), but it seems unlikely that sterling would still have been legal tender in 1969, when the novel was apparently completed (Lockett 1989, 286).

than just a single character between two poles. It shows the tension between the modern lifestyle aspirations of urban blacks and the restrictions on pay and housing that make these aspirations impossible to achieve, but it also offers ironic asides on the metropolitan ambitions of Johannesburg's white boosters, revealed in conversations among whites, and the considerable range of aspirations and values among the blacks. Based partly on Tlali herself, who had to work after financial constraints and a baby forced her to abandon her university studies in Lesotho and return to Johannesburg, Muriel is a young, educated black woman who works as a bookkeeper while being paid as a typist. Mr. Bloch, the (likely Jewish) owner of Metropolitan, comes to value Muriel's services but nonetheless pays her little more than the law requires, which is considerably less than that accorded white associates with less education; he also pays the more experienced Coloured technician less than his younger, barely competent Afrikaner coworker. Beyond this indictment of apartheid discrimination, however, Tlali creates vivid scenes that show the wide variety of black responses to city life and especially to urban habits of consumption, from Mozambican migrants buying radios to white-collar workers acquiring furniture to embellish otherwise drab Soweto houses. Although Tlali is critical of these consumers, photographs of many Soweto interiors by Goldblatt as well as Soweto-based photographers such as Alf Kumalo offer testimony to their inhabitants' aspirations.

In addition to showing the economic strain that debt places on Metropolitan's black customers, Tlali introduces characters whose behavior suggests more complex negotiations with the ways of urban capitalism colored by apartheid. Where Gordimer had Anna Louw criticize the "Robin Hood" romanticism of blacks who rationalize their hire-purchase defaults as political rebellion, Tlali's narrative is more sharply critical of the system that encourages this and other delinquent behavior by underpaying blacks while simultaneously promoting middle-class aspirations. The company truck driver Agrippa gets drunk on and off the job but the boss keeps him on because he repossesses unpaid merchandise without sympathy for its purchasers; his thirst for alcohol has, in the view of another worker, Adam, left Agrippa "like a dead thing" (52) without a sense of obligation to his wife and children, or a sense of the shame he might cause community members by repossessing merchandise in full view of neighbors, for which he gets a commission. Adam the messenger lives probably illegally in a storeroom annex, which he rents out to couples after hours and, like Phineas in Simon's "Monologue for Vanessa," charges extra for white men in the company of black women (33). Whereas the narrator emphasizes economic exploitation and white slights to her dignity, the narrative as a whole includes a full range of interactions that show how workplace relations in Johannesburg persisted in greater complexity than apartheid law supposedly allowed. It is these interactions that take "the reader's involvement beyond the act of recognition" (Ndebele 1991, 24) and toward an understanding of conflict and collaboration beneath the surface of the grand struggle.

Although the tumult of Soweto and the ever-widening revolt that would become the United Democratic Front (1983) and the Mass Democratic Movement (1988) created powerful sounds and images that often overshadowed ordinary life, some significant writing pressed beyond the spectacle of struggle to depict with "rigorous attention to detail" the "subjective capacity" of characters to ground their sense of commitment in "knowledge of themselves" as well as the "objective situation" (Ndebele 1991, 57, 56). While Ndebele takes his own fiction outside the bounds of this study by setting *Fools and Other Stories* in Charterston township near the city of Nigel, at the very end of the Reef line a hundred miles or so from Johannesburg, other stories, including some praised by Ndebele, return to ordinary life in Johannesburg in the twilight of apartheid and thus provide a fitting conclusion to this chapter. Bheki Maseko's story "Mamlambo" appeared in *Staffrider* in 1983 and was reprinted in *Ten Years of Staffrider* (Tlali et al. 1988) and the *Heinemann Book of South African Short Stories* (1994). Its tale of a magical snake slithering into the lives of ordinary Sowetans draws, as Ndebele suggests, on storytelling forms where the traditional oral mode has been modulated by the context of telling and listening on the overcrowded trains that link life in Soweto with work in Johannesburg (1991, 32). While the snake that domestic servant Sophie Zikode and her Malawian partner Jonas discover in the "maid's" room in the white suburb may be a powerful totem that could "bring fortune to anyone who accommodates it," as the opening mantra claims (Maseko 1994 [1985], 153), it disturbs the lives of Africans aspiring to modern urban life. Sophie and Jonas follow the traditional doctor's instructions to coax the snake into a suitcase and to leave it with an unwitting recipient in a public place—a task that favors the most anonymous of urban sites, the train station. The station platform and the woman who agrees to "look after" Sophie's suitcase (159) may seem anonymous, but the woman turns out to be the mother of Sophie's "ex-lover" Elias (160), who left her to return to his wife in small-town Ermelo. Maseko's story draws not only on rural tales of migration and of totem animals with power over displaced humans, but also on the urban forms of melodrama and anecdote that shaped earlier "train stories" like Themba's "Mob Passion" (see Chapter 2).[35] But, where Themba had no use for magic, Maseko mixes acts of revenge fueled by the supernatural with the conditions of migrant life in modern South Africa, and thus addresses an audience that straddles both worlds. It thus speaks more directly to popular audiences than the avowedly political prose of intellectuals like Serote or Tlali. Even though he ends the story with the couple's sentimental journey to rural Malawi, which most likely cannot support them, Maseko's mix of secular and supernatural in the city offers a critical synthesis that challenges both immediate audiences on the train and mediated literary (mostly white) readers to see the multiple dimensions of life in Johannesburg.

Although Ahmed Essop's early contribution to *Staffrider*, "Two Dimensions," told the story of a troubled relationship between a Black-identified Indian student and his white friend and thus fits the rubric of Black Consciousness, most of his many stories depict multidimensional encounters between Indians and others in his native Johannesburg. Essop received little attention in surveys of either South African literature or Indian diaspora fiction through the 1990s, but one US-based critic has recently devoted a book chapter to his work. Pallavi Rastogi notes the impact of anti-apartheid non-racialism on Essop's depiction of relationships across religious barriers (Muslim and Hindus among Indians) as well as racial ones (South Asians in dialogue as well as in conflict with English, Afrikaans, Jewish, and black South Africans); nevertheless, Rastogi still remains attached to locating "Indianness" in Essop's characters, however hybridized their identities may have become by contact with South Africa (Rastogi 2008, 50). While the Johannesburg-based critic Marcia Leveson notes that Essop places characters in particular districts (1996, 214), her reading focuses on Jewish characters, especially in the story "The Metamorphosis," without, however, following Essop's lead that takes the widow Naomi from near-west white but modest Mayfair, west of Pageview, to her new comrades in the neighboring mixed district of Fietas/Pageview. Although Essop refers to Pageview, officially a narrow parcel of land southwest of Vrededorp, his stories vividly convey his intimate knowledge of the whole area remembered by residents as Fietas, and of other inner-city districts like Fordsburg or Hillbrow, as well as Lenasia, the far-flung township beyond Soweto that was built on the former military base Lenz,

35. This suitcase with hidden, but disturbing, content might also echo "The Suitcase," a story by Themba's contemporary Mphahlele, in which the protagonist steals a suitcase that turns out to contain a dead baby (Mphahlele 1989 [1955]). More recently, a dramatic adaptation of Mphahlele's story by James Ngcobo has been revived several times since its premiere in 2007; "Mamlambo" was made into a short film by Paleso Letlaka-Nkosi in 1997.

to which many, including Essop, were relocated in the 1960s and 1970s.[36] In depicting the Johannesburg terrain occupied by Indians and others, Essop creates an urban world quite different from the more insular Indian communities captured by Durban-based writers like Ronnie Govender, and establishes points of fictional as well as environmental reference that resonate in recent fictions by writers depicting Indians and kindred in Johannesburg, from Achmat Dangor to Zinaid Meeran.

"The Hajji," Essop's most anthologized story, deserves acclaim for its poignant treatment of the pious but proud Hajji Hassen, who refuses to bring his fatally ill brother back home to Fordsburg, because Karim had abandoned the family years before to pass for white in Hillbrow, and despite appeals by the imam and others that he show the charity fitting for a *hajji* (a Muslim who has made pilgrimage to Mecca), he can bring himself to attend his brother's funeral only incognito. Like the others in his first collection *The Hajji and Other Stories* (1978), it focuses on everyday life in Fordburg and Fietas at a time before the uprooting of inner-city Indian communities in the 1970s. In contrast, his second and third collections, *Noorjehan and Other Stories* (1990) and *The King of Hearts and Other Stories* (1997), include several narratives that portray dissidents in open rebellion against apartheid. What is distinctive about these stories is not just that they show the plight of the dispossessed or some measure of solidarity between Indians and other South Africans but that they place these scenes in particular urban places. Thus "The Metamorphosis" not only charts the political awakening of Naomi but also uses residence to differentiate the class affiliations of Naomi's adult children, distinguishing between mining magnate Alexander and his trophy wife Esther in Houghton, and former communist Mark and his yogi wife Helen in Homestead Park near Mayfair (1997, 23). He also places other key sites in recognizable locations: the headquarters of the dissident women's group Pharos (modeled perhaps on the Black Sash, which protested apartheid removals in silent pickets and also provided legal aid to victims) are in an "ancient looking, ivy-covered stone house in Hillbrow" (25) that recalls another former mansion, now the Windybrow Theatre, hidden between the high-rises.

36. In *Fietas: A Social History of Pageview*, Nazir Carrim provides a map (1990, 7), which has Pageview bounded by Delarey Street on the east, Eleventh Street to the north, and Twenty-Third Street to the south, thus separating it from the larger district of Vrededorp. He claims that it had an "Indian character" but nonetheless goes on to document the mixed population (60 percent Indian; with the remaining 40 percent including blacks, Chinese, and others) that persisted until the strict enforcement of the Group Areas Act in the 1960s and 1970s. The fact that many Fourteenth Street merchants owned their homes and shops did not stop the government from dispossessing them (Carrim 1990, 126–42).

Also published in *Staffrider*, the story "Jericho Again" uses the biblical quotation from the *Book of Joshua* (6.21), "and they utterly destroyed all that was in the city" (Essop 1990, 42), to lend the story of Khalid and Layla the authority of a moral fable; however, their status as the last property owners to be evicted from Fietas in the 1980s after their neighbors have moved house to Lenasia and trade has moved to the Oriental Plaza (est. 1974), the Indian mall in Fordsburg, is precisely grounded in Johannesburg history.[37] One of several photographers to document these evictions, Goldblatt took pictures during the 1970s that show people in their homes and shops as well as the abandoned buildings afterward (2010, 158–75). Essop reinforces the documentary element of his fiction by locating Khalid and Layla's house and shop in the lively shopping strip of Fourteenth Street, where many merchants often lived above their shops, thus highlighting the flexible urban fabric that was anathema to apartheid ideologues. In turn, Nazir Carrim reproduces the story as a document in his *Social History of Pageview* (1990, 158–61) and juxtaposes it with the actual cases of the "last 67 families" evicted from Fietas in 1984 (176–81). More recently, Cabral's *Jozi Sketchbook* includes sketches and descriptions of Fourteenth Street and the Oriental Plaza (2010, 18–21). Essop also leads the reader beyond Fietas; his image of the "[white] official" driving down Delarey Street (1990: 42) draws attention to the street that connects Fietas with Fordsburg and thus leads indirectly to the central administration district of police and other government bureaucracies, and that commemorates the charismatic Boer general who died in 1914 trying to escape Johannesburg to join rebels against the Union government, and thus the irony of former rebel Afrikaners turned tyrants.[38] Shadowed by this history and by Delarey Street's function as

---

37. Rastogi uses the term "fable" in the title of her chapter "Essop's Fables" (2008, 47), but appears to go no further than the pun on Essop's name. While she illuminates his attention to politics and daily life, her reading does not fully examine Essop's practice of weaving together fabular and realistic modes of storytelling. Even a story that plays with the fabular form—such as "East-West," the tale of security policeman Borg transformed by contact with political detainee Ranjit into Yogi Satyananda, a follower of Gandhi and devotee of Krishna (1990, 59–72)—locates this moral tale of renunciation of violence against self and others in realistically depicted places: Lenasia, the township built by the government for Indians working in Johannesburg; and Tolstoy Farm, Gandhi's ashram built by his friend, architect Hermann Kallenbach, while Gandhi resided in South Africa in the early twentieth century.

38. Koos De La Rey was one of several generals from the Anglo-Boer War known as *bittereinders* (bitter-enders) who revived Nationalist sentiment when they refused to join the British Army in World War I. He died trying to run a roadblock that had been set up for the notorious Foster Gang in Johannesburg (Davie 2003). The street links Fietas with Fordsburg, via a subway that now boasts a mural depicting the history of the district (Davie 2011a). De La Rey continues to foster dissent in the post-apartheid era; he was the subject of a 2008 song by Bok van Blerk that has been interpreted by some as a call for another Boer uprising.

the dividing line between white and black "Vrededorp," the house's signature element, a stained-glass window featuring a purple lotus, initially offers testimony to the blend of European and Indian culture that characterized Fietas and then illuminates the climax with an image of spiritual as well as material resistance: "for an instant the setting sun seemed to concentrate all its fire into the stained glass bloom" (46), despite the apparent victory of the bulldozers demolishing their home. Goldblatt's *TJ* (2010) includes no such imagined image, but the book features a picture that invokes a similar response: a small sailing-ship mirror still fixed to the landing of a house on Twentieth Street catches the light long after its inhabitants have been forced to leave (172). While Essop was doubtless drawing on the memories of friends and family and his own experience rather than a photograph by someone outside the community, the coincidence of sympathies in the literary and the photographic record of a beautiful and poignant remnant of willful destruction is a noteworthy reminder not only of that destruction, but also of the will to resist it and the ongoing impulse to redress it.

Although *The King of Hearts and Other Stories* (1997) includes fables about abuses of power that might be perpetrated by a post-apartheid black elite aided by sycophants among the Indians, such as "The Silk Scarf" and "The Banquet," one of its most compelling stories and certainly the wittiest is "The Novel." This story has been noted for its meta-fictional play between the author of the novel *The Visitation* (which Essop published in 1980) and Asgar, a Fordsburg gangster. Asgar's self-representation draws on 1950s gangster glamour and so may recall the club owner Lucky Chaputra in Gordimer's *World of Strangers*, but Essop's treatment plays with his own inter-texts. Asgar claims that Gool (a common abbreviation of Goolam), the gang boss in *The Visitation,* is a portrait of himself, despite the narrator's disclaimer that "a novelist does not write about real people" (Essop 1997, 70), but its evocation of Fordsburg has so far escaped critical attention. The narrator mentions actual places in Fordsburg including, in addition to Oriental Plaza and the Lyric Cinema, a bookshop and other locations on Mint Road (1971), the Fordsburg extension of Delarey Street, as well as fictional locations on real streets, such as Asgar's club on Pioneer Road and "Ahmed's" house in Lilian Road that the narrator identifies as his own, even though Essop had by this time been forced to move to Lenasia. He also includes other significant locations, such as Zoo Lake, and the reservoir in Herman Eckstein Park opposite the Johannesburg Zoo in Parkview, a favorite haunt for Indian South Africans and a rare integrated Johannesburg park, even if there were no Indians officially living nearby.[39] Some fictional variations, such as the location of "Herald Publishers" in Hillbrow, serve to concentrate the action in inner-city districts with some notoriety, as against the office district Braamfontein where Ravan Press had begun operations, or north-suburban Randburg, the press's postal address at the time that it published this story, and thus to sharpen the edge of Asgar's visitation. As the story unfolds, Asgar changes his appearance to fit the description of Gool in the novel, tries to obtain a red convertible that looks like Gool's, and sets up scenarios that repeat scenes of intimidation from the novel, with the difference that Asgar pressures people to buy copies of "his" book that he has bought en masse from the publisher, whereas his likeness had compelled a merchant under his "protection" to take stolen lamps. However, when a potential buyer in Laudium, an Indian satellite of Pretoria reputedly more respectable than Fordsburg, humiliates Asgar by telling him to keep both books and check, he decides to follow the narrator's advice to stop copying the fictional Gool and invites him to celebrate by watching Marilyn Monroe at the Lyric. Although the last reference may date the characters and the author (Essop was born in 1931), it returns the action to home turf in Fordsburg, an area which, in the post-apartheid era, is once again dominated by Indian merchants both locally born and new arrivals.

Segue: Johannesburg's Centenary and the Elusive Pursuit of Integrated Urbanity

Essop's focus on Fordsburg returns us to key sites in the cultural history of Johannesburg, and in particular to the neighboring district of Newtown, where the Market Theatre had opened in June 1976. The commemoration of Johannesburg's centenary ten years later in September 1986 promoted the transformation of Newtown, which came to stand for a transformation of Johannesburg, from an industrial and commercial to a cultural precinct including a jazz club in a converted Beaux Art toilet and the Federated Union of Black Artists across from the Market. However, the renovations promoted by the press were mostly commercial, including a craft mall, restaurants, and

39. Herman Eckstein was a gold-mining magnate of Jewish descent who donated tracts of land to the city for parks. Despite this bequest, most people who use Zoo Lake are unaware of its official name. Only when William Kentridge introduced the character Soho Eckstein into his animated shorts, beginning with *Johannesburg, 2nd Greatest City after Paris* (1989), did Eckstein re-emerge, albeit ironically, as a representative of the city.

paving stones of South African cultural icons, in imitation of Hollywood. Moreover, the press response to the centenary showed some striking continuities with as well as predictable differences from the fiftieth anniversary Jubilee at the Empire Exhibition in 1936, which had been housed across the railway line, about a kilometer to the north of Newtown, in the Witwatersrand Showgrounds. As in 1936, press reports on the preparations for the commemoration mixed boosterish celebration of Johannesburg's aspirant world-class status with gossip about financial scandals erupting among the groups vying for control of the event (see Johannesburg Historical Society 1986). The centenary organizers also planned a pageant but, unlike the Empire Exhibition's staged history of the Union, the performance in 1986 favored the spectacular—mine dancers and fireworks—(see Christie 1986) and seemed little more than a rehearsal for tourist attractions housed in the new Gold Reef City theme park in Ormonde, south of the old mining terrain on Cabral's map. The buzz around the cheap nostalgia of the theme park seems especially striking in contrast to the paucity of comment on neglected historical structures, such as the skeleton of the old Park Station (1897; Cabral 2010, 5), rusting between the railway line and the new Newtown Cultural Precinct. The newspapers also published little on the more innovative structures of the year, such as Meyer and Pienaar's new wing of the Johannesburg Art Gallery (see Chapter 2) or controversial newcomers such as Helmut Jahn's reflective glass Diamond Building (1984), which cast blinding light on its Diagonal Street neighbor, the Johannesburg Stock Exchange building (1978–2000), and motorists and pedestrians in the street below (see Goldblatt 2010, 229).

While the white newspapers in 1936 had praised the labor of black workers, but had left to the black papers the task of tracking black dissatisfaction with the Johannesburg Jubilee, the press in 1986 acknowledged the more emphatic protest by contemporary blacks and the glaring contradiction between the last evictions from Pageview (Woodgate 1986), and the lack of events in Soweto on the one hand, and the organizers' claim to open the centenary to "all the people of our city" (Dalling 1985) on the other. Black response to this claim to include everyone in the centenary celebrations varied from skeptical to furious. Chipane Kgaphola's poem "Johannesburg 100," published in *Staffrider*, sarcastically urges his fellow blacks: "Mnt'onyama [black person] celebrate/ the big city comes of age/ forget your dark cold home in Soweto" (1988 [1986], 292). He focuses his ire on the consumerist character of the commemoration "celebrate mntanami [my child] celebrate/ what little you earn/ you have to return it" but ends by bringing up the coercion just below the surface: "CELEBRATE OR ELSE" (293–94). The poem may be blunt, but the imposition of a state of emergency that very year and the violent repression than topped even the 1970s only fueled rebellion in the townships. Just as the original Newtown had attempted to bury the troubled history of its predecessor districts of Brickfields and Coolie Location, which it forcibly replaced in 1913, the revitalization of Newtown in 1986 attempted to deflect attention from ongoing conflict over rights to the city. Unlike early renovations, however, this one exposed the city's troubled history rather than covering it up, as protests continued despite the violent repression of public gatherings.

The Market Theatre, which had become the city's preeminent anti-apartheid cultural institution by 1986, did not tackle the centenary controversies directly, but its powerful testimonial play from the year before, *Born in the RSA*, did address the political crisis, dramatizing public and private conflict in the state of emergency that was declared in 1985 and would last essentially until President F. W. de Klerk announced that Nelson Mandela would be granted unconditional release from his life sentence in 1990. Although the action of *Born in the RSA* takes place in Johannesburg and Soweto and characters mention several sites, from John Vorster Square to Wits University, from Dube Primary School to Sun City (a.k.a. Diepkloof Prison), this drama of repression and resistance, as the title implies, could have played out anywhere in the country (Simon et al. 1997, 91–126; Kruger 1999, 166–82). Where the Market Theatre's reputation, at home and abroad, rested on its staging of immediate and urgent responses to the apartheid present, Junction Avenue Theatre Company (JATC) instead concentrated on the critical—and playful—representation of competing South African pasts. Their *Sophiatown* (1986) dramatized the history of this distinctive district in a way designed not only to recover the lives and environments buried under Triomf but also to create the conditions for imagining a future integrated urbanity in and of Johannesburg.[40] Coming after a decade of experiment with dramatizing history in collaboration with the Wits History Workshop and in creating drama that addressed contemporary concerns of labor and politics, *Sophiatown*

40. For JATC's evolution and more detailed commentary and illustrations of the 1986 performance of *Sophiatown* and comparison with JATC's next—and last—Johannesburg play, *Love, Crime and Johannesburg* (1999), see Kruger (2004a, 256–80). For the definitive reading of *Love, Crime and Johannesburg*, see Becker (2010). I have included the analysis of *Sophiatown* in modified form here because the play's engagement with Johannesburg history and the occasion of its performance highlight, in contrast, the ahistorical boosterism of the centenary and thus merit review in this context.

refined the form and method honed in JATC's preceding history plays, such as *The Fantastical History of a Useless Man* (1976), the company's reaction to the sense of superfluity felt by many young whites at the time of the uprising, and *Randlords and Rotgut* (1978), a dramatized response to historian Charles van Onselen's study of the collusion between mining magnates and Afrikaner politicians in the liquor trade in 1890s Johannesburg (van Onselen 1982), which combined the testimonial theatre honed by the Market with a distinctly South African interpretation of Brecht's practice of critical historicization to illuminate the present (see Orkin 1995, 172–222; Kruger 2004a, 256–80). Junction Avenue's project to not only investigate the past but also to combine historical interpretation with, as Brecht has it, "delight in what is close and proper to ourselves" (Brecht 1998 [1954], 23, 290; 1992 [1964], 276), does not treat Brecht as a sacrosanct European classic. Rather, it appropriates not only Brecht's innovations on stage, but also his interest in probing, through both historicizing and interventionist representation, social relations in the house and in the world outside.

Performed first in the Market's smaller Upstairs Theatre in February 1986, *Sophiatown* moved to the main stage in April and ran again in September and October to commemorate the centenary. Revived the following year and again for Mandela's inauguration in 1994 and several times since, *Sophiatown* has become a standard text on university syllabi as well as a point of reference for many nostalgic recollections. Despite this influence, *Sophiatown* preceded the nostalgia boom that was largely a 1990s phenomenon and, while it acknowledges the affections of its former residents (such as Dan Mattera, whose memoir it quotes in conclusion), it nonetheless offers a more critical view. The performance of the play, along with the publication of interviews collected by the company (Stein and Jacobson 1986), and the republication, after the performance, of formerly prohibited Sophiatown texts like *Blame Me on History* (1963), the memoir of Bloke Modisane, who died in exile in 1985, encouraged the rediscovery of a historical model, however flawed, of an integrated urbane Johannesburg. The play was based on a serious prank: Nkosi and Nakasa advertised in the *Johannesburg Star* for a Jewish girl to come and stay with them. Out of the interaction between the visitor, Ruth, and the members of a Sophiatown household—from the matriarchal owner, Mamariti, and her daughter, Lulu, to the gangster Mingus, the numbers runner Fahfee, and the "situation," Jakes—JATC recreated a microcosm of the Sophiatown milieu, while also probing the connections and disconnections between Nkosi's "fabulous fifties" and the tentative integration of the 1980s. The situation of the "situation," Jakes, articulated the mixture of alienation and celebration in urban life. As Jakes remarks after Ruth introduces the household to Jewish Sabbath wine:

> God is One and God is Three and the ancestors are many. I speak Zulu and Xhosa and Tswana and English and Afrikaans and Tsotsitaal and if I'm lucky Ruth will teach me Hebrew. . . . And this Softown is a brand new generation and we are blessed with a perfect confusion. (Junction Avenue Theatre Company 1995, *At the Junction*, 180)

This celebration of "perfect confusion" marks a moment suspended in time, caught in the machine of apartheid that engineered this place and would soon demolish it. As director Malcolm Purkey remarked, the association of moments in the (anti)apartheid calendar (such as June 26, 1955, the declaration of the Freedom Charter) with numbers games constitutes a key structuring principle of the play (1995, 211). It also implies that the prediction of an imminent ANC victory at that time had something of a magic spell about it. Far from denigrating the Defiance Campaign and the history of struggle, this invocation bears witness to the intensity of the desire for change as well as the difficulty of achieving it. Ramoloa Makhene, as the numbers runner Fahfee, led this chorus of historical references but his presence on stage, along with veteran actors Gladys Mothlale as Mamariti and newer arrivals like Arthur Molepo (Mingus) and Patrick Shai (Jakes), also reasserted the continuity of a performance repertoire lost through repression or forgetfulness.

Sophiatown participates not only in the historical reconstruction of Sophiatown but also in contemporary debates about the legacy of the 1950s. The play engages with historical but unsuccessful initiatives of the Defiance Campaign (1951–) and the Freedom Charter (1955) in the context of the government's violent measures against so-called ungovernable townships in the 1980s. While celebrating the utopian potential of Sophiatown and the "situation's" view that memorialized it in the songs and stories of the period, it also acknowledges that this utopia was at best only partially there. The mass resistance to removals never materialized, in part because Sophiatown's poorer tenants saw the Meadowlands houses as an improvement on their overpriced backyard shacks. Nonetheless, *Sophiatown* emphasizes the value of memory, not merely for healing but for agitation. The songs that punctuate the domestic scenes in this play with comments on the struggle link the self-aware but insufficient urbanity of the *Drum* era and the militant cultural politics of the 1980s. The final song juxtaposes pathos and militancy, as the play concludes with a litany of those who were to die in exile and so links the time of the plot with the time of performance:

> And out of this dust Triomf rises. What triumph is this? Triumph over music? Triumph over meeting? Triumph over the future? . . . I hope that the dust of that triumph . . . covers these purified suburbs with ash. Memory is a weapon. Only a long rain will clean away these tears. (JATC 1995, *At the Junction* 204–5)

Invoking Don Mattera's recollection of the Sophiatown rubble as a prediction of its revival from his memoir *Memory Is a Weapon* (Mattera 1987; published abroad with the title *Sophiatown*), the song is both a lament and a call to arms. Mattera's own odyssey, from his birth to an Italian father and black mother in Western Native Township, now named Westbury, on the border of the formerly white Westdene, to other contested areas Sophiatown and Pageview, and back again, tracks the conceptual and emotional maps of inner-city denizens during apartheid and its aftermath. Confronted in the turbulent 1980s with the past of Sophiatown and the present of Triomf, this play proposes an alternative history, in Brecht's terms, the "not but" of what might have happened had conditions favored rather than disavowed integrated urbanity, and so also looks forward to a future, as yet hypothetical, post-apartheid era in which the false triumph of Triomf would be transformed in the image of an integrated city. Even if Triomf would by the year 2000 be reinvented as a newer and better Sophiatown, and its poorer neighbor Westbury would become the destination of tours offering a glimpse of built environments that recalled the Sophiatown that had been (Abrahams 2010), the vision of urbanity in yet another "New Town" would prove elusive in the edgy 1990s.

4 1996: EDGY CITY

The year 1996 marked the twentieth anniversary of the Soweto uprising but, whereas the uprising itself could be seen as the beginning of the end of apartheid, the commemoration of this watershed event took place in more uncertain times. The national elections of 1994 had ushered in South Africa's first democratically elected government with a president, Nelson Mandela, who was recognized as one of the world's most charismatic leaders. However, the interregnum that began with Mandela's release from prison in 1990 persisted beyond 1994 at the local level, where administrators and city council members who knew that they would be voted out by 1996 did nothing to manage the unregulated movement of capital and people that had begun already in the 1980s.[1] In Johannesburg, the city government that took office in 1996 had to tackle the late apartheid administration's neglect of the built environment, as well

1. The year 1996 also saw the first hearings of the Truth and Reconciliation Commission that began in the Eastern Cape, crucible of anti-apartheid resistance and Mandela's home turf. Since the TRC and its aftermath have received more attention overseas than any other South African topic, and since this institution's impact was nationwide rather than specific to Johannesburg, I will not be discussing it here. For my views on the TRC industry and pointers to useful books, see Kruger (2011).

as the problem of absentee owners and the irregular operators who took their place. It struggled to overcome not only the inequities of apartheid, but also the damage done by capital flight to the suburbs and by undocumented newcomers to the inner city, whose unregulated occupation of dilapidated structures exacerbated the problems of governance; the city government was unable until the turn of the century even to fix the boundaries between Johannesburg and other entities, let alone define the character of the city within these new boundaries.[2] As murder and other violent crimes soared to rates four times that of the United States in 1996 (Martin Shaw of the South African Institute for Security Studies; quoted by Bremner 1998, 53), edginess deepened into apocalyptic visions of a "long day's journey into Jo'burg night"(Varder 1998, 18–19). Writers, artists, planners, and citizens largely agreed that the gulf between extreme wealth and desperate poverty had widened *since* the election and that the future looked bleak (Bremner 1998; Swilling 1998).[3]

Despite the official end of apartheid, Johannesburg in 1994 was still burdened with its legacy. The geography of crime reflected not only the history of racial segregation, but also the *geo-pathology* of ever sharper divisions by wealth, in which the crisis of management was expressed as the inability to imagine the city as anything other than incurably divided.[4] Johannesburg appeared to planners and artists alike to be unimaginable as well as unmanageable; it seemed not merely to elude representation, but rather to sabotage it. The unresolved legacy of apartheid left the city with huge gaps between rich and poor, which were made manifest in the separation of affluent citadels from the urban fabric or from informal settlements housing the unemployed

---

2. Beavon's maps and analysis of the spatial restructuring of the metropolitan area in the period 1991–2000 (2004, 238–69) highlight the difficulties faced by the provisional Central Witwatersrand Metropolitan Chamber (1990–95) in compelling previously white self-governing municipalities to join historically black and deprived townships that had been managed by the government; he also criticizes the subsequently elected government (1996–) for taking too long to absorb thirteen different municipalities into a single city authority and thus to forge a single tax base from which to generate revenue for urban renewal and services.

3. This perception of crime in the 1990s was confirmed retrospectively by local and outside observers alike (Beavon 2004; Altbeker 2007; Murray 2008, 2011).

4. Una Chaudhuri defines geo-pathology as "the problem of place—and of place *as problem*" (1997, 55) but focuses primarily on the thematization of this problem, primarily in realist drama. Nonetheless, the resonance of the terms reaches beyond thematics; in a preliminary discussion of the crisis of imagination among Johannesburg planners as well as playwrights, I argued that geo-pathology defined not only dramatic representations of the city but also the decay of its urbanity as well as its social and economic power (Kruger 2001a, 224–25).

as well as those employed to serve the affluent, and the proliferation of commercial nodes competing with the erstwhile central business district (CBD). The public street became the locus of danger and decay, losing legitimacy to privatized enclaves of work or leisure or to administrative precincts that changed the historical CBD into a central administration district (CAD). The evacuation of the meaning as well as the structure of public space reinforced the perception of Johannesburg as a city of edges and fractures. As edgy city, potentially stimulating but mostly abrasive, it shifted from apartheid segregation—the injustices of which were still contested in public spaces—to a "city of walls" divided by class, in which, as Teresa Caldeira wrote of comparable environments in São Paolo, "encounters in public spaces" between the rich and the rest become not only "tense" and "framed by fears and stereotypes" (2000, 297), but also emptied of desire, sites of aversion rather than urbane attraction.

Despite this decline, efforts to reinvest in city space emerged in the interregnum between apartheid and post-apartheid governance. Even in the early 1990s, when the city council appeared passively to observe the decay of the city, the Central Johannesburg Partnership (CJP) from 1991 attempted to rebuild frayed links between absentee landlords and their inner-city properties. Johannesburg boosters like CJP principal Neil Fraser, or Christopher Till, former director of the Johannesburg Art Gallery, who invented the position of Director of Culture for Johannesburg and occupied it from 1991 to 1996, created showcase projects like the Johannesburg Biennale (1995 and 1997) and the Arts Alive Festival (ongoing since 1992) and expanded the Newtown Cultural Precinct beyond the Market Theatre to include the Worker's Library, the Dance Factory, Mega Music, the exhibition hall known as the Electric Workshop, and other spaces. Till maintained that the city could be "regenerated through culture" (Till 1996) but the new administration was not persuaded, and these efforts remained on a small scale, as major financial institutions moved to Sandton, including the Johannesburg Stock Exchange (JSE) in 2000.[5]

---

5. The modest returns of these renewal efforts were exaggerated by enthusiastically boosterish rhetoric. The cited interview with Till regretted the passing of his position as director of culture but celebrated his achievements as Chair of the Foundation for the Creative Arts (another Till invention) in a lavishly illustrated special issue of *ADA Magazine* (no. 14) on "Johannesburg: Cultural A–Z Update," which includes a map of Newtown developments to 1996 (88–89) and an editorial celebrating the city's "cutting edge of arts, culture, and finance" despite being "the most violent place in the country" (Sorrell 1996, 6). This issue appears to have been the last issue of the magazine.

Even as the affluent sought to protect their assets behind high walls and militarized security, however, previously marginalized groups claimed the inner city in the 1990s. Emboldened by the resurgence of hitherto suppressed opposition groups, black and white members of Gays and Lesbians of the Witwatersrand (GLOW) directed the first-ever Lesbian, Gay, Bisexual, Transgender, and Queer (LGBTQ) Pride Parade in 1990—the year of Mandela's release but also the start of the decade that saw the escalation of the AIDS epidemic. The parade (which participants that first year remembered as being more like a political march) followed inner-city routes, taking in Hillbrow as well as Braamfontein and in subsequent years other historic sites such as the Library Gardens (De Waal and Manion 2006). Although retreating to the northern suburbs from 2002 to 2004, it returned to the city in 2005, but by 2012 appeared to have settled on the area around Zoo Lake (GALA 2012) as a safer zone.

Also in the 1990s, as the state was unable to police its borders, African migrants from the north moved south to claim the inner city with less publicity but with perhaps more tenacity than public renewal projects. Although treated by state and street alike as a new unsettling phenomenon, African migrants followed in the wake of internal migrants who had begun to move into Hillbrow and other inner-city districts already in the 1970s. However, while the latter can be described as "returning natives," since many Indians and Coloureds had historic ties to Fordsburg and Fietas if not to Hillbrow, the migrants who penetrated the porous borders to the north came in unprecedented numbers. Those on work or student permits from Mozambique or Congo in the 1980s were in the 1990s joined by many more people who traveled without papers, sometimes on foot from as far away as Senegal or Ethiopia, in search of a better life in South Africa. Although they met with suspicion, especially from black South Africans from the townships or from rural areas competing for space and livelihood, these migrants helped to reanimate the inner city. As several urbanists, including Asef Bayat, Graeme Götz, and AbdouMaliq Simone have noted, the apparently "uncivil society of informal people" (Bayat 1997, 53) or unregulated migrants realized new forms of civic potential through mobilizing networks of "people (rather than bureaucratic institutions) as infrastructure" (Simone 2004a). Reformulating Michel de Certeau's "pedestrian enunciations" and "networks of moving and intersecting writing" by which the "migratory city *insinuates* itself" into the planned "concept city" (1988, 95; 1991, 144), Götz and Simone (2003) envisage a newly "animated city" (De Certeau 1988, 93; 1991, 142) rewriting ways of "becoming and belonging."[6] To those "post-metropolitan" urbanists like Edward Soja who caution against the romanticization of "gritty street-wise pluck" (1997, 28) in urban theory (and thus implicitly against granting street-level improvised networks legitimate space in conurbations shaped by vehicular traffic, such as Los Angeles and Johannesburg), Götz and Simone offer an account of migrant insinuations that animate a Johannesburg whose worldliness may be embodied less in the built environment of office towers mimicking the cities of Europe and North America, than in networks of transnational exchange on the street. Simone's investigations of the simultaneous Africanization of inner-city Johannesburg and the "globalization of African spatial practices" (1998) have drawn since the 1990s on comparisons with other African trading hubs such as Dakar or Douala. These investigations, together with the informal work by residents' organizations to encourage the informal interaction they call "*sawubona* culture" (culture of greeting; see Davie 2008) and the more systematic documentation by the African Centre for Migration and Society (ACMS) in Johannesburg, suggest that the informal but tenacious movements of migrants—practices that I have called instances of sustained precarity—revise northern notions of cosmopolitan worldliness to account for what ACMS researchers call the "tactical cosmopolitanism" (Landau and Haupt 2007) of migrants and their potential to enliven the city, despite threats of violence from informal nativist groups as well as the police.[7]

---

6. While the participle in the English translation "Walking in the City" emphasizes action and process, the original French "Marches dans la ville" connotes both literal "steps" and figurative "progress"; the subtitle *énonciations piétonnières* (148) highlights embodiment and performance, which disappears in translator Randall's "pedestrian speech-acts" (97). Randall's translation of "s'insinue" as "slips into" misses the potential incivility connoted by "insinuates." To highlight these connotations of de Certeau's influential text, references cite first the French original and then the translation. Several urbanists, from Steve Pile (1997) to Asef Bayat, have used the concept of insinuation in discussing the informal reformulation of the city street; Jennifer Robinson (1998) and AbdouMaliq Simone (1998) were the first to deploy de Certeau to analyze Johannesburg.

7. As these brief remarks suggest, the fear of foreigners expressed by poor South Africans, especially newcomers to the city from impoverished rural regions, did not suddenly erupt in the xenophobic riots of 2008 but had been simmering ever since the 1990s, when disappointment at the slow pace of change turned into resentment of those who appeared better able to compete for scarce resources. For comparison between internal and external migrants in South Africa since 1990 see Segatti and Landau (2011a) and for the longer historical view of one of the flashpoints in 2008, the dense district of Alexandra, see Bonner and Nieftagodien (2008).

Before trying to fathom the impact of imagined as well as enacted violence on city life, we should distinguish between the disorderly 1990s and the urban renewal since the 2000s. The preliminary efforts of the CJP, and the mayor's Inner City Office (ICO, 1999–2002), set the stage for renewal, but only with the Johannesburg Development Agency (JDA)—directed initially by Graeme Reid (2001–4) who had headed the ICO (1999–2001) and also contributed to the Pride Parade—did the city enact more substantial improvements to the built and social environment with the financial and logistical support of public-private partnerships under the aegis of the JDA, especially CJP and the private real estate firm Kagiso Urban Management, which absorbed the CJP in 2003.[8] These distinctions are not absolute; neither the city's extreme wealth gap nor the violence by both state and criminal agents has disappeared, and urban renewal projects since 2002 have met with mixed success. Nonetheless some working distinctions are in order. In 2004 geographer Keith Beavon delineated three periods: (1) 1991–95, from the initiation of the CJP to the first post-apartheid local elections; (2) 1996–2000, from the inauguration of the ANC-led city government to the absorption of residual apartheid-era municipalities like Randburg and Roodepoort, and the consolidation under an executive mayor of a single city management; and (3) 2001 to the open-ended present (2004, 237–39). Only with the third phase, which might be seen in retrospect to begin in 2002 with the mayor's long-term plans, articulated in *eGoli 2030* (updated in 2010 to *Joburg 2040*) for Johannesburg as a "world-class African city" (City of Johannesburg 2002a) and JDA's activation of Central Improvement Districts, did urban renewal begin in earnest. And only in mid-decade did the still-incomplete results, from street safety to the renovation of designated inner-city districts, emerge into public view.

I shall review twenty-first-century developments in the final chapter, but for now I will note that the recent urban renewal efforts should be measured

8. The relationship between the city, as represented by the JDA, and private firms, in particular KUM (now Urban Genesis), remains contested. Murray argues that KUM's legal obligation to manage commercial properties in the Central Johannesburg Business Improvement District, nearby Braamfontein, and other BIDs in the northern suburbs in return for levies (2011, 260–64) extends to "voluntary" management of government or heritage precincts including Constitution Hill, Newtown, and Wits (233–36), but supports the latter claim with interviews with KUM PR people, without discussing the more recent renovation of public sites in inner-city residential areas of Hillbrow, Berea, and Yeoville, or the JDA's role in soliciting the work of planners, architects, artists, and NGOs. For information, including budgets, see www.jda.org.

against the challenges that preceded them. While those who view the city from the optimistic perspective of the aspiring "Afropolis" may dismiss the nervousness of the 1990s as merely one instance of an allegedly "long tradition of loathing" (Nuttall and Mbembe 2008, 33), those who lived in Johannesburg in the 1990s generally tell a different story. As architect Lindsay Bremner noted in "Crime and the Emerging Urban Landscape of Johannesburg," in *blank___: Architecture, Apartheid and After* (1998), an important collection of visual and textual essays on built environments in the wake of apartheid, the media focused on the anxieties of the affluent but the areas "most vulnerable to murder, armed robbery, rape and violent assault" were those "least protected under apartheid," namely black townships like Soweto and more remote informal settlements like Orange Farm in the south or Diepsloot in the north, as well as the inner city (Bremner 1998, 55). In contrast, property crime targeted wealthier districts, increasing after the 1994 elections failed to produce the good life for the majority. The theft of cars and other valuables, including heists against cash transit vehicles, was often accompanied by violence, feeding suspicions that crime syndicates were emerging from ranks of decommissioned apartheid and anti-apartheid operatives who had not been absorbed into an effective post-apartheid force and whose weapons fueled criminal violence (59).

In keeping with perceptions of imagined as well as documented violence, narratives of gloom, doom, and crime dominated the early 1990s (especially in film thrillers like *Dangerous Ground* [1997] set partly in the dilapidated Ponte City), and persisted into the twenty-first century in films like *Jerusalema* (2008). Before these narratives became formulaic, however, Michael Hammon's cinematic fiction of car-jacking and murder in *Wheels and Deals* (1991), Paul Slabolepszy's dramatization of rent racketeering and other crimes in the play *Mooi Street Moves* (1992), and the circulation of arms and other stolen goods in the miniseries *The Line* (1994) set the tone with their depictions of violence as unpredictable and pervasive. This nervousness persisted to decade's end even as the city began to recover, as in, for instance, Nadine Gordimer's novel *The House Gun* (1998) and Junction Avenue Theatre Company's play *Love, Crime and Johannesburg* (1999).[9] While these works may

9. Since I will be focusing here on film and prose narrative responses to 1990s Johannesburg, readers interested in theatrical treatments might consult "Theatre, Crime and the Edgy City" (Kruger 2001a).

have white authors (in collaboration with black writers and performers), black Johannesburgers paint similar pictures of an edgy city, especially in visual narratives like Zola Maseko's film *The Foreigner* (1997) or in television drama targeting young black viewers, such as *Yizo Yizo* (1999–2002). Even accounts that temper this bleak picture with the resourcefulness of ordinary people making do in the dense and fractured environment of the high-rise inner districts, whether in nonfiction as in *Bleakness and Light*, Alan Morris's sociological study of Hillbrow (1999), or in fiction as in Phaswane Mpe's novel *Welcome to Our Hillbrow* (2001), highlight the odds against which their subjects struggle.

These narratives share not only a sense of exposure to unpredictable risks, whether from crime or contagion, but also an awareness of the impact of migration on Johannesburg. Migrants and other strangers have shaped the Johannesburg environment throughout its history, but their greater visibility and variety of origins in the 1990s provoked strong reactions from nativists who accused them of spreading AIDS and taking jobs and other resources. While some narratives return to the familiar figure of the rural migrant at a loss in the big city, they give the old story of "Jim comes to Joburg" new twists, either, as in *Mooi Street Moves* or Les Blank's film *Jump the Gun* (1996), by showing naive white men at sea in a mostly black inner city, or, as in John Ledwaba's *Jozi, Jozi* (1994), Slabolepszy's *Fordsburg's Finest* (1998), or Maseko's *The Foreigner* (1997), by exploring the woes of black foreigners (respectively: a comic Malawian, the grown daughter of political exiles, a Senegalese trader) unsure of their bearings among natives who shun them as *amaKwerekwere* ("those who talk funny") or even as aliens or zombies (Comaroff and Comaroff 1999). Migrants also haunt the margins of narratives that do not primarily portray them, from the world-weary Mozambican in *The Line* to the ambiguous Slav in Ivan Vladislavić's *The Restless Supermarket*. They may even be hard to distinguish from native protagonists, as are the cosmopolitan internal and external migrants in *Welcome to Our Hillbrow*. The inner city is the primary site of this encounter and its impact on the national and transnational character of Johannesburg in transition, even if some fictions from this period, such as *Wheels and Deals* or *The House Gun*, show affluent suburbanites as actual or potential victims of violent intruders from the townships. Especially in visual narratives (i.e., film and television), the built environment is more than an assemblage of landmarks, although skyline elements such as the Telkom Tower and Ponte City, which stand in for Hillbrow, are a shaping environment, shown to constrain and occasionally to enable rather than merely to house residents or migrants. If, as John

Matshikiza (son of Todd and a writer and actor himself) suggests, Johannesburg is an "unfinished movie" (2008, 222), these films, their characters on the make, the scenes and built environment they inhabit, and the images of the skyline, especially nocturnal images dissolving into darkness, highlight the fleeting perception of an environment whose meaning may lurk between frames.

The "Unfinished Movie" and the Scene of Crime

While *A World of Strangers* had a key character lament that "Johannesburg has no genre of its own" in the 1950s, writers, especially screen writers of the 1990s, found their signal genre in the thriller, in chilling stories of violent crime that captured the sense of dread and uncertainty that pervaded this period. The turn to the thriller may not have been surprising in the city of crime and grime but for the fact that these thrillers were created by filmmakers who had made their names in anti-apartheid activist documentary, tracking the re-emergence of public protest and of the anti-apartheid public sphere in the United Democratic Front (UDF), militant unions in the Federation of South African Trade Unions (FOSATU) and, from 1986, in the Congress of South African Trade Unions (COSATU), which continues to represent unions today. Grouped under the rubric of the Video News Service (VNS) and funded in part by overseas anti-apartheid organizations like the International Defence and Aid Fund, filmmakers identified with VNS risked arrest or worse to shoot guerrilla footage of demonstrations and clashes with police. They made films whose titles such as *Compelling Freedom* (1986) or *Fruits of Defiance* (1991) demonstrated their commitment to "making South Africa ungovernable" as the ANC slogan had it. In choosing the risky practice of filming on the front lines, VNS filmmakers can be compared to the better-known photographers associated with the agency Afripix and more controversially with the Bang-Bang Club, whose members included Ken Oosterbroek, who died while covering violence in Thokoza township just before the 1994 election. In addition to struggle footage, however, VNS members such as Brian Tilley, Angus Gibson, and Oliver Schmitz also made more complex narrative films. Tilley's *Mayfair* (1984) documented the return to this inner-city suburb (near Fietas) of Indians and others who had been expelled by the Group Areas Act in the 1960s and 1970s, and their negotiation of hostile responses from blue-collar whites defending what they considered their turf. In interviews with social historian Nazir Carrim, returnees preferred to live in a mixed rather than a "group" area (Carrim 1990, 156). In 1986, Schmitz collaborated with actor Thomas Mogotlane to make *Mapantsula* (1986). This film, which was initially banned but was later screened at home and abroad, followed the example of Lionel Rogosin in persuading the police to allow the director to film a cop drama at the police headquarters, but unlike *Come Back Africa*, it combined thriller elements including the capture and interrogation of its *pantsula*, or gangster-dandy protagonist Panic (Mogotlane), with simulated struggle footage of Soweto protests against police and rent increases, and concluded with the individualist Panic coming round to expressing solidarity with the role of protestor in which the police had initially cast him. This expression of solidarity, in the form of Panic's final "No!" to police manipulation, has encouraged the identification of this film with "militant revolutionary" products of "Third Cinema" (Maingard 2007, 155), although a revisionist reading by a black critic suggests that the gangster glamour implied by the title, which means something like "gangster dandy," outshines the message of solidarity (Magagodi 2002, 243–53).

Influenced by these anti-apartheid projects, filmmakers attempted to give the chaotic violence of the interregnum a political slant, and thus to provide narrative meaning for disturbing and apparently random acts. The reorganization of the SABC under the watchful eye of the new Independent Broadcasting Authority (1993–2006) and the repeal of censorship statutes prior to the 1994 election brought these former guerrilla filmmakers into the national broadcaster where they made documentaries like *Ordinary People* (1993; by Harriet Gavshon and Free Filmmakers) and new national narratives, as in *Soweto: a History* (1994) by Gibson and others. In particular, *The Line* (1994), a three-part miniseries directed by Tilley and written in part by Schmitz, followed a young activist couple in the period immediately prior to the watershed election of 1994, as they attempt to escape Soweto vigilantes working surreptitiously for police counterinsurgency forces by fleeing to an uncle running an illegal but benign shebeen in a congenial apartment block in Hillbrow, whose thriving interracial community defied the district's criminal reputation.[10] The plot carried anti-apartheid preoccupations, in particular

---

10. I discuss this series in greater detail in "Filming the Edgy City" (Kruger 2006) but its attempt to combine political themes and thriller form provides a useful point of comparison to the darker tone of *Wheels and Deals*.

battles between those associated with the UDF and the rising ANC on the one hand, and disgruntled minority parties with connections to the apartheid regime, such as the Inkatha Freedom Party (IFP) on the other, into the incipiently post-apartheid interregnum. The collusion between the police and Inkatha against activists or "comrades" associated with the ANC in the turbulent period immediately before the elections was convincing enough to provoke IFP death threats to the producers and actors. These death threats did not lead to murder (except for the fictional vigilante eliminated by his erstwhile police allies); the fictional story concluded with the activists and their family and friends celebrating this victory and their triumph over a nouveau riche black landlord who attempted to evict them and other tenants. Nonetheless the final party ends on a nervous note, as the wryly cynical Mozambican who had supplied the comrades with arms to combat the vigilantes warns the more optimistic South Africans against assuming the best of all possible worlds is yet to come.

While *The Line* attracted attention by attempting to render the violence of the early 1990s intelligible by inserting it into a familiar (perhaps outdated) narrative of political struggle and triumph, and had confirmed the ongoing power of this narrative in the political debate it engendered in 1994 and through its subsequent overseas circulation, *Wheels and Deals* (1991) has received comparatively little notice. Written, directed, and photographed by Michael Hammon and coproduced by the Deutsche Film und Fernseh-Akademie and Westdeutscher Rundfunk, the film lingers in the imagination in part because its depiction of cold-blooded violence *anticipated* the crime spike of mid-decade, and thus also the perception of violence as criminal rather than, as during the apartheid era, as an expression of political revolt. The sense that the evaporation of a coherent political narrative made violence appear brutally random had its visual counterpart in Hammon's intensely dark palette, which pushed to the limit nearly opaque black and white images reminiscent of classic noir, especially Jules Dassin's *Night and the City* (1950) and his even darker *Rififi* (1955).[11] Enhanced by the

11. It is plausible that Hammon's DFFA education included access to classic Hollywood cinema and the overseas work of blacklisted directors like Dassin. Richard Widmark, star of *Night and the City*, was a particular favorite with Sophiatown-era audiences, and references to him appear in *Drum* as well as texts by Chapman and others writing during the Sophiatown revival from the 1980s.

FIG. 4.1 Sello Maake kaNcube as BT in Michael Hammon's *Wheels and Deals* (1991). Courtesy of Michael Hammon. Reprinted with permission.

production design by Mark Wilby, *Wheels and Deals* depicts city and township spaces, often in nocturnal images that are almost totally black with only flickering streaks of light on fragments of faces, and so suggests the city's seemingly irredeemably dark future (fig. 4.1).[12] *Wheels and Deals* captured the contradictions of the transition in its portrayal of a young man ensnared in a car-theft syndicate that meets the demands not only of township dwellers underserved by taxis, but also of high-end consumers like the political elite of neighboring Swaziland, by combining the resources of seasoned Soweto criminals, corrupt policemen, and the "lost generation" of young men who traded education for activism or a more inchoate expression of anger in the apartheid period and beyond. Released at the outset

12. The film also has a German title (*Tödliche Geschäfte* [Deadly Business]) but was screened at home and on the festival circuit with the English title and Portuguese subtitles, perhaps for distribution in Mozambique. Hammon shares with Schmitz links to German film and television, but where Schmitz received critical attention at home and abroad for *Mapantsula*, which is still distributed in the United States by California Newsreel, the primary American distributor for African films, Hammon's South African films, *Wheels and Deals* and *Hillbrow Kids* (1999), have been eclipsed by his work as a cinematographer in Germany, on films like *Halbe Treppe* (a.k.a. *Grill Point*, 2002), *Cloud Nine* (2008), and *Halt auf freier Strecke* (2011) by East Berliner Andreas Dresen.

of the 1990s, the film anticipated with eerie prescience the atmosphere of apparently random violence and shadowy agents that would characterize Johannesburg at the height of the 1990s crime wave.[13] It evoked the chaos unleashed in Soweto and suburb alike by the unpredictable violent acts of those doing the syndicate's dirty work. It illuminated the chaos in part by showing the obsolescence of the plots of struggle and solidarity that drove anti-apartheid narratives like *Mapantsula* and that still animated partially post-apartheid narratives like *The Line*.

The plot traces the life and untimely death of BT (Sello Maake kaNcube in his debut film role; see fig. 4.1) who evolves from a naive young factory worker toward the *pantsula* bravado that would characterize the dandy villainous landlord he would portray in *The Line* in 1994. As Schmitz and Mogotlane did with Panic in *Mapantsula*, Hammon uses BT's clothes as an index of his changing social role, juxtaposing his progressively flashier garb not only with the drab wardrobe of the industrial worker but also with anti-apartheid T-shirts and, in the final frames, with the inconspicuous clothing he is wearing when the syndicate thugs shoot him in a muddy Soweto street. *Wheels and Deals* also shares with *Mapantsula* a plot that highlights the power of social conditions over the individual protagonists but, whereas Panic is swept up by the anti-apartheid struggle so that he appears at the end as a militant, even if he does not quite speak like one, BT is shown to be at least partly responsible for his fate. He chooses to abandon the path of resistance to the still-powerful combination of apartheid, capital, and the police, resistance represented by the union man Chippa (played by Ramoloa Makhene, who also wrote much of the dialogue and worked as casting and assistant director) in the quest to get what he wants—revenge, money, love—by whatever means come his way. BT's bravado is shadowed by self-doubt, especially in conversation with the union lawyer and love interest Alsina (played by

13. As Ingrid Palmary, Janine Rauch, and Graeme Simpson noted in 2003, violence associated with theft and burglary, especially car-jacking, increased after the 1994 elections but even more notable than an increase in reported crime was the shift away from rationalizing violence in political terms: "Although the violence that emanated from marginalization during the apartheid era was largely understood [...] as political (and therefore socially functional), continuity in the experience of marginalization during the early phase of democracy resulted in high levels of violence. These *new* patterns of violence were selectively relabeled as 'criminal' rather than 'political'" (Palmary et al. 2003, 104–5; emphasis in original). However, Antony Altbeker has suggested that these explanations need to be supplemented by an acknowledgment that policy favoring community policing and crime prevention rather than investigation and conviction has left criminals on the street to encourage others (2011, 45–65).

the American Kimberley Stark as an Americanized exile recently returned home). Maake's performance brings out his character's impulsive responses to challenges, such as his anger against the overbearing boss who fires BT's workmates and provokes the strike and agitation against union directives. His impulsiveness is highlighted when he rationalizes his first car theft as defiance of all "rules" and displays the stolen car to defy car syndicate leader Shabantu (Dominic Tyawa), who claims to dominate the market. Shabantu, whose name may allude to Soweto Councilman Lucas Tshabangu, who opposed anti-apartheid activity in 1976, blends seduction and bullying to ensnare BT, after he has used his police contacts to apprehend and imprison Chippa while he was driving the stolen car. Shabantu's sinister power rests above all on his ability to present himself as a respectable businessman running for mayor of the corrupt Soweto Council, all the while planning to maximize profits by building a taxi fleet from stolen minivans and leaving his hangers-on to face the risks of acquiring them.

Thus, while *Wheels and Deals* certainly draws on Maake's charm to sustain audience interest in the thriller plot, it does not overindulge in gangster glamour. BT's story forms part of a broader narrative of the turbulent interregnum, after Mandela's release had encouraged high expectations but before the country could elect a government that could begin to meet those expectations. The film depicts the high level of lawlessness in Soweto (to whose denizens the film is dedicated) but, as Bremner's article on crime would later confirm (1998, 53), also heralds the spread of violent crime from the townships, where residents had for decades been victims of corrupt cops as well as petty and organized criminals, into affluent districts, which had hitherto been shielded by a police force dedicated to white minority interests. Departing from the conventional noir plotting and the cover of darkness, Hammon suggests the perverse normalization of violence in the edgy city by showing murder in the light of day. The nocturnal view of the skyline to the north of the M2 expressway, shown as BT drives Alsina into the city, including trophy structures like Jahn's Diamond Building, may conjure the appeal of classic *noir*, but the violent act that turns BT from a car thief to a witness of and scapegoat for cold-blooded murder takes place in the morning. After taking several parked cars at night, the gang snatches a minivan as its white female owner is attempting to drive out of her walled property in an unnamed but clearly affluent northern suburb. Instead of driving away immediately, Shabantu's henchman Sipho (Beebee Mhlombo) shoots her at point-blank range in front of her children and two black servants. Although the cold long shot of the unnamed dead woman who is marked as progressive by the UDF sticker in her rear window is offset somewhat by BT's heated response and Sipho's threats to shut him up, Shabantu's cool collusion with his thugs' attempt to frame BT drains the emotion from the incident. Even though followed by scenes in which Chippa, Alsina, and her senior partner plan with BT to use the latter's testimony to expose Shabantu, the icy tone prevails as the thugs first stab BT's friend and fellow witness in his darkened shack and then mow BT down with a machine gun in broad daylight. The film ends as a crane shot moves the camera from a close-up of BT up to the rooftops, from which distance the body is reduced to detritus in the gutter.

This ending is indeed dark, despite the bright if smoggy light of day, but the director's concluding dedication "to the people of Soweto" suggests a counterpoint to the thriller plot that returns viewers to daily life in the township. The story takes place mostly in Soweto, in the houses, shacks, and shebeens of ordinary people as well as Shabantu's grandiose mansion and the chop shop where his lackeys change car colors, plates and serial numbers, with only occasional forays into the city. The dialogue also plays out in the languages of Soweto, where English is usually supplemented and often eclipsed by Zulu, Sotho, or, in the speech of young men in the film as in the streets, by *flaaitaal*. The environment displays mundane but telling signs of the apartheid legacy such as the scrawled "boycott" signs and the scarcity of steady work or reliable transport; it also shows the illegal but functional responses to that legacy and its chaotic aftermath. The chop shop's efficient work in camouflaging stolen vehicles or in the delivery of an intact stolen BMW to a buyer in Swaziland ground the noirish atmosphere in the socioeconomic realities of the interregnum and its particular manifestation in greater Johannesburg. The wealth gap is depicted not only in the contrast between the shacks, bare houses, and muddy tracks of Soweto and the bright lights, tall buildings, and suburban houses of the city but also in the sinister power of Shabantu, the black man who has enriched himself by exploiting the white system. Further, this film's focus on cars and taxis highlights the links among economic, geographic, and social pathology. In a sprawling conurbation where public transport has, like public space, been degraded for decades, aspirations to freedom can no longer be expressed in the public political gatherings that defined the anti-apartheid era; instead this aspiration finds expression in the consuming desire for a private car. Although it would be followed by better-distributed films such as Les Blank's *Jump the Gun* (1996), Oliver Schmitz's *Hijack Stories* (2003), or Ralph Ziman's *Gangster's Paradise/Jerusalema* (2008), which quotes both Hammon and Schmitz, as well as television narratives that depict the edgy city, *Wheels and Deals* deploys a powerful combination of genre plotting, visual evocation, and social critique of crime in the city that has yet to be matched.[14]

While *Wheels and Deals* followed its central characters from Soweto into the city and back again and remained true to their perception of the city as alien if alluring territory, its successors, especially on television, from *The Line* (1994) through *Yizo Yizo* (1999–2002) and *Gaz'lam* (2002–6) to *The LAB* (2006–9), show blacks at home in the inner city, even if their hold on inner-city districts remains precarious. While the visual narratives mentioned above, including those with avowed educational aspirations like *Yizo Yizo*, tend to rely on thriller plots and larger-than-life characters to capture audience attention (see Kruger 2006, 2009a, 2010a), some offer more modest and ultimately more compelling treatments of ordinary people in the inner city. Like *Wheels and Deals*, *The Foreigner* ends in the death of a sympathetic protagonist, suggesting that those who aspired to thrive in Johannesburg remained at the mercy of unremitting violence through the 1990s. However modest is this film (a fifteen-minute short) by Zola Maseko who later directed *A Drink in the Passage* (see Chapter 2), it merits attention for depicting Ponte City and the surrounding streets as an urban environment both forbidding and magical (as against the derelict backdrop of Darrell Roodt's thriller *Dangerous Ground* starring the American rapper Ice Cube [1997]) and for its anticipation of the topic that would not command cinematic attention until a decade later: the growing presence of African migrants first in Hillbrow, reputedly the densest square mile in Africa even before this wave of migration, and later in Berea and Yeoville, and the rise of xenophobic violence committed by locals against those deemed to be foreigners. Maseko himself was born abroad in 1967 to South African exiles and educated in Swaziland, Tanzania, and at the National Film and Television School in Britain and returned to South Africa only in the 1990s.[15] Although I have discussed this film on

---

14. *Hijack Stories* (Schmitz 2003) modifies the thriller formula in that it reverses the narrative of Schmitz's *Mapantsula*, whose gangster protagonist became an activist. Here, Sox (Tony Kgoroge) is a post-apartheid yuppie actor who hangs out with activist-turned-gangster Zama Zama (Raphula Seiphemo) and becomes sucked into the hijack business on the pretext of creating his character for a lucrative television series about a gangster, only to lose that role to his mentor, Zama Zama, whom the casting director finds more authentic.

15. According to an interview with the BBC on the occasion of a FESPACO Special Jury award for *Drink in the Passage* (BBC, 2002), Maseko was attacked by robbers who claimed that they were targeting foreigners. Even if hard to verify, this kind of claim on the part of opportunistic criminals was often reported in the press in the 1990s.

previous occasions (2006, 2009a), its evocative depiction of ordinary life and the built environment in the inner city call for inclusion here.

At a time when foreigners appeared on television mostly as predators in thriller narratives, *The Foreigner* depicted newcomers as crucial contributors to Johannesburg's urbanity. Koffi (Koffi Kouakou Gervais), a Senegalese Muslim doing a brisk trade in fresher produce than his South African competitors on Abel Road on the border between Berea and Hillbrow, befriends a street kid, Vusi (Bafana Matuta), whom he invites home for a good meal and new imported clothes (designed like Gervais's outfit by a local costumier Mabel Mofokeng), only to be beaten up and killed by envious locals, who rationalize their attack on the foreigner by implying that he not only "talks funny" but may also be an AIDS-spreading pederast. Despite his death at the end, the foreigner is at home here. His flat is in Ponte City, the fifty-four-story apartment building that, by 1998, accommodated many Francophone Africans and their small businesses, even if it was dilapidated enough for the owners to consider selling it to the police for a prison.[16] He walks the streets with a confidence that exemplifies what urbanist Jennifer Robinson saw in 1998 as new modes of "mobilizing" the previously "immobilized spaces" of apartheid (1998, 170). Although Maseko's film does not dwell on the national origins of his protagonist, Simone's essay, published in *blank____: Architecture, Apartheid and After* (1998), the same year as the film was broadcast on the cable channel MNET, demonstrates the hidden but noteworthy impact of networks of informal trade fanning out from Mauride clans in Senegal, who sustain these networks by relying on fellow Muslims to transport goods or to advance money to distant associates (Simone 1998).

The opening image of *The Foreigner*, filmed from a helicopter (production design by Wilby; aerial camera work by Jonathan Kovel) circling the tower, highlights Ponte City by leaving the cylindrical tower seemingly transparent in the city night as the camera pans slowly around the huge neon sign advertising Coca Cola on its roof. The sign indexes the impact of globalization on South Africa as well as the residual glamour of the International Style, while the inhabitants, revealed only later, demonstrate the *glocal* dimension of transnational capital flows as well as the local consequences, in the dilapidated common spaces, of this towering structure's

16. As journalist Lizeka Mda noted at the time, the Department of Corrections was attracted by the internal panopticon provided by the atrium (Mda 1998, 196–201).

inability to accommodate changes of use, function, and governance in a design that had been imported from the international modern register. The soundtrack, composed and played by Gervais, mixes Congolese *soukous* and Senegalese *mbalax* with the local jazz that punctuates films from *Mapantsula* through *Wheels and Deals* to *The Line* but is localized during a dream sequence by a South African female vocalist, Gloria Bosman. Before this epiphany, however, the opening sequence of the sign suspended in the sky gives way to nighttime at ground level, where a sex worker and her client snub two street children asking for money in return for cleaning his car. By day, the foreigner sets up his well-stocked produce stand in front of a 1950s mid-rise apartment block as drably functional as Ponte appears glamorous. The name of the block, Concordia, may be a convenient accident, but Maseko allows these and other details to augment Koffi's peaceable presence as he sells produce to well-dressed local customers and offers free food to street children. Over dinner with Vusi, Koffi reflects on the difference between political freedom in South Africa and the elusive economic freedom that other Africans are still chasing, remarking, "ignorance will kill us." As Vusi sleeps, the scene shifts to Ponte's atrium, where he appears wrapped in a glowing prayer shawl, which unravels and soars from the exposed bedrock at the base past the circular hallways as Bosman's voice sings "Africa Thina" (Africa Is Us) serenading an as yet utopian unity. Despite the dream, the foreigner's difference is marked by his dress, Muslim faith, and his conversation in English rather than the Zulu used by those insulting him with the epithet (*inja* ["dog"]) that blacks once reserved for apartheid policemen. Ending with Koffi's voice-over reiterating "ignorance will kill us," *The Foreigner* is didactic in the manner of the moral tales that shaped African storytelling long before film, but transforms this formerly rural practice by reinventing it on the urban street. *The Foreigner* uses an indigo palette against the saturated black of *Wheels and Deals,* which returns even in documentary treatment of street children, as in Hammon's *Hillbrow Kids* (1999). Maseko's pioneering depiction of the foreigner's search for a home in the edgy city sets the scene for later treatments of this xenophobia and hospitality in television drama with educational aspirations, such as *Yizo Yizo* (especially the final season of 2002, which takes place mostly in illegally occupied inner-city apartments), *A Place Called Home* (2006), or the rough but compelling videos in *Reflecting on Xenophobia* showcased by Film Makers against Racism (2008). These projects, like *The Foreigner,* avoid formulaic recycling of battles between natives and aliens to sketch a provisional drama of hospitality that, by making the supposed foreigner the host and the giver of gifts, challenges rigid distinctions between us and them that shape the post-apartheid as much as similar distinctions did the apartheid city.

Welcome to Our Hillbrow: Natives, Prodigals, and Other Aspirants in Africa's Densest District

While not an evident influence on Phaswane Mpe's *Welcome to Our Hillbrow* (2001), Maseko's *Foreigner* anticipates the generosity toward strangers that is the signature element of the novel's *Welcome* expressed to a degree still rare in Johannesburg. Praised for his depiction of "African cosmopolitanism" (Hoad 2007, 113–26) and "intra-African multi-culture" (Nuttall 2008, 202), Mpe was nonetheless not the first to write blacks back into the inner city nor to invoke an ethics of hospitality to accommodate Johannesburg's diversity. Even after Nkosi's celebration of the "intercultural bohemia" in the "fabulous fifties" had given way to portraits of anxious white migrants to the city in Simon's *Jo'burg, Sis!* (1974) or Roberts's *Outside Life's Feast* (1975), black writers emerged to depict the city from the vantage point of the township, as in Miriam Tlali's *Muriel at Metropolitan* (1975). At the close of the twentieth century, the figures of the native and the foreigner, apparently sharp, if not deadly antagonists, invited juxtaposition with more ambiguous figures whose identification played on the peculiarly South African meanings of "native," which has historically referred not to citizens by birth but to disenfranchised people of color. Taking "native" in its full range of meanings, the cast of *The Line* featured white natives of Hillbrow and nearby districts who would never call themselves natives but are forced by the ever edgier city to see themselves as foreigners. Similar figures include the Greek restaurant owner and patrons in Paul Slabolepszy's unpublished play *Victoria Almost Falls* (1994) or the cantankerous proofreader Aubrey Tearle doing battle with *The Restless Supermarket* (2001), the Hillbrow streets, and other "foul proofs of the world" (304) in Vladislavić's novel.

The representation of the tensions in 1990s Hillbrow between natives and foreigners, as well as tensions *within* each category, might be illuminated in brief contrast to the 1990s legacy of the Sophiatown removals, whose narrative depiction was featured in Chapter 2. Marlene van Niekerk's novel *Triomf* (1994) bears the name that the government gave the district when it moved whites into the territory that it had forcibly cleared of black residents in the 1950s. The Afrikaner Benade family at the center of this novel may appear too trapped in an insular world marked by sex, violence, and fierce family feeling to pay much attention to the imminent election of 1994 that would end the exclusive white welfare entitlements they depend on. Nonetheless, the novel brings the buried past of Sophiatown into the district of Triomf, which had been built on its ruins, by juxtaposing official with vernacular place names, Triomf with Sophiatown and Kofifi, as in the example of the return of Father Trevor Huddleston in a parade past the house in Martha Street accompanied by the African Jazz Pioneers celebrating "Kofifi," and thus anticipating the district's reversion to Sophiatown in the twenty-first century. The novel's depiction of notes and photographs in letters from the family's migration in the 1930s from the rural hinterland to the mixed district that whites call Vrededorp allows the protagonist Lambert to discover that his parents were siblings, a revelation that provokes him to kill his uncle-father in a violent but passing rage (Van Niekerk 1994, 308; 1999, 326). While bilingual writer Michiel Heyns reads the incestuous family secret ironically as the "inbred triumph of Afrikaner nationalism" (2000, 61), critic Nicole Devarenne highlights the undoing of Afrikaner Triomf in the novel's use of an Afrikaans whose promiscuous absorption of English and the words and accents of Coloured and black speakers of Afrikaans belies long-standing ideological claims for purity (2006, 105–20). None, however, note the distinctly urban inflection of this linguistic promiscuity or that the language of the Benades sounds like that of the mixed-up family in Du Plessis's *Siener in die Suburbs*, while the "southern" suburb looked much like Triomf in the twilight of apartheid, with small brick houses and yards littered with broken cars and other debris.[17]

The sanctioned migration of not-quite-urbanized white natives from inner-city Vrededorp to would-be suburban Triomf offers an initially sharp contrast to those people of color who had a more settled urban life than the rural whites did, until this life was disrupted by government orders to clear Fietas, just as Sophiatown had been cleared. But the return of these natives in the 1990s exploded tidy distinctions between natives and foreigners by racial or other markers. Although, as the previous paragraph indicates, other

17. These are not the last words to be said about this complex novel, which both Heyns and Devarenne illuminate. My point here is to bring out the urban dimension of *Triomf* and to place it in an unevenly acknowledged literary history of *urban* Afrikaans, which began around 1970 to depart from the rural and anti-urban bias of Afrikaans fiction and has since produced the similarly hybridized vernacular of Jeanne Goosen and Vincent Pienaar, among others.

districts were contested before Hillbrow, it is above all in Hillbrow whose acknowledged cosmopolitan air has made it appear simultaneously foreign to South African norms and appealing to South African outsiders, where this explosion took its most powerful form. While Slabolepszy and Vladislavić depict with differing levels of irony and sentiment the loss in the 1990s of a Europhile urbanity that the white South African imagination had conferred on Hillbrow in the 1970s, Achmat Dangor writes of migrants of color in *The Z Town Trilogy* (1990) and *Kafka's Curse* (1997) whose historic connection to inner-city districts from Doornfontein in the near east to Fordsburg and Fietas (vernacular name for both Vrededorp and Pageview) in the near west makes them, despite the countermeasures of the apartheid regime, returning natives to central Johannesburg.[18]

Although Dangor's returning natives are neither avowed cosmopolitans nor African in a narrow sense, his protagonists inhabit a Johannesburg opening up, at the turn of the twenty-first century, to a new worldliness. While the title of *Kafka's Curse* does not refer to a built environment (and was in any case suggested by Dangor's editor Vladislavić; see Dangor 2012), it nonetheless casts the protagonist, the Muslim Omar Khan who becomes identified as the Jewish Oscar Kahn, in a cosmopolitan light. "Kafka's curse" is an insult flung at Oscar by his white Anglo-Saxon Protestant (WASP) brother-in-law who despises his Jewish persona and suspects his hidden Muslim identity (9), which is revealed when Oscar's brother Malik, whose imperious religious pride resembles that of the eponymous hypocrite in Essop's story "The Hajji" (1978) (see Chapter 3), claims what is left of his body. Whereas the Hajji's brother and returning native Karim appears to die a natural death, Oscar seems to have been mysteriously suffocated by tree bark. The entwinement of Kafkaesque metamorphosis with the ancient Arabic tale of Majnun, who turns to dust while pining for Leila, links this South African tale of racial passing with multiple cultural flows between Jewish and Muslim, and West and East, across literary traditions from Arabic and Urdu to Afrikaans and German (see Kruger 2001b). Even though Oscar's migration takes him to a quiet suburb rather than the inner city, that suburb also speaks to Johannesburg's complex cultural and literary history. Parkside in this novel, as in *Cry, the Beloved Country* before it and Christopher Hope's *Heaven Forbid* (2002) thereafter, is the literary guise of Parkview (established in 1906). Identified

---

18. My comments here focus on Dangor's treatment of Johannesburg in these novels; for more detailed analysis of the trilogy and its literary sources and contexts, see Kruger (2001b).

initially by its Irish street names and appearing in all three novels as the home of a well-meaning but ultimately impotent English liberalism, the suburb is known for its proximity to Zoo Lake, which its benefactor Hermann Eckstein insisted remain integrated despite apartheid. Since the 1980s, it has been the favorite Sunday park for Indians in Johannesburg, an attachment that would receive satirical treatment in the post-apartheid era in, for example, Zinaid Meeran's novel *Saracen at the Gates* (2009) and Craig Freimond's and Riaad Moosa's comic film *Material* (2012).

While *Kafka's Curse* and Dangor's next novel *Bitter Fruit* (2001) have been published abroad and are therefore better known, his previous novel *The Z Town Trilogy* (1990) was the first to depict in fiction the so-called greying of Johannesburg in context—Hillbrow in the late 1980s—and thus provides a key comparison for Mpe's *Welcome* a decade later. In contrast with the sometimes feverish sensationalism of newspapers reporting on Coloureds and Indians in the inner city in the 1970s, Dangor's fiction draws on his family history of prior residence in the inner city (before being forced out of Fordsburg; Dangor 1998) and concurs with South African Institute of Race Relations (SAIRR) research documenting migrants who were returning to familiar neighborhoods rather than, as the government insisted, intruding on whites-only districts (see Pickard-Cambridge).[19] In *Z Town*, Jane Meraai flees an official Coloured township, which resembles the desperately overcrowded and politically tense Eldorado Park, after the death of her husband, a government-appointed Coloured Representative, at the hands of activists. Instead of choosing one of the older neighborhoods like Fordsburg or Fietas, designated white but reverting in the late 1980s to their historical diversity, Jane finds an inconspicuous dwelling in an apartment block in Klein Street, Hospital Hill, whose grand name of Mount Manor, like many in greater Hillbrow, contrasts with its actual dilapidation and "musty smell of mould and disinfectant" (1990, 46).[20] Here she finds welcome anonymity alongside a

19. Morris's sober analysis of the changing class and racial demographics of Hillbrow (1999) provides an instructive contrast to the newspaper cuttings he deposited in Wits's Cullen Library. Although some articles document plans for urban renewal and the provision of parks and leisure centers, many indulge in sensationalist treatment of crime and misery (see Morris 1971–93).

20. I use the term "greater Hillbrow" to include Hospital Hill (on the southern slope) in the larger view of the district, which extends in vernacular understanding from Clarendon Place and the historic boundary marker of Randeslaagte, one of the original farms on which the city was built, south beyond Hillbrow's official border with Hospital Hill at Pretoria Street, to Wolmarans Street and Joubert Park.

motley group of migrants, including white "expatriates from Mozambique and Angola" and young "refugees from the rich, who smoked *dagga* [cannabis] on the pavements and decried the wealth of their parents" (48), and seeks some measure of friendship with other single women, "divorcees or young widows" (48), which the narrative identifies by station not by race. Jane attracts a lover, Yusuf "Joe" Malik, a Muslim doctor turned Black Consciousness poet, who can neither fully conquer her "sensuous enigma" (59) nor persuade her to share his politics. Dangor highlights the enigma by wrapping Jane in several guises; she arrives from the township in a drab black dress and stockings, changes into cheap but sexy dresses that match the promiscuous flux of life in Hillbrow, but occasionally dons traditional Muslim garb when they visit Malik's family. The narrative departs from a realist depiction of the urban environment at the moment when a bird, which may be Jane, visits Malik in detention in John Vorster Square (86). The occasion allows Malik and Dangor to link this visitation with the Gujarati poet Iqbal's reflection on imprisoned birds, and with other political prisoners like Ahmed Kathrada who have invoked the same poet, and thus with a wider cosmopolitan view that looks beyond the apartheid era encapsulated by structures of surveillance and punishment like John Vorster Square, to the city yet to come.

The year *Z Town Trilogy* was published, 1990, also saw the inauguration of another event in Hillbrow that hoped to usher in a more open city yet to come: the first LGBTQ Pride Parade in South Africa, which took place on October 13. Beginning on this occasion at the offices of the SAIRR in Braamfontein—the anti-apartheid organization that had documented the informal reintegration of the inner city (see Chapter 3)—and continuing into Hillbrow to end at Pieter Roos Park on the border between Hillbrow and Parktown, the parade took in streets that represented a hitherto unacknowledged history of gay life in Hillbrow and the adjacent neighborhoods. Led by Simon Nkoli, the recently released anti-apartheid detainee and founder of Gays and Lesbians of the Witwatersrand (GLOW) (see Nkoli 1995), the organizers emphasized the kinship between anti-apartheid and anti-homophobic resistance, and the ANC issued a statement calling for the "scrapping of all discriminatory legislation" (quoted in De Waal and Manion 2006, 43), even though not all stakeholders were willing to embrace an overt connection with as yet unauthorized anti-apartheid activities and many of the several hundred marchers hid their faces under paper bags rather than more theatrical drag or disguise (12–49). By 1999, despite Nkoli's death from AIDS, the annual parade had grown to include tens of thousands of South African and international participants; the event received the public endorsement of recently inaugurated President Thabo Mbeki, as well as an invitation to include a GLOW delegation celebrating "Pink September" (De Waal and Manion 2006, 126) at the Heritage Day festivities on the weekend of September 22.

This commemoration is striking for both its landmarks and its omissions. The 1999 parade culminated with the honorary renaming of a central corner in Hillbrow, at Twist and Pretoria Streets, in honor of Nkoli, and the documentation by Shaun de Waal and Anthony Manion identifies the nearby Highpoint Centre and the Harrison Reef Hotel's gay-friendly Skyline Bar as key sites for the emergence of a post-apartheid LGBTQ public sphere. They appear nonetheless to have missed the fact that this Heritage Day commemorated the one hundred and thirteenth anniversary of Johannesburg's foundation, and with it, the long history of political parades well before the anti-apartheid era. The parade's characteristic mix of political march and carnival highlights not only its avowed anti-apartheid provenance but also a perhaps unexpected resonance of Bosman's "Johannesburg riot" both in a light and in a serious vein. Bosman's stance of ironic contrariness and his refusal to toe any political line has its echoes in the political and even anti-political fractions and factions of pride participants and the element of play in the parade, but his account of the violent edge of anarchism is also a reminder of the darker side of public parades and their political alliances. While the official invitation to LGBTQ organizers to join Heritage Day parades in 1999 constituted a public acknowledgment of their history in the city and of their future participation in its becoming, as part of the human infrastructure highlighted by AbdouMaliq Simone, the event has not escaped violent responses, including the rape of female participants and, more recently, resurgent homophobia in ANC ranks, both perhaps leading to the return of the event to the relative safety of Zoo Lake in recent years.[21]

In *For the City Yet to Come* (2004b), Simone links the urban spatial practices of transitional Johannesburg to the street-level flows and interactions documented in other African trading hubs from Dakar to Douala but, while

---

21. De Waal and Manion include a first-person account by a woman who was raped by two men in Hillbrow during the night after the 2000 parade and who had to suffer police incompetence and contempt before seeing the perpetrators eventually convicted ("Rose" quoted by De Waal and Manion 2006, 130–31). As reported in the *Johannesburg Mail and Guardian*, violence against people perceived to belong to sexual minorities continues around the country, and the Zuma presidency (since 2009) has seen a resurgence of homophobic rhetoric from public officials (Dawes 2012).

his reflections undoubtedly rest on direct observation, the title of his study implicitly acknowledges the capacity of fiction to conjure into being a city that eludes the designs of planners. Simone's celebration of people as infrastructure, as well as the imaginative dimension of urban spatial practices, recalls *Welcome to Our Hillbrow*, the sole novel by Phaswane Mpe who died—most likely of AIDS—in his thirties. Although published in 2001, the novel depicts Hillbrow in the 1990s, marking dates from the death of a young man from a "strange disease [. . .] AIDS" in 1990 to the FIFA (Soccer) World Cup match that took place in France in 1998 (2001, 1). The narrator's opening remarks contrast the latter event, in which the defeat of the perennially dismal national team Bafana Bafana (the name means "boys, boys"), even before the international competition in Europe, left the city quiet, with the occasion in 1995 when a rare victory for the team provoked reckless celebrations in the Hillbrow streets, which resulted in death and injury. The novel has provoked not only many critical responses, but also imitations like Niq Mhlongo's *Dog Eat Dog* (2004) and Kgebetli Moele's *Room 207* (2006), which share *Welcome*'s attention to the unpredictability of life and death in Hillbrow but tend to celebrate the survival of the fittest with an easy cynicism, in contrast to *Welcome*'s generous if also ironic portrayal of neighbors living or dead, native or foreign, kin or strangers.

The welcome to strangers that is the keynote of *Welcome to Our Hillbrow* echoes in the distinctive public art work designed by Maya Marx, inspired by the novel. By etching the segmented parts of a key sentence from Mpe's novel into steel plates supporting new concrete steps up Pullinger Kop, one of Hillbrow's steepest inclines (completed in 2008), this work enables a corporeal response to the proffered words of *Welcome* (fig. 4.2). The words chosen for the steps come from the end of the first chapter, entitled "Hillbrow—the Map":

> All these things that you have heard seen heard about felt smelt believed disbelieved shirked embraced brewing in your consciousness would find chilling haunting echoes in the simple words. . . . Welcome to our Hillbrow. (Mpe 2001, 27; ellipsis in original)

While rather abstract when read in isolation, this sentence concludes a chapter that traces a detailed map of greater Hillbrow from south to north, "from Wolmarans Street on the fringes of Johannesburg downtown, to Clarendon Place, at the boundary [and the Randjeslaagte Boundary Marker] of the serene Parktown suburb [established by the Randlords more than a

Fig. 4.2 *Welcome to Our Hillbrow*. 2008. Detail of laser-cut steel on concrete tread, Pullinger Kop. Photograph and work copyright by Maja Marx. Reprinted with permission.

century ago but inhabited today by cultural figures like Nadine Gordimer]" (2) and from Berea in the east to Braamfontein and the University of the Witwatersrand in the west (2–3). Written in the second person by an unnamed narrator who welcomes a series of interlocutors (some named, some not) to Hillbrow with direct address as "you," the map is remarkably accurate, even when the narrator shifts from documentary to irony, as he draws attention to the sex workers "near the corner of Quartz and Smit Streets" just south of the notorious Quirinale Hotel, suggesting that "men were advised to beware the menace of increasingly aggressive prostitutes . . . a few men had allegedly been raped there recently. . . . Welcome to our Hillbrow"(5). He goes on to provide directions to "Cousin's Place" implicitly from Park Station, the transit point for migrants since the Reverend Kumalo, and explicitly northward along Twist Street from Wolmarans—"past Esselen, Kotze, and Pretoria Streets"—to Vickers Place in Caroline Street (6) in Hillbrow's original triangle, a few blocks from the boundary marker. The specificity of these directions suggests not only that the speaker knows the route, but also that he has learned it recently. In other words, he is likely not a native, but rather a migrant who wants to show off his newly acquired "native" knowledge to an even more recent arrival.

Despite this show-off element, the itinerary invites readers familiar with Hillbrow to note the author's distinction between well-known sites like the Highpoint Centre and those, like the side street Caroline, which is sometimes confused with the more trafficked Catherine Street on the "border between Hillbrow and Berea" (8), and also to recall the repeated appearance of the Catherine Street boundary and buildings marking it, in particular Coniston Court and Concordia, in the films *The Line* (1994) and *The Foreigner* (1997), as well as the Chelsea Hotel mentioned in the novel. The epigraph from W. E. B du Bois, "this narrative is no fiction," may be Mpe's motto (2001, vii), but the map is no less imaginative for being accurate. Mpe's representation of the dense human habitation in Hillbrow draws on multiple media, words, images, and sounds, from his dizzying enumeration of built structures, whether mundane like supermarkets Spar, Checkers, and OK Bazaar (8), or dramatic, such as the Highpoint Centre, to lyrics and music from Neil Diamond's "Sweet Caroline" (8) to "See the World through the Eyes of a Child" by local band Stimela (25) (Nguni: "Train"), whose name evokes both jazz saxophonist John Coltrane and the exemplary vehicle of migration since *Jim Comes to Joburg*.

He does not, however, mention the two iconic structures that frame the Hillbrow skyline even though they appear on the cover of the book: Ponte City, the tallest residential building in Africa, and the even taller Telkom Tower, which was by the late 1990s the brand of Johannesburg, featured on the city's official website. Reflecting on this omission in an essay "On the Hillbrow Tower" accompanied by David Goldblatt's 1971 image of the structure then known as the Post Office tower, Mpe stated only that he did not mention the tower because his "characters and [he] had no direct dealings with it" (Mpe 2005, 54). Nonetheless, this explanation hints at other pertinent historical facts: the tower was named for J. G. Strijdom, the prime minister who oversaw the removal of blacks from the inner city in the 1950s and was still called by this name in the late apartheid period (1989) when Mpe first visited Hillbrow. Addressing the cover artist, the late Fikile Magadlela "who left this world before [Mpe] could meet him personally," Mpe acknowledged that the tower had become "a symbol of what it means to be in Jozi" and of as yet unexplored "opportunities and challenges posed by change" (54), suggesting a note perhaps more optimistic than in the novel. Published posthumously in *Johannesburg Circa Now* (2005), a collection of verbal and visual essays edited by photographers Terry Kurgan and Jo Ractliffe, who had been working with African aspiring commercial photographers in Joubert Park, Mpe's essay and tribute to the deceased illustrator Magadlela invite reflection on the visual as well as textual imagination of the inner city initiated at roughly the same time as and in a similar location to *Our Hillbrow*.[22]

Like the photographers in the park and like Mpe himself, the characters in his novel claiming rights to "our Hillbrow" are recent arrivals in a district that appears to have no officially native residents, even if it accommodates people who, like Dangor's characters, can claim to be returning natives. In the novel's first chapter, the withholding of hospitality or fellow feeling has an initially "chilling" aspect for the named characters and other migrants (27). The opening pages depict random violence in the streets as well as battles between avowed natives and the people they target as the *amaKwerekwere* (lit: "people who talk funny"; fig: "barbarians") allegedly pouring into Hillbrow from "Mozambique Zaire Nigeria Congo Ivory Coast Zimbabwe Angola Zambia from all over Africa" (Mpe 2001, 26) but as shown by the earlier fictions and demographic studies cited above, those avowed natives were themselves also migrants to the city from impoverished rural areas or unstable townships. The narrator's primary interlocutor is Refentše, whose origins in far northern Tiragalong and whose use of the Pedi language (related to Sotho), as well as his literary aspirations, align him with Mpe. Although Pedi proverbs and other allusions to his home village punctuate the text, Refentše also shares with his author a generosity toward strangers matched by a skeptical response to the claims of blood kin. While he disdains the habits of his cousin (who bears no other name than his family badge) and the latter's friends, who shake down migrants for cash and sex, he is willing to engage strangers such as an unnamed and apparently homeless man in regular and "mutually warm greetings" (16), which anticipate the informal sociology of "*sawubona* culture" (the culture of greeting, using the standard Nguni form which translates as "still seeing you"; see Davie 2008) in the decade after the novel appeared.

While "*sawubona* culture" certainly instantiates the "tactical cosmopolitan" practices documented by formal as well as informal sociologists in Johannesburg, it does not banish the edginess of these encounters. Readers hoping to find in *Welcome to Our Hillbrow* an "unconditional hospitality" of the radical kind imagined by Jacques Derrida should keep in mind not only

22. This project, initiated by Terry Kurgan, Jo Ractliffe, and the Joubert Park Project, brought vernacular photographers and their work in Joubert Park into the Johannesburg Art Gallery, which had historically turned its back on the park. JPP (2000–2009) went on to renovate Drill Hall as a venue for arts, culture, and urban renewal.

the threats of violence between strangers but also the tensions that erupt even in the elective affinities that reimagine kinship. Derrida himself, even as he evokes an utopian hospitality without conditions, recognizes that inclusion and exclusion are "inseparable" (1997, 75; 2000, 79). While the narrator's "you" in *Welcome* addresses characters—and readers—inclusively, it also interpellates characters who do not initially share Refentše's generosity and who thus resist inclusion in "our" Hillbrow. Refentše's fellow Tiragalong migrant and first love Refilwe rejects Refentše's friendship by spreading rumors that her rival Lerato is a foreigner, even though her name (Lerato means "heart") identifies her origin as Pedi even if she hails immediately from Alexandra, which had been a mecca for internal migrants for decades longer than Hillbrow. Yet, in the wake of Refentše's suicide through a "spectacular jump from the twentieth floor in Van der Merwe Street, after he had chosen his *LeKwerekwere* [in the Pedi/Sotho variation of the term usually rendered with the Nguni prefix "ma" (sing) or "ama" (plural)] woman over her" (116), Refilwe begins to come round to his point of view. Eventually, after her experience as a foreign student in Oxford (where Mpe himself studied), and before her own death from AIDS, she learns to appreciate the power of generosity to create elective community in a potentially hostile environment.

Perhaps because he writes "notes from heaven" (29), a place defined less by religious authority than by the power of the imagination, Refentše has an inclusive view and an accommodating ear with which to harmonize the voices of his Tiragalong homies and *amaKwerekwere,* while his compatriot Refilwe learns from living abroad in England with her Nigerian lover to "look at life from many sides" (116) and thus to acknowledge her affinity with *amaKwerekwere* and other erstwhile strangers as the "more widely used term: *African"* (102) is applied to her in England, and to reclaim that affiliation from white natives who might express their disdain for Africans as unwelcome foreigners, doomed like Thomas Hardy's Jude the Obscure, a character alienated by class rather than race, to toil on the edges of English society. This reclamation is expressed in imaginative acts from giving the name Jude the Obscure to a pub that welcomes expatriates, to inviting the reader to see in Refilwe's "expanding consciousness" nothing less than a "welcome to the world of our humanity" (113).

Although Refilwe's death from AIDS, like Refentše's from love, invites the response of mourning that Hoad calls an "elegy for African cosmopolitanism" (2007, 113), the novel concludes in a generous spirit, in recollection of the "fair taste of the sweet and bitter juices of life" (Mpe 2001, 124) and thus, as Hoad goes on to suggest, a eulogy not only for the many untimely dead but also for a cosmopolitan culture that, despite the odds, is "very much alive"

(2007, 114) in Johannesburg. Mpe's portrayal of characters dying and living in Hillbrow and elsewhere acknowledges the geo-pathology of the city and confronts the specter of incurable disease, but nonetheless allows for at least partial redemption from calamity. As *Welcome to Our Hillbrow* concludes, "the memory of those who live with us and after us" is "the archive that those we left behind keep visiting and revisiting, digging this out, suppressing or burying that" (2001, 124). Transforming Mpe's archeological metaphor, the products of the "linguistic chisels" in his characters' hands and in his own recollection in the later essay (2005, 54) into concrete and steel, the *Welcome to Our Hillbrow* steps chiseled into Pullinger Kop in 2008 have done more than

Fig. 4.3 *Welcome to Our Hillbrow*. Laser-cut steel on concrete tread and risers. 2008. Photograph and work copyright by Maja Marx. Reprinted with permission.

merely commemorate the dead (fig. 4.3). The steps not only honor the "desire lines" or "informal paths that pedestrians prefer to [...] official routes" (Shepherd and Murray 2007, 1) and thus aid Hillbrow walkers in scaling this forbidding incline, they also facilitate uses that have given unexpected meaning to Mpe's "linguistic chisels": young students on their way to school in groups or accompanied by elders, including those who appear to be non-English-speaking migrants, have used the words chiseled in the steps as prompts for informal English lessons, reading the words aloud as they move up and down the hill. We shall return to the institutional context for this project and others like it in the final chapter of this book, but it is worth noting here that these impromptu performances pick up a note of hope and solidarity amid the ongoing cacophony of voices and claims in Hillbrow that Mpe's novel had already expressed in 2001.

Hearing Mpe's eulogies as songs of solidarity as well as of mourning suggests an affinity between *Welcome to Our Hillbrow* and the only other novel that stands out on this terrain: *Kontrei* (2003) by the writer known only as Kleinboer. Response to this book at the time of its release focused on the graphic depiction of sex between the narrator, an Afrikaner living in Yeoville with Lungi his partner of sorts and her son Jomo, and a rotating roster of African sex workers in 1990s Hillbrow brothels, especially in the Royal Park and the Quirinale Hotels. *Kontrei*, which translates as region, district, or territory, and here more colloquially as "home turf," invites but also eludes comparison with the elective community of migrants in "our Hillbrow."[23] Both narrators share a sense of solidarity in anonymity, as well as an ambivalent attachment to the linguistic rather than the ideological heritage of their strictly religious families (whether African Christians in rural Tiragalong in the far north of South Africa or Afrikaner Calvinists in working-class Benoni just east of Johannesburg). Mpe's English—witty, slangy, and

23. See reviews of the Afrikaans edition cited as blurbs for the English translation: Antjie Krog notes the narrator's "obsessive" writing and search for sex, and André Brink calls the novel a "fucking good book" (quoted in Kleinboer 2006, i). However, Koos Kombuis (André Le Toit)'s attempt to hail the narrator as an "activist [...] against the bigoted laws of the apartheid regime" (quoted in Kleinboer 2006, back cover) is belied by history. Interracial sex as an act of rebellion appears in 1950s fiction from Gordimer to Themba. Even if one focuses only on Afrikaans, that taboo was broken by Brink's *Kennis van die Aand* (1973; translated as *Looking on Darkness*, which was published in 1974), whose indictment of apartheid includes not only celebrations of sex but representations of torture and other serious crimes, which provoked the state to ban the book. Finally, apartheid laws criminalizing sex across the color line were repealed before 1990; Kleinboer's novel may have transgressed Afrikaner Calvinist notions of propriety but it broke no laws.

lyrical by turns—alludes not only to writers in English from J. M. Coetzee to Thomas Hardy, but also to sources ranging from advertising jingles to the proverbs of his ancestors expressed in their native Pedi. Kleinboer's Afrikaans can be bluntly vulgar, as in "Op die hoek van Leyd en Nuggetstraats in die Goudstad is klont vervang deur kont en hardehoed deur kondoom (on the corner of Leyd and Nugget Streets in the Golden City, *lump* has been replaced by *cunt* and hard hat by condom)" (Kleinboer 2003, 13; translation modified by Kruger).[24] But it can also invoke the Old Testament, citing *Spreuke* ("Proverbs" or "sayings") about the mysteries of *vreemde vroue* ("strange or foreign women")—"For the lips of a strange woman drip honey-syrup (*drup heuningstroop*) [. . .] but her end is bitter as wormwood, sharp as a two-edged sword" (Prov. 5:3–4)—or contrasting Paul's prohibition, "Know ye not that your bodies are the members of Christ? Shall I then take the members of Christ and make them the members of a harlot? [*No*] God forbid" (1 Cor. 6:15) in the New Testament and God's injunction to Hosea in the Old Testament: "Go forth and take unto *thee a whore-woman and whore-children* (*hoervrou en hoerkinders*)" (Hos 1:2; Kleinboer 2003, 33). In the course of his wandering, the narrator alludes to texts from high (Breyten Breytenbach's surreal poetry in Afrikaans) to low (soap opera in English).[25] But, where Mpe's narrator dismisses the Heaven in the "Big Book" as a religious or ideological fiction indistinguishable from the other place whose imaginary terrors "live in the skulls and hearts of the people" (2001, 111) and suggests instead that "God and the gods of our happiness were more likely to be found in Hillbrow and Oxford and Tiragalong" (111), and thus that heaven occupies terrestrial and secular ground in "the world of our humanity" (113), a state of fellow feeling that transcends not only prejudice but also individual striving and competitiveness, Kleinboer's narrator remains, for all his avowed affection for the women whose bodies he rents

24. The published English translation is wordy and euphemistic: "nugget has been replaced by 'nookie' and the hard hat worn underground by a condom [for a different kind of drilling]" (Kleinboer 2006, 9–11). The bracketed phrase is translator Fouché's addition.

25. Kleinboer's scripture is the Afrikaans *Bybel* of 1933. In keeping with its archaicisms, I have used the Authorized (King James) Version rather than the circuitous translation (here: "an adulterous wife and the children of un-faithfulness" [2006, 31]), with modifications in italics to highlight untranslated connotations from the Afrikaans. The book also invites international comparisons; Joan Hambridge's praise, "Kleinboer is the Michel Houllebecq of Afrikaans" (quoted in Kleinboer 2006, i), alludes to the love affair with France that has moved Afrikaans writers since Brink and contemporaries, Breytenbach, and Etienne Le Roux, among others, found inspiration there in the 1960s. This link is reinforced by the book's design; blue text on the plain white cover replicates the covers of Gallimard, Minuit, and other French presses.

but whose lives he bypasses, at one remove from other people. His novel ends not with a shared or imagined heaven but with the defense of turf: the narrator, secure for the moment in his HIV-negative status, offers only clinical observation of behavior, as he turns in the end to his solitude and his obsession with writing, even while Lungi appears to succumb to AIDS and to fatalism as she and Jomo pack their bags and leave. To be sure, the narrator's stringent refusal of the dubious comfort or closure of generic plots, whether thrillers or melodramas, keeps this curious but compelling story free of the contrived climaxes of many other Hillbrow tales on screen or page.[26] But, as a devotee in the "Church of God the utterly indifferent" citing Kurt Vonnegut's *Sirens of Titan* (Kleinboer 2003, 34; 2006, 34), he secures his place for himself alone, even though the women he has known may be ill or dying—and women in the city beyond this fiction continue to suffer violent assault in a country that still has one of the highest rape rates in the world.

While the title of the English version of *Kontrei, Midnight Missionary* (2006), stresses an obvious pun on the missionary position and thus gives sexual and social power to the narrator that he would disavow, attributing it rather to the women whom he pays to satisfy his hunger, the cover photograph by Guy Tillim takes us back to the "world of our humanity" evoked by Mpe, perhaps telling us more about the lives of those living in Hillbrow than the "midnight missionary" allows. This photograph originally appeared in Tillim's book *Jo'burg*, which unfolds literally in concertina format. The series of images follows something of a narrative line, beginning with outside establishing shots of dilapidated, dangerous, but densely inhabited buildings (fig. 4.4) and moving inside to shots of people in hallways and on the stairs, continuing with pictures depicting life, work, and leisure in crowded inner-city rooms. These people range from an old white caretaker to small black children and include young men and women, some professionals like a nurse, many apparently only intermittently employed but evidently surviving in this daunting, dangerous, but still somehow hospitable environment. The book concludes with images of employees from the private eviction firm familiarly

26. In this category, I would place formulaic if absorbing thrillers like the miniseries *Crossing the Line* (Tilley 2005), as well as prose fiction that appears to aim for television options, such as *Stadt des Goldes* (Golden City) by Norman Ohler (2003 [2002]). The latter was published in South Africa as *Ponte City* but despite vivid descriptions of this landmark tower, the story is marred by a rather predictable conflict between criminal Nigerians and the good German journalist. In the light of the photograph and the title *Midnight Missionary* (both likely chosen by the publisher rather than the author), it is plausible that the English translation of *Kontrei* was also marketed on generic lines. Whatever the reason, it has not received the kind of literary attention given to the original.

Fig. 4.4 A fire threatens the Miller Weeden building on Twist Street. © Guy Tillim 2005. Courtesy of Stevenson Gallery, Cape Town and Johannesburg.

Fig. 4.5 Eviction aftermath, Noverna Court, Paul Nel Street, Hillbrow. © Guy Tillim 2005. Courtesy of Stevenson Gallery, Cape Town and Johannesburg.

called the Red Ants, interspersed with the remnants of lives rudely interrupted. As suggested by the nurse's uniform still hanging in the closet among the debris (fig. 4.5), the evicted inhabitants of these and other buildings were not only drifters, but also often people with aspirations to a good life in the city and skills that ought to help them do so.

Street Addresses and Other Mapmaking Essays

Mpe's combination of pedestrian maps of the flatland and the celestial imagination of the welcoming city yet to come may not be the first fiction to track the transformation of Johannesburg's central districts, but it offers nonetheless a distinctive addition to a series that might be said to begin with Dangor's *Z Town* and continue with the evocative visual narratives from *Wheels and Deals* through *The Line* to *The Foreigner* and Tillim's photo-essay to Khalo Matabane's part-documentary, part-fiction film about Somali and other migrants, *Conversations on a Sunday Afternoon* (2005), to Cabral's *Jozi Sketchbook* (2010). It also alludes to the cosmopolitan city that used to be, evoked more than half a century before by Nkosi, Themba, and friends. But these attempts to encompass the elusive and allusive city also invite comparison with the Johannesburg narratives of a writer whose contribution includes not only his own work but also his editorial investment in other writers like Dangor: Ivan Vladislavić. While publishing fiction already in the 1980s, Vladislavić's public engagement with Johannesburg began in the 1990s, with short stories and with his editorial contribution to *blank___: Architecture, Apartheid and After* (1998), an exhibition and anthology of visual and verbal essays on the unsettling spatial practices of urban dwellers in the apartheid, anti-apartheid, and post-anti-apartheid built environment, and continued to explore that environment up to the post-apartheid present. *Blank* has historical and analytical value as a document of 1990s views on built environments—urban, suburban, and anti-urban—but it also plays with this material, mixing fiction and even downright fakery with documentation. "Essay" here should be read generously to include "experiment," the characteristic mode of a writer who has always refused rigid distinctions between documenting and imagining urban space.

The project's title—the word "blank" in lower case followed by a line marking an element that has been blanked out, or is yet to be filled in—registers equivocation; the arrangement of the pieces compounds the uncertainty. The "Map of Contents" plots authors on a grid, A through J and 1 through 13, along with topics such as "fortification," "planned divisions," or "informal invasions," and one or two temporal markers such as "1960s." Although the combination of letters and numbers provides a visible segmentation of the book (and will therefore be used in the bibliography for reference to items in the book), the grid does not appear to arrange author, topic, or location according to a standardized chronological or topographic order or "conceptual map" (1998, 6). A list of "biographies" is included but is initially obscured by the headings that itemize contributions by grid placement first and then only by name so that, for instance, Vladislavić's essay on "Street Addresses: Johannesburg" concludes the list (1998, 17) under "V" but is identified first by its grid position (E11—somewhere in the middle) rather than his name. Further, the "index" of concepts and names of persons and places seems aleatory, as the length of explanation does not always match the theoretical or historical importance of the entry. While District Six, the integrated Cape Town neighborhood destroyed by mid-twentieth-century apartheid fiat, receives a succinct editorial annotation, Johannesburg receives only a series of references to other points on the grid, and Soweto no entry at all, even though this and other townships feature in several entries.

These schemata seem designed less to instruct those who know little about "apartheid and after" than to distract those who think they know with disorienting directions. This arrangement does not prevent the reader from finding enlightening documentation of urban spatial practices in greater Johannesburg, including apartheid social engineering in Soweto, the responses of local architects since Rex Martienssen to the international modern movement, or contemporary accounts of urban planning crises that registered the urgent concerns of the 1990s, such as the tensions between anti-apartheid urban activists and post-apartheid powerbrokers in the ANC (Swilling 1998, E8). Juxtaposed with these elements of excavation, documentation, and truth-telling, however, are those that play with the historical record and thus highlight both the objective difficulty of keeping up with radical changes in South African cities and the volatility of subjective reactions to this experience. For example, Lizeka Mda's short essays on Johannesburg sites she calls "City Quarters" (D10) qualify as journalism in that they record the material evidence of dilapidation, as in Ponte's grimy halls and overcrowded apartments, but draw on literary sources, including Italo Calvino's *Invisible Cities* (1974), to illuminate the palimpsest of different urban environments layered on the same site (Mda 1998, 200). And Stephen Hobbs's "erasure" of street signs and other guiding marks in photographs of the aspiring cultural precinct of Newtown (E10) highlights the dilapidation of a street corner named for nineteenth-century powerbrokers Carl Jeppe and F. J. Bezuidenhout (more recently renamed Miriam Makeba Street) at a moment when "signs of order and regulation [. . .] appeared to function purely as decoration" (Hobbs 1998, 301) while contrasting retrospectively with the site now at the heart of the precinct whose new street names reflect the post-apartheid celebration of anti-apartheid cultural figures like "Mr. *Drum*," Henry Nxumalo, and with Hobbs's expanded view as principal partner of Trinity Session and curator of major urban art projects in the twenty-first century.[27]

Although hidden in the middle of *blank*, Vladislavić's text "Street Addresses: Johannesburg" is exemplary for several reasons: first, his collection of notes represents a synecdoche, enacting in miniature the assemblage of the whole volume; second, it deploys juxtaposition rather than chronological order to spark connections across space and time in a manner that mirrors his overall editorial strategy; third, looking forward, it establishes a mode of composition—note taking, provisional arrangement, and later reassembly—that shapes his subsequent writing on Johannesburg. While Vladislavić has resisted typecasting as "purely an interpreter of Johannesburg" (quoted in Thurman 2011, 50), his work reflects an abiding connection to his adopted city and to what critic Ralph Goodman calls, in an essay on the Johannesburg notes as published in *Portrait with Keys* (2006), the *affect* of this "idiosyncratic cartography" (2011, 279). Vladislavić's fiction, especially *The Restless Supermarket* (2001) and *The Exploded View* (2004), has received more critical attention, notably since the international publication of *Portrait*, the special issue of the South African journal *Scrutiny2* (2006) and a critical anthology, *Marginal Spaces* (Gaylard 2011a), but his writing on the border between fiction and documentary is just as original. "Street Addresses" invites reading in juxtaposition not only with the augmented set of notes published in *Portrait* but also with other pieces from the 1990s that trace the edge between imagined and documented itineraries in the present as well as excavate layers of inner-city districts laid out since the 1880s.

The author highlights this edge by prefacing his numbered notes in "Street Addresses" with an essay on the "unequal exchange of directions" that occurs when strangers in the city ask natives for advice (Vladislavić 1998, 305). The

27. Carl Jeppe represented Johannesburg in the *Volksraad* (parliament) of the South African Republic, which was toppled by the British in the Anglo-Boer War; his brother Sir Julius was a mining, finance, and real estate magnate. F. J. Bezuidenhout owned the farm Doornfontein, much of which was leased to prospectors after gold was discovered nearby in 1886 (Musiker and Musiker 2000, 67, 101, 149). For Nxumalo, see Chapter 2.

standard map of the inner city reproduced on the verso page may offer the appearance of objective information (even if many street names have changed in the decade and a half since publication), but the preface ends by discarding the map that the author identifies with his advice-giving father in favor of the decidedly literary idea, prompted by Robert Louis Stevenson and Walter Benjamin, that "getting lost is not always a bad thing. One might even consider misdirecting a stranger for his own good" (306). The notes that follow juxtapose the lived experience of sites and dates and the pragmatic realism of the author's foil and interlocutor (identified as his brother Branko) who measures chance encounters, such as those initiated by pregnant women and their companions asking for directions to the Marymount Maternity Hospital near the author's house in central-near-eastern Kensington, by "statistical probability" (306), with vignettes that scramble facts and fictions. Although this Kensington is a modest district settled by white workers in 1897 and flavored since the 1970s by South Africans of Portuguese descent formerly resident in Mozambique, the Marymount Hospital was, as Vladislavić notes, the birthplace of generations of white people from across Johannesburg, including the author of this book. Despite its modest appearance, the name of the district alludes to London's Kensington Gardens, a gesture that might have pleased proofreader and amateur etymologist Aubrey Tearle. Although Tearle and his haunt, the Café Europa, in *The Restless Supermarket* were invented by Vladislavić, other cosmopolitan Hillbrow establishments mentioned—namely, Cafés de Paris, Zurich, and Wien (310)—did indeed exist in 1989, the date in the note. Conversely, the note on the Gandhi House on the border between Kensington and Troyeville (established 1891)—marked on Cabral's map by the change from Troyeville's tight grid to Kensington's more irregular streets hugging the hill (rather than by the sign somewhat too far east)—asserts the authority of the National Monuments Council (307), whose plaque identifies the house as the abode of Mohandas Gandhi and his family from 1904 to 1906 but does not mention that the Council identified the wrong house and thus invented a monument, until redirected to his correct abode at 11 Albemarle Street, Troyeville (sketch: Cabral 2010, 54–55).[28]

28. *Portrait with Keys* includes the note on the misidentified house (Vladislavić 2006, 19), as well as a new note on the historically verified one (172–73). Museum Africa now houses a permanent exhibition on Gandhi in Johannesburg with a map showing his law offices and other sites, but there are also private attempts to cash in on his fame, including the Satyagraha Guest House at 10 Pine Road, Orchards, in the house that Gandhi briefly shared with architect Hermann Kallenbach (opened in 2011). For a full list of sites, see http://www.joburg.org.za/culture/built-heritage/gandhi-in-joburg/about-gandhi-in-johannesburg.

Alongside heritage sites, the author chronicles the decline of the Carlton Centre, once the "centre of it all" (307), reduced to an almost empty shell in the mid-1990s, sketches "walking goodbyes" (309–10) tracking the city in the company of friends about to leave Johannesburg for good, and weighs the relative merits with an artist friend Jeff of a "Wall of Remembrance" and a "Hyperama of Sentimental Value" (311), which might owe something to the Crystal Palace in London as well as to its namesake megastore in Johannesburg, but also hypothetically requisitions affect-laden objects from "every person in the Greater Johannesburg area" to recollect the city that "is passing away" (310). This invented space in which "objects hung suspended, attached by nothing but spaces to the names of the people who once loved them" (311) offers a fugitive tribute to this city in which streets and concrete structures appear no more stable than lines on a screen.

This tension between the ironic but loving treatment of "Sentimental Value" and the purportedly sober documentation of streets, structures, and neighborhoods, each of which undergoes transformation on a different timescale, animates Vladislavić's books, from *The Restless Supermarket* to *Portrait with Keys*, but it takes a curious turn in texts that juxtapose narrative with photograph. Although this juxtaposition takes deliberate shape in the pairing of Vladislavić's novel *Double Negative* (2010) with Goldblatt's photo-essay *TJ* (2010), whose title alludes to the license plate marker for Johannesburg that had largely disappeared by the 1980s, its earlier appearance in two temporally and spatially separated texts, the story "The Book Lover" (1996) and the essay on the photographs that inspired it (2005), stages a compelling encounter between fact and fiction, documented and imagined truth. While the story has been read, along with its companions in *Propaganda by Monuments* (1996), Vladislavić's second story collection, as "postcolonial satire" in which the targets of critique include the narrator's aspirations to find in abandoned books a kind of cosmopolitan identity, this story has none of the explicitly political barbs that characterize writers like Salman Rushdie, to whom Gaylard compares Vladislavić (2005, 130–31). Although the author may mock his narrator's attachment to the tattered remnants of urbanity in 1990s Johannesburg, his account of this quest also dwells on—and in—the vividly rendered nostalgia that this character appears to share with the author of "Street Addresses."

Unlike the more famous title story of *Propaganda by Monuments*, which follows an unlikely but hilarious correspondence between a post-Soviet translator and a post-apartheid entrepreneur hoping to acquire one of the Lenin statues discarded by the Russian state for his rural South African inn, "The Book-Lover" makes no emphatic claims for transnational resonance. Rather, it insinuates references to distant places and times into precisely localized vignettes. The story's opening sentences, "I first came across Helena at the Black Sash Fête. Of all the second-hand book sales in Johannesburg, this one had the finest catchment area—good, educated, moneyed liberal homes. Thanks to the brain drain and death itself there is always a large and varied selection" (Vladislavić 1996, 79), introduce Helena as the narrator's object of desire, while locating the story in realistic time and space. After 1990, secondhand booksellers were flooded with books that had been suppressed for a generation: those banned by the apartheid government, alongside those discarded not only by emigrants but also by returning exiles or the heirs of deceased dissidents who might have owned the book in which the narrator first finds the signature "Helena Shein." Possession of Trevor Huddleston's memoir *Naught for Your Comfort* (see Chapter 2) might mark Helena as a liberal of the "fabulous fifties," but it also marks the moment of rediscovery for 1990s readers of an entire generation of writers who had been banned, and of a literary culture fostered by pre-apartheid urban institutions like Vanguard Booksellers (Vladislavić 1996, 81), which served generations of readers, black, white, and other, from the early 1930s to the early 1970s.[29] While the moment focuses on Huddleston's reputation as the "dauntless one" (81) and on the fiction of his contemporaries Herman Charles Bosman and Harry Bloom long enough to activate the historical resonance of 1956, it does not dwell on the political affect of that date. Instead, the narrative turns to another South African title, Sarah Gertrude Millin's novel *The Burning Man* (1952), to stimulate the reader's curiosity about the meaning of "book lover" as the narrator's reflection on Millin's character "God intoxicated" and "intoxicated by sex" (82) segues into the narrator's discovery of an apparent insect bloodstain in the *Pocket Book of Poems and Songs for the Open Air,* which seems to generate first a fleeting "breeze" and then an oddly agitated aftermath: "I found myself in my own breakfast nook again, hot and bothered, with the pungent scent of crushed geraniums on my hands" (83).

These moments of arousal recur with ever greater force as the narrator finds himself confronted, in a series of bookshops and other locations, by Helena Shein's books "doing their utmost to attract [his] attention" (86), as his approval of her interest in "serious" writing (87) from Huddleston to

29. In the 1990s, Phambili (Nguni for "forward"), a bookshop with leftist inventory similar to the old Vanguard, opened at 22 Plein Street, around the corner from one of its predecessor's locations on Joubert, but it too has since closed.

Luigi Pirandello, Ilya Ehrenberg, and Leo Tolstoy, is troubled by her taste in Barbara Cartland's romances. As citations from Cartland's *Ghost of Monte Carlo* and the overheated prose from an admirer's letters found between its pages seep into the narrator's previously sober account of himself, the "book lover" indulges in increasingly obsessive acts, especially after he discovers a black and white photograph, presumably of Helena and her parents, hidden in the Huddeston book. Smitten by her "statuesque beauty . . . her dark eyes, her olive skin" (99) in contrast to the "two dumpy looking Europeans" next to her, he resorts to "ripping off the jackets" of other books, "fondling their boards and flaps" in a vain search for more relics. The story ends after the narrator goes in search of the street corner in one of the photographs and, despite the elapse of more than thirty years between her time and his, apparently finds the house in Orange Grove where he glimpses a woman in appropriate 1950s dress looking "not a day older." As he follows, the "book in my pocket thumped like a heart in my chest" (104). While this story certainly invites ironic amusement (especially as the last words puncture the penultimate melodramatic line with a wry editorial point: "On the cool fabric of her blouse, between her sculpted shoulder-blades, I saw in English Times the legend: THE END—and I walked towards it" [104]), it leaves a residue of affect that persists nonetheless.

The trajectory that the narrator follows from bookshop to bookshop, from the flagship Vanguard to smaller stores like Yeoville Books, traces a legend on a map that marks sites of urban attachment as well as urbane irony. These traces may have their origins in personal experience (Vladislavić lived in the central near-northeastern district Yeoville in the 1980s), but they also revisit the social history of the inner city. In the 1980s, Yeoville still housed long-standing Jewish residents and institutions along with more recent waves of students and bohemians, but over the course of the 1990s, the bohemians, bookshops, and eventually most of the Jews made way for African migrants moving over from Hillbrow and Joubert Park, the inner-city districts to the southwest. While Hillbrow's high-rise built environment encourages anonymity, Yeoville's low-rise moderate density has favored street and community interaction. The evident decline of the district in the 1990s, due to government neglect and informal appropriation (Beall et al. 2002; Roux 2010), and its hoped-for resurgence in the twenty-first century spearheaded by Francophone African entrepreneurs and picked up by the JDA, have been accompanied by the recollections of former residents, including photographer Kurgan's exhibition *Hotel Yeoville* (see Zvomuya 2013) and by the local research of architects, planners, and their students through Wits University

Architecture School's Yeoville Studio (Beni-Gbaffou 2011), which has investigated the complex socio-economy of informal living arrangements that meet residents' needs in the district (Beni-Gbaffou 2012).

Vladislavić does not dwell on Yeoville but his writing follows the route from Hillbrow, the site of his novel *The Restless Supermarket*, through Yeoville to other districts abutting Louis Botha Avenue, the northbound artery on the eastern side of the city, in search of material traces of his imagined stories. Returning to the story in 2005, he published the essay "Helena Shein" on the character and the photographs that inspired her in *Johannesburg Circa Now* (2005), a compilation that foregrounds both Hillbrow and Joubert Park. In the essay, Vladislavić recounts his failure to find a source image that showed all three characters that made his story. Faced with this lack of evidence, he concludes that he "had put together two separate images" (one showing a young woman with an older woman, likely her mother, and another with the older woman and man) but had later "forgotten the process entirely"; the "fictional composite had come to seem so much more like the truth that it caused [him] to invent a source" (2005, 62). He also casts a skeptical eye on his narrator's claim that the house was in Orange Grove (established 1904), noting that the brick houses he identified with northeastern Johannesburg could just as well have been in eastern satellite towns like Boksburg (63). Nonetheless, his "troubling relationship with these anonymous people . . . who now look to [him] like 'Helena and her parents'" expresses an abiding attachment to the urban environment that they appear to inhabit. The bus line may be "no. 30" as in the picture (2005, 60) rather than "bus route 15" (1996, 102) as in the story, but the bus would still take a rider, as it does the narrator, from the bus terminus, formerly Van der Bijl now Gandhi Square, along Louis Botha Avenue, the northbound artery on the eastern side of the city, past Yeoville to Orange Grove, tracing a route that matches the historical journey of families like the Sheins. Although neither narrator nor author allude to ethnicity, Shein means "beautiful" in Yiddish; Orange Grove and Highlands North (also mentioned in "The Book Lover") had, as did Yeoville, substantial Jewish communities throughout the twentieth century. What figures in this trace is not so much a personal attachment that the non-Jewish author may have to Jewish individuals in Johannesburg (which is not the critic's affair), than the ways in which both story and essay code this part of the urban fabric as both Jewish and cosmopolitan. Tied to the 1950s, the thread connects the "bohemia" celebrated by Lewis Nkosi and the Jewish leftist Fanny Klenerman who presided over the Vanguard, but also carries less favorable associations. Both the dark-eyed beauty and her dumpy parents recall the ambiguous portrayals of Jewish physiognomy that persist beyond avowedly anti-Semitic texts like Black's *Helena's Hope Ltd.* (1984 [1910]) to portraits in Nadine Gordimer's early stories and her first novel *The Lying Days* (1953) (Leveson 1996). Unlike Gordimer's ambivalent engagement with her heritage, or the ironically exoticized dark-eyed beauty in "The Book-Lover," the essay on "Helena Shein" affirms familiar, even familial, ties that link author, characters, and the urban fabric that holds them together, as the last words of the essay suggest: "I keep thinking that if 'Helena Shein' and I were to bump into one another, she would recognise me" (2005, 63). Unlike the imagined Hyperama of Sentimental Value in "Street Addresses" with wares culled "from every Johannesburg resident" (1998, 311), this is a site of intimate recognition in the interstices between large structures real or imagined.

It is the interstices between monuments, rather than the landmarks themselves, that give Vladislavić's urban fabric its distinctive texture in the essays from "Street Addresses" to *Portrait with Keys* (2006). The latter's cover image—the implosion in 1983 of Van Eck (built in 1937 as ESCOM) House, a skyscraper with setbacks and a pinnacle that exemplified the Empire Exhibition era's local adaptations of American art deco—may suggest historical documentary, and the table of contents from Point A and Point B may imply a topographical and chronological order to guide the reader from one moment to the next and thus fill the gaps of space and time in the narrator's life. Despite this implication, the book is replete with spatial detours and temporal misdirections, from the mislabeled Gandhi House to the defunct tram lines, which functioned in this reader's memory for several years *after* the "early sixties" when Vladislavić (then still in Pretoria) had them buried (2006, 60). The essays overall span over two decades. One recalls a rare snowfall that occurred in 1981, and others refer to moments after 2000, such as the draining of Bruma Lake (another of the city's artificial reservoirs; east of Dewetshof on Cabral's map) to search for bodies and serial murder clues that, despite this grisly image, inspires a reflection on Johannesburg as "Venice of the South." Although this and other reservoirs of water are man-made, they have been endorsed over the course of the twentieth century by "birds," "grass" (94), and other flora and fauna whose migration to the verdant northern suburbs confirms the naturalization of these cultivated gardens as "socio-nature" (Foster 2012).

Most "portraits," however, probe the rough edges between old and new in the turbulent 1990s. Alert to the narrator's suggestion to "misdirect a stranger for his own good" (Vladislavić 2006, 61), readers should not expect an orderly chronology but should rather treat the epigraphs to "haunted places" (Point

A) and "anachronisms" (Point B) as invitations to undertake their own inventory and reassembly of "Jo'burg and What-What," as the subtitle has it. As suggested by the citation from de Certeau, "haunted places are the only ones people can live in," this process calls for a city walker rather than a highway driver. While the book includes essays on cars, these deal not so much with driving and not at all with romantic notions of freeway freedom, but rather with the problems of parking and locking cars, and retrieving them from guards, thieves, and dubious drifters. The most vividly rendered vignettes focus, like the introductory remarks on getting strangers out of their cars, on scenes of walking and talking. The walker-narrator of *Portrait* may have something in common with de Certeau's pedestrian enunciator, as several readers have claimed (Gaylard 2011b; Goodman 2011; Nuttall 2011), but he is not a *flâneur* in the romantic sense applied by Anglophone commentators seduced by French perfume. The *flâneur* from Baudelaire to his translator Benjamin yokes together the affluent urban stroller, who can afford to ride but chooses to walk, with an idle loiterer (its mundane meaning in French) looking for trouble.[30] Both figures are invariably male, as are Vladislavić's narrators. As I noted a decade ago (2001a, 241–42), and Andie Miller's essays on walking (2010) recently reiterated, women walking the streets in Johannesburg face more risks than pleasures. *Portrait* sketches the overlap between both strolling and loitering, while acknowledging the differences of class and history that separate them.

Portrait's walker-narrator may move in slow motion relative to the vehicles that could mow him down, but navigating Johannesburg streets demands vigilance to distinguish between neighbors and criminals and the wit to see comedy as well as danger in confusing them. Vladislavić's citation of Lillian Hellman's *pentimento* as a guiding metaphor for the layering of memoir suggests that the layers in this memoir, like the Ndebele design under the whitewashed walls of a nearby house (2006, 92), are best explored not by the sharply vertical thrust of the prospector—despite the city's mining history and its reimagination in William Kentridge's animated charcoal drawings in *Mine* (1991), where a coffee-plunger might morph into a drill or a shaft to unearth skulls and other buried relics. Instead the exemplary figure may be

30. In everyday French, *se flâner* means to loiter, as in the sign *Defense de flâner* or "No Loitering." Even allowing for the literary affect accreted by the noun, the *flâneur* from Baudelaire to Benjamin is invariably male and the privileges he claims are not automatically granted any female *flâneuse*; the feminine form has never been common and, for both Baudelaire and Benjamin, would be more likely to be "streetwalker" than "stroller."

the scavenger looking out of the corner of his eye or sometimes only a little beyond his feet. The author of these *Portraits* collects not only scavenged scraps, but the scavengers themselves. He identifies these as neighbors, loiterers, and those passing through, from latter-day hunter-gatherers stealing metal manhole covers to the soon-to-be exiled friends charged with gathering items of sentimental value to be added in remembrance to the Great Wall of Jeff, to the resolute Johannesburger Kentridge himself, who haunts an essay about a scavenger walking over scorched earth "charcoal on the hoof" to find "three porcelain insulators thrown down from the pylons by ESCOM electricians, as beautiful as vases," or a drawing of the same, characteristically marked by repeated erasure "a signature. smudged lines. pencil stubs" (Vladislavić 2006, 127), such as those that feature in animations from *Johannesburg, 2nd Greatest City after Paris* (1989) to *Felix in Exile* (1994) and beyond (Kentridge 2001, 84–100). These images, along with animations of the pylons themselves, the mine dumps, and the mine headgear, stirringly evoke the urban environment inhabited by *Woyzeck on the Highveld* (1993), the multimedia adaptation of Georg Büchner's *Woyzeck.* The play had first reached the Johannesburg stage and Kentridge's attention in Barney Simon's production at the Arena in Doornfontein in 1975, but this adaptation (the first of several collaborations between Kentridge and the Handspring Puppet Company) combined the power of Büchner's proletarian tragedy, the moving force of puppets in close harmony with puppeteers, and the music of migrant workers, to transform the familiar local story of the odyssey to the city traced in narratives from *Jim Comes to Joburg* to *Welcome to Our Hillbrow* Although most of Vladislavić's interlocutors are white, his allusion to Kentridge's sketches reminds the reader of the many more black people walking city streets on a daily basis.

Acts of walking, talking, and observing at street level shape Vladislavić's account of this allegedly un-walkable city, but his subjects are ordinary people rather than tragic protagonists. For his sorties he draws reinforcements not only from contemporaries like Kentridge but from writers and teachers, whether those he knew directly, such as Lionel Abrahams whose poem provides the caption for the imploding skyscraper on the cover of the book, or those who came before, especially Herman Charles Bosman, who appears first as the murderer of his "step-brother in the family home in Bellvue" next to Yeoville (Vladislavić 2006, 44). Although Bosman wrote about the 1926 murder and his subsequent prison sentence in *Cold Stone Jug* (1949), the house bears no plaque or other trace of his erstwhile habitation. Nonetheless, Bosman reappears in Vladislavić's references at the end of *Portrait.* Although unmentioned in the final essay, his spirit haunts the walk that the author takes from City Hall, where Bosman, like his Jeppe High schoolmate Bernard Sachs, observed political speeches, to the Library Gardens outside the Johannesburg Public Library, where Bosman also worked. On the way a strike by security guards is met by police in riot gear, and the ensuing tumult and teargas propel the author and others over the street hawkers' scattered wares—oranges, bubble gum, and sundries—into the library lobby to a scene that "looks and sounds like a market place" (195). With a nod to "The Book-Lover," he adds, "a hubbub as if every unread book had begun to speak at once" and concludes his book with a tactile response to reading matter, "when I lick my finger to turn the page, it tastes like orange juice" (195). Thus *Portrait with Keys* passes "from the company of people into the company of books" (191), while holding on to unlikely but not unheard-of tastes ingrained in their pages. Its last words come to rest in the library building itself, which has housed traces of Johannesburg and what-what since it opened in 1935. This building, which survived the dark days and dank smells of the 1990s, closed temporarily in 2009, but its reopening after renovation on Valentine's Day in 2012 provides the hinge to this anniversary year, centenary of the ANC and of the storied district of Alexandra, and the point of reference for the final chapter.

5 2012: CITY IN THE WORLD

The year 2012 marks the centenary of the African National Congress (founded in 1912 as the Native National Congress) and of the establishment of Alexandra as freehold township for African property owners; it was also the ten-year anniversary of the "iGoli [Johannesburg] 2030" vision statement for Johannesburg as a "world class African city," which appeared in 2002, the year that Johannesburg's metropolitan boundaries were finally settled. Even if the new plan for "Joburg 2040" floated in 2010 suggested that the full realization of the city's urban renewal might take longer than anticipated, the centenaries provided the opportunity for public commemoration of the governing party and of new public structures in Alexandra and Soweto, as well as the inner city, in the years since the Johannesburg Development Agency (JDA) began public-private partnerships to renovate Johannesburg. Under the leadership of Graeme Reid (2001–4) and Lael Bethlehem (2004–10), projects included the restoration of Drill Hall and the construction of the Constitutional Court on the site of the Old Fort in the inner city (both 2004) or the renovation of Soweto spearheaded by Amos Masondo, veteran of the 1976 uprising and Johannesburg mayor from 2000 to 2010, with structures like the much-visited Hector Peterson Museum in Orlando (2002; see

Bremner and Subirós 2007, 80–83) and the rather alienating Walter Sisulu Square on Freedom Square in Kliptown (2006; Goldblatt 2010, 268–69). Temporary installations, from artists' billboards by photographer Jo Ractliffe and others for *Tour Guides of the Inner City* in 2000, to *Hail the Dead Queen*, Mary Sibande's images of "Sophie," a black woman in a royal blue Victorian maid's costume, hung on city buildings in 2010 in tandem with the artist's gallery performances of the role. Public-private partnerships also implemented quality of life improvements, reclaiming residential buildings, regenerating degraded environments—such as Moroka Dam in Soweto (2003), the Jukskei River in Alexandra (2007), and inner-city parks in Hillbrow, Berea, and Yeoville (2007–9)—and developing transport hubs in the city (Faraday, 2003), Soweto (Baragwanath, 2006), or in the partly formalized settlement of Diepsloot (2011).

The very existence of Diepsloot challenges the world-class aspirations of Johannesburg's public planners and the commercial ambitions of private developers. The settlement that began in 1991 as a cluster of shacks in the district formerly known as Halfway House between northern Johannesburg and southern Pretoria is now a "dense dark patch in a sea of surrounding greenery" (Harber 2011, 7), including some formal housing and administration buildings, as well as shacks accommodating at least two hundred thousand people (18–19). The proximity of poor squatters to wealthy estates has provoked ire among the affluent (Bremner 2004, 29–38; Murray 2011, 283–319), and the claims of Diepsloot residents to shelter and other rights have interfered with the expansion of these luxury estates, which feature imitation Tuscan villas (Montecasino) or English country houses (Dainfern), golf courses, exclusive schools, electrified fences, and other services (Czeglédy 2003, 21–46; Murray 2011, 310). Wary of charges of racism, property owners have voiced their dissatisfaction in the guise of newfound concern about frog habitats threatened by shack builders (Harber 2011, 7–18), rather than in explicit rejection of poor black neighbors. However, the fissures exposed by Diepsloot go deeper than the familiar wealth gap between rich whites and poor blacks. They reveal new contradictions between the ANC's promises of a good life for all and the struggle over scarce resources in this settlement and others, such as Orange Farm southwest of Soweto. The battle for resources has been exacerbated by the ANC's renovation of sites relevant to struggle history at the expense of current petitioners. While the redevelopment of Alexandra, including the Mandela Yard Interpretation Centre, new housing, and the greening of the Jukskei, was prompted by the township's historic association with the bus boycotts that erupted three-quarters of a century ago, it purged the flood plain and other crowded areas of thousands of informal settlers, who have been dumped on Diepsloot from the mid-1990s to the present.

While the contradictions exposed by informal settlements do not negate the ongoing efforts of urban renewal, they invite questions about the unequal distribution of resources. These contradictions have provoked popular frustration, whether in direct protest action against corrupt bureaucrats and other perceived fat cats, or in outbursts targeting the even more precarious existence of migrants and other foreigners real or imagined, which exploded with deadly force in May 2008 (Hassim et al. 2008; Film Makers Against Racism 2009; Segatti and Landau 2011a). Despite the establishment of the City Migrant Office, which opened in 2007 before the xenophobic eruption of 2008, and the contribution of researchers and others to better understanding of the aspirations of internal as well as avowedly foreign migrants, tensions at ground level continue to simmer. While efforts to tackle crime and grime had been rather piecemeal in the 1990s, the promulgation in 2002 of the "Egoli 2030" plan signaled the city managers' global aspirations to systematic city management. The transformation of aspirations into urban renewal may have been uneven, but the years since the plan have seen significant developments. The former CBD has become more of a central administration district (hence: CAD) comprising government, corporate, and cultural precincts, as well as trade—developments that have improved order and activity at street level. This renewal has not resolved tensions, but it has made more visible and potentially more manageable the fault lines between the center (or zones competing for central status, from the CAD to putative new CBDs like Sandton) and peripheral zones like Diepsloot, between native and foreign, drivers and walkers, and other binaries that mark the divide between haves and have-nots. Although the reclamation of the inner city has proceeded piecemeal, zone by improvement zone, by the end of the first decade of the twenty-first century it heralded the local effects of collaboration between art and planning to create conditions for work, play, and urban civility.

Before looking at particular enactments of this precarious movement between play and productivity we should review key framing concepts. Jennifer Robinson's suggestion that it is the *ordinary* rather than exceptional or elite modern city that celebrates an "enchantment" with the "production and circulation of novelty and innovation" (Robinson 2006, 7) may be tempered by a necessarily critical *de-enchantment* of the "wonder city" in the face of discontent about inequity and broken promises. However, Robinson's choice of words reinforces the idea that managing the city requires imagining it in new ways. As Henri Lefebvre wrote on the eve of May 1968, at a time of brewing discontent among students and migrants on the Paris periphery, these groups claimed their right to the city through ordinary as well as extraordinary acts. The very act of inhabiting a city entails "play with the elements of the social whole," an activity that has gravity even when playful (1968, 138; 1996, 172). Moreover, artistic practice in the city is effective not because it prettifies surface elements, but because it tests new models of appropriating space and time. As structures of enchantment, public art, performances, and other imaginative representations of "cities yet to come" (Simone 2004b) test the limits of social and imaginative exchange by marking and unmarking boundaries between extraordinary acts and ordinary activity, between subjunctive hopes and indicative facts, between precarity and endurance, and between play and productivity.

Although Lefebvre is apparently not a point of reference for planners or artists in Johannesburg, his vision of the city reached South Africa by way of Bogotá, capital of Colombia. Despite evident differences, Johannesburg's rates of violent crime, especially murder, had exceeded Bogotá's by the 1990s (Brennan-Galvin 2002, 128), and the cities suffered similar high rates of economic inequality and an urban form that restricted the majority's access to resources. Recent communication between Bogotá and Johannesburg has, however, allowed for the sharing of possible solutions in the realm of culture as well as planning. In the 1990s, Bogotá mayor Antanas Mockus, an immigrant from Lithuania, tackled problems of social disorder from chaotic traffic to violent crime by beginning with small but surprising acts, such as deploying mimes to direct traffic. We can describe these acts in the first instance as theatrical in that they drew crowds who applauded or booed the mimes' antics, but in the last instance as performative in the efficacious sense, in that they created space and time for pedestrians and heralded changes in urban planning and practice to enhance public space and public transport. These events were the first in a series organized by Mockus, who proposed remedies to the deterioration of public space in Bogotá such as car-free days to encourage bicyclists and pedestrians, men-free nights for women alone, and restrictions on the hours of liquor sales and gun buy-back programs. Although Mockus's implementation of these quality of life improvements and other attempts to transform "cultural agency" into social action (Sommer 2006, 1–13) had to contend with entrenched moneyed interests in city and regional government (Buendía 2010, 20), popular consensus on these measures allowed Mockus's successor Enrique Peñalosa to implement durable social interventions. Peñalosa invested in green spaces, schools, public transportation, and bicycle paths instead of additional highways, and he mandated the use of public transport at least one day a month (by rotating restrictions on private vehicles) to encourage citizens of all classes to act as stakeholders in these services.

The combination of performative play and social engagement in Bogotá's urban renewal is relevant to Johannesburg because the cities share significant built and social environment features: low density sprawl, sharp income and quality of life inequality, and a history of planning for the rich at the expense of the poor. At the Urban Age conference organized by the London School of Economics, Peñalosa contrasted Bogotá's implementation of "transport as social justice"—spending on Bus Rapid Transit (BRT) rather than on more expressways—and what he called "quality of life equality" despite income inequality—creating parks, playgrounds, and other public amenities—with Johannesburg's struggle to meet its own goals (Peñalosa 2006). In the wake of this conference and the Inner City Summit in 2007, Johannesburg officially added public performance to its existing plans for "enhancing the urban environment, increasing the enjoyment of public space and building social cohesion" (City of Johannesburg 2007, 2). More recently, they have developed the Bus Rapid Transit system Rea Vaya (Let's go), the Portuguese slogan suggesting the influence on Johannesburg not only of Spanish-speaking Bogotá but also of Brazilian cities like Curitiba. As in Bogotá, BRT has been planned to formalize the informal and often dangerous services offered by minibus taxis to and from black districts since the 1980s and in the city at large since 1990 (Venter 2013). In addition, Rea Vaya aspires to provide a more affordable complement to the high-profile provincial project, the Gautrain, which links Johannesburg's Park Station with central Pretoria, and both central stations with the Johannesburg (O. R. Tambo) Airport. The implementation of Rea Vaya beyond the routes between Soweto and the city appears to be stalled, however, casting some doubt on claims that BRT is "eroding the socio-spatial legacies of apartheid" (Foster 2009, 178), as dedicated street lanes and artistically wrought bus stops on the near-north routes to formerly white districts like Auckland Park have yet to see buses.[1]

1. This comment is drawn in the first instance from my own experience attempting to use the BRT network in 2012 and my quest for an explanation for the delay in implementation from Rea Vaya officials. For a professional evaluation, see Christoffel Venter's analysis (2013), which includes comparison with Bogotá and a history of the fiercely competitive and often violent minibus taxi industry, which Rea Vaya has attempted to partly replace by granting taxi owners shared ownership and drivers an opportunity to train as bus operators. Despite an overall optimistic assessment, Venter concedes that the long-term success of Rea Vaya will depend not only on resolving tensions between taxi companies on the one hand and passengers and the government on the other, but also on persuading car owners to use the service, which has evidently not yet happened on the northern routes through more affluent districts.

These impediments, acknowledged and unacknowledged, to enhancing citizens' access to the city have not gone unnoticed; public intellectuals of the so-called born-free generation, who reached maturity after apartheid, have shown a healthy impatience with the government's inability to get beyond its self-representation as the party of liberation to deliver on post-liberation promises voiced in published criticism of "the poverty of ideas" in public life (Gumede and Dikeni 2009). There is also a robust interest in holding the powerful to account, as indicated by nationwide protests against the Freedom of Information (or government secrecy) bill of 2011 or against social problems—for example, housing in the inner city or tensions between taxi companies and BRT passengers. At the same time writers have acknowledged tangled roots as well as uncertain outcomes of these tensions: the obstructionist behavior on and around Rea Vaya fomented by taxi companies eager to capitalize on traffic to the stadiums during the FIFA World Cup in 2010 generated not only media-fueled outrage, but also short stories exploring the anxieties of taxi drivers and other stakeholders (see, for example, Norman 2010). Further, the dissident memorialization by emerging institutions like the Center for Historical Re-enactment reanimates ordinary apartheid history in sites like the former Pass Office and other buildings on the margins of improvement districts to show that the post-apartheid state has yet to overcome structural poverty, inequality, and the deepening wealth gap in present-day Johannesburg.

While the previous chapters of this book have concentrated on the temporal imagination of Johannesburg, and thus on narrative in fiction and film as the medium for recollecting and reanimating multiple strands of history from the familiar to the hardly known, this final chapter will revisit the spatial practices and structures discussed in the first chapter to highlight the excavation and reanimation of space at the present moment. While several artists in this chapter talk of "reactivating" neglected spaces, I prefer to speak of *reanimating* them, because this term highlights the role of people breathing life into spaces, and thus the performative contribution of people to urban life that Simone encapsulates in "people as infrastructure" (2004a). Simone's analogy between human agents thinking and living in the city, and the social networks and structures they create and sustain, emerges from years of observing the informal but effective exchanges among African migrants north and south, but his ideas have circulated globally. Drawing on Simone's concept to illuminate the social turn in American and European performance and installation art, Shannon Jackson argues that evaluating art as social practice requires moving beyond attachment to the idea of art as anti-institutional transgression to pay more attention to "art forms that help us to imagine sustainable social institutions," thus highlighting the appeal and the difficulty of creating and maintaining "forms of inter-dependent support" including the coordinated labor of planning, building, and social repair (2011, 14). The responses to reanimated spaces in Johannesburg indicate, however, that those claiming rights to the city are not content to play the role of "supporting public," but rather demand to be included as agents in the creation of meaningful work and productive networks.

The investigation of spatial practices around and through the built environments of Johannesburg allows us to track the transformation of diffuse space into definite places saturated with meaning. As I have suggested, following Lefebvre, the concept of "structures of enchantment" highlights the contribution of both work and play, the pedestrian and the exceptional, the lived and the imagined to the transformation of "desire lines" into legitimate paths in the city. While the idea (if not the term) of structures of enchantment has historical precedents, most notably in the goal of making Johannesburg "Africa's Wonder City" in the 1930s (an important but unacknowledged point of comparison with current "world-class" aspirations), artists and other citizen-agents today invoke "desire lines" to reflect a more democratic understanding of rights to the city. The term "desire lines" joins the planner's acknowledgment of "informal paths that pedestrians prefer to [. . .] using a sidewalk or other official route" (Shepherd and Murray 2007, 1) with the pedestrian's improvisation and the performers' imagining of new ways through the city. This ongoing emphasis on the ways "pedestrian enunciations" remake the city, in the phrase coined by de Certeau (1991), may invite disdain by those who favor the view from the driver's seat (Graham 2009, 68–69). Nonetheless, despite planning that has favored vehicular traffic in a manner comparable with other sprawling (but richer) conurbations like Los Angeles, 30 percent of all journeys in 2006 took place on foot (Burnett and Sudjic 2007, 198), public transport (including minibus taxis) costs five times what it does in Mexico City (Burnett and Sudjic 2007, 246–47), and the unfinished implementation of planned BRT routes as of mid-2012 suggests that similar numbers still walk. Although most of these pedestrians are poor and black and might prefer commuting on wheels, there is a subculture even among the affluent few who choose to walk (Miller 2010). Urban interactive art that aims at reclaiming the street for ordinary activity as well as exceptional acts may seem odd to those who mythologize the car, but the reimagination of Johannesburg encompasses both the routine and the surprising.

Against the dystopian drama on display in theatres and on television in the 1990s, and the crime thrillers and other bleak stories that still appeal to consumers today, spatial practices on the street have tested new ways of seeing *people as infrastructure*—that is, as valuable elements of urban order rather than as criminals or foreigners, as performers of new modes of belonging and becoming in what I would call a *drama of hospitality*. Especially in an era of intensified migration around the world, Johannesburg and other cities of the south offer opportunities to rethink divisions between natives and foreigners, cosmopolitans and xenophobes, us as them. It is important to remember that most migrants to Johannesburg are South Africans and include speakers of major languages from Zulu and Sotho to English and Afrikaans, as well as border languages like Tsonga or Portuguese, which may be perceived as foreign because they are spoken in Mozambique but which have also been spoken in South Africa for decades. More recently, francophone migrants from the Democratic Republic of Congo (since its 1980s days as Zaire) have been joined by others from as far away as Senegal and (more or less) Anglophone migrants from Nigeria and Ghana. Although contemporary press reports focus on Africans, Johannesburg has also attracted refugees from conflict zones such as the Balkans and other points in Eastern Europe as well as economic migrants from East and South Asia (Peberdy 2009).[2]

Skeptics may argue that a drama of hospitality may be out of place in the wake of violent nativists in peri-urban townships like Alexandra, who in May 2008 attacked those they called *amaKwerekwere* ("people who talk funny"), displaced over ten thousand, and killed over sixty, a third of them South African (Hassim et al. 2008, 1–2). As Loren Landau, Aurelia Segatti, and others at the African Centre for Migration and Society (ACMS) in Johannesburg show, however, these numbers are small in comparison to both the nineteen

---

2. My focus here is on intra-African migrants, because these are demonized by South Africans as *amaKwerekwere*, but Asian and European migration should also be noted. Migration from Eastern Europe was encouraged by the late apartheid regime in an effort to increase the number of whites; this migration continued for a decade or so after the demise of the Soviet Union but later tapered off. Closer ties with India and Pakistan after 1994 led initially to more migration, especially to historical Indian communities like Fordsburg, but the twenty-first century has seen more trade and cultural exchange than new settlement. In contrast, South Africa's new alliance with mainland China after 1994 continues to this day to encourage migration. In Johannesburg, new Chinese settlement in the northeastern district of Cyrildene has outstripped the old quarter along Commissioner Street. Nonetheless, Chinese economic activity in South Africa has been on a small scale compared to China's extraction of resources elsewhere—in Mozambique and Zambia, for example, which proceeds often without employing or otherwise compensating local people.

million on the move across Africa (Segatti 2011, 12) and to the under-documented numbers of people that have unofficially crossed into South Africa since the borders reopened in 1994. Best estimates in the appendix to Segatti and Landau's study suggest that about 6 percent of the total population of fifty million comes from elsewhere in Africa, and about 10 percent of migrants reside in the gateway city of Johannesburg (Segatti and Landau 2011b, 146).[3] To put this in perspective, Segatti and Landau note that Toronto's foreign-born population is close to 40 percent of the whole (Segatti and Landau 2011b, 146), suggesting that even in affluent cities with more stable populations, divisions between host and guest, native and foreign, us and them, require revision. As Landau has argued in an aptly titled paper "Hospitality without Hosts" (2012), the fluid populations of Johannesburg's inner city constitute overlapping as well as competing migrant groups rather than clearly defined fronts of natives versus foreigners. Focusing exclusively on xenophobic behavior obscures the degree to which migrants in the inner city have found ways of coexisting (see videos by Film Makers Against Racism). We may distinguish between sites of poverty and displacement on the edges, which have seen eruptions of violence against alleged foreigners, and inner-city districts whose denizens show a capacity for productive improvisation that manages to reimagine the edgy city in ways that might enable the realization of urban civility in a truly cosmopolitan city. This reading of urban civility takes "cosmopolitan" in its broadest senses, as the acceptance of multiple affiliations and the reimagining of citizenship and civility to include strangers and non-kin. I am drawing here on Ulrich Beck and Natan Sznaider's understanding of the "realistic" cosmopolitanism of transnational migrants, as against the "ideal-typical model" of the wealthy first-world traveler (Beck and Sznaider 2006), and on ACMS representation of migrant practices as instances of "tactical cosmopolitanism" (Landau and Haupt 2007), but would stress that "cosmopolitan" here is less a concept than a combination of affiliations and practices whose improvisation might enact new ways of interacting across multiple desire lines.

Focusing on spatial practices does not mean ignoring historical investigation. On the contrary, excavation of particular places requires attention

3. Although great attention and anxiety in the government and across society have focused on alleged foreigners, the number of transborder migrants to Johannesburg is still dwarfed by numbers from impoverished regions of rural South Africa: in 2010 over 30 percent of the population of Gauteng, dominated by Johannesburg, came from somewhere else in South Africa (Segatti and Landau 2011b, 151–55).

to the competing histories layered there, and thus understanding the multiple meanings and possible answers to the question posed by urbanist Kevin Lynch: "What time is this place?" Lynch addressed primarily architects, planners, and preservationists, but the question provokes the reimagination of city space in art and performance as well as building. As Lynch suggests, "restoration" alone "cannot easily reconstruct the circumstance that created a place" (1972, 32), whether a recognized landmark or a site of repressed memory, nor allow that any such place may bear traces not only of different times but also of a series of actions that may have created, changed, or buried a succession of structures and environments. Although Johannesburg's cycles of demolition and renovation every generation or so may make it seem an unlikely site for archeology or restoration, research on particular sites demonstrates the potential for historical reanimation against amnesia. In some rare cases, a historic structure marks the *places that mark time*, to paraphrase Lynch, in that their successive roles over time help us track not only the history of that one building, but of its neighbors as well. Beginning with the Market Theatre's reanimation of the old Fruit Market in 1976 but accelerating in the last decade with the renovation of Drill Hall as a site of artistic and urbanist experiment, theorists and practitioners from performers and other artists to urban planners both formal and informal have activated and analyzed productive networks linking play and work, management and imagination, planning and performance, belonging and becoming.

From Tour Guides to Passages: Reanimating the Inner City

The heading of this section refers to two projects, ten years apart, which contest received views of the historical city and attempt to imagine and to enact the city yet to come. *Tour Guides of the Inner City* was created by Stephen Hobbs, then curator of the Market Theatre Gallery, in collaboration with the Urban Futures Conference at a moment—the year 2000—when the Johannesburg Inner City office was still struggling to extend urban renewal beyond the limits of the Newtown Precinct, as an ironic response to the proliferation of heritage tours that had begun in the 1990s with destinations as different as Parktown and Soweto. In 2010, another young curator, Gabi Ngcobo, investigated a different corner of the inner city, the building in south-central Albert Street that formerly housed the Pass Office, the brutal initiation point for most black men entering Johannesburg, from the vantage point of her Centre for Historical Re-enactments in a converted industrial space in Doornfontein, once Johannesburg's premier residential district. These two distinct moments are important not only for their originality but because they highlight the long-term networking of organizations that occupy the space between individual creations and major institutions, and the time between 2000 to the present. The key institutions here are Joubert Park Project (founded in 2000; housed in Drill Hall from 2004 to 2009), and Trinity Session (founded in 2002 by Hobbs and Marcus Neustetter and housed at various sites from Newtown in the near northwest to the Maboneng Precinct in the near southeast). Trinity Session was by 2012 the primary curator of public art in urban renewal projects from Soweto to Diepsloot and inner-city points in between, so the perspectives of partners Hobbs and Neustetter are particularly illuminating for their long-term assessment as against newer but more derivative interventions funded by international organizations such as the German-sponsored Goethe Institute.

Before turning to these institutions, we can get a sense of the complexities of collaboration by briefly looking at a project that is better known, especially outside South Africa: Constitution Hill. Opened in 2004, ten years after the advent of democracy, the structure emerged from the remarkable cooperation among different stakeholders, including Constitutional Court judges Albie Sachs and Johann Krieger—who saw landmark potential in the dilapidated structures, including the notorious Number Four prison that the Department of Prisons had abandoned in the 1980s—Gauteng Province and its development agency Blue IQ, the city's JDA, and preservationists in the National Monuments Council, who initially opposed any demolitions. The latter were eventually persuaded that the new Court should replace the former Awaiting Trial Block, incorporating bricks from the demolished building, located on the crest of the hill overlooking both north and south. The complex was thus deliberately placed at a key vantage point in the inner city and designed (by Paul Wygers of Johannesburg-based Urban Solutions) to be open and accessible to pedestrians—in contrast to the Apartheid Museum, which was built on a busy thoroughfare south of the city to fulfill the statutory obligations of its for-profit neighbor and sponsor Gold Reef City to provide educational programming. Since the formal opening on Human Rights Day on March 21, 2004, the Constitutional Court building and contiguous structures (by Andrew Makin, Janina Masojada, and Durban-based Omm Design Workshop) have claimed their place on the city skyline alongside familiar landmarks like the Hillbrow Tower (Law-Viljoen and Buckland 2007). At ground level, the complex's integration of the new court building with the Old Fort, Cellblock Number Four, and the Women's Prison, which now houses the South African Gender Commission, and of museum installations combining the taped voices of former inmates and the live voices of guides who have a stake in the site as, for instance, the children of former inmates or the beneficiaries of constitutional change like provision for sexual minorities, demonstrates the combined power of multiple spatial practices to shape the visitors' experience (Kruger 2008, 2009b). This is an important institution as well as a landmark structure, but since the complex and its functions have been amply documented in the books compiled by museum consultant Lauren Segal (2006) and arts editor Bronwyn Law-Viljoen (2007, 2008), this chapter will focus on lesser-known spaces that deserve more attention.

Although they are not the only institutions that have labored at the interface between art and urban renewal to create works that interact with their environments and the people in them, Joubert Park Project (2000–2009) and Trinity Session (2002–present) and their associates have lasted longer than most, and have shaped the practice and the understanding of this interface more than singular landmarks like Constitution Hill or artworks that may represent their surroundings and inhabitants but that remain aloof from them, such as *Firewalker* by William Kentridge and Gerhard Marx.[4] Trinity Session was incorporated only in 2002, but the company's profile emerged in outline in Hobbs's *Tour Guides of the Inner City*, the cultural program that complemented the Urban Futures Conference, which was organized by Wits University in 2000 and published in part in *Emerging Johannesburg* (Tomlinson et al. 2003). Hobbs's "Erasing Landmarks" photomontage for *blank___* (1998) had imagined the disappearance of urban traces like street names, but his *Tour Guides* project invited conference participants and others to recover the city that had become alien even to locals. The opening exhibition at the Market Theatre Gallery carried the inner city on Atlas's shoulders, as the logo suggests (fig. 5.1); the silhouetted city includes towers Ponte (on the left) and Hillbrow in the center. The gallery displayed a city map around the wall and a scale model on the floor to provide preliminary guidance for the tours to come. A pink bus decorated by Alistair McLaughlin took visitors on a tour of formal and informal drive-in cinemas; a projector was set up at empty walls

4. *Firewalker*, a steel silhouette inspired by women food vendors who carry braziers of coal on their heads to commuter interchanges where they ply their trade, is a beautiful object in a striking location at the southern foot of the Mandela Bridge but, unlike the interactive work that I discuss in the rest of this chapter, does not engage with its real-life subjects or their customers; for a range of essays on the design, construction, and reception of the work, see Barstow and Law-Viljoen (2011). Gerhard Marx, who is married to Maja, has also collaborated with theatre practitioners.

Fig. 5.1 *Tour Guides of the Inner City*, Johannesburg, 2000. Exhibition logo by Stephen Hobbs. Reprinted with permission.

along the route to screen artists' films, and the final screening took place at Top Star Drive-in, abandoned on top of one of Johannesburg's distinctive mine dumps, where animations by Kentridge including *Johannesburg, 2nd Greatest City after Paris* and *The History of the Main Complaint* were shown. Other works included *Under Heaven (Alien/Native)* by Marlaine Tosomi, in which postcards alternating with the words "alien" and "native" were to be dropped by plane on to the Electric Workshop in Newtown where the conference was taking place on July 11, 2000, but they landed instead near South African Breweries (a multinational that now owns a majority share in Miller) and reached the delegates by way of enterprising street children trying to sell them back (Hobbs 2000, 3).

Among images displayed on fifty-two abandoned billboards in inner-city locations, three became the germ of *Johannesburg Inner City Works* by photographer Jo Ractliffe. Assembled from 2000 to 2004, this series of "strips"—four or five still images juxtaposing sometimes views of the same building or street facade, and more often images from separate points along a well-known thoroughfare like Commissioner Street—speaks to curator Hobbs's interest in signs that disorient the viewer who might expect clear directions through the city, as well as Ractliffe's interest in taking pictures that seem inadvertent rather than purposeful. Taken with a Holga disposable camera with the framing device removed, the images overlap in and out of focus and are sometimes separated by sharp edges, more often blurring over the next shot. As

Ractliffe describes them, these images represent a "city of slippages" in which "buildings, people and streets catch you unawares and hover, half-blurred on the edge of your vision" (2004, 10). Images glimpsed fleetingly on the edge of vision would seem to escape explicit scripting; indeed art critic Sean O'Toole suggests that these images are appealing because they "say nothing" (2005, 26). Many strips register images caught as if from a passing car or from a pedestrian's eye seeing a building from an unfamiliar angle. This element of surprise mobilizes the previously "immobilized spaces" of apartheid (Robinson 1998, 170). The images may appear to register less the purposeful pedestrian enunciations that Robinson borrows from de Certeau than a kind of serendipity that might well be dangerous in Johannesburg, but purposeful enunciations can still emerge from them. Although Ractliffe does not use captions or other signposts, her image track along Commissioner Street reminds us indirectly of the literary traces of this long thoroughfare, from Bosman to Sepamla, and directly of Vladislavić; a roof-top pink plastic elephant appearing in several images along the strip may recall (or may have inspired) the ground-level facsimile that opens *The Restless Supermarket* (Vladislavić 2001, 3). These images of Commissioner Street also anticipate political debates about changing street names, including this one and its as yet intact historical reference to the gold-mining past. As city politicians run out of streets once named after mining-era officials or Afrikaner bureaucrats and now dedicated to struggle heroes (Mandela, Gandhi, Beyers Naudé), cultural icons (Miriam Makeba, Henry Nxumalo), or lesser-known ANC political figures, it may well lose, despite the cost to government and private tenants, its relatively neutral reference to the city's emergence from the gold industry.

Despite many images caught in the corner of the eye, some of Ractliffe's strips strike the viewer as formally framed, while others more subtly invoke scenes of scripted action or layered images from other places or narratives. The images that form the strip of Constitution Hill were taken mostly from the vantage point of the rampart, which, in the official narrative of the site, provides the "perfect place to give visitors . . . a physical and historical overview of the landscape in which the new Constitutional Court sits" (Segal and Cort 2006, 125). The strip (Ractliffe 2004, 17; reproduced in larger format in Segal and Cort 2006, 131–32) begins on the left with a low angle shot along the site of Number Four, the former black male prison documented by Gosani and Nxumalo in the 1950s. The rest of the strip, however, places at the center a doubly exposed image from the ramparts of the Court and the built environment beyond and frames this central image with two variations on the same shot from an even higher angle that reduces pedestrians to immobile figures on a model. Other images are less overtly theatrical but still hint at city scripts not of the photographer's making. The strip that traces the Mandela Bridge, which appears in countless logos and other city representations (and more modestly on Cabral's map as a vertical line just east of the Newtown sign), undoes the commercialized image by taking in a random pedestrian on the left. In the center, there are two iterations of a huge headshot the size of the office block behind it. This image from *Tour Guides of the Inner City* (2000) is identified by O'Toole as the "screaming boy" by Ruth Motau (2005, 26), but he also quotes an inner-city resident who claims that the boy is crying from happiness, not pain (20). Motau's image was replaced soon after by an advertisement for Johnny Walker whiskey, but the facade has gone on to host other images such as Mary Sibande's *Sophie*. Far from saying nothing, these layered images offer multiple narratives and interpretations, inviting the viewer to fit them into one or more of a series of scenarios without, however, immobilizing the series into a single master narrative.

If *Inner City Works* seems restlessly to move across formerly dormant urban sites to reanimate multiple traces and dramas within them, *CityScapes* brings more formally scripted acts to sites whose civic meaning might appear more mixed. These performances reanimate both monumental and more humdrum sites in unexpected ways. *CityScapes* (2003), as described by its creator Jay Pather, "juxtaposed South African dance styles against the sites within which they were performed." These included events in privately owned spaces at the opposite ends of Johannesburg's urban spectrum. At the Carlton Centre, symbol of the apartheid building boom through the early 1970s, and of the hollowed-out CBD in the 1990s, "*pantsula* dancers in pin-stripe suits and attache cases . . . play out a story of survival on a moving escalator," while on Sandton (now Mandela) Square at the heart of the upstart but *effective* CBD of Sandton City, close to the new home of the JSE, a group of "Shembe, Indian and ballet dancers" observe an "encounter between a rural woman and an urban skateboarder" (Pather 2005, 66). Despite the public visibility of these performances and their engagement with Johannesburg's late capitalist urban fabric, defined by private ownership of quasi-public spaces, the scene that invites Pather's recollection as well as the video work of collaborators like Ractliffe is the more intimate if not more private *Hotel* (Ractliffe 2007). Representing the *CityScapes* project in *Johannesburg Circa Now* (2005), the text and photo-essay anthology introduced in Chapter 4, this performance took place before a small audience in a room in the Devonshire Hotel in Braamfontein (across the bridge from Newtown) that had yet to see the urban renewal that would revive the district with new hotels, restaurants, and galleries around 2010.

Once described as grand, the Devonshire in 2003 housed "stranded budget travelers" (Pather 2005, 66) alongside other transients such as businessmen and their evening escorts, but became something of a fortress when most of Braamfontein's businesses closed at night. The performance harnessed this space of transient meetings to dramatize an edgy encounter between a slight "small and reticent" younger white man, whom Pather describes as a "typical small business businessman" and a large, older black women, a "new arrival to the city" (66). The vulnerability implied by this description is overshadowed by her bulk and his lightness and by both performers' fragmented monologues, which suggest prior acquaintance—perhaps a scenario in which the woman served as a domestic worker in the house where the man grew up and where she provided comfort to this "strange boy" in the face of unknown anxieties. The encounter in the hotel room varied from moments of quiet comfort and closeness to others of frenetic activity in which the man ran and jumped frantically over walls and furniture while the woman sits musing; the edge of violence and despair raises questions about this and other "lawless spaces" in the inner city (66); the encounter ended as the man collapses on a bed and an apparition emerges from a closet to carry him off. Face caked in white *umcako* (makeup that alludes to the face-paint traditionally donned by Xhosa male initiates), the androgynous figure wore urban leather pants, sunglasses, and brown tulle—the very oddness of which suggested the improvised vocabulary of "belonging and becoming" that urbanists Götz and Simone identified with the new denizens of inner-city hotels. Although this otherworldly figure may seem to have nothing obvious to do with migrants in search of the good life, his spookiness resonates with the zombie characteristics attributed to the *amaKwerekwere*, African aliens allegedly invested with powers to spirit away local livelihood. Even though the renovation of Braamfontein in the decade since this work has added theatres, restaurants, rooftop clubs, and other hallmarks of urban nightlife to the district, the shadows behind the shiny new surfaces remain.

Johannesburg Circa Now documents above all the work of the Joubert Park Project (JPP), whose participants included, in addition to editors Ractliffe and Terry Kurgan, Bea Venter, Joseph Gaylard, and Dorothea Kreutzfeldt. JPP began in 2000 by animating events in Joubert Park, the inner-city park (marked by the black patch south of Hillbrow on the map) that has staged Johannesburg's contradictory history of public space in the social gulf between the gallery and the surrounding lawn, which was by the turn of the century used almost exclusively by inner-city blacks. JPP brought together art photographers and students with commercial photographers who take wedding pictures and the like in the park. Projects included building portable studios to enable portraitists to frame their subjects with theatrical backdrops and displaying both studios and portraits in the gallery that had been ignored by most patrons of the park. Although not mentioned by JPP members, this project had significant historical resonances: as Santu Mofokeng had shown in his exhibition of abandoned studio portraits, "The Black Photo Album," these studio arrangements reflected a century-long, if little-known, tradition in African photography.[5] JPP's work also encouraged further attention to both park and gallery by other artists: Zola Maseko's 2002 film *A Drink in the Passage* (see Chapter 2) registers the resonance of contemporary debates about access to and ownership of the gallery as a repository of art and as an inner-city landmark.

Subsequent JPP collaborations tackled directly the issue of the rights of ordinary people to the city. In 2002, JPP and Trinity Session worked with the JDA and the private firm VMA Architects to formalize informal trade and traffic in Faraday Interchange, a site under the freeway linking a railway siding with an informal taxi hub since the 1990s, by building stalls in response to users' expressed needs (Ben-Zeev and Gaylard 2006; Bremner and Subirós 2007; Deckler, Graubner, and Rasmuss 2006). In 2002, JPP began work on Drill Hall. This historic site of dramas as different as the Rand Revolt and the Treason Trials (see Chapters 1 and 2) had been abandoned by the Rand Light Infantry in the 1990s and was subsequently occupied by squatters and gutted by fire. JPP became the major tenant in 2004 and shared the complex with Johannesburg Child Welfare and later the Keleketla Community Library until 2009, highlighting their common concern with youth as well as urban cultural renewal. Although the public gallery space was dominated by a permanent exhibition highlighting the Treason Trial, the names of spaces within it, such as the Point Blank Gallery, recalled the hall's military history while accommodating temporary but more immediately relevant exhibitions.[6] *Notes to Home* (2006)

5. Before he gained renown for his own black-and-white photographs of South Africans in urban and rural settings, Mofokeng collected formal photographs of Africans, which he displayed in the exhibition "The Black Photo Album: Look at Me." Their poignant reflection of the subjects' aspiration to dignity despite oppression was deepened by Mofokeng's account (1996, 81) of finding these photographs, some from as early as the 1890s, abandoned in the darkrooms of newspapers where he worked in the 1980s and 1990s.

6. The renovations by Michael Hart and associates (documented by Deckler, Graubner, and Rasmuss, 2006) preserve the historic character of the complex, which was built in the Transvaal vernacular style predominantly of brick with a corrugated iron roof painted a characteristic red, while opening up spaces leading to the central parade ground to direct the bright Highveld sun through glass curtain walls into the Point Blank Gallery.

featured exchanges between artists and migrants from Mozambique, Angola, and Congo, and *KinBeJozi*, a collaboration among artists in Kinshasa, Bern, and Johannesburg, displaying work in all three cities from November 2006 to January 2007. Congolese artist Pathy Chindele created *Living/Waiting Room* after negotiations with taxi companies and drivers at the Noord St. rank, who were reluctant to yield any street space that might be used by taxis. Chindele built a temporary structure that served by day as a shelter for waiting passengers and by night as a dwelling for the artist, so he could observe the traffic rhythms over the course of twenty-four hours.

This imaginative engagement with traffic rhythms and the conflicting claims of pedestrians and drivers anticipated a more complex series of events, exhibitions, and performances that together constituted JPP's most ambitious project. *Cascoland* in Johannesburg (2007) was the second is a series of events facilitated by Dutch partners Fiona de Bell and Roel Schoenmakers combining art, work, and social interaction within South African communities, beginning in 2006 with Crossroads, a historic informal settlement outside Cape Town that defied apartheid removals in the 1980s, and continuing after Johannesburg with the enhancement of pedestrian paths and desire lines linking home, work, and leisure sites in the Indian Ocean port of Durban in 2008. The work for Cascoland Johannesburg began well before the formal public festival in March 2007. *Cascoland: Interventions in Public Space, Drill Hall, Johannesburg* (de Bell and Schoenmakers 2008) documents detailed preparations and the festival days, beginning with a "pre-laboratory phase" (2004–January 2007) including a scouting visit in 2005, and the evaluation of the venue, the Drill Hall Precinct, in November 2006 with SharpCity, the group of architects who had restored the complex in 2004.[7] Work continued with a laboratory phase (February 2007) including inner-city research on the denizens of the neighborhood, workshops with local schools and youth groups, and performances and installations designed to encourage locals to participate before the advent of the formal festival. Other collaborators included people working on the interface between performance and social intervention, among them micro-architectural and digital projects led by instructors at Wits, architect Hannah Le Roux, digital arts producer Christo Doherty, urban researcher Ismael Farouk, and Rangoato Hlasane, co-director of the

7. Comments about the laboratory and preparatory phases are drawn from my interview with Cascoland principals Fiona de Bell and Roel Schoenmakers in Amsterdam in 2009. Comments about the public festival are drawn from my personal observations supplemented by the above interview and the published document.

Keleketla Library, later Keleketla Media Project, which would take over JPP's lease on Drill Hall in 2010.[8]

From the outset, this interaction mediated between work and play, informal activity and purposeful acts, to built structures and scripts for the complex I have called the "drama of hospitality." From January through March 2007, de Bell and Schoenmakers lived in Drill Hall, so as to track the everyday rhythm of activity around the building, from the foot traffic at dawn to the taxi jams throughout the day and the sudden intrusion of unidentified sounds at night, and to observe the spatial practices of commuters, vendors, or wanderers. Also in January, Cascoland members Bert Kramer, Jair Straschnow, and Nkosinathi Ngulube acted directly on this built environment by replacing the forbidding concrete barrier around the Drill Hall complex with an open-work steel fence, and by incorporating into the fence retractable steel tables and benches for use by street entrepreneurs, including hairdressers and mechanics. This open iron fence maintained clear sight-lines to secure the threshold between inside and out with three entrances under surveillance, but also reconfigured the relationship between those inside the building and those outside to enable more communication than the old concrete wall had allowed. At the front, on Twist Street, the entrance was identified from March by the "Urban Playmobile," an oblong volume of purple fabric over a steel frame, designed by SharpCity. Although made of flimsier material, the playmobile, with its transient but vividly hued presence in the evolving post-apartheid city, recalled in smaller scale the red InfoBox that marked Potsdamer Platz, which in the Cold War era was a minefield behind the Berlin Wall, as a site of construction and urban imagination in the 1990s, at the time of the radical transformation of post-communist Berlin, the city

---

8. In addition to designing architectural projects in greater Johannesburg, Le Roux also supervised the *Urban (and) Fabrics* project in 2005. Working in what was then an informal mix of manufacture and retail in the long-standing garment district in the inner-city east, Le Roux, Katherina Rohde, and students from the Wits Architecture School created micro-architectural structures (moveable fences, tables, chairs, and so on) to persuade suspicious South African traders to take their wares on to the sidewalk, so as to compete with African migrant traders already used to this practice, and to encourage more interaction with potential customers; see Le Roux and Rohde (2005) and Kruger (2008). These small-scale efforts were later expanded by the JDA's plans to turn the garment district into the city's Fashion Kapitol. For the work of Keleketla, which means "participate" in Sotho and Tswana, see http://keleketla.org. Although former JPP principals Gaylard and Kreutzfeldt are listed as board members of Keleketla and the website promises a link to JPP's tenure in Drill Hall, this link is broken, reflecting the ephemeral character of art and urban practice collaborations, even in this case of ten years of work.

that follows Johannesburg in the Urban Age Project's *Endless City* volume (Burdett and Sudjic 2007).[9]

The formal festival, which ran from March 9–18 in 2007, included performances inside the Drill Hall as well as public art and other playful activities outside, which were free, but it also included opportunities for entrepreneurs to, for example, sell food or fix cars (de Bell and Schoenmakers 2008, 14–15). As the above chronology indicates, however, the borderlines between preparation and featured event, or between laboratory experiment and public performance, tend to blur. Behind the Drill Hall on Quartz Street (one of many whose names reflect the city's gold-mining history), the off-white walls of the long-shuttered cinema multiplex served as an outdoor screen for films on local themes. The Drill Hall itself hosted staged shows such as the Swenkas, dance-parades of men in swanky suits; their name honors former downtown outfitters Kaye and Swank, who catered largely to black customers, many of whom added flamboyant touches to their suits. It also housed overnight gatherings, dubbed the "inner city Xperience," on the rooftop, with dinner and breakfast served in the courtyard between buildings inside the complex. Outside events took place in surrounding streets and in escorted walks along the three-block path from parking at the JAG to the Drill Hall. The organizers deployed high school students to patrol the pedestrian crossings, local women to clean a long-shuttered public toilet dating from the Edwardian Beaux Arts period (which the organizers opened efficiently but without a permit), and members of the Tsusanang Youth Project to install and man a temporary swimming pool in the basement. They also provided space around the perimeter for food sellers, barbers, and car repair services by (primarily Mozambican) mechanics, who used the new retractable iron tables on the fence. This appropriation of street space for pedestrian and performative enunciations of both the ordinary and extraordinary kind is more significant than formal performance inside contained spaces, because they enact claims of rights to city space that cannot be taken for granted here.

Like Chindele's experimental appropriation of taxi space, local artist Maja Marx challenged taxi drivers' impunity on the streets by painting eccentric

9. As I suggested in *Post-Imperial Brecht*, sweeping analogies between post-communist and post-apartheid trends would be tendentious (2004a, 8) but the ambiguous legacies of struggle against oppression and of socialist ideologies, as well as the tensions between the newly rich and the still poor, invite comparative analysis. Notwithstanding the different histories and locations of these two cities, the similarity between these markers highlights their place to urban environments, whose past as well as present have been alike characterized by periods of social upheaval, as well as radical transformations of architectural and street spaces.

zebra crossings for pedestrians. Her "pedestrian poetry" combined the artist's preoccupation with shaping urban and other landscapes by writing on them (Marx 2009a) with practical, if temporary, solutions to conflicts between drivers and walkers. Marx and her collaborators, who included the Mozambican mechanics who set up informal shop in the area by day, worked on the pedestrian poetry at night from one o'clock to five o'clock in the morning—the only time when no taxis were running. They dressed in orange traffic-repair jackets to deflect police interference as well as to reflect the lights of the occasional oncoming vehicle. They painted white lines and script that, at a distance, looked like zebra crossings but on closer approach revealed a series of slogans (2009b). These included statements appropriate to strangers in the district, whether those from the affluent northern suburbs lured to the inner city by a cultural festival, or migrants in search of a livelihood: "I walk in two worlds" marked the crossing between Joubert Park and the JAG (fig. 5.2), which occupy two contiguous but radically separate worlds, and the formerly gracious but now dilapidated art deco apartments on the other side. "These are bridgeable divides" led to the bridge across the railway line, which links Twist Street and the Drill Hall to the Noord St. taxi rank and "I am in and out of place," which marks the point where Twist becomes Troye Street and Joubert Park the CAD. While the migrants were not in

FIG. 5.2 *Pedestrian Poetry: Two Worlds*. Zebra crossing; white paint on tarmac. Bok/Twist Streets. March 2007. Photograph and work copyright by Maja Marx. Reprinted with permission.

a formal sense visitors to the cultural event, their involvement was more than incidental. To complete her designs, Marx had to check them from above; to gain access to the roofs of surrounding buildings, she employed the Mozambican mechanics once again, this time as informal interpreters to talk to their compatriots working as janitors in these buildings. Once complete, the crossings were patrolled by high school students and neighborhood youth (rather than the Western convention of elementary-school children) old enough to challenge taxi drivers who ignored the rights of pedestrians. These crossings served not only as pedestrian crossings, but also as a stage for real conflicts and improvised choreography by Marx between pedestrians trying to cross and taxi drivers trying to run them off the street. While the taxi drivers' aggressive behavior implied that they did not think of themselves as players in this drama, the successful attempt, albeit temporary, to change their behavior for the pedestrians' benefit suggests the potential for productive negotiation as well as play. Neither Marx nor the Dutch organizers of *Cascoland* knew of Mockus and his mimes in Bogotá but their own interventions, especially the re-presentation and reclamation of pedestrian space, suggest an affinity not only with the form of intervention, but also with the social structures that enable or constrain it.[10]

This ensemble of theatrical and social acts, whether avowedly ephemeral or hopefully sustained, is admittedly precarious. Although *Cascoland* impressed on participants the power of performance and other urban spatial practices to bring together people of very different walks of life on precarious urban terrain, local traces of the event were hard to spot two years after the festival. *Cascoland*'s stated objective was "to activate the public function of [inner-city locations like] Drill Hall and Quartz Street by audience participation and mobilization" (de Bell and Schoenmakers 2008, 12). De Bell also quotes JPP's Kreutzfeldt corroborating "a massive influx of inner city audiences to the Drill Hall" (4), but her colleague Hannah Le Roux, reflecting on the source meaning of *casco* as the "hull of a boat," wondered if Cascoland might be less a foundation for durable transformation on the ground than a "vehicle for escape" (quoted in de Bell and Schoenmakers 2008, 155). Some elements of Cascoland were indeed ephemeral. The Urban Playmobile and other temporary structures designed for the short festival have vanished.

10. My interviews with Marx, de Bell, and Gaylard confirmed that Mockus was not a point of reference—but the semblance nonetheless suggests the power of a playful response to problems with urban management and civility.

The playful pedestrian crossings and the spectators who commented on them have also disappeared, leaving ordinary pedestrians to engage in the serious business of daily crossing at their own risk.

Nonetheless, some elements remain while others have migrated to other inner-city sites. The fence/workbench structures around Drill Hall remain in use by the mechanics and other street entrepreneurs. In the surrounding streets, Mozambicans, Zimbabweans, and others who make a living capturing, selling, and hiring out shopping carts (locally: "trolleys") inspired JPP researcher Ismael Farouk to initiate the Trolley Project in the area in 2009, designing new, more mobile carts and working with the city toward legalizing the trolley pushers (Farouk 2012, 308–9). Other buildings in the neighborhood, extending south and east to the Garment District, are today fully occupied by small and medium-sized businesses ranging from legal garment manufacture to the more dodgy—but nonetheless profitable—production of fake identity documents (Gaylard 2009). Architectural researchers Hannah le Roux and Naomi Roux's "social biography" (2012, 312–13) of one such structure shows how the former Medical Arts Building has been transformed, mostly by Ethiopian migrants, into Majesty Wholesalers, selling imported goods or offering Internet services behind doors that still advertise doctors' offices. The organized walks from the JAG to the Drill Hall to introduce visitors to the environment around the venue resonated, on a larger scale, with the fan walks before and after FIFA (Soccer) World Cup matches in 2010, from parking lots or transport hubs to the city stadium in Ellis Park, near Doornfontein, or Soccer City in Soweto, or on a smaller but perhaps more durable scale, projects developed by Johannesburg Child Welfare to establish "safe routes" for children moving between Drill Hall and nearby sites like St Mary's Cathedral (Holtmann 2013).

Hillbrow has seen public art and urban renewal complement the efforts of joint public-private ventures like the Johannesburg Housing Company and Ekhaya (At Home) Neighbourhood Association to reclaim hijacked buildings in the interests of stable working-class and lower-middle-class tenants and to raise the level of urban civility in this dense high-rise district full of strangers to each other and to the city. The unnerving experience of unpredictable encounters persists in the district, as encapsulated in the opening chapter of *Welcome to Our Hillbrow*: "All these things [. . .] would find chilling haunting echoes in the simple words. . . . Welcome to our Hillbrow" (Mpe 2001, 27). But, in the years between the publication of these words and their laser-etched metal markers up Hillbrow's most forbidding hill in Marx's 2008 project, the tension between the "chilling" anticipation of unpredictable, if not always criminal, acts and the persistent attempts, through tracing and retracing desire lines and other modes of conceptual and embodied mapping, to render the terrain legible, or as Lynch had it "imageable" (1960, 9) and thus useable, has not been definitively resolved—but it has been at least mitigated by the combined efforts of residents, artists, and the city. In his analysis of cognitive mapping, especially on the productive dialectic between formal urban planning and the subjective maps drawn and walked by district denizens, Lynch argued that "we need an environment that is not only well organized but that is poetic and symbolic as well" (1960, 119). Although Lynch does not feature in the comments of planners, artists, or residents of Hillbrow, his reflections on the symbolic power of place, like Lefebvre's structures of enchantment, test new "models of appropriating space and time" at the intersection of the "city as art and the art of life" (Lefebvre 1968, 139; 1996, 173), thus highlighting the realist imperative behind the power of imagination.

As part of the long-term urban renewal of Hillbrow that began in 2005 with the renovation of the Hillbrow Hospital on the one hand, and with the Johannesburg Housing Authority supporting tenants' groups to maintain order on the other, the JDA moved in 2007 to upgrade parks and other public amenities in conjunction with Ekhaya. While the renovation of the parks and public institutions has not automatically led to the reclamation of buildings whose absentee landlords allowed their take-over by syndicates and other illegal rent collectors (Murray 2011, 137–71), this work has secured a base for the ongoing work on housing, led for more than a decade by activist Josie Adler of Ekhaya, to improve living conditions inside apartment blocks (Bush and Velna 2011; Sithole 2011; Mabotja 2012) and in public places—in particular, the multiyear Hillbrow, Berea Yeoville (HBY) art and parks projects coproduced by the JDA and Trinity Session (HBY: 2008). Before working with the JDA, Trinity Session partners Hobbs and Neustetter had developed informal contacts in Hillbrow, including Congolese and Nigerian nightclub managers—contacts which enabled them to penetrate the district to a degree rare for South Africans. Even so, Hobbs relates (2007) that, when he and Neustetter went to Hillbrow to take photographs that would later form the core of their portfolio for the Dakar Biennale, they were stopped by men urging them not to carry their photographic equipment openly, lest they be robbed. These men, part of a growing Senegalese community in Hillbrow, became Trinity Session's informants, whose accounts of their journeys overland from Dakar to Hillbrow and whose informal maps of Dakar (reminiscent of those Lynch gathered from residents of Boston, Jersey City, and

Los Angeles) became part of the Dakar exhibition. In Johannesburg again, Trinity Session exhibited these documents with images of Hillbrow storefronts whose French signage suggested Senegal rather than South Africa.

The opening at the University of Johannesburg's Art Museum in July 2007 included conversation with principal informant Ali Jaiteh and others and culminated in an organized walk from the university to Hillbrow (for documentation, see Trinity Session and Ngwedi Design 2008). This seven-kilometer (4.6 miles) outing constituted a pedestrian enunciation of multiple meanings. It drew in part on the example of *Tour Guides of the Inner City* but offered a more complex interaction with layers of past and present in the city from the turbulent 1920s to the apartheid boom circa 1970 to the open-ended present. In the first place, the University of Johannesburg, while functioning today as an integrated post-apartheid institution, occupies the campus of the former Afrikaner Nationalist bastion, the Randse Afrikaanse Universiteit, and its fortress architecture still evokes the *laager* mentality of its founders (see Chapter 3). Moving up and away from the campus, the walk took more than twenty participants (several black and white South Africans and a few European tourists) southeastward along the Brixton ridge, past the landmark Brixton Tower, which served the apartheid regime for broadcasting and surveillance (fig. 5.3). Below the ridge is the neighborhood that fomented the Rand Revolt

FIG. 5.3 *Hillbrow/Dakar/Hillbrow*. Exhibition and walk. Brixton Tower, Johannesburg, July 2007. Photograph by Stephen Hobbs. Reprinted with permission.

of 1922 in which the migrants of the day (English from Cornwall, Irish from Ulster, or Afrikaans from the South African hinterland) rebelled against the government. Brixton had little foot traffic on this Saturday afternoon (but has since attracted arts and culture professionals, students, and other committed or incidental pedestrians; see Davie 2011b). Fietas, the next suburb on, had more foot traffic, but not to the extent of its heyday chronicled by historians (Carrim) or storytellers (Essop). By contrast, Hillbrow was as usual crowded with people willing to sell merchandise—or advice—to members of this procession, as well as to engage them in conversation (fig. 5.4). An Afrikaans reporter from the Johannesburg paper *Die Beeld* described the event as a *staptog*, more like an odyssey or at least a hike than a mere walk or a "tourist outing (*toeriste-uitstappie*)." The term *staptog* highlighted this event's symbolic partnership to Hobbs's and Neustetter's initial hike through Hillbrow followed by their trip to Dakar, as well as the physical demands of six hours of hiking from Auckland Partk to Hillbrow and back (Lambrecht 2007). Acknowledging the occasion *as* occasion (Lambrecht's "first time in Hillbrow since the 1970s") and as the "performance-*deel*" (performance-part; "performance" in English) of the exhibition, Lambrecht also emphasized the cosmopolitan social interaction that characterized the occasion by beginning the article by describing the sharing of food, and the communal watching of a

Fig. 5.4 *Hillbrow/Dakar/Hillbrow*. Exhibition and walk to Hillbrow, Johannesburg, July 2007. Photograph by Stephen Hobbs. Reprinted with permission.

Wimbledon tennis match and the Nigeria-South Africa soccer match on television in Chez Ntemba (a Congolese club chain with a branch in Hillbrow), and by talking to Trinity Session's primary Senegalese informant Ali Jaiteh and others about their changing experience of the district from the mayhem of the 1990s and early 2000 to a situation improved not only by more visible CCTV and police, but also by more civility on the part of the population, and more evident orderliness of apartment buildings and their inhabitants, whom the press has in the past usually depicted as dilapidated or disorderly. Immersing participants in new environments, rather than merely inviting spectatorship of new images, distinguishes this event from many subsequent exhibitions of Johannesburg photographs, however absorbing many of these have been, such as Sally Gaule's *Jo'burg Gini* (2009), which used the Gini coefficient, the standard measurement of the wealth gap in specific countries or cities, as a point of departure for thoughtful images of Johannesburg's extreme contrasts, or Kutlwane Moagi's *Split Facades* (2012), which captured city pedestrians reflected in the shiny surfaces of city buildings that they would be unlikely to enter.

With this context in view, Marx's steps rising up Pullinger Kop, the narrow, steep park on the border between Hillbrow and Berea, reappear in this chapter as part of a larger project of inner-city renewal. While Marx's articulate street crossings to the Drill Hall have long since faded, their legacy and that of Mpe's influential novel come together in more durable form in the concrete steps emblazoned with steel strips etched, word by word, with the quotation from "Hillbrow—the map" (see fig. 4.3). Sounding out the words has become an informal exercise in English practice, and perhaps in repetition a kind of ritual for schoolchildren and their adult companions ascending or descending the hill. Since the majority of Hillbrow residents are migrants, whether internal, from rural South Africa, or transnational, from Africa and beyond, for whom English is at best a second language, this improvisation creates a common ground for people whose paths might not otherwise cross.

Because these performances remain informal and unscripted (in the sense that students and others reading the steps aloud are not subject to a director or a set schedule), they remain largely invisible beyond the circle of people who continue to use the steps on a regular or even occasional basis. Their status *as* performance may well be challenged, certainly if they are compared with the more overtly scripted professional performances staged in Hillbrow during the FIFA World Cup in mid-2010. Of the latter, the series that received the most international attention was *X-Homes: Hillbrow*, in large part because of its international origins. This series of performances in Hillbrow locations included its notoriously broken-down apartment building and the Hillbrow Boxing Club was the Johannesburg iteration of a franchise devised in the original German as *X-Wohnungen* by Berlin-based Matthias Lilienthal in 2002, and later exported to cities across the world from São Paolo to Warsaw (Siemes 2010). In Hillbrow, performances included a mise-en-scène scripted and directed by Mpumelelo Paul Grootboom, who had shocked Johannesburg with graphically violent plays such as *Cards* (2004), about sex workers, their clients, and bosses in a Hillbrow brothel, and *Foreplay* (2009), a local adaptation of *Der Reigen* (*La Ronde*; Kruger 2010b), Arthur Schnitzler's clinical examination of sex and violence, for the age of AIDS. Grootboom's scenario in the St. Antony's apartment building on Wolmarans Street, at the southern edge of Hillbrow, required patrons to climb nine flights of barely lit stairs to a run-down apartment where space in a room was allegedly for rent to share with the owner, two young men, and a woman apparently very ill with AIDS. Their arrival appeared to provoke a fight in which the owner's boyfriend, waving a knife, protested the prospect of another tenant and attempted to get the visitors to take sides. Whether one finds this performance "amazing," as did local reporter Ray Maota (2010) or "social porn," as did German reporter Christof Siemes (2010), or an uneasy mixture of the two, it is undoubtedly unnerving in its intrusion on the intimate space of visitors pulled by sheer proximity and bodily contact into participating in a drama occurring too close to be framed as theatrical (Gillespie 2012). The scenario reproduces not only Grootboom's trademark scripted violence but also a view of lawlessness in Hillbrow that suggested the depths of the 1990s rather than the uneven but persistent revival since 2000. In contrast the performance on the steps, while perhaps only inadvertent, suggests the power of ordinary acts—even if the prompts, in this case the lettered metal strips, may disappear—to claim and hold rights to the city.

While these are small-scale projects, they have formed part of an ongoing collaboration between stakeholders on the street and the JDA. Even in the ongoing negotiation over contested territory, the evidence for greater civility is not merely subjective. The JDA has documented increased local use of the Hillbrow parks as well as neighborhood efforts at conflict resolution. Ekhaya, in collaboration with the South African Police Service, the Community Policing Forum, and Pikitup (city trash collection), has produced better management of buildings by both landlords and tenants as well as improvements in city services (Bush and Velna 2011; Davie 2008; Mabotja 2012). It has also encouraged public interaction with events like an annual Safe New Year campaign to discourage formerly notorious Hillbrow practices like throwing goods and people out of high-rise windows on New Year's Eve, as well as community socialization of new arrivals unfamiliar with urban apartment life. In this context, ongoing artistic projects including not only the *Welcome to Our Hillbrow* steps but also interactive play areas and design projects by and for children using recycled tires, tree stumps, and other found materials in the parks below thus complement the work of socialization or social work in the broadest sense.[11] The interaction among artists, structures, and patrons of the parks also encourages a sense of ownership that has protected them from the type of appropriation that has destroyed more expensive monumental sculpture harvested for scrap metal. As Trinity Session's Marcus Neustetter notes about the steel silhouettes in Donald Mackey Park, also on the Hillbrow-Berea border, and artist Marco Cianfanelli's interaction with the soccer players who inspired the sculptures, these remained intact when the park benches were vandalized "perhaps because they were engaged in the process, [. . .] they have come to appreciate these objects as having added value to the environment" (2011, 37).

While this sense of ownership of public works is not universal—as Hobbs has since noted (2012), toilet parts have been stolen from the Diepsloot Transport Hub because they can be repurposed as long-lasting wicks for lighting fuel—even its partial emergence suggests the potential of urban civility, as does the performance in celebration of a sculpture installation marking fencing in Diepsloot. These may be small steps but they nonetheless suggest that the tenacious collaboration of art and ordinary spatial practices is producing not merely the objects of urban renewal but the subjects, the people as infrastructure, required to maintain it.

Places of Light and Times of Shadow: Pass-ages to Maboneng

As Trinity Session's work shows, the interface between art and urban renewal remains a sharp edge that can produce vanguard experiments but may not include those who attempt to connect the vanguard to ordinary social practices. The gap in Johannesburg between those who see artworks mostly as objects for profitable appropriation and those who aspire to use art to imagine and

11. For information about artists and projects, see Trinity Session and Ngwedi Design (2008). Although JPP was not listed as a group member of the design team, its principal members, such as Farouk, Gaylard, and Kreutzfeldt managed several projects.

to create new social wholes cannot be conjured away but it can, as Neustetter suggests, be negotiated with skill and imagination to the benefit of all stakeholders. To address this question of stakes in the collaborations between art and urban renewal, I will turn to the more recent development of another district, whose success as an urban environment will rest not only on the gentrification of buildings and blocks that attract cultural producers and consumers, but on its effective integration of non-artistic inhabitants of nearby informally repurposed structures, who sometimes find employment working in gentrifying enterprises, and also seek broader rights to call the district home. I have in view the southeastern edge of the inner city, at the opposite end from the near-northwestern Newtown Cultural Precinct, which began nearly forty years ago. The new developments include not only a designated arts precinct, Maboneng or "Place of Light," which was inaugurated in 2009 in the district whose historical name, "City and Suburban," still recalls the era of mining concessions, but also less visible projects in neighboring Marshalltown to the west and Doornfontein to the northeast. The gentrified portion of the precinct extends little more than two blocks along Fox Street (fig. 5.5), the street

Fig. 5.5 Industry and art in City and Suburban, Johannesburg, March 2012. Photograph copyright by Loren Kruger.

Fig. 5.6 Jewel City Wall, Johannesburg, March 2012. Photograph copyright by Loren Krüger.

that leads to the formerly grand but now rather shabby Carlton Centre more than a kilometer further east, if the road were not blocked by the fenced and guarded Diamond Precinct (fig. 5.6). Nonetheless, the developers claim on the dedicated website that Maboneng is an "integrated urban neighborhood." It touts its urban aspirations under the address of Main Street, which runs parallel to Fox a block to the south, between the refurbished brick compound of Arts on Main (2009) and the new structure Main Street Life (2011), two blocks west, even though the entrance and street addresses are on Fox. Arts on Main includes branches of long-standing institutions like the Goodman Gallery, which stages intimate performances for festivals such as Dancing All over Johannesburg (2012; see Kruger 2013, 97), and studios of renowned artists like Kentridge, alongside the work of younger artists and entrepreneurs, and outlets for design companies such as Black Coffee and Love Jozi. These companies and others were commissioned to each design a room in the 12 Decade Hotel, the "art hotel" on the top floor of Main Street Life, which has upscale apartments on the lower floors. Each room in the hotel features furniture and fittings inspired in some way by one of the city's twelve decades. One block north on Commissioner Street in a former factory is Trinity Session's unadorned exhibition space, which housed the company's tenth anniversary light and photograph show in March 2012 and which the Maboneng website imagines as the future home of a Museum of African Design (MOAD).

Before returning to Maboneng, we should look briefly at artistic projects on the shadowy margins of this Place of Light. While Maboneng celebrates the city's aspirations for future affluence in a precinct that combines high art with relatively expensive accommodation to attract young, upwardly mobile urbanites, the grandly named but modestly housed Center for Historical Reenactment (CHR 2010–2012; located in a repurposed industrial building in End Street, Doornfontein, owned by former JPP principal Bea Venter) gathers artists primarily of the post-apartheid generation in a collaborative effort to explore the meaning of specific times and places, in particular the ordinary, everyday aspects of apartheid legacy eclipsed by official exhibitions of the struggle's heroes. Where JPP's reanimation of Drill Hall had acknowledged its long history but memorialized chiefly the heroic part of the Treason Trials in its permanent exhibition, CHR curator Gabi Ngcobo and her colleagues chose to "reactivate" the former Pass Office at 80 Albert Street, on the southern edge of the inner city in Marshalltown, where the daily routines of apartheid bureaucrats had made criminals of ordinary South Africans, including older relatives of the artists, who sought a livelihood in the city.[12] The building and its business had been incorporated into cultural representation decades before in the recollections of Fugard, whose brief employment there inspired his first play, *No Good Friday* (1958), and the work of his collaborators Kani and Ntshona, who created *Sizwe Bansi Is Dead* (1972) in response to a photograph of a man whose broad smile and new suit portrayed in their expert view a man with his pass in order (image: Kruger 1999, 157). Although abandoned even before the end of apartheid as indicated by Goldblatt's 1991 photograph of the entrance with scars on the concrete where the official metal signs had been (2010, 257), the former Pass Office was in 2010 not completely invisible: the Johannesburg Housing Company had built the Elangeni (In the Sun) housing complex in the same street in 2002 (Bremner and Subirós 2007, 104–7) and the Albert Street School had opened to accommodate refugee children sheltered at the time in the Central Methodist Church several blocks north on Pritchard Street. In May 2010, the school

12. Ngcobo's reactivation of the term "reactivate" (Jacobs 2010), used by Cascoland and JPP in 2007, is probably no coincidence, given that CHR shared space in a building reclaimed for residential, work, and exhibition purposes by Bea Venter more than a decade ago.

had hosted performances and exhibitions by the children presided over by the Methodist bishop of Johannesburg, Paul Verryn, and the Solidarity Peace Trust leader Reason Machengere, from Zimbabwe (Berger and Steyn 2010).

Running from July 24 to August 1, 2010, *Pass-ages: References and Footnotes* took as its primary point of departure the pass or "reference book" that all people designated Bantu were required to carry by the apartheid government, and its various aliases, from the vernacular Afrikaans *dompas* (stupid pass) used by those who had to carry it, to the official Afrikaans *bewysboek*, which, as Louise Bethlehem notes, means "proof-book" (Bethlehem 2010), and thus designates a document that was supposed to prove the bearer's legitimate access to the city but, as the poems by Serote and Sepamla attest (discussed in Chapter 3), more often gave the authorities an excuse to declare the carrier out of bounds. The exhibition also revived a key photograph published in *Drum*, "Young Boy Stopped for his Pass as White Plainclothesman Looks On," whose title omits a crucial player in this picture: the black uniformed policeman who was required to humiliate his fellow African in front of his white boss. The photograph by Ernest Cole was displayed in multiple iterations on a wall in the unadorned space. The posthumous legacy of the photographer was commemorated not only by the reiteration of his picture but also by documentation of his life by collaborator Sean Jacobs published in the exhibition "newspaper": born black as Ernest Levi Tsoalane Kole, he applied to be classified "Coloured" in 1966 (Jacobs 2010), which freed him from the requirement of carrying the pass. but not of the indignities of segregation that applied to all so-called non-whites. This history of racial discrimination at once personal and collective was reanimated by Kemang wa Lehulere, whose video installation reenacted the "pencil test," the arbitrary but fateful routine enacted by apartheid bureaucrats who declared that hair that gripped the pencil inserted there had to be "Bantu," whereas hair that let the pencil fall was straight enough to be labeled Coloured. In retrospect, the terms invite ironic reading: apart from the apartheid branding, the meaning of *bantu* is simply "people," which implies that the supposedly superior Coloured was a non-person and thus that apartheid racial categories were ideological constructs.

Whereas *Pass-ages* attempted to reanimate the labor of the past in a particular place in the contemporary city, CHR's 2011 project *Xenoglossia* alluded to the cosmopolitan present and future of Johannesburg but staged the work within the CHR gallery space. Ngcobo began with an abstract definition of xenoglossia as the "rare condition of speaking a language entirely unknown to the speaker" (Ngcobo 2010, 3), but the installations tracked the concrete South African problem of the persistent gap between the country's eleven official languages and the lack of multilingual competence among many of the country's most privileged citizens. While speakers of African languages, say Zulu, usually understand related languages, in this case Xhosa or Ndebele, as well as some English or Afrikaans, native speakers of English are often still ignorant of African languages, a fact recognized by artists whose works are mentioned by Ngcobo, like Ernestine White's "I do not speak Xhosa" and Brett Murray's "I must learn to speak Xhosa" (2010, 5). But although Ngcobo alludes to the 1976 Soweto uprising against the imposition of Afrikaans and calls the ongoing labeling of migrants speaking other languages as *amaKwerekwere* a "sensitive matter" (3), the work by colleagues wa Lehulere and Donna Kukama, *An Unknown Grammar of Inhabiting a Text*, an assemblage of textual objects in several languages, appears to speak more to the theoretical interests of artists and critics than the more immediate concerns of migrants who have been subject to linguistic trials such as the notorious "elbow test," which has been used by native speakers of dominant languages like Zulu to challenge the citizenship of speakers of other languages (including border languages like Venda or Tsonga) to name elbows and other body parts in Zulu or face violent consequences (Gqola 2008, 214–8).

In foregrounding the production of schooled artists and the consumption of their work by affluent patrons and audiences, CHR narrows the gap between their work and the more prestigious art housed in Arts on Main in the Maboneng Precinct, which includes downtown branches of long-standing institutions like the Goodman, which stages intimate performance for festivals such as Dancing All over Johannesburg (2012; see Kruger 2013), and studios of renowned artists like Kentridge, alongside enterprises run by members of the same cohort as the CHR group, and outlets for design companies such as Black Coffee and Love Jozi, which designed a room each in the 12 Decade Hotel, while opening the gap between art and the social practices outside the gallery. As indicated by my emphasis on institutions here and throughout, this gap does not express an essential distinction between avowedly autonomous art and allegedly heteronomous social activism, but rather the functional differences between institutions with more or less cultural legitimacy and the ideology that privileges autonomy over engagement (see Kruger 1992, 11–25, 185–87).

The gap between autonomous art and engaged practice on Johannesburg streets emerges in the work of artists who represent engagement but perform it, rather than practice it in the streets. In February 2012, for instance, the

Ninox Gallery in Arts on Main exhibited works in oils, fabric, and other materials by the Nigerian-born, Texas-based artist Olaniyi Rasheed Akiresh, also known as Akindiya, reflecting his African-Indian affiliations. It also provided the staging ground for a performance on February 26 called, in Xhosa, *Isicelo* (petition), in which the artist, his face and body partly covered by silk thread and tape similar to the material in the exhibited sculpture, walked from Arts on Main to Main Street Life, handing out copies of a petition in English and Xhosa advocating the rights of migrants to the city, while taking photographs of children in the neighborhood, which were then exhibited in the gallery. While alluding to the pressing problem of migrant rights, the performance left them at the margins of the artwork and did not interrogate the artist's representation as privileged international traveler. Akindiya's work more closely resembles the cerebral and ultimately disconnected representation of foreign languages in *Xenoglossia*, rather than the *Cascoland* collaborators' engagement simultaneously with the forms of the art, such as the pedestrian poetry created by migrants and artist, and its contribution to the ongoing transformation of social practice, such as the negotiation of street space and time by drivers and walkers.

Similarly, in November 2012, Goethe on Main, the Maboneng outpost (or in-post) of the Goethe Institute, sponsored two performance events under the rubric *Traversing the City's Spine.* Although curator Lien Heidenreich-Seleme made no mention of either *Tour Guides of the Inner City* or *Hillbrow/ Dakar/Hillbrow*, her key words were still "tour" and "inner city," and this project bears a striking, if refracted, resemblance to these pioneering projects. Prompted by now-familiar questions like "What is public space in Jozi? Who uses it? Who is allowed in or kept out?" (Heidenreich-Seleme 2012), two groups of artists, the first led by choreographer Sello Pesa (this group was called *In House*) and the second convened by musicians and hip hop performers (and called *Utopias*) led participants from Arts on Main to the Carlton Centre and Park Station on foot, from where they traveled in the first instance to Soweto and the second to Alexandra and back to the inner city. In both cases, participants were encouraged to follow a guide who had them, in Heidenreich's words, "acting funny," so as to encourage reactions from those on the streets, while also reacting to staged scenes, such as a white-faced figure lying on the ground near an open first aid kit. Pesa, whose previous work, *Inhabitant* (2011), had also invited participants to make sense of strange behavior (the artist rolling in the street or darting through traffic), described the *In House* project in conversation with Heidenreich as an opportunity to "displace" artists and participants in interior or exterior locations that compelled them to reassess their position in the society around them.[13] Perhaps overly concerned to create a spectacle, this event did not allow for improvisation of engagement both with strangers and with people embedded in their districts, and thus with the exploration of the performative dimension of ordinary interaction that might modify the intrusion of the tourist, as *Hillbrow/Dakar/Hillbrow* had revised *Tour Guides* with the enactment of hospitality in Chez Ntemba and beyond.

These avowedly artistic performances capture, perhaps inadvertently, the institutional and ideological contradictions shaping Maboneng and the arts precinct as a distinct and often policed entity, among them the contradiction between art as play and art as commodity, and between the expressed goal of integration and the ongoing fact of segregation, by class and status if no longer by race. While the "integrated urban neighborhood" appears confidently in the present tense (as in "Maboneng *is* a an integrated urban neighbourhood") on a website otherwise saturated by the future tense, the site touts optimistic projections of developer Jonathan Liebmann's big plans, such as the as yet hypothetical MOAD that is advertised as the Museum of African Design but appears to function more as a hypothetical event space for rent, but the private police force's apprehension of those that wander into the zone suggests at best insufficient integration (Rees 2013). As has been noted throughout this book, boosterish discourse is Johannesburg's home language but does not always match the actually existing altercations between glossy aspirations and gritty improvisation. While Arts on Main houses major Johannesburg galleries and designers, whose products attract tourists from abroad and from Johannesburg's northern suburbs, the interaction between residents, visitors, and workers suggests more complicated interaction that may or may not add up to a drama of hospitality or durable urban renewal. The hotel, which offers artists reduced rates in return for a donated work, boasts rooms with intriguing but often whimsical and ahistorical elements, which suffer from basic oversights such as a paucity of practical electrical outlets and a security

13. *Inhabitant* by Pesa and Vaughn Sadie was sponsored by Goethe on Main in March 2011 and revived the Bag Factory studio on the border between Newtown and mixed industrial/residential Fordsburg in October 2012. Pesa's performance involved rolling in the street (to the consternation of drivers and walkers), while Sadie talked from a lectern to spectators seated on folding chairs on the sidewalk. Despite their claim that each space "changed" the performance (Pesa and Sadie 2012), their response to these environments (and sites further away, like Istanbul), remained rather abstract, in that they did not engage the ordinary inhabitants or passers-by on the margins of Cultural Precincts to the degree executed by the Joubert Park Projects and Trinity Session.

door whose mechanism broke down in March 2012 and apparently on other occasions before and since.

Against this evidently uneven production of "world-class" experiences or commodities, the drama of hospitality and the potential for urban renewal may take place in more informal settings. Although the hotel does not advertise the fact, many of the staff live in the area, in low-slung brick buildings similar to the Arts on Main complex with minimal but, according to worker-informants, functional services; these buildings are situated among the motor repair and light industrial production businesses and continue through most of the blocks between Maboneng and the banking district nearly two kilometers to the west, and toward Doornfontein in the east. While this is not the urban playground touted on the website, this occupation represents a significant departure from apartheid-era segregation and a return to a more distant past of urban integration before apartheid, when diverse communities of working people lived in the inner city. To be sure, this accommodation is not always happy. In early 2013, people who had been living in a light industrial structure, the former Radiator Centre at 238 Main Street, and paying rent to a local building hijacker posing as a landlord, were evicted by a foreign national better able to claim ownership of the building (Bauer 2013); they ended up spending nights under the M2 freeway near the sealed-off Jewel City (fig. 5.6). Renters in other converted buildings, including workers at the hotel and surrounding businesses, appear to have retained their places in the district.

Ironically for the Place of Light, it is at dusk that an integration of sorts becomes more visible. While yuppies, buppies, and other members of the affluent classes, including many in the Main Street Life apartments, enjoy sundowners at the cluster of bars and restaurants along the Fox Street strip, working-class residents and their children play soccer in the street or ride skateboards donated by the community organization Nollie Faith. While spokespeople for this and other community organizations express skepticism about developers' plans to offer housing for a range of income levels and complain that economic segregation has replaced racial discrimination in the district (Rees 2013), this street-level interaction offers a small, tentative, but workable model for urban civility. In contrast to the inner-city norm, where dwellings and workplaces are subject to strict biometric security, this improvised *straatwerf* (Dutch/Afrikaans for a working street temporarily claimed as a neighborhood play yard; de Bell and Schoenmakers 2009) encourages what local commentators call *sawubona* culture, marked by habits of greeting and interaction at the street level and pedestrian pace (Davie 2008; Bush and Velna 2011). The standard Zulu greeting *sawubona* can be parsed as "we are still seeing you" or "we see you again" (after an absence). Extended to strangers as well as neighbors, the greeting may offer an antidote to the "elbow test" imposed on alleged foreigners, even if some local speakers of Pedi, Sotho, Tswana, and other languages perceive Zulus to be less willing than they are to speak others' languages (Slabbert and Finlayson 2002, 249).[14] The interaction between people across barriers of class, ethnicity, and aspiration—whether visual, gestural, or perhaps less often verbal—constitutes an informal and still tentative version of what folklorist Elaine Lawless has called "reciprocal ethnography" (1992, 311), as against the more academically "reflective" mode of the ethnographer writing her subjectivity into her observations. This engagement is reciprocal insofar as it encourages interaction between different groups of people inhabiting intersecting spaces—an engagement that may be as yet uneven but that takes steps toward mutual acknowledgment along desire lines that may reweave rather than undo the frayed urban fabric.

The practice of acknowledging the presence of a familiar person or even of a stranger as though she were familiar enough to greet, before questioning the reason for that presence, might be translated as the performance of civility or, in social terms, as the transformation of ways of belonging and becoming. In a city where walking and talking can be risky even by day and where many districts appear to be sealed tight at night, this is in part a plebeian African reiteration of what veteran urbanist Jane Jacobs called the "sidewalk ballet," the "intricacy of sidewalk use," and the "constant succession of eyes" that maintain a "complex order" on city streets that may appear to outsiders to be disorderly (Jacobs 1992 [1961], 50). Johannesburg is not New York and the sidewalk ballet is not art. Nonetheless, this activity can certainly be claimed as *performance* because it creates a measure of form and grace pulled at some risk out of improvised responses to the edgy city, as *writing* because it provides a record and thus implicitly a shareable script for reiteration elsewhere, and as *building* because it extends the literal sense of making dwellings and other structures of labor and habitation, and to the figurative sense of making and sustaining connections. Identified in the introduction to this book as the tenacious habitation and re-imagination of

14. This perception was confirmed more recently (2007, 2012) in informal conversations with Sotho speakers, who expressed disappointment or even annoyance that white people, including this writer, allegedly "always learn Zulu, never Sotho."

the edgy city, the *sustained precarity* expressed in this informal choreography of play and labor on the Johannesburg street and sidewalk, and in the surrounding buildings, suggests that this activity on a Saturday at dusk in what is as yet a fraction of the edgy city might yet merit the city the praise-name the "Place of Light."

REFERENCES

Note: To indicate the institutional sources of collectively authored or edited work and thus to avoid a long string of sources labeled "anonymous," this list of references catalogues unattributed texts under the newspaper, magazine, or organization that published them or, in the case of unpublished materials, the association responsible for their release. Books and articles originally published in South Africa are, where possible, represented by local editions so as to highlight the contribution of South African presses to the cultural history of Johannesburg.

Abrahams, Michael. 2010. Westbury Township: A Place of Dreams. *Demotix: The Network for Freelance Photojournalists*. http://www.demotix.com/news/353194/westbury-township-place-dreams#media-353190. Podcast.

African World, eds. 1935. Johannesburg's Jubilee . . . An Exclusive Interview with Mr. B. M. Bellasis. *African World* 2 (March): 227–29.

Alexander, Caryn. 2010. Transforming the Region: Supermarkets and the Local Food Economy. *African Affairs* 109 (434): 115–34.

Alfred, Mike. 2003. *Johannesburg Portraits*. Johannesburg: Jacana Media.

Altbeker, Antony. 2007. *A Country at War with Itself: South Africa's Crisis of Crime*. Johannesburg: Jonathan Ball.

———. 2011. Crime and Policing: How We Got It Wrong. In *Opinion Pieces by South African Thought Leaders*, edited by Max du Preez, 45–65. Johannesburg: Penguin SA.

Baldwin, James. 1968. Sidney Poitier. *Look Magazine* 32, no. 15 (July 23): 50–58.

Ballenden, G[eoffrey]. 1936. The City's Army of Native Workers. *Johannesburg Star*, September 22, n.p.

Balseiro, Isabel. 2003. *Come Back Africa*: Black Claims on "White" Cities. In *To Change Reels: Film and Film Culture in South Africa*, edited by Isabel Balseiro and Ntongela Masilela, 88–111. Detroit: Wayne State University Press.

Bantu People's Theatre. 1936. Bantu People's Theatre, Draft Constitution, SAIRR. AD843/RJ/Kb 28.

———. 1940. *Bantu Peoples Theatre Festival*, SAIRR. AD843/RJ/Kb 28: 4.

Bantu World (BW). 1934. Africans Celebrate Emancipation Centenary. *Bantu World*, June 9, 4.

———. 1936a. The Lucky Stars. *Bantu World*, April 11, 17.

———. 1936b. The Lucky Stars to Perform at the Empire Exhibition. *Bantu World*, May 30, 17.

———. 1936c. City Celebrates Its Birthday. *Bantu World*, September 26, 2.

———. 1936d. Africans Participate in Jubilee Pageant. *Bantu World*, September 26, 3.

Barker, Harley Granville. 1922. *The Exemplary Theatre*. London: Sidgwick and Jackson.

Barnard, Rita. 2004. Oprah's Paton, or South Africa and the Globalization of Suffering. *English Studies in Africa* 47 (1): 85–107.

Barstow, Oliver, and Bronwyn Law-Viljoen, eds. 2011. *Firewalker: William Kentridge, Gerhard Marx*. Johannesburg: Fourthwall Books.

Bauer, Nikolaus. 2012. Ponte's Fourth Coming: An Urban Icon Reborn. *Johannesburg Mail and Guardian*, April 20. http://mg.co.za/article/2012-04-20-pontes-fourth-coming-an-urban-icon-reborn.

———. 2013. Eviction Nightmare on Main Street. *Johannesburg Mail and Guardian*, January 11, http://mg.co.za/article/2013-01-10-eviction-nightmare-on-main-street.

Bayat, Asef. 1997. Un-civil Society: The Politics of the Informal People. *Third World Quarterly* 18 (1): 53–72.

Beall, J., O. Cranshaw, and S. Parnell. 2002. *Uniting a Divided City: Governance and Social Exclusion in Johannesburg*. London: Earthscan.

Beavon, Keith. 2004. *Johannesburg: The Making and Shaping of the City*. Pretoria: UNISA Press.

Beck, Ulrich, and Natan Sznaider. 2006. Unpacking Cosmopolitanism for the Social Sciences: A Research Agenda. *British Journal of Sociology* 57 (1): 1–23.

Becker, Florian. 2010. Capitalism and Crime: Brechtian Economies in *The Threepenny Opera* and *Love, Crime and Johannesburg*. *Modern Drama* 53: 159–86.

Beittel, Mark. 2003. "What Sort of Memorial?" *Cry, the Beloved Country* on Film. In *To Change Reels: Film and Film Culture in South Africa*, edited by Isabel Balseiro and Ntongela Masilela, 70–87. Detroit: Wayne State University Press.

Beni-Gbaffou, Claire, ed. 2011. *Leaving Yeoville*. Johannesburg: Wits School of Architecture and Yeoville Studio. http://www.wits.ac.za/academic/ebe/archplan/4866/yeoville_stories.html.

———. 2012. *Yeoville Housing Stories*. Johannesburg: Wits School of Architecture and Yeoville Studio. http://www.wits.ac.za/academic/ebe/archplan/4866/yeoville_stories.html.

Ben-Zeev, Kerem, and Joseph Gaylard, eds. 2006. *The Drill Hall*. Johannesburg: Joubert Park Project.

Berger, Iris. 1992. *Threads of Solidarity: Women in South African Industry 1900–1980*. Bloomington: Indiana University Press.

Berger, Laurin, and Lisa Steyn. 2010. Life as a Refugee Child: A Story Through Art. *Johannesburg M&G*. http://www.m.co.za/multimedia/2010-05-25-life-as-a-refugee-child-story-through-art. Podcast.

Berman, Marshall. 1982. *All That Is Solid Melts into Air: The Experience of Modernity*. New York: Simon and Schuster.

Bethlehem, Louise. 2004. "A Primary Need as Strong as Hunger": The Rhetoric of Urgency in South African Literary Culture under Apartheid. In *South Africa in the Global Imaginary*, edited by Leon de Kock, Louise Bethlehem, and Sonja Laden, 95–116. Pretoria: UNISA Press.

———. 2010. By/way of Passage. *Johannesburg Workshop on Theory and Criticism*, July 29, http://jhbwtc.blogspot.com/2010/07/byway-of-passage.html.

Biko, Stephen Bantu. 1978. *I Write What I Like*. New York: Harper and Row.

Black, Stephen. 1984 [1910]. Helena's Hope Ltd. In *Three Plays*, edited by Stephen Gray, 127–81. Johannesburg: AD Donker.

Blair, Les, director. 1996. *Jump the Gun*. London: Channel 4. DVD.

Bloom, Harold, Pat Williams, et al. 1961. *King Kong—An African Jazz Opera*. London: Collins.

Bonner, Philip, and Noor Nieftagodien. 2008. *Alexandra—A History*. Johannesburg: Wits University Press.

Boraine, Andrew, Owen Crankshaw, Carien Engelbrecht, Graeme Götz, Sithole Mbanga, Monty Narsoo, and Susan Parnell. 2006. The State of South African Cities a Decade after Democracy. *Urban Studies* 43 (2): 259–85.

Bosman, Herman Charles. 1981. *Collected Works*. 2 vols. Edited by Lionel Abrahams. Johannesburg: Jonathan Ball.

———. 1986. *Bosman's Johannesburg*. Edited by Stephen Gray. Cape Town: Human and Rousseau.

Brecht, Bertolt. 1992 [1964]. Appendices to the Short Organum. In *Brecht on Theatre*, edited and translated by John Willett, 276–81. New York: Hill and Wang.

———. 1998 [1954]. Nachträge zum kleinen Organon. In *Werke: Grosse kommentierte Berliner und Frankfurter Ausgabe*, vol. 23, 289–95. Frankfurt: Suhrkamp.

Bremner, Lindsay. 1998. Crime and the Emerging Landscape of Post-Apartheid Johannesburg. In *blank____: Architecture, Apartheid and After*, edited by Hilton Judin and Ivan Vladislavić, B2, 48–63. Rotterdam: Netherlands Architecture Institute.

———. 2004. *Johannesburg: One City, Colliding Worlds*. Johannesburg: STE.

———. 2010. *Writing the City into Being: Essays on Johannesburg 1998–2008*. Johannesburg: Fourthwall Books.

Bremner, Lindsay, and Pep Subirós, eds. 2007. *Johannesburg: Emerging/Diverging Metropolis*. Mendrisio, Switzerland: Mendriso Academy Press.

Brennan-Galvin, Ellen. 2002. Crime and Violence in an Urbanizing World. *Journal of International Studies* 51 (1): 123–45.

Brink, André P. 1973. *Kennis van die Aand*. Cape Town: Buren Publishers.

———. 1974. *Looking on Darkness*. London: W. H. Allen.

———. 1978. *Gerugte van Reën*. Cape Town: Human and Rousseau.

———. 1979. *'N Droë Wit Seisoen*. Johannesburg: Taurus.

———. 1983. *Mapmakers: Writing in a State of Siege*. London: Faber and Faber.

———. 1984a. *A Dry White Season*. Harmondsworth: Penguin.

———. 1984b. *Rumours of Rain*. Harmondsworth: Penguin.

Buendía, Felipe Cale. 2010. More Carrots Than Sticks: Antanas Mockus's Civic Cultural Policy in Bogotá. *New Directions for Youth Development* (125): 19–32.

Burdett, Richard, and Deyan Sudjic, eds. 2007. *The Endless City: The Urban Age Project by the London School of Economics and Deutsche Bank's Alfred Herrnhausen Society*. London: Phaedon.

Bush, Demelza, and Vuvu Velna. 2011. Hillbrow: The Danger Zone Some Call Home. *Johannesburg M&G,* March 15. http://mg.co.za/multimedia/2011-03-15-hillbrow-the-danger-zone-some-call-home. Podcast.

Butler, William. 1911. *Sir William Butler: An Autobiography*. London: Constable.

Cabral, Zafrica [Zubair Hassem]. 2011. Interview with SABC2 at the Ruin of the Old Park Station of 1897. *Architecture ZA*, January 30. http://www.youtube.com/watch?v = UX3yT-RaVZA. Podcast.

———. 2010. *Gold in Graphite: Jozi Sketchbook*. Text by Somayya A.E. Johannesburg: Kufica Publishing.

Caldecott, Charles H. 1853. *Descriptive History of the Zulu Kafirs*. London: John Mitchel.

Caldeira, Teresa. 2000. *City of Walls: Crime, Segregation and Citizenship in São Paolo*. Berkeley: University of California Press.

———. 2009. From Modernism to Neo-liberalism in São Paolo. In *Other Cities, Other Worlds: Urban Imaginaries in a Globalizing Age*, edited by Andreas Huyssen, 51–77. Durham: Duke University Press.

Campbell, Roy. 2002 [1930]. The Zulu Girl. In *The New Century of South African Poetry*, edited by Michael Chapman, 83. Johannesburg: AD Donker.

Cape Town Pageant Committee. 1910. *Historical Sketch & Description of the Pageant Held at Cape Town on the Occasion of the Opening of the First Parliament of the Union of South Africa*. Cape Town: Pageant Committee

Carman, Jillian. 2003. Johannesburg Art Gallery and the Urban Future. In *Emerging Johannesburg: Perspectives on the Postapartheid City*, edited by Richard Tomlinson, Robert Beaurigard, Lindsay Bremner, and Xola Mangcu, 231–56. London: Routledge.

Carrim, Nazir. 1990. *Fietas: A Social History of Pageview*. Johannesburg: Save Pageview Campaign.

Celli, Louise. 1937. South African Dramatists. *South African Opinion*, May 15, 13–14.

Chakrabarty, Dipesh. 1992. Postcoloniality and the Artifice of History: Who Speaks for Indian Pasts? *Representations* (37): 1–26.

Chapman, Michael. 1989. Drum and Its Significance for Black South African Writing. In *The Drum Decade: Stories from the 1950s*, edited by Michael Chapman, 183–232. Pietermaritzburg: University of KwaZulu-Natal Press.

———. 2007 [1982]. Introduction. In *Soweto Poetry: Literary Perspectives*, edited by Michael Chapman, 3–15. Pietermaritzburg: University of KwaZulu-Natal Press.

Chapman, Michael, and Achmat Dangor, eds. 1982. *Voices from Within: Black Poetry from Southern Africa*. Johannesburg: AD Donker.

Chaudhuri, Una. 1997. *Staging Place: The Geography of Modern Drama*. Ann Arbor: University of Michigan Press.

Chipkin, Clive. 1998. The Great Apartheid Building Boom: 1964–74. In *blank———: Architecture, Apartheid and After*, edited by Hilton Judin and Ivan Vladislavić, E4, 248–67. Rotterdam: Netherlands Architecture Institute.

———. 1993. *Johannesburg Style: Architecture and Society 1880s–1960s*. Cape Town: David Philip.

Christie, Roy. 1986. Cast of 12,000 to Celebrate SA. *Johannesburg Star*, January 15.

Clay, Paddi, and Glynn Griffiths. 1982. *Hillbrow*. Cape Town: National Books.

Comaroff, Jean, and John L. Comaroff. 1999. Alien-Nation: Zombies, Immigrants, and Millennial Capitalism. *CODESRIA Bulletin* 3 (4): 17–28.

———. 2012. *Theory from the South: Or How Euro-America Is Evolving toward Africa*. Boulder, CO: Paradigm Books.

Cooper, Saths, and Pandelani Nefolovhodwe. 2007. Steve Biko and the SASO/BPC Trial. In *We Write What We Like; Celebrating Steve Biko*, edited by Chris van Wyk, 110–15. Johannesburg: Wits University Press.

Coplan, David. 2008. *In Township Tonight!* 2nd ed. Chicago: University of Chicago Press.

Corbey, Raymond. 1993. Ethnographic Showcases: 1870–1930. *Cultural Anthropology* 8: 338–69.

Couzens, Tim. 1985. *The New African: A Study of the Life and Work of H. I. E. Dhlomo*. Johannesburg: Ravan Press.

Couzens, Tim, and Essop Patel, eds. 1982. *The Return of the Amasi Bird: Black South African Poetry 1891–1981*. Johannesburg: Ravan Press.

Crocker, H. J. 1936. The Exhibition Opens. *The Almanac*, October, 44–46.

Czeglédy, André. 2003. Villas of the Highveld. In *Emerging Johannesburg: Perspectives on the Postapartheid City*, edited by Richard Tomlinson et al., 21–42. London: Routledge.

Dalling, Dave. 1985. The Big Centenary Debate. *The Star*, November 1.

Dangor, Achmat. 1990. *The Z Town Trilogy*. Johannesburg: Ravan Press.

———. 1997. *Kafka's Curse and Other Stories*. Cape Town: Kwela Books.

———. 1998. Apartheid and the Death of South African Cities. In *blank———. Architecture, Apartheid and After*, edited by Hilton Judin and Ivan Vladislavić, F10. Rotterdam: Netherlands Architecture Institute.

———. 2012. Personal communication at the Johannesburg launch of *The Cambridge History of South African Literature*, March 10.

Dart, Raymond. 1931. The Ancient Iron-smelting Cavern at Mumbwa. *Transactions of the Royal Society of South Africa* 19 (1): 379–427.

Davie, Lucille. 2002. When War Came to Joburg's Streets. *Joburg*, March 18, http://www.joburg.org.za/index.php?option=com_content&view=article&id=280&catid=38&Itemid=51.

———. 2003. Foster Gang: Raiders of the Secret Cave. *Joburg*, January 3, http://www.joburg.org.za/index.php?option=com_content&task=view&id=244&Itemid=51.

———. 2008. Making Hillbrow a Neighbourhood. *Joburg*, www.jda.org.za/2008/10mar_hlb.stm.

———. 2011a. Long Live Fietas. *Joburg*, February 21, http://www.joburg.org.za/index.php?option=com_content&view=article&id=6254&catid=122&Itemid=20.

———. 2011b. Brixton: The Caring Suburb. *Joburg*, June 20, www.joburg.org.za/index.php?option=com_content&view=article&id=6682&catid=88&Itemid=266#ixzz1OoLd17m.

Davis, Peter. 1996. *In Darkest Hollywood: Exploring the Jungles of Cinema's South Africa*. Athens: Ohio University Press.

———, ed. 2004. *Come Back Africa: Lionel Rogosin, A Man Possessed*. Johannesburg: STE Publications.

Dawes, Nic. 2012. Editorial: Gay Rights—Proud but Vigilant. *Johannesburg Mail and Guardian*, May 10, http://mg.co.za/article/2012-05-10-gay-rights-proud-but-vigilant.

De Bell, Fiona, and Roel Schoenmakers, eds. 2008. *Cascoland: Interventions in Public Space. Drill Hall, Johannesburg, South Africa, 2007*. Rotterdam: Episode.

———. 2009. Interview with Loren Kruger. Amsterdam, March 16.

De Certeau, Michel. 1988. Walking in the City. In *The Practice of Everyday Life*, translated by Steven Randall, 91–110. Berkeley: University of California Press.

———. 1991. Marches dans la ville. In *L'invention du quotidien*, vol. 1, Arts de faire, 139–64. 2nd ed. Paris: Gallimard.

Deckler, Thorsten, Anne Graubner, and Henning Rasmuss, eds. 2006. *Contemporary South African Architecture in a Landscape of Transition*. Cape Town: Double Storey Press.

Derrida, Jacques. 1997. *De l'hospitalité. Anne Dufourmantelle invite Jacques Derrida à répondre*. Paris: Calmann-Lévy.

———. 2000. *Of Hospitality: Anne Dufourmantelle Invites Jacques Derrida to Respond*, translated by Rachel Bowlby. Stanford: Stanford University Press.

De Waal, Shaun, and Anthony Manion, eds. 2006. *Pride: Protest and Celebration*. Johannesburg: Jacana Media.

Dhlomo, Herbert I. E. 1985. *Collected Works*, edited by Tim Couzens and Nicholas Visser. Johannesburg: Ravan Press.

Diala, Isadore. 2006. André Brink and Malraux. *Contemporary Literature* 47 (1): 91–113.

Dikobe, Modikwe. 1979. We Shall Walk. In *Labour, Township and Protest: Studies in the Social History of the Witwatersrand*, edited by Belinda Bozzoli, 104–8. Johannesburg: Ravan Press.

Dlamini, Jacob. 2009. *Native Nostalgia*. Johannesburg: Jacana Media.

Douglass, Frederick. 1999 [1893]. Introduction. In *The Reason Why the Colored American Is Not in the World's Columbian Exposition*, edited by Robert Rydell, 3–20. Urbana: University of Illinois Press.

Drum Magazine. 1953. Negro Show Sweeps the World (on World Tour of *Porgy and Bess*). *Drum*, August, 7.

Dubois, William E. B. 1989 [1903]. *The Souls of Black Folk*. New York: Bantam.

Dubow, Saul. 1987. Race, Civilization and Culture: The Elaboration of Segregationist Discourse in the Interwar Years. In *The Politics of Race, Class, and Nationalism in Twentieth Century South Africa*, edited by Shula Marks and Stanley Trapido, 71–94. London: Longman.

Ellis, Stephen, and Tsepo Sechaba. 1992. *Comrades against Apartheid: The ANC and the South African Communist Party in Exile*. London: James Curry.

Empire Exhibition, Johannesburg. 1936a. *Amptlike Gids: Rykstentoonstelling, Suid-Afrika/Official Guide: Empire Exhibition, South Africa*. Johannesburg: Empire Exhibition.

———. 1936b. Vhavenda Terrified by ISCOR Works. *Star-Mail News Bulletin*, December 7, 2.

Erlmann, Veit. 1991. *African Stars: Studies in Black South African Performance*. Chicago: University of Chicago Press.

———. 1999. "Spectatorial Lust": The African Choir in England, 1891–93. In *Africans on Stage: Studies in Ethnographic Show Business*, edited by Bernth Lindfors, 107–35. Bloomington: Indiana University Press.

Essop, Ahmed. 1978. *The Hajji and Other Stories*. Johannesburg: Ravan Press.

———. 1980. *The Visitation*. Johannesburg: Ravan Press.

———. 1990. *Noorjehan and Other Stories*. Johannesburg: Ravan Press.

———. 1997. *The King of Hearts and Other Stories*. Johannesburg: Ravan Press.

Farouk, Ismael. 2012. The Trolley Project. In *Afropolis: City, Media, Art*, edited by Kerstin Pinther, Larissa Förster, and Christian Hanussek, 308–9. Johannesburg: Jacana Media.

February, Vernon. 2007 [1982]. Sipho Sepamla's *The Soweto I Love*. In *Soweto Poetry: Literary Perspectives*, edited by Michael Chapman, 82–83. Pietermaritzburg: University of Kwa-Zulu-Natal Press.

Filewod, Alan. 1990. National Theatre, National Obsession. *Canadian Theatre Review* 62: 5.

Film Makers against Racism (FAR). 2009. *Reflecting on Xenophobia: Documentary Film Makers Respond to the Violent Xenophobic Attacks That Hit South Africa in 2008*. Cape Town: Human Rights Media Trust. DVD.

Foster, Jeremy. 2008. *Washed with Sun: Landscape and the Making of White South Africa*. Pittsburgh: University of Pittsburgh Press.

———. 2009. From Socio-nature to Spectral Presence: Re-imagining the Once and Future Landscape of Johannesburg. *Safundi: Journal of South African and American Studies* 10 (2): 175–213.

———. 2012. The Wilds and the Township: Articulating Modernity, Capital, and Socio-nature in the Cityscape of Pre-apartheid Johannesburg. *Journal of the Society of Architectural Historians* 17 (1): 42–59.

Freimond, Craig, and Riaad Moosa. 2012. *Material*. Johannesburg: SterKinekor. DVD.

Furner, A. Stanley. 1925. The Modern Movement in Architecture, Part 1. *South African Architectural Record* 10 (40): 87–89.

———. 1926a. The Modern Movement in Architecture, Part 2. *South African Architectural Record* 11 (41): 6–8.

———. 1926b. Johannesburg and the Need for a Civic Survey. *South African Architectural Record* 11 (42): 31–34.

GALA: Gay and Lesbian Archive. 2012. Joburg Pride Parade. http://www.gala.co.za/events/2012/October/joburg_pride.htm.

García-Canclini, Néstor. 2009. Mexico City 2010: Improving Globalization. In *Other Cities, Other Worlds: Urban Imaginaries in a Globalizing Age*, edited by Andreas Huyssen, 79–95. Durham: Duke University Press.

Garreau, Joel. 1991. *Edge City: Life on the New Frontier*. New York: Doubleday.

Gaule, Sally. 2005. Alternating Currents of Power: From Colonial to Post-Apartheid in Newtown, Johannesburg. *Urban Studies* 42: 235–61.

Gaylard, Gerald. 2005. Postcolonial Satire: Ivan Vladislavić. *Current Writing* 17 (1): 129–48.

———. 2011a. Introduction. *Marginal Spaces: Reading Ivan Vladislavić*, edited by Gerald Gaylard, 1–20. Johannesburg: Wits University Press.

———. 2011b. Migrant Ecology in the Postcolonial City in *Portrait with Keys*. In *Marginal Spaces: Reading Ivan Vladislavić*, edited by Gerald Gaylard, 287–308. Johannesburg: Wits University Press.

Gaylard, Joseph. 2009. Interview with Loren Kruger. Johannesburg, September 3.

Gevisser, Mark. 1995. A Different Fight for Freedom: Gay and Lesbian Organizations from the 1950s to the 1990s. In *Defiant Desire: Gay and Lesbian Lives in South Africa*, edited by Mark Gevisser and Edwin Cameron, 14–86. New York: Routledge.

Gillespie, Kelly. 2012. Interview with Loren Kruger. Johannesburg, February 25.

Glasser, Mona. 1960. *King Kong—A Chronicle*. London: Collins.

Goga, Soraya. 2003. Property Investors and Decentralization. In *Emerging Johannesburg: Perspectives on the Postapartheid City*, edited by Richard Tomlinson et al., 71–82. London: Routledge.

Goldblatt, David. 2010. *TJ: Johannnesburg Photographs 1948–2010*. Rome: Contrasto.

Goodman, Ralph. 2011. Ivan Vladislavić's *Portrait with Keys:* Fudging a Book by Its Cover. In *Marginal Spaces: Reading Ivan Vladislavić*, edited by Gerald Gaylard, 276–86. Johannesburg: Wits University Press.

Gordimer, Nadine. 1962 [1958]. *A World of Strangers*. Harmondsworth: Penguin.

———. 1998. *The House Gun*. New York: Farrar, Straus, Giroux.

Gordon, Robert. 1999. Bain's Bushmen: Scenes at the Empire Exhibition. In *Africans on Stage: Studies in Ethnographic Show Business*, edited by Bernth Lindfors, 266–89. Bloomington: Indiana University Press.

Gosani, Bob. 2005. *Tauza: Bob Gosani's People*, edited by Mothobi Mutloatse and Jacqui Masiza. Johannesburg: Bailey African History Archive.

Götz, Graeme, and AbdouMalique Simone. 2003. On Belonging and Becoming in African Cities. In *Emerging Johannesburg: Perspectives on the Postapartheid City*, edited by Richard Tomlinson, Robert Beaurigard, Lindsay Bremner, and Xola Mangcu, 123–47. London: Routledge.

Goudvis, Bertha. 1925. *Where the Money Goes and Other Plays*. Johannesburg: Sterling Printing Company.

Gqola, Pumla Dineo. 2008. Brutal Inheritances: Echoes, Negrophobia and Masculinist Violence. In *Go Home or Die Here: Violence, Xenophobia and the Re-invention of Difference in South Africa*, edited by Shireen Hassim, Tawana Kupe, and Eric Worby, 209–22. Johannesburg: Wits University Press.

Graham, James. 2009. Exploding Johannesburg: Driving in a Worldly City. *Transcultures/Transtext(e)s* 5: 67–83.

Gready, Paul. 1990. The Sophiatown Writers of the 1950s: The Unreal Reality of their World. *Journal of Southern African Studies* 10 (1): 139–64.

Grootboom, Mpumelelo Paul. 2009. *Foreplay*. Adapted from Arthur Schnitzler's *Der Reigen* (*La Ronde*). London: Oberon.

Gumede, William, and Leslie Dikeni, eds. 2009. *The Poverty of Ideas: South African Democracy and the Retreat of Intellectuals*. Johannesburg: Jacana Media.

Gwala, Mafika Pascal. 1982. *No More Lullabies*. Johannesburg: Ravan Press.

Hammon, Michael, director. 1991. *Wheels and Deals*. Johannesburg and Berlin: Deutsche Film und Fernsehakademie/WDR. PAL video.

Hammon, Michael, and Jacqueline Görgen, directors. 1999. *Hillbrow Kids*. Johannesburg and Berlin: MNET and Zweites Deutsches Fernsehen. PAL video.

Harber, Anton. 2011. *Diepsloot*. Johannesburg: Jonathan Ball.

Harber, Anton, and Malcolm Purkey. 2002–5. *Hard Copy*. Johannesburg: Curious Pictures. Television series.

Hassim, Shireen, Tawana Kupe, and Eric Worby, eds. 2008. *Go Home or Die Here: Violence, Xenophobia and the Re-invention of Difference in South Africa*. Johannesburg: Wits University Press.

Hatfield, Frank. 1936. Romance of Johannesburg's Building Boom. *Johannesburg Star*, January 25, 10–11.

Hegel, Georg W. E. 1956 [1899]. *The Philosophy of History*, translated by J. Sibree. New York: Dover.

Heidenreich-Seleme, Lien. 2012. Traversing the City's Spine through Art. Video interview by Lauren Clifford-Holmes and Koketso Dlongolo. *Johannesburg Mail and Guardian*, December 5, http://www.mg.co.za/multimedia/2012-12-05-traversing-the-citys-spine-through-art. Podcast.

Herbert, Robert K., and Richard Bailey. 2002. The Bantu Languages: Socio-historical Perspectives. In *Language in South Africa*, edited by Rajend Mesthrie, 51–78. Cambridge: Cambridge University Press.

Heyns, Michiel. 2000. The Whole Country's Truth: Confession and Narrative in Recent White South African Writing. *Modern Fiction Studies* 46 (1): 42–66.

Hirson, Baruch. 1979. *Year of Fire, Year of Ash: The Soweto Revolt: Roots of a Revolution?* London: Zed Books.

Hoad, Neville. 2007. *African Intimacies: Race, Homosexuality and Globalization.* Minneapolis: University of Minnesota Press.

Hobbs, Stephen. 1998. Erasing Landmarks: Cnrs. Bezuidenhout and Jeppe Streets. In *blank___: Architecture, Apartheid and After*, edited by Hilton Judin and Ivan Vladislavić, E8. Rotterdam: Netherlands Architectural Institute.

———. 2000. Inside the Outside: an Artist's View of Johannesburg. Text for exhibition *Total Global: South Africa*, Museum of Modern and Contemporary Art, Basel.

———. 2007. Interview with Loren Kruger. Johannesburg, July 19.

———. 2012. Interview with Loren Kruger. Johannesburg, March 1.

Hoffmann, Arthur, and Ann R. Hoffmann. 1980. *They Built a Theatre: The Story of the Johannesburg Repertory*. Johannesburg: AD Donker.

Hofmeyr, Isabel. 1988. Popularizing History: The Case of Gustav Preller. *Journal of African History* 29: 521–35.

Hofmeyr, Johannes H. 1986 [1926]. Peter Pan among Cities. In *Reef of Time: Johannesburg in Writing*, edited by Digby Ricci, 114–15. Johannesburg: AD Donker.

Holtmann, Barbara. 2013. The Best Life for Every Child: Connecting St Mary's Cathedral and the Drill Hall on a Safe and Clean Route. *Faces of the City Seminars*, Wits School of Architecture, March 19.

Hope, Christopher. 2002. *Heaven Forbid*. London: Macmillan.

Hughes, Langston. 1976 [1966]. Black Influences in the American Theatre, Part 1. In *The Black American Reference Book*, edited by Mabel M. Smythe, 690–711. Englewood, NJ: Prentice Hall.

Hyslop, Jonathan. 2008. Gandhi, Mandela and the African Modern. In *Johannesburg: The Elusive Metropolis*, edited by Sarah Nuttall and Achille Mbembe, 119–36. Durham: Duke University Press.

Jackson, Shannon. 2011. *Social Works: Performing Art, Supporting Publics*. London: Routledge.

Jacobs, Jane. 1992 [1961]. *The Death and Life of Great American Cities*. New York: Vintage.

Jacobs, Sean. 2010. The Pass Office: From Kole to Cole, Passages, References & Footnotes. http://africasacountry.com/2010/07/27/the-pass-office/.

Johannesburg, City of. 2002a. Vision. Chapter Five of *iGoli 2030* (2002) www.joburg.org.za/feb_2002/2030-vision.pdf.

———. 2002b. *iGoli 2030: Short Version*. www.joburg.org.za/feb_2002/2030-shortversion.pdf.

———. 2007. Public Performance Policy. www.joburg.org.za.

Johannesburg Historical Society. 1986. *Centenary Scrapbook, Wits University Cullen Library Historical Papers A972f* 11.3.

Johannesburg Star 1936a. Native Iron Smelters. September 12, 12.

———. 1936b. Native Smithy at Exhibition (caption to photograph). September 17, 22.

———. 1936c. The Birth of the City (Jubilee supplement). September 21, n.p.

———. 1937. Red Rand at the Library Theatre. December 3, 26.

Jonas, Kurt. 1936. Towards a Philosophy of Architecture. *South African Architectural Record* 21 (1): 1–12.

Jonker, Ingrid. 2002 [1965]. The Child (Who Was Shot Dead by Soldiers in Nyanga). Translated by Jack Cope. In *The New Century of South African Poetry*, edited by Michael Chapman, 167–68. Johannesburg: AD Donker.

Judin, Hilton, and Ivan Vladislavić, eds. 1998. *blank———: Architecture, Apartheid and After*. Rotterdam: Netherlands Architectural Institute.

Junction Avenue Theatre Company. 1995. Sophiatown. In *At the Junction: Four Plays by the Junction Avenue Theatre Company*, edited by Martin Orkin, 134–222. Johannesburg: Wits University Press.

Kabane, M. L. 1936. The All-African Convention. *South African Outlook* (August): 185–89.

Kane-Berman, John. 1978. *Soweto: Black Revolt, White Reaction*. Johannesburg: Ravan Press.

Karis, Thomas, and Gail M. Gerhart. 1997. *From Protest to Challenge: A Documentary History of African Politics in South Africa; Vol. 5: Nadir and Resurgence, 1964–79*. Bloomington: Indiana University Press.

Kavanagh, Robert "Mshengu". 1981. Introduction and Commentary. In *South African People's Plays*, edited by Robert Kavanagh, ix–xxxi, 126–28. London: Heinemann.

———. 1985. *Theatre and Cultural Struggle in South Africa*. London: Zed Books.

Kelly, Mary, ed. 1938. *Conference on African Drama, 1938*. London: British Drama League.

Kentridge, William. 2001. *William Kentridge* (Exhibition Catalog). Curators: Neil Benezra, Stacy Boris, and Dan Cameron. New York: Harry Abrams, Museum of Contemporary Art.

Kgaphola, Chipane L. 1988 [1986]. Johannesburg 100. In *Ten Years of "Staffrider": 1978–1988*, edited by Andries Walter Olifant and Ivan Vladislavić, 292–94. Johannesburg: Ravan Press.

Khoapa, Benny. 1972. Arts and Entertainment. *Black Review* 2: 201–11.

King, Anthony. 1990. *Global Cities*. London: Routledge.

Kleinboer. 2003. *Kontrei*. Cape Town: PRAAG.

———. 2006. *Midnight Missionary*. Translated by Jaco Fouché. Cape Town: Zebra Press.

Klenerman, Fanny. 1916–83. Correspondence and interview transcriptions. Wits University Cullen Library Historical Papers: Fanny Klenerman Collection: A2031.

Korda, Zoltan, director. 1951. *Cry, the Beloved Country*. Screenplay by Alan Paton and John Howard Lawson. London: London Film Productions. DVD.

Krikler, Jeremy. 2005. *White Rising: The 1922 Insurrection and Racial Killing in South Africa*. Manchester: Manchester University Press.

Kruger, Loren. 1992. *The National Stage: Theatre and Cultural Legitimation in England, France and America*. Chicago: University of Chicago Press.

———. 1999. *The Drama of South Africa: Plays, Pageants and Publics since 1910*. London: Routledge.

———. 2001a. Theatre, Crime, and the Edgy City in Post-Apartheid Johannesburg. *Theatre Journal* 53: 223–52.

———. 2001b. Black Atlantics, White Indians, and Jews: Locations, Locutions, and Syncretic Identities in the Fiction of Achmat Dangor and Others. *South Atlantic Quarterly, Special Issue: Atlantic Genealogies* 100 (1): 111–43.

———. 2004a. *Post-Imperial Brecht: Politics and Performance, East and South*. Cambridge: Cambridge University Press.

———. 2004b. Theatre for Development and TV Nation: Educational Soap Opera in South Africa. In *African Theater and Performance*, edited by John Conteh-Morgan and Tejumola Olaniyan, 155–75. Bloomington: Indiana University Press.

———. 2006. Filming the Edgy City: Cinematic Narrative and Urban Form in Post-Apartheid Johannesburg. *Research in African Literatures* 37 (2): 141–63.

———. 2007. White Cities, Diamond Zulus, and the African Contribution to Human Advancement: African Modernities at the World's Fairs. *TDR–Journal of Performance Studies* 51 (3): 19–45.

———. 2008. Performance and Urban Fabrics in the Inner City. *Theater* 38 (1): 4–17.

———. 2009a. *Africa Thina*: Xenophobic and Cosmopolitan Agency in Johannesburg's Film and Television Drama. *Journal of Southern African Studies* 35 (March): 237–52.

———. 2009b. Democratic Actors and Post-Apartheid Drama: Contesting Performance in Contemporary South Africa. In *Contesting Performance: Emerging Sites of Research*, edited by Jon McKenzie, Heike Roms, and C. J. Wan-ling Wee, 236–54. New York: Palgrave Macmillan.

———. 2010a. Critique by Stealth: Aspiration, Commodification and Class in Post-Apartheid Television Drama. *Critical Arts, Special Issue: Cultural Economy and Media* 24 (no. 1): 75–98.

———. 2010b. Review of *Foreplay* by Mpumelelo Paul Grootboom, Market Theatre, Johannesburg. *Theatre Journal* 62 (3): 453–54.

———. 2011. Beyond the TRC: Truth, Power, and Representation in South Africa After Transition. *Research in African Literatures* 42 (2): 184–96.

———. 2012. *What Time Is This Place?* Continuity and Conflict in Urban Performance Sites: Lessons from Haymarket Square. In *The Politics of Space: Theatre and Topography*, edited by Erika Fischer-Lichte and Benjamin Wihstutz, 45–63. London: Routledge.

———. 2013. Dancing All Over Johannesburg: Twenty-fourth Annual Dance Umbrella (review). *Theatre Journal* 65 (1): 95–99.

Krut, Riva. 1984. The Making of a South African Jewish Community in Johannesburg, 1886–1914. In *Class, Community and Conflict. South African Perspectives*, edited by Belinda Bozzoli, 135–59. Johannesburg: Ravan Press.

Kunene, Daniel P. 1981. Ideas under Arrest: Censorship in South Africa. *Research in African Literatures* 12 (4): 421–39.

Kurgan, Terry, and Jo Ractliffe, eds. 2005. *Johannesburg Circa Now: Photography and the City*. Johannesburg: Terry Kurgan Books.

Lambrecht, Bettie. 2007. Kuns as verkenning as kuns. *Die Beeld,* July 19. www.onair.co.za.

Landau, Loren. 2012. Hospitality without Hosts: Mobility and Community in Africa's Urban Estuaries. Presentation at Wits Institute for Social and Economic Research (WISER), March 19.

Landau, Loren, and Irann Haupt. 2007. Tactical Cosmopolitanism and Idioms of Belonging. Insertion and Self-exclusion in Johannesburg. Migration Studies Working Papers #32. http://www.migration.org.za/working-paper/working-paper-32-tactical-cosmopolitanism-and-idioms-belonging-insertion-and-self-exclusion.

Lawless, Elaine. 1992. "I Was Afraid Someone like You . . . an Outsider . . . Would Not Understand." Negotiating Differences between Ethnographers and Subjects. *Journal of American Folklore* 105: 302–14.

Law-Viljoen, Bronwyn, and Angela Buckland. 2007. *Light on a Hill: Building the Constitutional Court of South Africa*. Johannesburg: David Krut.

Law-Viljoen, Bronwyn, and Ben Law-Viljoen. 2008. *Art and Justice: The Art of the Constitutional Court of South Africa*. Johannesburg: David Krut.

Lefebvre, Henri. 1968. *Le droit à la ville*. Paris: Anthropos.

———. 1996. Rights to the City. In *Writings on Cities*. Translated by Eleonore Kofman and Elizabeth Lebas. Oxford: Blackwell.

Le Roux, Hannah, and Katherine Rohde, eds. 2005. *Urban (and) Fabrics: A Project by Students of Architecture*. Johannesburg: Witwatersrand University School of Architecture.

Le Roux, Hannah, and Naomi Roux. 2012. Majesty Wholesalers: The Biography of a Building. In *Afropolis: City, Media, Art,* edited by Kerstin Pinther, Larissa Förster, and Christian Hanussek, 312–13. Johannesburg: Jacana Media.

Leveson, Marcia. 1996. *The People of the Book: The Image of the Jew in English South African Literature*. Johannesburg: Wits University Press.

Lewis, David. 1997. Black Workers and Trade Unions. In *From Protest to Challenge: A Documentar History of African Politics in South Africa, 1882–1990,* edited by Thomas Karis, Gwendolen Margaret Carter, and Gail M. Gerhart, 189–220. Bloomington: Indiana University Press.

Lindfors, Bernth, ed. 1999. Introduction. In *Africans on Stage: Studies in Ethnographic Show Business,* vii–xiii. Bloomington: Indiana University Press.

Linscott, A. P. 1937a. Mr. van Gyseghem and the Bantu Players. *South African Opinion,* January 23, 15.

———. 1937b. Mr. van Gyseghem and the Pageant. *South African Opinion,* January 23, 15–16.

Lloyd, T. C. 1935. The Bantu Tread the Footlights. *The South African Opinion*, March 6, 3.

Lockett, Cecily. 1989. The Fabric of Experience: A Critical Perspective on the Writing of Miriam Tlali. In *Women and Writing in South Africa: A Critical Anthology*, edited by Cherry Clayton, 275–86. London: Heinemann.

Love, Harry, ed. 1984. *The Australian Stage: A Documentary History*. Sydney: University Press of New South Wales.

Lukács, György. 1955 [1936]. Erzählen oder Beschreiben? *Probleme des Realismus* I: 197–242. Berlin: Aufbau.

———. 1971. Narrate or Describe? In *Writer & Critic and Other Essays,* edited and translated by Arthur Kahn, 110–48. New York: Grosset and Dunlap.

Lynch, Kevin. 1960. *The Image of the City*. Cambridge, MA: MIT Press.

———. 1972. *What Time Is This Place?* Cambridge, MA: MIT Press.

Mabotja, Kgopi. 2012. *Ekhaya* Moves into North Hillbrow. *Joburg,* February 22, http://www.joburg.org.za/index2/php?option=com_content&view=article&id=7761&catid=88&Itemid=266#ixzz1nqbu2Wbj.

Magagodi, Kgafela oa. 2002. Refiguring the Body: Performance of Identity in *Mapantsula* and *Fools*. *Theatre Research International* 27: 243–58.

Maingard, Jacqueline. 2007. *South African National Cinema*. London: Routledge.

Makhudu, K. D. P. 2002. An Introduction to Flaaitaal (or Tsotsitaal). In *Language in South Africa*, edited by Rajend Mesthrie, 398–406. Cambridge: Cambridge University Press.

Mandela, Nelson. 1995. *Long Walk to Freedom*. Boston: Little, Brown.

Maota, Ray. 2010. Hillbrow Takes Centre Stage. *Joburg*, July 9, http://www.joburg.org.za/index2.php?option=com_content&task=view&id=5425&pop=1&page=0&Itemid=26.

Maqina, Mzwandile. 1975. *Give Us This Day*. Johannesburg: Ravan Press.

Marcuse, Herbert. 1968 [1935]. The Affirmative Character of Culture. In *Negations: Essays in Critical Theory*, translated by J. Shapiro, 113–35. Boston: Beacon Press.

Marks, Shula. 1986. *The Ambiguities of Dependence*. Johannesburg: Ravan Press.

Martienssen, Rex. 1935. Editorial. *South African Architectural Record* 20 (6): 149–55.

Marx, Maja. 2009a. *Maja Marx Public Art*. CD-ROM supplied by the artist.

———. 2009b. Interview with Loren Kruger. Johannesburg, September 9.

Maseko, Bheki. 1994 [1985]. Mamlambo. In *The Heinemann Book of South African Short Stories*, edited by Denis Hirson and Martin Trump, 153–61. London: Heinemann.

Maseko, Zola, director. 1997. *The Foreigner*. Johannesburg: La Sept Arte/Channel Four/Primedia. PAL video.

———. 2002. *A Drink in the Passage*. Johannesburg: MNET/Max-D-TV/National Film and Video Foundation. PAL video.

Mashinini, Tsietsi. 1977. Interview with Black TV, New York, January 9. *Wits Historical Papers: Soweto Uprising: A2953* Interviews A11.

Masilela, Ntongela. 2003. The Beginnings of Film Culture in South Africa. In *To Change Reels: Film and Film Culture in South Africa*, edited by Isabel Balseiro and Ntongela Masilela, 15–30. Detroit: Wayne State University Press.

Masondo, Amos. 2007. Johannesburg: State of the City Address, March 8. http://www.joburg.org.za.

Matabane, Khalo. 2005. *Conversations on a Sunday Afternoon*. Johannesburg: Matabane and SterKinekor Home Entertainment. DVD.

Matshikiza, John. 1999. An Incomplete Masterpiece. *Johannesburg Mail and Guardian*, February 4, p. 11.

———. 2008. Instant City. In *Johannesburg: The Elusive Metropolis*, edited by Sarah Nuttall and Achille Mbembe, 221–38. Durham: Duke University Press.

Matshikiza, Todd, Pat Williams, et al. N.d. *King Kong—A Jazz Opera. Original Cast Recording*. Paris: Celluloid (under license from Gallo, South Africa).

———. 1982 [1961]. *Chocolates for My Wife*. Cape Town: David Philip.

Mattera, Don. 1987. *Memory Is a Weapon*. Johannesburg: Ravan Press.

Mazrui, Ali, and Maurice Tidy. 1984. *Nationalism and New States in Africa*. London: Heinemann.

Mbembe, Achille. 2008. Aesthetics of Superfluity. In *Johannesburg: The Elusive Metropolis*, edited by Sarah Nuttall and Achille Mbembe, 37–67. Durham: Duke University Press.

McArthur, Stuart. 1979. *McArthur's Universal Corrective Map of the World*. Melbourne: Melbourne University Press. http://www.odt.org/southupmaps.htm.

Mda, Lizeka. 1998. City Quarters: City Spine, Faraday Station, KwaMayiMayi and Ponte City. In *blank____: Architecture, Apartheid and After*, edited by Hilton Judin and Ivan Vladislavić, D10 196–201. Rotterdam: Netherlands Architecture Institute.

Meeran, Zinaid. 2009. *Saracen at the Gates*. Johannesburg: Jacana Media.

Menell, Irene. 1994. Interview with Loren Kruger. Parktown, Johannesburg, September 20.

Merrington, Peter. 1997. Masques, Monuments, and Masons: The 1910 Pageant of the Union of South Africa. *Theatre Journal* 49: 1–14.

Mesthrie, Rajend. 2002. Introduction. In *Language in South Africa*, edited by Rajend Mesthrie, 1–8. Cambridge: Cambridge University Press.

Mhlongo, Niq. 2004. *Dog Eat Dog*. Cape Town: Kwela.

Miller, Andie. 2010. *Slow Motion: Stories about Walking*. Johannesburg: Jacana Media.

Miller, Duncan. 2002. Smelter and Smith: Iron Age Metal Fabrication Technology in Southern Africa. *Journal of Archeological Science* 29: 1083–1131.

Modisane, William "Bloke." 1986 [1963]. *Blame Me on History*. Johannesburg: AD Donker.

Moele, Kgebetle. 2006. *Room 207*. Cape Town: Kwela.

Mofokeng, Santu. 1996. The Black Photo Album: Look at Me: 1890–1950. In *Standard Bank National Arts Festival: Souvenir Program*, 81. Grahamstown: Grahamstown Foundation.

Mokadi, Aubrey. 2003. *Narrative as Creative History*. Randburg: Sedibeng Publishers.

Mokoena, Aubrey. 1991. Interview with Gail Gerhart [date not specified]. *Wits University Cullen Library Historical Papers: Soweto Uprising: A2953* Interviews A11.

Morobe, Murphy Mafiso. 1991. Interview with Gail Gerhart [date not specified]. *Wits University Cullen Library Historical Papers: Soweto Uprising: A2953* Interviews A11.

Morris, Alan. 1971–93. Hillbrow Newspaper Cuttings. *Wits University Cullen Library Historical Papers: Alan Morris Collection*: A2755/2.

———. 1999. *Bleakness and Light: Inner-city Transition in Hillbrow*. Johannesburg: Wits University Press.

Morris, James [Jan]. 1958. *South African Winter*. New York: Pantheon.

Mpe, Phaswane. 2001. *Welcome to Our Hillbrow*. Pietermaritzburg: University of KwaZulu-Natal Press.

———. 2005. On the Hillbrow Tower. In *Johannesburg Circa Now: Photography and the City*, edited by Terry Kurgan and Jo Ractliffe, 54–55. Johannesburg: T. Kurgan Books.

Mphahlele, Es'kia. 1989 [1955]. The Suitcase. In *The Drum Decade: Stories from the 1950s*, edited by Michael Chapman, 73–78. Pietermaritzburg: University of KwaZulu-Natal Press.

———. 2002. *Es'kia: Education, African Humanism, Social Consciousness, Literary Appreciation*. Edited by James Ogude et al. Cape Town: Kwela.

Mtimkulu, Oupa Thando. 1978. Four Poems. *Staffrider* 1 (1): 21.

Mumford, Lewis. 1996 [1937]. What Is a City? In *The City Reader*, edited by Richard Le Gates and Frederic Stout, 183–88. London: Routledge.

Municipal Magazine. 1935. Empire Exhibition. Johannesburg, June, 1.

Murray, Martin J. 2008. *Taming the Disorderly City: The Spatial Landscapes of Johannesburg after Apartheid*. Ithaca: Cornell University Press.

———. 2011. *City of Extremes: The Spatial Politics of Johannesburg*. Durham: Duke University Press.

Musiker, Naomi, and Reuben Musiker. 2000. *A Concise Historical Dictionary of Greater Johannesburg*. Cape Town: Francolin Publishers.

Mzamane, Mbulelo. 1982. *Children of Soweto*. Johannesburg: AD Donker.

———. 1984. Introduction. In *Selected Poems*, by Sipho Sepamla, 9–16. Johannesburg: AD Donker.

Nakasa, Nat. 1963–64. Correspondence with Can Themba. *Wits University Cullen Library Historical Papers: Nathaniel Nakasa Collection: A2696/B*.

———. 1989 [1959]. The Life and Death of King Kong. In *The Drum Decade: Stories from the 1950s*, edited by Michael Chapman. 25–29. Pietermaritzburg: University of KwaZulu-Natal Press.

Ndebele, Njabulo. 1983. *Fools and Other Stories*. Johannesburg: Ravan Press.

———. 1991. *The Rediscovery of the Ordinary: Essays on South African Literature and Culture*. Johannesburg: Congress of South African Writers.

Ndlovu, Sifiso Mxolisi. 1998. *The Soweto Uprisings: Counter-memories of June 1976*. Johannesburg: Ravan Press.

Neustetter, Marcus. 2011. The Art Intermediary: Interview with Oliver Barstow. In *Fire Walker: William Kentridge, Gerhard Marx*, edited by Oliver Barstow and Bronwyn Law-Viljoen, 35–41. Johannesburg: Fourthwall Books.

Ngakane, Lionel. 1997. Thoughts on My Life in Film. *South African Theatre Journal* 11: 261–68.

Ngcobo, Gabi. 2010. *Centre for Historical Reenactments*. http://centerforhistorical reenactments.blogspot.com.

Ngwenya, Thengani. 2012. Black Consciousness Poetry. In *The Cambridge History of South African Literature*, 500–522. Cambridge: Cambridge University Press.

Nicol, Mike. 1991. *A Good-looking Corpse: The World of DRUM, Jazz and Gangsters, Hope and Defiance in the Townships of South Africa*. London: Secker and Warburg.

Nkoli, Simon. 1995. Wardrobes. In *Defiant Desire: Gay and Lesbian Lives in South Africa*, edited by Mark Gevisser and Edwin Cameron, 249–57. New York: Routledge.

Nkosi, Lewis. 1965. *Home and Exile*. London: Longman.

———. 2002. *Underground People*. Cape Town: Kwela.

———. 2006. *Mandela's Ego: A Novel*. Cape Town: Umuzi.

Norman, Xoli. 2010. Verloren [Lost]. In *Elf: Fußballgeschichten aus Südafrika*, translated by Thomas Brückner, edited by Manfred Loimeier, 55–69. Wuppertal: Peter Hammer Verlag.

Nuttall, Sarah. 2008. Literary City. In *Johannesburg: The Elusive Metropolis*, edited by Sarah Nuttall and Achille Mbembe, 194–217. Durham: Duke University Press.

———. 2011. The Invisible City: Surfaces and Underneath. In *Marginal Spaces: Reading Ivan Vladislavić*, edited by Gerald Gaylard, 327–37. Johannesburg: Wits University Press.

Nuttall, Sarah, and Achille Mbembe. 2008. Introduction: Afropolis. In *Johannesburg: The Elusive Metropolis*, edited by Sarah Nuttall and Achille Mbembe, 1–33. Durham: Duke University Press.

Nxumalo, Henry. 1989a [1951]. Birth of a Tsotsi. In *The Drum Decade: Stories from the 1950s*, edited by Michael Chapman, 18–23. Pietermaritzburg: University of KwaZulu-Natal Press.

———. 1989b [1954]. Mr. Drum Goes to Jail. In *The Drum Decade: Stories from the 1950s*, edited by Michael Chapman, 35–47. Pietermaritzburg: University of KwaZulu-Natal Press.

Ohler, Norman. 2003 [2002]. *Ponte City* (*Stadt des Goldes* [Reibeck: Rowolt]). Translated by Robert Bertelsmann. Cape Town: David Philip.

Olifant, Andries Walter, and Ivan Vladislavić, eds. 1988. *Ten Years of Staffrider: 1978–88*. Johannesburg: Ravan Press.

O'Meara, Dan. 1996. *Forty Lost Years: The Apartheid State and the Politics of the National Party. 1948–1994*. Athens: Ohio University Press.

Orkin, Martin. 1991. *Drama and the South African State*. Manchester: Manchester University Press.

———, ed. 1995. Introduction. In *At the Junction: Four Plays by the Junction Avenue Theatre Company*, 1–15. Johannesburg: Wits University Press.

O' Toole, Sean. 2005. Saying Nothing. In *Johannesburg Circa Now: Photography and the City*, edited by Terry Kurgan and Jo Ractliffe, 19–28. Johannesburg: Terry Kurgan Books.

Outspan. 1936. The Pageant of the Provinces. May.

Pabale, Makoena. 2011. Miners' Strike Remembered. *Joburg*, September 27, http://www.joburg.org.za/index.php?option=com_content&view=article&id=280&catid=38&Itemid=51.

Palmary, Ingrid, Janine Rauch, and Graeme Simpson. 2003. Violent Crime in Johannesburg. In *Emerging Johannesburg: Perspectives on the Postapartheid City*, edited by Richard Tomlinson et al., 101–22. London: Routledge.

Pather, Jay. 2005. Hotel. In *Johannesburg Circa Now: Photography and the City*, edited by Terry Kurgan and Jo Ractliffe, 66–67. Johannesburg: Terry Kurgan Books.

Paton, Alan. 1987 [1948]. *Cry, the Beloved Country*. New York: Scribners.

———. 1961. A Drink in the Passage. In *Debbie Go Home: Stories*, by Alan Paton, 87–96. London: Jonathan Cape.

Pearson, Mike, and Michael Shanks. 2001. *Theatre/Archeology*. London: Routledge.

Peberdy, Sally. 2009. *Selecting Immigrants: National Identity and South Africa's Immigration Policies, 1910–2008*. Johannesburg: Wits University Press.

Peck, Richard. 1992. Condemned to Choose, but What? Existentialism in Selected Works by Fugard, Brink, and Gordimer. *Research in African Literatures* 23 (3): 67–84.

Peñalosa, Enrique. 2006. Opening Statement: Transport as Justice. Urban Age Johannesburg Conference. www.urban-age.net/03_conferences/conf_johannesburg.html.

Pesa, Sello, and Vaughn Sadie. 2012. Interviews recorded in Lauren Clifford-Holmes, Inhabitant, *Johannesburg Mail and Guardian*, October 12, mg.co.za/multimedia/2012-10-12-inhabitant-1. Podcast.

Peterson, Bhekizizwe. 2000. *Monarchs, Missionaries and African Intellectuals: African Theatre and the Unmaking of Colonial Marginality*. Trenton: Africa World Press.

Pickard-Cambridge, Claire. 1989. *The Greying of Johannesburg*. Johannesburg: South African Institute for Race Relations.

Pile, Steve. 1997. Opposition, Political Identity and Spaces of Resistance. In *Geographies of Resistance*, edited by Steve Pile and Michael Keith, 1–32. London: Routledge.

Platzky, Lauren, and Cheryl Walker. 1985. *The Surplus People: Forced Removals in South Africa*. Johannesburg: Ravan Press.

Plomer, William. 1984. *The South African Autobiography*. Cape Town: David Philip.

Purkey, Malcolm. 1995 [1993]. Sophiatown—The Play. In *At the Junction: Four Plays by the Junction Avenue Theatre Company*, edited by Martin Orkin, 210–13. Johannesburg: Wits University Press.

Ractliffe, Jo. 2004. Johannesburg Inner City Works, 2000–2004. In *Selected Colour Works*, by Jo Ractliffe. Johannesburg: Warren Siebrits Modern and Contemporary.

———. 2007. Interview with Loren Kruger, March 29.

Rand Daily Mail. 1935a. Exhibition Designs Criticised. *Rand Daily Mail*, June 20, 10.

———. 1935b. André van Gyseghem, Pageant Master. *Rand Daily Mail*, July 10, 10.

———. 1936a. A New Johannesburg in 50 Years. *Rand Daily Mail*, April 20, 10.

———. 1936b. Immediate Start to a New Bridge. *Rand Daily Mail*, June 4, 12.

———. 1936c. Johannesburg will Rub Shoulders with the World. *Rand Daily Mail*, September 15, 22.

———. 1936d. Three Mile Procession Celebrates Johannesburg's Jubilee. *Rand Daily Mail*, September 22, 14.

———. 1936e. Africa's Wonder City (Jubilee Supplement). *Rand Daily Mail*, September 23, n. p.

———. 1956a. The Big Sweep: High Treason Suspects Crowded into the Old Fort. *Rand Daily Mail*, December 6, 1.

———. 1956b. Treason Trial in Pictures. *Rand Daily Mail*, December 21, 14.

———. 1956c. Treason Case: Prisoners Freed on Bail. Allegations: Plans to Overthrow State and Set up People's Democracy. *Rand Daily Mail*, December 21, 1.

Rastogi, Pallavi. 2008. *Afrindian Fictions: Diaspora, Race and National Desire in South Africa*. Columbus: Ohio State University Press.

Rees, Malcolm. 2013. Maboneng Precinct: I am an Island. *Johannesburg Mail and Guardian* March 11: http://mg.co.za/article/2013-03-08-maboneng-i-am-an-island.

Ricci, Digby, 1986. Introduction. In *Reef of Time: Johannesburg in Writing*, edited by Digby Ricci, 9–17. Johannesburg: AD Donker.

Roberge, Paul T. 2002. Afrikaans: Considering Origins. In *Language in South Africa*, edited by Rajend Mesthrie, 79–103. Cambridge: Cambridge University Press.

Roberts, Sheila. 1975. *Outside Life's Feast*. Johannesburg: AD Donker.

Robinson, Jennifer. 1998. (Im)mobilizing Space, Dreaming of Change. In *blank____: Architecture, Apartheid and After*, edited by Hilton Judin and Ivan Vladislavić, D7, 163–71. Rotterdam: Netherlands Architecture Institute.

———. 2002. Global and World Cities: A View from Off the Map. *International Journal of Urban and Regional Research* 26: 531–54.

———. 2003. Johannesburg's 1936 Empire Exhibition: Interaction, Segregation and Modernity in an African City. *Journal of Southern African Studies* 29: 759–89.

———. 2006. *Ordinary Cities between Modernity and Development*. London: Routledge.

Rogosin, Lionel, director. 2010 [1959]. *Come Back Africa*. Paris: Carlotta Films. DVD.

R[othmann], M[imie] E. 1936. By die Rykskou: Bantoe, Boesman . . . en Witman. *Die Burger*, November 7, 14.

Routh, Guy. 1950. The Bantu People's Theatre. *Trek* (October): 20–23.

Roux, Naomi, ed. 2010. *Yeoville History*. Johannesburg: Wits School of Architecture and Yeoville Studio. http://www.wits.ac.za/academic/ebe/archplan/4866/yeoville_stories.html.

Royston, Robert. 1973. Introduction. In *To Whom It May Concern: An Anthology of Black South African Poetry*, edited by Robert Royston, 3–10. Johannesburg: AD Donker.

Sachs, Bernard. 1959. *South African Personalities and Places*. Johannesburg: Kayor.

Sampson, Anthony. 1956. *Drum: A Venture into the New Africa*. London: Collins.

———. 1983. *Drum: An African Adventure and Afterwards*. London: Hodder and Stoughton.

Sanders, Mark. 1994. Responding to the "Situation" of Modisane's *Blame Me on History*: Towards an Ethics of Reading in South Africa. *Research in African Literatures* 25 (4): 51–68.

Sassen, Saskia. 1991. *The Global City: London, New York, Tokyo*. Princeton: Princeton University Press.

———. 2000. The Global City: Strategic Site/New Frontier. *American Studies* 41 (2/3): 79–95.

Schadeberg, Jürgen. 1987. *The Fifties People of South Africa: The Lives of Some Ninety-Five People Who Were Influential in South Africa During the Fifties, a Period Which Saw the First Stirrings of the Coming Revolution*. Johannesburg: Bailey's African History Archive.

Schechner, Richard. 1994. *Environmental Theater*. New York: Applause Books.

Schmitz, Oliver. 2003. *Hijack Stories*. Berlin: Xenos Pictures/Paradis Films. DVD.

Schmitz, Oliver, and Thomas Mogotlane. 1986. *Mapantsula*. Johannesburg: Max Montocchio. DVD.

Segal, Lauren, and Sharon Cort, eds. 2006. *Number Four: The Making of Constitution Hill*. Johannesburg: Penguin. SA.

Segatti, Auriela. 2011. Introduction. Migration to South Africa. Regional Challenges vs. National Interests. *Contemporary Migration to South Africa: A Regional Development Issue*, edited by Aurelia Segatti and Loren Landau: 9–29. Washington, DC: World Bank.

Segatti, Aurelia, and Loren Landau, eds. 2011a. *Contemporary Migration to South Africa: A Regional Development Issue*. Washington, DC: World Bank. 2011.

———. 2011b. Appendix. *Contemporary Migration to South Africa*: 137–65.

Sepamla, Sipho, [Sydney]. 1976. *The Blues Is You in Me*. Johannesburg: AD Donker.

———. 1977. *The Soweto I Love*. Cape Town: David Philip.

———. 1984a. *Selected Poems*, edited by Mbulelo Mzamane. Johannesburg: AD Donker.

———. 1984b. *A Ride on the Whirlwind*. London: Heinemann African Writers Series.

Sepamla, Sipho, in conversation with Jaki Seroke, Miriam Tlali, and Mothobi Mutloatse. 1988. Black Writers in South Africa. (African Writers Association discussion, 1981). In *Ten Years of "Staffrider": 1978–1988*, edited by Andries Walter Olifant and Ivan Vladislavić, 303–17. Johannesburg: Ravan Press.

Serote, Mongane [Wally]. 1972. *Yakhal'inkomo*. Johannesburg: Renoster Press.

———. 1981. *To Every Birth Its Blood*. London: Heinemann African Writers Series.

———. 1982. *Selected Poems*. Edited by Mbulelo Mzamane. Johannesburg: AD Donker.

———. 2007. Interview with Michael Chapman. In *Soweto Poetry: Literary Perspectives*, edited by Michael Chapman, 112–15. Pietermaritzburg: University of KwaZulu-Natal Press.

Shepherd, Nick, and Noeleen Murray. 2007. Introduction. In *Desire Lines: Space, Memory, and Identity in the Post-Apartheid City*, edited by Noeleen Murray and Nick Sheperd, 1–11. London: Routledge.

Shezi, Mthuli. 1980. Shanti. In *South African Peoples Plays*, ed Robert Kavanagh, 63–84. London: Heinemann.

Siemes, Christof. 2010. Prügel unterm Regenbogen: Das Theaterprojekt "X-Homes" in Johannesburg. *Die Zeit*, July 15, 48.

Simon, Barney. 1974. *Jo'burg, Sis!* Johannesburg: Bateleur Press.

———. 1986. Hey Listen. In *Market Plays*, edited by Stephen Gray, 109–33. Johannesburg: AD Donker.

Simon, Barney, and the Market Theatre cast. 1984. Cincinatti. In *South African Theatre: Four Plays and an Introduction*, edited by Temple Hauptfleisch and Ian Steadman, 166–235. Pretoria: HAUM.

———. 1997. Born in the RSA. In *Four Workshopped Plays*, edited by Pat Schwartz, 91–127. Johannesburg: Wits University Press.

Simone, AbdouMalique. 1998. Globalization and the Identity of African Urban Practices. In *blank____: Architecture, Apartheid and After*, edited by Hilton Judin and Ivan Vladislavić, 175–87. Rotterdam: Netherlands Architecture Institute.

———. 2004a. People as Infrastructure: Intersecting Fragments in Johannesburg. *Public Culture* 16: 407–29.

———. 2004b. *For the City Yet to Come: Changing African Life in Four Cities*. Durham: Duke University Press.

Sithole, Ayanda. 2011. High Density, High Hopes. *Johannesburg Mail and Guardian*, November 3, http://mg.co.za/printformat/single/2011-11-03-high-density-hopes.

Slabbert, S., and R. Finlayson. 2002. Code-switching in South African Townships. In *Language in South Africa*, edited by Rajend Mesthrie, 235–57. Cambridge: Cambridge University Press.

Slabolepszy, Paul. 1994. Victoria Almost Falls. Unpublished playscript.

———. 1998. Fordsburg's Finest. Unpublished playscript.

———. 1999 [1992]. Mooi Street Moves. In *Drama from a New South Africa*, edited by David Graver, 113–53. Bloomington: Indiana University Press.

Slosberg, Bertha. 1939. *Pagan Tapestry*. London: Rich and Cravan.

Soja, Edward. 1997. Six Discourses on the Postmetropolis. In *Imagining Cities: Scripts, Signs, Memory*, edited by Sally Westwood and John Williams, 19–30. London: Routledge.

Sole, Kelwyn. 1988. Days of Power: Depictions of Politics and Community in Four Recent South African Novels. *Research in African Literatures* 19 (1): 65–88.

Sommer, Doris. 2006. Introduction. In *Cultural Agency in the Americas*, edited by Doris Sommer, 1–16. Durham: Duke University Press.

Sorrell, Jennifer. 1996. Editorial. *ADA [Architecture Design Art] Magazine* 14: 6, 88–89.

South African Institute of Race Relations (SAIRR). 1977. *South Africa in Travail: Evidence Submitted to the Cilliers Commission, January 1977.* Johannesburg: SAIRR.

South African Mining and Engineering Journal. 1935. South Africa's Forthcoming Empire Exhibition. May 18, n.p.

Sowden, Lewis. 1937. *Red Rand.* Unpublished playscript. *Wits University Cullen Library Historical Papers*, A406.

———. 1956a. At Start Songs; At End Drawn Guns. Historic Court Was Scene of Confusion. *Rand Daily Mail*, December 20, 1.

———. 1956b. A Day of Panic and Alarm in Court. *Rand Daily Mail*, December 21, 1.

Stein, Pippa, and Ruth Jacobson, eds. 1986. *Sophiatown Speaks.* Johannesburg: Junction Avenue Press.

Stephanou, Irene, and Leila Henriques. 2005. *A World in an Orange: Creating Theatre with Barney Simon*, edited by Lionel Abrahams and Jane Fox. Johannesburg: Jacana Media.

Stewart, Jacqueline. 2005. *Migrating to the Movies: Cinema and Black Urban Modernity.* Berkeley: University of California Press.

Stevenson, Robert, director. 2007 [1937]. *King Solomon's Mines.* London: Gaumont-British. DVD.

Stone, Gerald L. 2002. The Lexicon and Sociolinguistic Codes of the Working-class Afrikaans-speaking Cape Peninsula Coloured Community. In *Language in South Africa*, edited by Rajend Mesthrie, 381–97. Cambridge: Cambridge University Press.

Sullivan, Louis. 1988 [1896]. The Tall Office Building Artistically Considered. In *Louis Sullivan: The Public Papers*, edited by Robert Twombly, 103–12. Chicago: University of Chicago Press.

Swanson, Donald, director. 1949. *Jim Comes to Joburg.* Johannesburg: Warrior Films.

———. 1951. *The Magic Garden.* Johannesburg: Swan Film Productions.

Swilling, Mark. 1998. Rival Futures: Struggle Visions, Post-Apartheid Choices. In *blank____: Architecture, Apartheid and After*, edited by Hilton Judin and Ivan Vladislavić, E8. Rotterdam: Netherlands Architecture Institute.

Theal, George McCall. 1922. *History of Africa South of the Zambesi, 1505–1795.* 3rd ed. London: Allen and Unwin.

Thema, R. V. Selope. 1934a. Before the Advent of the White Man, the Dead Ruled the Living with a Rod of Iron in Bantu Society. *Bantu World*, May 12, 8–9.

———. 1934b. Honour the Great Emancipators. *Bantu World*, June 2, 1.

———. 1936. Editorial. *Bantu World*, January 18, 4.

Themba, Can. 1972. *The Will to Die.* London: Heineman African Writers Series.

———. 1985. *The World of Can Themba*, edited by Essop Patel. Johannesburg: Ravan Press.

———. 1989 [1955]. Baby, Come Duze. In *The Drum Decade: Stories from the 1950s*, edited by Michael Chapman, 109–13. Pietermaritzburg: University of KwaZulu-Natal Press.

Thorndike, Sybil. 1935. African Art Forcing Its Way to Realisation. *Bantu World*, March 2, 1.

Thurman, Christopher. 2011. "I take up my spade and I dig." Verwoerd, Tsafendas and the Position of the Writer in the Early Fiction of Ivan Vladislavić. In *Marginal Spaces: Reading Ivan Vladislavić*, edited by Gerald Gaylard, 46–69. Johannesburg: Wits University Press.

Till, Christopher. 1996. Interview with Jennifer Sorrell, *ADA Magazine*, 14, 37.

Tilley, Brian. 1984. *Mayfair*. Johannesburg: Video News Service. PAL video.

———. 1994. *The Line*. Johannesburg/London: Afrovision and Channel Four. PAL video.

———. 2005. *Crossing the Line*. Johannesburg: Big World Cinema. TV broadcast.

Tillim, Guy. 2005. *Jo'burg*. Johannesburg: STE Publishers.

Titlestad, Michael. 2012. Writing the City after Apartheid. In *The Cambridge History of South African Literature*, edited by David Attwell and Derek Attridge, 676–94. Cambridge: Cambridge University Press.

Tlali, Miriam. 1987 [1975]. *Muriel at Metropolitan*. London: Longman.

———. 1998. Interview with Rosemary Jolly. In *Writing South Africa*, edited by Rosemary Jolly and Derek Attridge, 141–48. Cambridge: Cambridge University Press.

———. 2005 [1980]. *Amandla*. Vanderbijlpark: Vaal University Press.

Tlali, Miriam, Jaki Seroke, Sipho Sepamla, and Mothobi Mutloatse. 1988. Black Writers in South Africa (African Writers Association discussion, 1981). In *Ten Years of "Staffrider": 1978–1988*, edited by Andries Walter Olifant and Ivan Vladislavić, 303–17. Johannesburg: Ravan Press.

Tlali, Miriam, with Mike Kirkwood, Mr. X, Mrs. Leah Koae, and Mrs Sebenzile Lekota. 1978. Soweto Speaks with Miriam Tlali. *Staffrider* 1 (1): 2–6.

Tomlinson, Richard, Robert A. Beaurigard, Lindsay Brem, and Xolela Mangcu, eds. 2003. *Emerging Johannesburg: Perspectives on the Postapartheid City*. London: Routledge.

Trinity Session (Stephen Hobbs and Marcus Neustetter). 2007. *UrbaNET: Hillbrow/Dakar/Hillbrow*. www.onair.co.za.

Trinity Session (Stephen Hobbs and Marcus Neustetter) and Ngwedi Design. 2008. Public Artworks Program for Hillbrow/Berea/Yeoville Phase One. www.onair.co.za.

Twala, Dan. 1937. Bantu People's Theatre. Letter to J. R. Rheinhallt Jones. South African Institute of Race Relations, July 31, AD843/RJ/Kb28.2.2.

Umteteli wa Bantu (UwB). 1933. This Day of Freedom. August 5, 2.

———. 1934. The Emancipation Centenary Celebration. June 9, 2.

———. 1936. Africans' Contribution to Development of the Witwatersrand. October 19, 5.

Van der Waal, Gerhard-Mark. 1986. *Van Mynkamp tot Metropolis*. Johannesburg: Human Sciences Research Council.

———. 1987. *From Mining Camp to Metropolis*. Johannesburg: Human Sciences Research Council.

Van Niekerk, Marlene. 1994. *Triomf.* Cape Town: Quellerie.

———. 1999. *Triomf.* Tranlated by Leon de Kock. Johannesburg: Jonathan Ball.

Van Onselen, Charles. 1982. *Studies in the Social and Economic History of the Witwatersrand. Vol. I: New Babylon; Vol. II: New Nineveh.* London: Longman.

Van Warmelo, N. J., and G. P. Lestrade. 1932. *Contribution to Venda History, Religion, and Tribal Ritual.* Pretoria: Government Printer.

Van Wyk, Chris. 1988. Interview with Andries Olifant. In *Ten Years of "Staffrider": 1978–1988,* edited by Andries Walter Olifant and Ivan Vladislavić, 165–77. Johannesburg: Ravan Press.

Varder, M. 1998. Reliving a Long Day's Journey into Jo'burg Night. *Johannesburg Mail and Guardian,* January 16, 18–19.

Venter, Christoffel. 2013. The Lurch towards Formalisation: Lessons from the Implementation of BRT Johannesburg, South Africa. *Research in Transportation Economics* 39 (1): 114–20.

Viennale. 2000. Cry, the Beloved Country. In *Blacklisted: Movies by the Hollywood Blacklist Victims: A Retrospective,* 118–19. Vienna: Vienna International Film Festival.

Visser, Nick. 1976. South Africa: The Renaissance That Failed. *Journal of Commonwealth Literature* 9 (1): 47–59.

Vladislavić, Ivan. 1996. The Book Lover. In *Propaganda by Monuments and Other Stories,* by Ivan Vladislavić, 79–104. Cape Town: David Philip.

———. 1998. Street Addresses: Johannesburg. In *blank____: Architecture, Apartheid and After,* edited by Hilton Judin and Ivan Vladislavić, E11, 304–13. Rotterdam: Netherlands Architecture Institute.

———. 2001. *The Restless Supermarket.* Cape Town: David Philip.

———. 2005. Helena Shein. In *Johannesburg Circa Now: Photography and the City,* edited by Terry Kurgan and Jo Ractliffe, 60–63. Johannesburg: T. Kurgan Books.

———. 2006. *Portrait with Keys: Joburg & What-What.* Cape Town: Umuzi.

———. 2010. *Double Negative—a Novel.* Rome: Contrasto.

Watson, Stephen. 1990 [1986]. The Shock of the Old: What's Become of 'Black' Poetry? In *Selected Essays,* by Stephen Watson, 80–92. Cape Town: Carrefour Press.

Weber, Max. 1989. *Science as Vocation.* Translated by Michael John. London: Unwin.

———. 1992 [1921]. Wissenschaft als Beruf. *Gesamtausgabe* 17: 87–105. Tübingen: JCB Mohr. Humboldt.

Williams, Raymond. 1981. *Politics and Letters.* London: Verso.

Woodgate, Shirley. 1986. Pageview: Ghosts Not at Rest. *Johannesburg Star,* 26 August.

Woodham, Jonathan. 1989. Images of Africa and Design at the British Empire Exhibitions between the Wars. *Journal of Design History* 2 (1): 15–33.

Workshop '71. 1981. Survival. In *South African People's Plays,* edited by Robert Kavanagh, 128–73. London: Heinemann.

Ziman, Ralph. 2008. *Jerusalema: Gangster's Paradise.* Johannesburg: Muti Films. DVD.

Zvomuya, Percy. 2013. An Outsider's Yeoville Insights (review of Terry Kurgan's *Hotel Yeoville* Exhibition). *Johannesburg Mail and Guardian,* March 8. http://mg.co.za/article/2013-03-08-00-an-outsiders-yeoville-insight.

ARCHIVAL COLLECTIONS IN JOHANNESBURG UNLESS OTHERWISE STATED

Johannesburg Public Library: Strange Africana Collection: not as yet accessible online

Market Theatre: Programs and Newspaper Cuttings: www.markettheatre.co.za

University of the Witwatersrand Cullen Library Historical Papers: www.historicalpapers.wits.ac.za

- Johannesburg Empire Exhibition
- Johannesburg Historical Society
- Klenerman (Fanny): accounts, correspondence, and interviews relevant to Vanguard Booksellers
- Morris (Alan). Newspaper cuttings and Hillbrow research materials
- Nakasa (Nathaniel) Collection
- South African Institute of Race Relations
- Sowden (Lewis) Collection
- Soweto Uprising: interviews, newspaper cuttings, and photographs

University of the Witwatersrand, Gay and Lesbian Archive: www.gala.co.za

National English Literary Museum, Rhodes University, Grahamstown, South Africa: http://www.ru.ac.za/static/institutes/nelm/

- Gluckman (Leon): *King Kong* Collection
- Market Theatre Collection
- Simon (Barney) Collection

Private Collections

- De Bell (Fiona) and Schoenmakers (Roel): Cascoland, www.cascoland.com
- Gaylard (Joseph): pamphlets and online documentation of Joubert Park Project, http://artmap.co.za/312/joseph+gaylard/
- Goldblatt, David: photographs, http://www.goodman-gallery.com/artists/davidgoldblatt
- Hassem (Zubair): graphite drawings and maps, kufica@ovi.com
- Hobbs (Stephen): photographic, video, and online documentation of Trinity Session, www.onair.co.za
- Le Roux (Hannah): *Urban (and) Fabrics* and other architectural and design documents.
- Marx (Maja): photographic and CD-ROM documents, www.majamarx.com
- Menell (Irene): *King Kong* material
- Purkey (Malcolm): *Junction Avenue Theatre Company* and *Market Theatre* documents
- Ractliffe (Jo): photographs, http://www.stevenson.info/artists/ractliffe.html
- Schadeberg, Jürgen: photographs, http://jurgenschadeberg.com/
- Tillim, Guy: photographs, http://www.stevenson.info/artists/tillim.html

INDEX